THE WRITINGS AND LATER WISDOM BOOKS

Society of Biblical Literature

The Bible and Women
An Encyclopaedia of Exegesis and Cultural History

Edited by Christiana de Groot, Irmtraud Fischer,
Mercedes Navarro Puerto, and Adriana Valerio

The Bible and Women
Hebrew Bible/Old Testament
Volume 1.3: The Writings and Later Wisdom Books

THE WRITINGS AND LATER WISDOM BOOKS

Edited by

Christl M. Maier and Nuria Calduch-Benages

SBL Press
Atlanta

Copyright © 2014 by SBL Press

All rights reserved. No part of this work may be reproduced or transmitted in any form or by any means, electronic or mechanical, including photocopying and recording, or by means of any information storage or retrieval system, except as may be expressly permitted by the 1976 Copyright Act or in writing from the publisher. Requests for permission should be addressed in writing to the Rights and Permissions Office, SBL Press, 825 Houston Mill Road, Atlanta, GA 30329 USA.

Library of Congress Cataloging-in-Publication Data

Escritos y otros libros sapienciales. English.
 The Writings and later Wisdom books / edited by Christl M. Maier and Núria Calduch-Benages.
  pages cm. — (The Bible and women: an encyclopaedia of exegesis and cultural history ; no. 1.3)
 Includes bibliographical references and index.
 ISBN 978-1-62837-057-7 (paper binding : alk. paper) — ISBN 978-1-62837-058-4 (electronic format) — ISBN 978-1-62837-059-1 (hardcover binding : alk. paper)
 1. Women in the Bible. 2. Women in Judaism. 3. Bible. Hagiographa—Criticism, interpretation, etc. I. Maier, Christl M., editor. II. Calduch-Benages, Núria, editor. III. Society of Biblical Literature.
 BS575.E8613 2014
 223'.06082—dc23   2014036283

Printed on acid-free, recycled paper conforming to
ANSI/NISO Z39.48-1992 (R1997) and ISO 9706:1994
standards for paper permanence.

Contents

Abbreviations vii

Introduction
Christl M. Maier and Nuria Calduch-Benages 1

Part 1: Tracing the Living Conditions of Women

The Lives of Women in the Postexilic Era
Tamara Cohn Eskenazi 11

Female Names and Gender Perspectives in Chronicles
Sara Japhet 33

Part 2: "Good" and "Bad" Women? Images of Women in Israel's Wisdom Tradition

Personified Wisdom: Contexts, Meanings, Theology
Gerlinde Baumann 57

Good and Evil Women in Proverbs and Job: The Emergence of Cultural Stereotypes
Christl M. Maier 77

Between Misogyny and Valorization: Perspectives on Women in Qoheleth
Vittoria D'Alario 93

Good and Bad Wives in the Book of Ben Sira: A Harmless Classification?
Nuria Calduch-Benages 109

CONTENTS

PART 3: WOMEN'S VOICES AND FEMALE METAPHORS IN POETIC TEXTS

Ancient Near Eastern Pictures as Keys to Biblical Metaphors
Silvia Schroer 129

Feminine Symbols and Metaphors in the Psalter
Donatella Scaiola 165

On Gendering Laments: A Gender-Oriented Reading of the Old Testament Psalms of Lament
Ulrike Bail 179

Lamentations and Gender in Biblical Cultural Context
Nancy C. Lee 197

Shulammite: The Woman "at Peace" in the Song of Songs
Gianni Barbiero 215

PART 4: AMBIVALENT ROLE MODELS: WOMEN IN NARRATIVE TEXTS

Ruth and Naomi Reclaim Their Lives and Memories
Miren Junkal Guevara Llaguno 237

Interpreting Esther: Categories, Contexts, and Creative Ambiguities
Susan Niditch 255

Susanna, Example of Virtue and Daniel's Female Counterpart
Isabel Gómez-Acebo 275

Bibliography 289
Contributors 317
Index of Ancient Sources 323

Abbreviations

AB	Anchor Bible
ADAJ	*Annual of the Department of Antiquities of Jordan*
AfO	*Archiv für Orientforschung*
AnBib	Analecta biblica
AOTC	Abingdon Old Testament Commentaries
BA	*Biblical Archaeologist*
BBB	Bonner biblische Beiträge
BBET	Beiträge zur biblischen Exegese und Theologie
BETL	Bibliotheca ephemeridum theologicarum lovaniensium
BHS	Biblia Hebraica Stuttgartensia
Bib	*Biblica*
BibInt	*Biblical Interpretation*
BibIntS	Biblical Interpretation Series
BibOr	Biblica et orientalia
BJS	Brown Judaic Studies
BK	*Bibel und Kirche*
BKAT	Biblischer Kommentar Altes Testament
BN	*Biblische Notizen*
BThS	Biblisch-theologische Studien
BVC	*Bible et vie chrétienne*
BZ	*Biblische Zeitschrift*
BZAW	Beihefte zur Zeitschrift für die alttestamentliche Wissenschaft
CBQ	*Catholic Biblical Quarterly*
CurBS	*Currents in Research: Biblical Studies*
DBSup	Dictionnaire de la Bible: Supplément. Edited by Louis Pirot and André Robert. Paris: Letouzey et Ané, 1928–.
EgT	*Eglise et théologie*
ErIs	*Eretz Israel*
ExpTim	*Expository Times*
FAT	Forschungen zum Alten Testament
FCB	Feminist Companion to the Bible

FRLANT	Forschungen zur Religion und Literatur des Alten und Neuen Testaments
HBS	Herders Biblische Studien
HKAT	Handkommentar zum Alten Testament
HTR	*Harvard Theological Review*
ICC	International Critical Commentary
IBC	Interpretation: A Bible Commentary for Teaching and Preaching
ITC	International Theological Commentary
JAAR	*Journal of the American Academy of Religion*
JANES	*Journal of Ancient Near Eastern Studies*
JAOS	*Journal of the American Oriental Society*
JBL	*Journal of Biblical Literature*
JBQ	*Jewish Bible Quarterly*
JHNES	Johns Hopkins Near Eastern Studies
JSJSup	Supplements to the Journal for the Study of Judaism in the Persian, Hellenistic, and Roman Periods
JSOT	*Journal for the Study of the Old Testament*
JSOTSup	Journal for the Study of the Old Testament: Supplement Series
KAT	Kommentar zum Alten Testament
KHC	Kurzer Hand-Commentar zum Alten Testament
LCL	Loeb Classical Library
LD	Lectio divina
LHBOTS	Library of the Hebrew Bible/Old Testament Studies
NCB	New Century Bible
NEchtB	Neue Echter Bibel
NovTSup	Novum Testamentum Supplements
NRTh	*La nouvelle revue théologique*
NTOA	Novum Testamentum et Orbis Antiquus
OBO	Orbis Biblicus et Orientalis
OIP	Oriental Institute Publications
OLA	Orientalia lovaniensia analecta
OTG	Old Testament Guides
OTL	Old Testament Library
OtSt	Oudtestamentische Studiën
QD	Quaestiones disputatae
RIBLA	*Revista de interpretación bíblica latino-americana*
RivB	*Rivista biblica italiana*
RivBSup	Supplements to Rivista biblica italiana
SubBi	Subsidia biblica
RTL	*Revue théologique de Louvain*

RStB	*Ricerche storico bibliche*
SBAB	Stuttgarter biblische Aufsatzbände
SBS	Stuttgarter Bibelstudien
SBLDS	Society of Biblical Literature Dissertation Series
SBT	Studies in Biblical Theology
SemeiaSt	Semeia Studies
SNTSMS	Society for New Testament Studies Monograph Series
SOTSMS	Society for Old Testament Studies Monograph Series
SUNT	Studien zur Umwelt des Neuen Testaments
TD	*Theology Digest*
TDOT	*Theological Dictionary of the Old Testament.* Edited by G. Johannes Botterweck and Helmer Ringgren. Translated by David E. Green. 15 vols. Grand Rapids: Eerdmans, 1974–2006.
TLOT	*Theological Lexicon of the Old Testament.* Edited by Ernst Jenni and Claus Westermann. Translated by Mark E. Biddle. 3 vols. Peabody, Mass.: Hendrickson, 1997.
TP	*Theologie und Philosophie*
TUAT	*Texte aus der Umwelt des Alten Testaments.* Edited by Otto Kaiser et al. 3 vols. Gütersloh: Gütersloher, 1982–2002; new edition, 2004–.
VT	*Vetus Testamentum*
VTSup	Supplements to Vetus Testamentum
WBC	Word Biblical Commentary
WMANT	Wissenschaftliche Monographien zum Alten und Neuen Testament
WUNT	Wissenschaftliche Untersuchungen zum Neuen Testament
ZAH	*Zeitschrift für Althebräistik*
ZAW	*Zeitschrift für die alttestamentliche Wissenschaft*
ZBK	*Zürcher Bibelkommentare Altes Testament*
ZTK	*Zeitschrift für Theologie und Kirche*

Introduction

Christl M. Maier and Nuria Calduch-Benages

This volume belongs to the ambitious international project of an encyclopaedia of exegesis and cultural history named "The Bible and Women." The project seeks to provide an ecumenical, gender-sensitive interpretation and reception history of the Bible, with a focus on European theological research and Western religious history.[1]

When we undertook the task of editing one volume on the Hebrew Bible in the framework of this encyclopaedia, we embraced the idea as promising and trendsetting. Within the course of the work, however, we gradually became aware of the challenge of collecting texts of authors from four linguistic domains that simultaneously reflect different traditions of exegesis and various scholarly contexts. We are pleased that biblical scholars from five different European countries, Israel, and the United States have contributed to this volume. Each of them is a well-known expert in her or his field of study in their respective linguistic domain. As their essays were originally written in English, German, Italian, or Spanish, they represent diverse social contexts, which differ in terms of gender relations and gender theories, as well as diverse religious affiliations.

1. The Scope and Structure of the Volume

The essays presented in this volume cover the third part of the Hebrew Bible canon, the so-called Writings (*Ketuvim* in Hebrew), plus some later wisdom traditions in the books Ben Sira and Wisdom (*Sapientia Salomonis*). The biblical wisdom tradition that forms an integral part of the ancient Near East-

---

1. For the scope, hermeneutics, and goals of the project, see the introduction in volume 1.1, *Torah* (ed. Irmtraud Fischer and Mercedes Navarro Puerto, with Andrea Taschl-Erber; Atlanta: Society of Biblical Literature, 2011), 1–30. A shorter form is also available on the project's website at: http://www.bibleandwomen.org/EN/descripcion.php.

ern tradition produced a coherent stream of texts throughout the first millennium BCE and into the Christian era. This coherence was disturbed by the decision to include only the books of Proverbs, Job, and Qohelet into the Hebrew canon. Ben Sira—long known as the Greek translation of a Hebrew original that could be fragmentarily recovered only in modern times—and the originally Greek book of Wisdom belong to the canon of the Greek translation of the Hebrew Bible, the Septuagint, and therefore may also be treated in volume 3.1 of this project (Pseudepigrapha and Apocrypha). We included in this volume Nuria Calduch-Benages's essay on "good" and "bad" wives in Ben Sira because this wisdom book reiterates the cultural stereotypes that emerge in Proverbs and presents them to a Jewish-Hellenistic audience. With regard to gendered images of both the divine and humanity, the interpretation of personified wisdom, which first appeared in Prov 1–9, would be incomplete without considering its development in the later wisdom tradition. This connection is demonstrated in Gerlinde Baumann's article on the wisdom figure and in a passage of Silvia Schroer's essay on iconic traditions behind Lady Wisdom.

Due to its formation in the second century BCE, the prophetic book of Daniel was not integrated into the canon as part of the Prophets but ended up in the Writings. For Daniel, we asked Isabel Gómez-Acebo to include the Greek expansions on Susanna in order to demonstrate the first step of the book's reception history, which introduces a female protagonist and, thus, gender issues. These threads of wisdom tradition motivated us to deal with the sapiential writings despite their separation within the Jewish and Christian canon.[2]

The essays of this volume are gathered under four headings. The first group of articles traces the living conditions of women, either through a socio-historical reconstruction of Jewish life in Persian-period Judah or through an analysis of family and clan relations in postexilic genealogies.

The next set of essays treats the Israelite wisdom tradition with its numerous female figures: Lady Wisdom and the "strange" woman, the king's mother and the strong woman, the "good" and the "bad" wife. All four articles not only underline the highly judgmental presentation of women and their roles in wisdom but also discuss their societal function and demonstrate that some texts are not as androcentric as commonly assumed.

The third part of the volume assembles articles about women and gender relations in single books, some poetic and others prose. They aim either at

---

2. For the original plan to divide the volumes with regard to the canons, see Fischer, Navarro Puerto, and Taschl-Erber, *Torah*, 11–21.

reconstructing women's experience and contexts of living or at unfolding the meaning of female metaphors. For instance, Psalms and Lamentations mostly talk implicitly or generally about women. Their gendered images, however, contribute to the metaphors used for God as well as to the metaphor of the community as a female body.

The essays of part 4 explore narratives about great female protagonists, such as Ruth, Esther, and Susanna, who prove their wit and strength in situations of conflict. While some essays interpret these protagonists as examples of virtue and faith, they also demonstrate that these female figures may be ambivalent role models for contemporary female readers.

2. Contents and Genres of the Writings

With regard to contents, literary style, and genre, the Writings assemble very different texts, which may be variously classified. Some offer poetry, such as the books of Psalms, Proverbs, Song of Songs, Lamentations, and Qohelet, to which Job may be added despite its short narrative frame. Proverbs, Job, and Qohelet (with Ben Sira and Wisdom) clearly belong to the wisdom tradition and thus have a didactic purpose. Psalms, Song of Songs, and Lamentations provide prayers, songs, and liturgical texts, albeit of very different tone and contents. Ruth, Esther, and Dan 1–6 contain narratives of brave women and men in Diaspora who, despite adverse conditions, succeed through faith and righteousness. Daniel 7–12 holds prophetic visions, which in symbolic camouflage announce the forcible end of subsequent Greek and Hellenistic rulers. Ezra-Nehemiah is a historiographical narrative about the rebuilding of Jerusalem and the reestablishment of a Judean community after the exile. Chronicles replicates the history of the Judean kingdom from a postexilic perspective starting with nine chapters of the genealogies of "all Israel."

Regarding this collection of rather diverse texts, most of which were written or edited in the Persian and early Hellenistic period, it is obvious that they present vastly different gender relations. Yet all texts are clearly products of a patriarchal society in which a person is first determined by social status, that is, as free person or slave, then by social class, and within the same class by gender, age, and other factors.[3] While the biblical texts mirror this pyramid of social hierarchy called patriarchy, some of them also represent voices of the marginalized or criticize hegemonic discourses of power. Due to this intriguing feature of the biblical texts—the inclusion of a variety of voices and

---

3. See Fischer, Navarro Puerto, and Taschl-Erber, *Torah*, 9–10.

perspectives—many different interpretations may emerge depending on the hermeneutic position of the interpreter.

The Writings that form the third part of the Hebrew Bible canon were produced in Jerusalem and its environs from the fifth to the beginning of the second century BCE, a period of political and economic crises, in which different empires dominated Judah. Therefore, most of their authors may not have known each other and did not communicate their views to one another. Since their texts have been assembled in the same corpus, however, their differing views on women and gender issues may now be perceived as a written discourse on gender hierarchy, societal values, and power relations. In relating each book to a specific date and location, which may be more or less evident, modern Bible scholars may detect some development of views and arguments, or seemingly persistent ideas. Evidently, the Writings, with their numerous strong female figures, offer modern readers a fascinating tapestry of women's lives and roles as perceived by ancient authors.

3. The Range of Approaches to the Texts

The attentive reader of this volume will realize that the articles differ in the methodology they bring to the biblical texts. Therefore, we asked each author to briefly introduce her or his hermeneutics and approach at the beginning of the essay.

Tamara Cohn Eskenazi aims at reconstructing the lives of women in the postexilic era through biblical and extrabiblical sources, introducing readers to the economic and social situation in Persian-period Yehud, the formative period for some of the Writings. Sara Japhet's treatment of Chronicles as a history of Israel that is based on previous accounts in Samuel and Kings as well as on local Judean traditions of the early Hellenistic period demonstrates how a historiographical narrative is shaped by the interests of its authors. She reads the bone-dry genealogies of Chronicles, which modern recipients often intentionally ignore, as a countervoice to the strong rejection of marriages with foreign women advocated in Ezra-Nehemiah and Prov 1–9.

The articles about the wisdom tradition focus on the portrayal of female characters with a critical eye on the ideologies these characterizations promote. From a gender-sensitive perspective, such characterization of women and their roles in society is neither neutral nor merely descriptive, but often prescriptive by offering role models for ancient readers, both men and women. As Gerlinde Baumann elaborates, the figure of personified wisdom enriches the imagery of the divine, yet was also used to promote a certain ethics and behavior in leading circles of the Persian and Hellenistic period.

In contrast, the cultural stereotypes of the "strange" and the "strong" woman in Proverbs and the "good" and "bad" wives in Ben Sira generated role models for women in a patriarchal society and an upper-class milieu. Christl Maier and Nuria Calduch-Benages discuss both the benefits and the risks of such stereotyping. Similarly, Vittoria D'Alario interprets notions about women in Qohelet as alternating between misogyny and appreciation. She also demonstrates how wisdom texts that have long been named "misogynist" may offer astonishing insights into the authority and power of women.

In keeping with the other volumes on the Hebrew Bible canon, Silvia Schroer examines relations between texts and iconographic traditions that result from a common cultural set of motifs. The ancient Near Eastern images of creation and world order as well as gods and goddesses presented on artifacts of Syrian-Palestinian art provide a fuller understanding of many of the metaphors in poetic texts like Psalms, Song of Songs, and Proverbs.

Where dating is impossible on account of a long tradition history of single texts, such as the book of Psalms, Donatella Scaiola focuses on emblematic feminine symbols like the mother metaphor, which adds to the imagery of both the divine and the holy city of Jerusalem. Ulrike Bail and Nancy Lee use the method of gendering voices in the text, proposed by Athalya Brenner and Fokkelien van Dijk-Hemmes, to interpret various songs of lament. By pointing to intertextual links between Ps 55 and the story of Tamar (2 Sam 13), Bail is able to read a lament psalm as a prayer that encourages victims of sexual violence to voice their grief. In Lamentations, Lee detects a strong female voice that takes the lead in expressing complaint about God's violent punishing. This voice, she argues, represents the experience of women and may even belong to a female composer. In reading the female protagonist of the Song of Songs through the lens of the wisdom tradition in Gen 2–3, Gianni Barbiero argues that the empowerment of Shulammite does not contradict a fulfilling love attachment.

The articles on female protagonists in narrative texts analyze their characterization with regard to explicit or implicit gender hierarchies and to women's options for finding their place in a patriarchal world. Miren Junkal Guevara Llaguno interprets Ruth and Naomi as women who reclaim their life and memory to become a source of empowerment for female readers in their struggle for life. Susan Niditch discusses a range of feminist readings of the Esther figure and demonstrates that the expectation and worldview of the interpreter is key to Esther's reception. By revealing the subtleties of the biblical character, the interpreters demonstrate that their diverse readings of Esther are based on rather ambivalent images of women. Isabel Gómez-Acebo interprets the figure of Susanna, whose story has been added to the original text, as a female counterpart to Daniel. Susanna's struggle against gender hierarchies gives way to the idea that a people's liberation can only be completed if both men and women fight for it.

The essays of this volume do not offer exhaustive or exclusive interpretations of the Writings. Their common characteristic is to focus on gender issues, power relations, and ideologies within the texts and in current interpretations. The latter belong to the texts' reception history in Western academic circles, which until recently have been dominated by male scholars and therefore often prolonged the inherited androcentric tradition. Most of the articles do not deal explicitly with the reception history of the Hebrew writings, but many do offer a critique of incomplete or gender-biased interpretations by either arguing against standardized exegesis or by carving out countertraditions that lead to new, gender-sensitive readings of these texts.

The translation of German, Italian, and Spanish contributions into English is a complex task insofar as scholarship differs in the respective linguistic domains, especially with regard to the interpretation of single biblical books as well as to feminist issues. We tried to translate the essays into comprehensible English and in some instances included footnotes that indicate which translations of the Bible have been used. Through more detailed biographical notes on our authors, we try to illuminate these different traditions of research.

4. Acknowledgments

The research colloquium held in Marburg in July of 2011, in which most of the authors submitted their first theses to a critical discussion, was generously sponsored by the German Research Foundation (DFG). The department of Protestant Theology at the University of Marburg supported the colloquium by providing rooms, administrative support, and student assistants. We thank both institutions for fostering our research. For their assistance in organizing the colloquium, we thank Mareike Schmied, Andrea Schönfeld de Weigel, and Maurice Meschonat.

In 2011, our project was awarded the Leonore Siegele-Wenschkewitz Prize, named after the German church historian Leonore Siegele-Wenschkewitz (1944–99). With this award, the Verein zur Förderung Feministischer Theologie in Forschung und Lehre e. V., the Protestant Church of Hesse and Nassau, and the Protestant Academy Arnoldshain honor studies or projects that promote feminist theology or gender studies in theological contexts. We are grateful for this endorsement of our work and have spent the award money on the translation of some essays.

We especially thank our esteemed authors for their willingness to contribute to this volume, their cooperation in the colloquium, their open-mindedness to all our requests regarding their articles, and their patience to wait for publication in four different languages. We greatly appreciate the work of our translators, some of whom were so generous as to dedicate their skills without compensation. Our thanks also go to Spencer Kasko, student at Yale University Divinity School, who reviewed the English essays, and Miriam Tabea Kraaz, who helped with the editing of the final manuscript in Marburg.

We are very grateful to the project's main editors for entrusting us with the edition of this volume and for supporting our work in every step of the process. Finally, we thank the Society of Biblical Literature for their cooperation in bringing this book into print.

Marburg and Rome, April 2014

Part 1
Tracing the Living Conditions of Women

The Lives of Women in the Postexilic Era

Tamara Cohn Eskenazi

A major interpreter of life in the fourth century BCE describes the household as primarily a productive economic unit, with the woman in charge of turning raw material into foodstuff and textile into other goods. The wife's successful management determines the well-being of the household.

> A wife who is a good partner in the estate carries as much weight as her husband in attaining prosperity. Property generally comes into the house through the exertions of the husband but it is mostly dispensed through the housekeeping of the wife. If these activities are performed well, estates increase, but if they are managed poorly, estates diminish. (Xenophon, *Oeconomicus* 3.14–15)[1]

These words do not come from a twenty-first-century feminist scholar (though they could) but from Xenophon, writing in the fourth century BCE. His book *Oeconomicus* describes in detail the running of the household as the backbone of Greek society. Xenophon devotes half of the book to the wife and her roles. Such extensive information about the household and its management, with its division of labor, is unique. Also uniquely, the author constructs a dialogue between a husband and wife, giving the unnamed wife an opportunity to speak about herself and her wishes.

In Xenophon's account, the wife in an affluent agricultural household had full administrative and other authority for what transpired indoors. Her work and her husband's were viewed as interdependent. Her economic, emotional, and physical contribution was recognized as equal to her husband's, both partners potentially endowed with the same spiritual and moral virtues. The success of the household depended on the mutual contributions of both spouses. If the wife's skills and education came to surpass the husband's, he

---

1. Sarah B. Pomeroy, *Xenophon, Oeconomicus: A Social and Historical Commentary with a New English Translation* (Oxford: Clarendon, 1994), 121.

readily transferred the greater authority and responsibility to her.² However, Xenophon also makes it clear that the wife he describes did not originally possess any of these requisite skills but was trained by her husband when, at fifteen, she married. Her sole qualifications when she first married were weaving and the ability to control her appetite.

Although Xenophon describes an Athenian household at the outskirts of Athens, several factors make his book relevant for information about women in postexilic/Persian-period Judah. First, Xenophon gives us a firsthand description of someone's reflection about the lives of women, dated to the period under study, namely, the Persian period. Second, the agrarian world he depicts resembles that of Judah in terms of geography and climate, and produces some of the same crops (grapevines, olive trees, date palms). Third, his description also corresponds to what modern scholars construe on other grounds for women in antiquity; for example, the tasks Xenophon assigns to the woman correspond to much in Carol Meyers's "Archaeology—A Window to the Lives of Israelite Women."³ These also conform to what Hennie Marsman depicts in her study of Israel and its surrounding cultures.⁴ Fourth, this description in Xenophon largely corresponds also to that of the "woman of valor" in Prov 31:10–31, the most extensive biblical description of an ideal wife, her duties, abilities, and worth.

These various parallels between Xenophon and Proverbs are just some of the hints of common features in perceptions about women in the contemporaneous ancient world. They suggest that exploring such contemporaneous sources can help shed light on women's lives in the postexilic period and on interpreting their representations in the Bible. When handled critically and with care, the numerous and diverse sources from classical Greece and other neighboring cultures enable scholars to hypothesize about possible similarities or developments, and fill in gaps in the biblical sources.

For this reason I will first (1) briefly describe the postexilic period, and then (2) review representative extrabiblical sources (from Greece, Egypt, and

---

2. See Ibid., 143.

3. See Carol Meyers, "Archaeology—A Window to the Lives of Israelite Women," in *Torah* (ed. Irmtraud Fischer et al.; The Bible and Women: An Encyclopaedia of Exegesis and Cultural History 1.1; Atlanta: Society of Biblical Literature, 2011), 19–21. See also Meyers, "Grinding to a Halt: Gender and the Changing Technology of Flour Production in Roman Galilee," in *Engendering Social Dynamics: The Archaeology of Maintenance Activities* (ed. Sandra Montón-Subías and Margarita Sánchez-Romero; BAR International Series 1862; Oxford: Archeopress, 2008), 65–74.

4. Hennie J. Marsman, *Women in Ugarit and Israel: Their Social and Religious Position in the Context of the Ancient Near East* (Leiden: Brill, 2003).

Mesopotamia) in order to envision wider cultural trends in the postexilic/Persian period. Finally (3), I will place within these contexts the contribution of the biblical sources in order to understand the lives of women in the postexilic period.

1. The Postexilic/Persian Period (Sixth–Fourth Century BCE)

Reckonings of the postexilic period usually begin in 539/538 BCE, which coincides with the emergence of the Persian Empire that dominated the ancient Near East until 333 BCE. According to the Bible and archaeology, Judah was devastated in 587/586 BCE by the Babylonians. Jerusalem and its temple were destroyed, and important segments of the population were deported (in 597 and 587 BCE and after). Recent archaeological studies suggest that the population in Judah was reduced to 20 percent or at most 30 percent of its former size.[5]

Ezra-Nehemiah is the only biblical narrative that explicitly depicts postexilic Judah. According to Ezra-Nehemiah, Judah was repatriated during the Persian period. The returnees came in three major waves: the first reinstated the cult and rebuilt the temple (Ezra 1–6); the second, guided by the priest and scribe Ezra, reformed the community by prohibiting marriage with "foreign" women (Ezra 7–10); the third, guided by Nehemiah the governor, rebuilt Jerusalem's walls (Neh 1–7). In mid-fifth century BCE, when the restoration was complete, the community rededicated itself, vowing to abide by the teachings of the Torah and demonstrating its allegiance (Neh 8–13).

The census list in Ezra-Nehemiah records that over 42,000 returned from exile to Judah (Ezra 2/Neh 7). When the number for the named groups of men are added, the "men" tally at about 30,000, which implies that the list includes some 10,000 women (or women and children). This ratio between women and men is credible in light of general information about other voluntary migrations in which men, especially young and unmarried, more often undertake arduous transplanting.

However, the reliability of the list(s) is highly contested. The sum total for repatriates conflicts with archaeological data. Excavations show no evidence of a sudden influx of such proportion; furthermore, excavations indicate that Judah remained poor and sparsely populated throughout the Persian period. Some scholars therefore suppose that the list is a compilation of several stages

---

5. Avraham Faust, "Settlement Dynamics and Demographic Fluctuations in Judah from the Late Iron Age to the Hellenistic Period and the Archaeology of Persian Period Yehud," in *A Time of Change: Judah and Its Neighbours in the Persian and Early Hellenistic Periods* (ed. Yigal Levin; New York: T&T Clark, 2007), 23–51.

of return, spanning the whole period and/or an expanded census list of the cumulative record of the entire Jewish community in Judah over decades. Nevertheless, the overall picture of several returns and some serious reconstruction in the fifth century BCE is credible, even if the numbers are heavily inflated. Judah/Yehud did recover and became more developed by the beginning of the Hellenistic period. The fifth century is a likely time for immigration in light of other developments in the region, such as increased commerce on the coast and the end of the Persian wars with Greece (dated to the Peace of Kallias in 449 BCE).

According to Ezra-Nehemiah, Babylonian Jews and the empire helped subsidize the reconstruction. But Judah remained unquestionably very poor. Archaeologists conclude that of the 108 newly established sites, 49 were small, less than 5 dunams (1.25 acres). Significantly, 372 sites were not resettled in the Persian period and 27 never again.[6]

Yet some texts point to some level of affluence among a few. The items for the temple and the priests suggest that this class of cult professionals was well supported. Ezra-Nehemiah includes among the returning exiles 7,337 slaves (Ezra 2:65//Neh 7:67) and 200 male and female singers (Ezra 2:65//Neh 7:67). Although the number of slaves is proportionately small, it bespeaks a class with means, as does the presence of singers (Qoh 2:8 also mentions female singers, where they are acquired for pleasure by the speaker, who claims to be exceedingly wealthy). Nehemiah, the Jewish governor, claims to pay from his own (not communal) resources for regularly hosting over 150 people at his table (Neh 5:17). Perhaps the strongest evidence is Neh 5, where poor Judeans[7] (men and their wives) complain that their land, homes, and children are seized by their more affluent compatriots, with their daughters especially vulnerable (Neh 5:1–13).

All sources thus concur that postexilic Judah was small, struggling to survive economically, and rebuilding its identity as a minority group in a multi-

---

6. Thirteen sites were of 6–10 dunams; 13 were of 11–20 dunams; 18 were larger than 20 dunams. For another 15, no size is given; see Diana Edelman, *The Origins of the Second Temple: Persian Imperial Policy and the Rebuilding of Jerusalem* (London: Equinox, 2005), 59. These recent studies effectively contradict the claims of scholars who in the 1990s promoted the view that most of the territory of Judah and Benjamin outside of Jerusalem was only little affected by the Babylonian conquest and destruction. See, e.g., Hans M. Barstad, "After 'the Myth of the Empty Land': Major Challenges in the Study of Neo Babylonian Judah," and Bustenay Oded, "Where Is 'The Myth of the Empty Land' to Be Found?—Myth versus History," both in *Judah and the Judeans in the Neo Babylonian Period* (ed. Oded Lipschits et al.; Winona Lake, Ind.: Eisenbrauns, 2003), 3–20, and 55–74, respectively.

7. It is customary now to refer to the inhabitants of Judah/Yehud in the Persian period as "Judahites." I use "Judean" because it is the term more familiar to the general reader.

ethnic milieu. Avraham Faust depicts it as a "post collapse society," a technical term for a society that has undergone traumatic destruction and seeks to restore an infrastructure. Biblical sources reflect a debate about the new way forward as a colonized people. This includes a debate about criteria for membership, prompted by the loss of earlier established markers.[8]

According to Ezra-Nehemiah, women were an important component of the community. Their presence is acknowledged in every stage of reconstruction; however, they are not typically named, and their most prominent role in Ezra-Nehemiah is as "foreign wives" who are deemed a threat.

2. Extrabiblical Sources

While most biblical texts for the postexilic period focus on events in the province of Judah, Jewish postexilic communities coexisted in Diaspora, and kept their ties to Judah. Diaspora communities reflect a modicum of affluence and stability among these transplanted Judeans. In the Bible, the book of Esther depicts life in Persia itself. But the extrabiblical evidence is found primarily in two major Jewish Diaspora centers in the Persian period: the archives from Elephantine, Egypt, and documents from different communities in Babylonia. Other valuable information about women's lives comes from classical Greece, where diverse sources are more abundant. Although Greek sources do not specifically pertain to Jewish women, they augment our understanding of how women in the Persian period (in a neighboring culture) were perceived socially, legally, and economically. These multiple sources serve as a backdrop to the sparser sources from the Bible and the archaeology of Judah.

2.1. Women in Classical Greek Sources

As Sarah Pomeroy observes, Xenophon "is the first Greek author to give full recognition to the use-value of women's work, and to understand that domestic labour has economic value even if it lacks exchange value."[9] And yet, Xenophon's praise of the wife's worth is not typical of Xenophon's society and is probably not typical of biblical society. We learn elsewhere from Xenophon that most Greeks denigrate manual work that can be performed by women and slaves, having leisure as their ideal. This attitude may also represent a biblical view, at least in some circles. For this reason, we must guard against

---

8. See Faust, "Settlement Dynamics," 43–46.
9. Pomeroy, *Xenophon, Oeconomicus*, 59.

equating productivity with prestige, against supposing that the importance of women's work generated widespread appreciation for women.

2.1.1. Women in Athenian Sources from the Persian Period

A fourth-century BCE text describes women's roles in Athens this way: "courtesans [ἑταίραι] we keep for pleasure, concubines [παλλακαί] for our daily attendance upon our person, but wives for the procreation of legitimate children and to be the faithful guardians of our households."[10] How, then, does Xenophon's depiction of the happy couple, cited on the first page of this article, match what other sources disclose about Athenian women in the classical period? The Athenian οἶκος, home, was—as Xenophon depicts it—a production unit. It could include an extended family with several adult sons and their own spouses and offspring, as well as parents and unmarried daughters. It would also include slaves and possibly concubines. In all this the Athenian household parallels the biblical household, the בית.

Similarities are less certain in regard to women's legal status, marriage practices, inheritance laws, and the like. According to Athenian laws, women were not independent persons. A woman's father or husband was her κύριος, legal "lord" and master. A woman's marriage was arranged by her male relative and comprised two stages: the contract between the males and the actual marriage, γάμος, when the bride physically joined the groom's home. Her dowry, which was an optional gift by her father to the couple, however, was returned in the case of divorce or the husband's death. Divorcing a wife was easy: the man simply sent her away and returned the dowry.[11] Divorcing a husband was more difficult. Although a woman could do so, she had to appear before an official and provide a document in order to get a divorce. Her dowry had to be returned in this case as well; it went to the original giver (her father or brother). It is not clear whether her husband could block the divorce.[12]

A childless widow had to return (with her dowry) to her father's house. If with children, she could remain in the husband's household. This was the only situation in which a woman had a choice. A widow or divorcée could remarry,

---

10. Pseudo-Demosthenes, *Against Neaera* 122 (fourth century BCE; cited in Mary R. Lefkowitz and Maureen B. Fant, *Women's Life in Greece and Rome: A Source Book in Translation* (Baltimore: Johns Hopkins University Press, 1992), 82.

11. See Douglas M. MacDowell, *The Law in Classical Athens* (Ithaca, N.Y.: Cornell University Press, 1978), 87.

12. Ibid., 88.

with her original κύριος making the arrangement. Her husband "on his deathbed or in his will could give his widow, with dowry, to a new husband."[13]

Athenian laws carefully delineated the transmission of property through the male line. A widow did not inherit her husband's property. It went instead to their children or to the husband's siblings. When a man died without a son or grandson, his daughter was provided with a male kin who was to marry her and produce children who inherit.

2.1.2. The Gortyn Code (Fifth Century BCE)

The extensive Gortyn Code from Crete is one of the most complete law codes from the fifth century BCE. Its laws are primarily family laws, regulating issues of marriage, inheritance, adoption, rape, and adultery. These laws suggest that women enjoyed a relatively high position in Gortyn when compared with Athens,[14] with parity between women and men in certain areas. Women, like men, could own property, retain it in marriage, and dispose of it at will. Both spouses were equally entitled to usufruct. Widows inherited on par with male kin. Daughters inherited alongside sons. However, a son inherited two portions of parental property and a daughter only one. Witnessing of legal arrangements required free men as witnesses, not women. Marriages were arranged by male relatives (VIII.20–22) and male witnesses (VI.1–2). Women could initiate divorce and take what they brought into the house—a certain amount of money as well if the man was the cause of the divorce.[15] But, whereas what a man added to the household remained his, the woman could take away only half of what she had added to the household.

The laws of Gortyn assume legal social stratification, with free citizens as the aristocracy that controls the three governing bodies.[16] The other groups were the ἀρεταίροι, that is, free persons excluded from political rights, serfs, and slaves. Tribes were still important, especially in the case of an heiress (she was expected to marry within the tribe). A woman's status was either her own—if the man joined her household—or the husband's—if she joined his (VII.1–10, 15).

---

13. Ibid., 89, citing Demosthenes 27.5, 45.28 (see 266n189).

14. Ronald F. Willetts, *The Law Code of Gortyn, Edited with Introduction, Translation and a Commentary* (Berlin: de Gruyter, 1967), 25. In what follows, in-text references are to the column and line number(s) of the Gortyn Code.

15. Ibid., 29.

16. These bodies are the κόσμος/κόσμοι, the Council of Elders, and the Assembly, the latter with limited power, mentioned only once in the code in relation to adoption.

Ronald Willetts, who has translated and commented extensively on the laws of Gortyn, observes that some of the stringent measures imposed on violators of these laws imply that "abuses against women's rights of tenure must have been markedly on the increase."[17]

2.2. Babylonian/Mesopotamian Sources

Babylonian sources for this period include the Murashu banking records from Nippur[18] and archives and marriage contracts from the Egibi family.[19] Additional information comes from the recently studied documents from or associated with al-Yahudu, a town in Babylonia named, presumably, after the original homeland of its chief inhabitants, namely, Judean exiles. Some of the names in these documents are of Jewish origin and more visibly indicate thereby exiled Judeans who live in Babylonia.

In her detailed examination of the material, Christine Roy Yoder documents some of the ways that women in Mesopotamia played various roles in the economy.[20] She notes that the sources depict women as household managers, some of whom "manufactured textiles, traded in the marketplaces, and might own properties"; nonroyal women "engaged in a wide range of skilled and unskilled professions in numbers equivalent or greater than men."[21] The Murashu banking records and other Mesopotamian documents demonstrate that women were able to conduct their husband's business affairs, such as distributing and receiving payments.[22] They also initiated business transactions, making and taking loans, managing property, and accruing interests. They were also parties in the sale and purchase of slaves and land.[23]

---

17. Willetts, *The Law Code of Gortyn*, 21.
18. See the Murashu tablets published by Matthew W. Stolper, *Entrepreneurs and the Empire: The Murašû Archive, the Murašû Firm, and Persian Rule in Babylonia* (Leiden: Nederlands Historisch-Archaeologisch Instituut te Istanbul, 1985).
19. See especially Martha T. Roth, "The Dowries of the Women of the Itti-Marduk-Balatu Family," *JAOS* 111 (1991): 19–37.
20. Christine R. Yoder, *Wisdom as a Woman of Substance: A Socio-economic Reading of Proverbs 1–9 and 31:10–31* (BZAW 304; Berlin: de Gruyter, 2001).
21. Ibid., 71.
22. Ibid., 59–60, 66.
23. Ibid., 59–60, 66–67. Transactions by royal women appear in Veysel Donbaz and Matthew W. Stolper, *Istanbul Murašû Texts* (Leiden: Nederlands Historisch-Archaeologisch Instituut te Istanbul, 1997), e.g., 114 [no. 44] and CBS 5199, cited by Yoder, *Wisdom*, 66. Nonroyal women's transactions are documented, e.g., in Nbn 741 and Camb 279, cited by Yoder, *Wisdom*, 60. For a fuller account, see Yoder, *Wisdom*, 58–68.

Of special interest are marriage contracts and dowry accounts. Although the vast majority of them record transactions between men, in which the bride is spoken of but not herself a legal partner, a few of these show that women were legal persons entitled to give and receive property and also to bequeath it. One document from the Egibi family archives records that a woman bequeathed property to her granddaughter as part of a dowry arrangement. In a document from al-Yahudu, the bride's mother is named as the person from whom the groom requests the daughter in marriage. This mother is also the recipient of some silver in this process.[24] The presence of the bride's brother, who is recorded in the document, indicates that the mother is not the only surviving family member and underscores the authority that the mother possesses. Although not typical of the contracts, since most of the others are between men, such examples establish that a woman could constitute a legal partner in a legal transaction in Babylonia. The Egibi family archives also show that a woman could receive property from her father as well as her husband. The dowries of the affluent brides in this archive usually include two to ten slaves, as well as silver.

2.3. The Jewish Community in Elephantine, Egypt

The over one hundred Elephantine papyri from fifth-century BCE Egypt provide the most extensive information about Jewish women's lives in the Persian period. They come from a garrison of Judeans who lived with Egyptian neighbors and were serving the Persian king. The archives trace via legal transactions the lives of several women and show that women could marry and divorce as they wished, on equal footing with men. They could own and dispose property independently, even when married, and could bequeath it equally to their male and female offspring. The documents indicate great mobility across class, ethnicity, and religious boundaries. Tapmut was an Egyptian slave woman who married a Judean man (K 2).[25] Twenty-two years later she was granted her freedom (K 5). But fifteen years after their marriage, Anani, her husband, transferred half of his house to her (K 4), with the entire house to be hers upon his death. They both bequeathed it to their children, to be divided equally between their son and daughter, Yehoshima. Although she

---

24. Moussaieff tablet, translated and analyzed by Kathleen Abraham, "West Semitic and Judean Brides in Cuneiform Sources from the Sixth Century B.C.E. New Evidence from a Marriage Contract from *al-Yahudu*," *AfO* 51 (2005–6): 198–219.

25. Emil G. Kraeling, ed., *The Brooklyn Museum Aramaic Papyri: New Documents of the Fifth Century B.C. from the Jewish Colony at Elephantine* (New Haven: Yale University Press, 1953). Since Kraeling numbered the documents, they are referred to as K 1, K 2, etc.

began as a slave, Tapmut later held a position comparable to her husband's in the local Jewish temple to the God Yahu, presumably a Yahwistic temple (K 12:1).[26]

Another woman, Mibtahiah, was initially married to a Judean man. Her father granted her property upon marriage, specifying that it must remain hers, not her husband's (C 7);[27] her husband apparently died before they had children. Mibtahiah then married an Egyptian architect/builder and became his business partner. They subsequently divorced amicably and divided their many possessions, at which point she married his Egyptian partner, who later took a Hebrew name (a sign of officially becoming a Jew?), and with whom she bore children who were given Yahwistic names.

The marriage contracts of all the women—the earliest extant Jewish marriage contracts so far—specify that either spouse can initiate a "no-fault" divorce, each taking back what he or she brought to the marriage. The initiating spouse pays a designated "divorce money" (K 12; K 7). The מהר (*mohar*), that is, the gift by the groom to the bride or her family, is not returned to the groom in either case (C 7). The wife inherits her husband's property upon his death if there are no children (C 7). These marriage contracts are construed as an agreement between men—the groom with the father or master of the bride. However, other documents, such as loans or deeds of conveyance, list the woman as an actual contractual partner (C 8; C 10; K 10). Although women are sometimes parties to the contract, the witnesses are invariably men. Women are also active contributors to the local Jewish temple. About half of the 103 persons who are mentioned in one document as contributors of money or gifts of monetary value to the temple are women (C 22).

The marriage documents list the woman's belongings and give us a sense of a "trousseau": the affluent daughter of Tapmut, Yehoshima, in 420 BCE, brought with her several garments of linen and wool, silver objects including utensils, a mirror, olive oil, and balsam oil, some light furniture as well as "cash" (K 7). Her mother brought to the marriage in 449 BCE only one wool garment, some balsam ointment, a mirror, and a few shekels (K 2). Yehoshima's wealth came to her from her father and indicates that her mother, the former slave Tapmut, married a prosperous man.

More can be garnered from these documents, but for our purpose it suffices to say that this community displays legal parity in the postexilic/Persian period between Jewish women and men. Importantly, women were

---

26. The term for the office, לחן for him, לחנה for her, is not fully understood. A later meaning of the term suggests something related to music or chanting.

27. Arthur E. Cowley, ed., *Aramaic Papyri of the Fifth Century B.C.* (Oxford: Clarendon, 1923). These documents are named C 1, C 2, etc.

economically protected in marriage and in divorce. Although not as frequently represented in extant documents, we see throughout that women controlled their resources and were able to engage in commerce, buy and sell property, and undertake loans. In this way community, ethnic, religious, and social boundaries were permeable.

2.4. Conclusions Regarding Women's Status and Legal Position

The preponderance of evidence suggests that the disenfranchisement of women in Athens is an exception to the more widespread position of limited but definite legal rights for women in terms of marriage, divorce, property, and inheritance. The practices in contemporaneous Jewish communities such as those in al-Yahudu and Elephantine are especially suggestive. The biblical evidence implies a similar situation when we look at the book of Ruth or Proverbs. In Ruth 4 we learn that Naomi is disposing of family land and that Ruth is likewise entitled to it. Proverbs 31:14 and 17 likewise claim that the woman is able to negotiate commercial transaction on behalf of the household.

3. Postexilic/Persian Period Biblical Sources

Three sources unambiguously pertain to the postexilic period: Ezra-Nehemiah, Esther, and Proverbs. Evidence from Ruth is more difficult to assess because the book depicts an earlier era, even though it most likely emerges from the postexilic period.

3.1. Women in Ezra-Nehemiah

Ezra-Nehemiah includes women at key points, although—with one exception—it never mentions their names.[28] The most important texts are those "covenantal" texts that describe the public reading and the pledge to uphold the Torah. Whereas Moses' instructions in Exod 19:15 ("do not go near a woman") have rendered women's presence at the Sinai revelation somewhat ambiguous,[29] Neh 8 specifies twice that women were present at the formal postexilic public reading and accepting of the Torah (8:2–3). This event,

---

28. For an overview on feminist research, see Christiane Karrer-Grube, "Ezra and Nehemiah: The Return of the Others," in *Feminist Biblical Interpretation: A Compendium of Critical Commentary on the Books of the Bible and Related Literature* (ed. Luise Schottroff and Marie-Theres Wacker; Grand Rapids: Eerdmans, 2012), 192–206.

29. See the discussion by Elaine Goodfriend, "Yitro," in *The Torah: A Women's Commentary* (ed. Tamara Cohn Eskenazi and Andrea L. Weiss; New York: UTJ, 2008), 407.

sometimes reckoned as a "second Sinai"[30] with enduring consequences, marks the sustained transformation of the Judeans into "the people of the Book." It records the presence of women as recognized, active partners in the formally constituted community.

Women are also integral to the communal pledge in Neh 10:1–29. We read about the vow of "the rest of the people, the priests, the Levites, the gatekeepers, the singers, the temple servants, and all who separated themselves from the peoples of the lands to [follow] the Torah of God, their wives, sons and daughters, all who know enough to understand, join with their noble brothers, and take an oath with sanctions to follow the Torah of God" (Neh 10:29–30). Other texts attest to the perceived power of women and their influence. Of special interest is the female prophet Noadiah, who appears as an opponent of Nehemiah. Nehemiah singles her out for curses, along with his chief adversaries—the governor of Samaria and the high official Tobiah: "O my God, remember against Tobiah and Sanballat these deeds of theirs, and against Noadiah the prophetess, and against the other prophets that they wished to intimidate me!" (Neh 6:14). In placing Noadiah on par with other leaders, Nehemiah's denunciation indicates that her position carried weight. Nehemiah does not deny her authority as prophet. Unfortunately, we know nothing further about her.

The crisis of the so-called foreign wives highlights most vividly the importance of women and their influence, even if in terms of the danger they might pose. According to Ezra 9:1–2, returning exiles, especially their leaders, have married women from among "the people[s] of the land." Ezra 9 likens the activities of these women to those of the Canaanite nations that Israel was commanded to shun and even destroy upon entering the land centuries earlier (see, e.g., Deut 7:1–6; 23:4–7).

It is not clear whether the opposed women in Ezra 9–10 actually belong to other ethnicities (Moabites, etc.) or merely are charged with being like them (Ezra 9:1–2); in other words, are they in fact foreign or only deemed that way because they belong to Israelite or Judean groups that did not go into exile or do not share the ethos of those responsible for Ezra-Nehemiah? Either way, the crisis Ezra 9–10 depicts is based on the assumption that women whose religious practices do not conform to the current standards of Ezra-Nehemiah should be expelled. The intermarrying men—not the women—are the targeted offenders, with the greatest opposition directed

---

30. See Tamara Cohn Eskenazi, "Ezra-Nehemiah," in *The Women's Bible Commentary* (ed. Carol A. Newsom et al.; 3rd ed.; Louisville: Westminster John Knox, 2012), 192–200, here 199.

against priests, who, according to Lev 21, are prohibited from marrying foreign women. Ezra 10 records that the priests promise to send their foreign wives away (10:19), whereas the fate of the other wives is not mentioned in Ezra-Nehemiah.[31]

Foreign wives are opposed by Nehemiah as well. He writes: "Also at that time, I saw that Jews had married Ashdodite, Ammonite, and Moabite women; a good number of their children spoke the language of Ashdod and the language of those various peoples, and did not know how to speak Judean" (Neh 13:23–24 NJPS). Nehemiah soon declares that foreign wives caused even King Solomon (centuries earlier) to sin (13:26), and subsequently expels the priest who married a woman from Samaria.

Although the situations in Ezra 9–10 and Neh 13 are markedly different, they contribute some important insights into the status of women in the household and the community. Class and economic issues seem to be at work since upper-class Judeans are marrying upper-class members of the surrounding nations, perhaps, like Solomon, for the purpose of cementing political and economic alliances. The clear message in Ezra-Nehemiah is that from here onward exogamous marriages, that is, marriages with outsiders, are forbidden. They threaten the cohesion of the community and undermine its devotion to God.

Certain conclusions regarding women can be drawn: First, women appear to be loyal to their own traditions. They perpetuate their own cultural and religious practices rather than adapt to those of their husbands. Second, women are influential. Their commitment to their own culture and religion is so definitive that they and their offspring must be excised when there are differences with the man's. This issue seems to be of greater concern in the postexilic era—as well as in contemporaneous Athens, where a similar law was enacted in 451—perhaps because citizens now play a greater role in the community's religious and political life. Such circumstances, in which families often determine policies, disclose a greater concern with shared norms than is required when binding authority is imposed by a monarch from above. Third, women are not automatically absorbed into the religious and cultural life of their husbands. They are expected to retain their traditions. Fourth, the children go with the mothers. Even if it may not be correct to speak here about examples of matrilineal descent, this indivisible bond granted mother and child is noteworthy. Fathers do not retain custody of the children. Although

---

31. Ezra 10:44 is ambiguous; most English-language translations insert a verse from 1 Esdras, which specifies that these women were expelled, but this is not found in the Hebrew Bible. The number of men who intermarried is about 110, with seventeen belonging to cultic officials.

some modern interpreters express an understandable dismay over the decision to expel children, separating the children from their mother would have justified a louder outcry. Finally, although women are present among those supporting the decision (Ezra 10:1), the "foreign" women themselves are not addressed and they do not voice their position.

Membership in the postexilic community seems to have been a highly contested issue in the postexilic community, when earlier identity markers, such as birthplace, no longer applied in the same way and when the fledgling community was small and a minority in Judah, and even more so in Diaspora. Isaiah 56:3–8 is one of several postexilic texts that respond to the challenge, taking a different position from Ezra-Nehemiah, by welcoming foreigners. The book of Ruth describes how a Moabite woman enters the Judean household—despite the prohibition in Deut 23:4–7 and the objections in Ezra-Nehemiah—becoming the ancestress of Israel's most celebrated king, David.

3.2. Women in the Book of Ruth

As if a response to the exclusion of foreign women in Ezra-Nehemiah, the book of Ruth illustrates how a Moabite woman is welcomed into the community in Judah and becomes the great-grandmother of Israel's greatest king. Moreover, whereas women are silent in Ezra-Nehemiah, they are the eloquent protagonists in Ruth. Although situated at the time of the Judges (eleventh century BCE), the book of Ruth most likely was written in the postexilic era and represents a different answer from Ezra-Nehemiah as to whether a foreign woman may join the community.[32]

No biblical book concentrates on women and their lives more than the book of Ruth. Yet, while the book extols the determination of Ruth the Moabite and celebrates her and Naomi's resourcefulness, it also illustrates the limits of women's capacity to succeed without reliance on male authority. It thereby shows a world in which women can initiate actions but one in which official decisions are conferred or confirmed by men. Ruth preserves the typical pattern in the ancient world in which women can exercise power to achieve their goals but must also recruit men to their cause because men have the requisite authority.[33]

---

32. See Frederick Bush, *Ruth/Esther* (WBC 9; Waco, Tex.: Word, 1996), 18–30; Tamara Cohn Eskenazi and Tikva Frymer-Kensky, *Ruth* (JPS Bible Commentaries; Philadelphia: Jewish Publication Society, 2011), xvi–xix.

33. For another interpretation of the story of Ruth and Naomi, see the essay by Miren Junkal Guevara Llaguno in this volume.

Carol Meyers highlights the presence of a community of women in Ruth.[34] The women of Bethlehem surround Naomi when she arrives there (1:19). They reappear at the end (4:13–14) and define the meaning of the story with "a child is born to Naomi," who is to care for her in old age (4:14–15), and they also name that child (4:17). Yet one is also struck by the prior isolation of Ruth and Naomi, who are widows and probably poor: In the many months between the arrival in chapter 1 and the birth in chapter 4, Ruth and Naomi are home alone, except when Ruth is in the field, working close to Boaz's "girls," with whom there is no recorded interaction. The picture offered by the book is one in which absence of support is striking. This comports well with the hardships that widows experience in the rest of the Bible (see, e.g., the widow in 2 Kgs 4:1), and with the castigations in prophetic literature on account of the oppression of widows.

A couple of additional insights can be gleaned: first, that "girls" work in the field, gathering grain—an occupation also familiar from Egyptian paintings; second, that women in Ruth's position were likely to be harassed if they were not in the company of other women, because they were either foreign or poor (see Ruth 2:16, 22).

In terms of legal rights, Ruth 4 indicates that a woman could inherit familial property, either as usufruct or as outright possession. This follows from the fact that Naomi's husband's land does not revert to the nearest male kin but, rather, remains under Naomi's control (4:3). The fact that Boaz negotiates on behalf of Naomi and Ruth leaves unsettled the issue as to their legal or official capacity to undertake transactions. We cannot tell whether Boaz acts on the women's behalf because they are disqualified or because he gallantly spares them the arduous task.

An unusual reference to the mother's house in Ruth 1:8 most likely refers to the mother's jurisdiction as the context wherein a widow may find temporary respite while waiting to find a husband. This mention contrasts with the expectation that widows will return to their father's house elsewhere in biblical texts (e.g., Gen 38:11; Lev 22:13). As Carol Meyers observes, the term highlights women's role in "effecting nuptial agreements," which involve "perspicacity and diplomacy."[35] Meyers concludes that "in the survival of 'mother's

---

34. See Carol Meyers, "'Women in the Neighborhood' (Ruth 4.17): Informal Female Networks in Ancient Israel," in *Ruth and Esther* (ed. Athalya Brenner; FCB 2/3; Sheffield: Sheffield Academic, 1999), 110–127; Meyers, "Returning Home: Ruth 1:8 and the Gendering of the Book of Ruth," in *A Feminist Companion to Ruth* (ed. Athalya Brenner; Sheffield: Sheffield Academic, 1993), 85–114.

35. Carol Meyers, "'To Her Mother's House': Considering a Counterpart to the Israelite *Bet ab*," in *The Bible and the Politics of Exegesis: Essays in Honor of Norman K.*

house' as a counterpart to the usual term for family household as the fundamental unit of society, the wisdom and power of women in ancient Israel become fleetingly visible."[36]

Women in Ruth are deemed the pivot on which historical developments swing.[37] The Davidic genealogy at the end of the book (4:18–22) links the past (with Tamar's son Perez in 4:18, but also earlier with Tamar; see 4:12, where Tamar is named) and the national future. The names in the concluding genealogy are all of men. But the story's elaborate depiction of women's roles, and the naming of Tamar, Ruth, and Naomi as progenitors (see 4:12–13, 17) also illustrates how this male genealogy, like all genealogies, is the work of women, in this case resourceful and courageous women. Granting such credit to women is particularly perceptible in Persian-period biblical texts and suggests a more overt recognition of women's place in the culture and its literary works.

Orit Avnery sheds a certain light on the phenomenon by suggesting that Ruth and Esther are a literary attempt to cope with the existential realities of the Jewish community in the Persian period. Specifically, their stories focus on marginalization of an "other" who needs access to power—a position akin to that of the Jewish community under Persian imperial rule.[38] She points out that women are the best protagonists for the exploration because women are simultaneously "other" (brought from outside into the family) and, insofar as they stand for the "home," are also "insiders."

3.3. Women in the Book of Esther

The book of Esther focuses on Jewish life in Diaspora during the Persian period. Like the book of Ruth, it places a woman at the forefront and illustrates her capacity to exert power, this time in the highest echelons of society. As a story of an exceptional woman in an exceptional situation (a queen in Persia), it offers but little evidence concerning the lives of ordinary women. Still, its very presence in the Bible sheds light on perceptions about women in the postexilic/Persian period.[39]

Gottwald on His Sixty-Fifth Birthday (ed. David Jobling et al.; Cleveland: Pilgrim, 1991), 39–51, here 50.

36. Ibid., 51.

37. See Orit Avnery, "The Threefold Cord: Interrelations between the Books of Samuel, Ruth and Esther" [Hebrew] (Ph.D. diss., Bar Ilan University, 2011), 105.

38. Ibid., 1–13.

39. For another interpretation of the book of Esther, see the essay of Susan Niditch in this volume.

The book of Esther is more fiction than history and concerns a royal woman whose life in the court does not represent the common experience of women. Probably the most important information about women that Esther offers is its claim that women can exercise power in the political arena: Vashti's refusal to obey the king launches a national crisis for the crown, and Esther's tact and daring determine policies that rescue her people. Although Esther has no authority in the court and must achieve her goals by coaxing her man, she exercises authority in the Jewish community from which the book emerges. This phenomenon is itself a cultural statement about women in the postexilic era, even if the reality of women's lives differs. Thus, at the book's end, we learn that a woman's official letter has an authoritative role in Jewish life. Regardless of any historical accuracy, the story confirms and establishes Esther's instructions as binding on all generations.

> Queen Esther daughter of Abihail, along with the Jew Mordecai, gave full written authority, confirming this second letter about Purim. Letters were sent wishing peace and security to all the Jews, to the one hundred twenty-seven provinces of the kingdom of Ahasuerus, and giving orders that these days of Purim should be observed at their appointed seasons, as the Jew Mordecai and Queen Esther enjoined on the Jews, just as they had laid down for themselves and for their descendants regulations concerning their fasts and their lamentations. The command of Queen Esther fixed these practices of Purim, and it was recorded in writing. (Esth 9:29-32 NRSV)

The Hebrew verb translated in 9:29 as "gave full written authority" is feminine singular, unambiguously showing that Esther is the author of the letter. The point is made again in the last verse of this passage. As scholars note, there are clear signs that Mordecai's name was inserted at a later point.[40] Earlier layers of the text assert more clearly the singularity of Esther's role. But enough is preserved in the canonized version to show that an author articulated and a Jewish community accepted Esther's instructions as perpetually binding.

Along with this astounding affirmation, one also discerns most women's helplessness. Young women are rounded up at the king's whim and sent to his bed, whether willing or not (2:1-8). Esther herself risks death by approaching him unbidden (4:10-17). In addition, as a queen, Esther is confined to the palace, interacting even with her relative via an intermediary. Such is the portrait of a most privileged woman's life in the book of Esther. These details

---

40. See, e.g., David J. A. Clines, *Ezra, Nehemiah, Esther* (NCB; Grand Rapids: Eerdmans, 1984), 331.

reflect circumscribed lives for women even as the book highlights the extraordinary achievements of one extraordinary young woman.

3.4. Women in Proverbs

The book of Proverbs is considered an "instruction manual" aiming to educate elite men. It depicts women as a major force to be reckoned with. Good women determine a man's fate as successful and happy; "evil" women lead to his destruction. The latter constitute a perennial temptation for the young men whom the author of Proverbs addresses.[41]

The book is framed with messages concerning women. The last chapter begins with the instructions of King Lemuel's mother (31:1–9); it is followed by the lengthy acrostic poem of praise about "the capable wife" (Prov 31:10–31), which ends the book. The poem is the most explicit biblical text depicting the roles and responsibilities of a woman. Beginning with "A capable wife who can find? She is far more precious than jewels" (31:10 NRSV), it presents the household as an economic center for the production and dissemination of food and clothing, with the woman in full charge. The Hebrew is sometimes rendered as "a woman of valor," a translation that catches the sense of power embedded in the Hebrew, where the word חיל ("strength") describes the woman, a term elsewhere possessing military or other forms of power. Her tireless activities benefit her family and beyond. She controls the purse from which charity is bestowed upon the poor. The household is ביתה, "her household" or "her house," her בית (31:15, 21).

The poem specifies a number of things, almost all of them consistent with how Xenophon describes women's household activities and what scholars such as Carol Meyers have concluded on the basis of other sources such as material culture/archaeology for the Judean highland. In Proverbs, the wife is personally in charge of providing food for the household (31:15), and buys and plants fields and vineyards (31:16). She acquires flax and wool (31:13) and weaves both clothes and textile furnishing for the household (31:18, 21–22), as well as textiles that she sells for profit (31:24). She manages the (female) staff well (31:15) and is generous to the poor. She is a good administrator (31:27), whose virtues and skills secure the well-being of her entire family, bringing profit (31:21). The family's wealth is due to her, not her husband's, diligence. The focus throughout is on her competence as an administrator, much in the manner we find in Xenophon.

---

41. For an interpretation of the stereotypes of the "good" and "evil" woman in Proverbs see the essay by Christl M. Maier in this volume.

Interestingly, although we learn that she is a mother—her children praise her according to 31:28—nothing further is said about child care in this concluding poem. Thus Prov 31:10–31 does not mention the activities that most intensely would have occupied a woman's life, namely, giving birth and rearing children. Nonetheless, Proverbs elsewhere articulates the importance of maternal teaching in the socialization and education of the children (1:8; 6:20). In addition, we get a hint about a woman's intimate bond with her child when King Lemuel's mother addresses the king as "My son … son of my womb … son of my vows!" (31:2) before imparting teachings that include warnings about dangerous women.

Proverbs contrasts the wife, depicted as a deer (5:19)—a gentle creature, always able and ready to satiate—with the seductive, "foreign," and "strange" woman (5:3–14; 6:20–35). As Christl Maier suggests (in this volume), that woman is sexualized as an adulteress who leads young men to their destruction with her brazen behavior in public and the invitation to her bedroom in 7:1–27. Setting aside the tendentious nature of the passage as a warning, and the inevitable hyperbole, we can nevertheless discern certain facets of a woman's life in the depiction of the wayward or "foreign" woman. First, we learn that the woman has made vows and offered a sacrifice of well-being, her שלמים offering (7:14–15). These details suggest that women were making vows and fulfilling them, that they were able or expected to bring an offering themselves, even when married, and that, in certain circumstances, they were able to determine who could enjoy eating the remains of the offering with them. This picture largely corresponds to rules concerning the well-being offerings in Lev 7:11–21 and 22:21 and rules about women's vows in Num 30. The passage is thus helpful in establishing the independence of women in this area of sacrificial offerings. Second, her words take the reader into a luxurious bedroom. The woman says: "I have decked my couch with covers of dyed Egyptian linen; I have sprinkled my bed with myrrh, aloes, and cinnamon" (7:16–17). The מרבדים, "covers," appears also in Song of Songs and Prov 31:22, where it is one of the items the woman weaves.

4. Conclusions

Several conclusions emerge. The postexilic community in Judah was small, struggling for its physical and religious survival in the midst of a multiethnic milieu under foreign rule. As in the preexilic period, women's chief responsibilities centered on the household. Their significance and power in this domain were readily acknowledged. An important difference resulted from the greater poverty of Judah in the postexilic period, which would have made women's lives more strenuous. Certain groups, however, lived in relative affluence, which enabled women greater freedom and independence.

In describing a woman's life, the sources concur that making bread and weaving were central tasks. Both tasks were arduous in antiquity. It took three hours to produce enough flour for a family of six. The technological development of the mill in the Roman period alleviated some of this hardship, but in the Persian period this work was still, indeed, "grinding" work.[42] The requisite physical exertion is acknowledged by Xenophon when the husband recommends that his wife undertake it periodically—but only periodically—as a form of physical exercise. Archaeological remains show the physical damage and distortion to the body that resulted from such work.[43] For this reason, as both Xenophon and Prov 31 indicate, a wife would have needed household help, slaves in Xenophon, "her maids" (NJPS) or "servant girls" (NRSV) in Prov 31:15. Most agrarian households in impoverished postexilic Judah would not have had the luxury of such help, and depended on the women's ability to shoulder the work themselves—Ezra 2:65//Neh 7:67 mentions only 7,337 male and female slaves when listing the over 42,000 people who populated the province of Judah. Without slaves, a woman's life would have been constant drudgery. Given the poverty of the province of Judah, we can conclude that for most women in postexilic Judah economic hardships resulted in a qualitatively different life from those of Xenophon's happy homemaker, with the exception of the small elite depicted in Prov 31.

Legal empowerment of women is evident in the sources where their rights as wives, heirs, and legal agents are made manifest. Greater recognition of women's legal position and rights, together with a shift toward broader communal responsibility for different strata of the Judean community, may account for why women's own ethnicity and background become relevant in matters concerning membership in the community. In Athens and Judah, women were no longer merely absorbed into their husband's household and group but were also identified in terms of their own. Both Athens in 451 BCE and Ezra-Nehemiah (in accounts situated in 458 and 444 BCE) restricted legitimate marriages that qualified offspring for communal membership, and both communities legislated against intermarriage. A woman's ethnic and religious affiliation mattered in new ways. Nonetheless, as Ruth illustrates, intermarriage was possible when a woman prioritized a commitment to Israel's God and to the Israelite people and disassociated herself from foreign origins.

---

42. See Meyers, "Grinding to a Halt," 65–74.
43. Ibid.

Concomitantly, the sources display women's impact and the importance of the home more prominently than do sources about earlier periods. This development may be linked to the changed political and social circumstances at work. With the demise of the autonomous state and the reconstruction of life as a subjugated nation under imperial control, the home gains new recognition as the arena in which decisive events take place.

Female Names and Gender Perspectives in Chronicles

Sara Japhet

The book of Chronicles abounds with women. It mentions by name over sixty women—more than any other single biblical book—refers to quite a few anonymous women, usually in relation to others, such as "the wife of *x*," "the daughter of *y*," "the mother of *z*," and several times mentions women as a group.[1] Some of the names and their bearers are also mentioned in other biblical works, and were most probably taken over from these sources, while others are peculiar to Chronicles. Chronicles' testimony on the topics of

---

1. The women of Chronicles have not received much attention in biblical scholarship. For previous discussions, see Alice L. Laffey, "I and II Chronicles," in *The Women's Bible Commentary* (ed. Carol A. Newsom and Sharon. H. Ringe; Louisville: Westminster John Knox, 1992): 110–15; Marie-Theres Wacker, "Books of Chronicles: In the Vestibule of Women," in *Feminist Biblical Interpretation: A Compendium of Critical Commentary on the Books of the Bible and Related Literature* (ed. Luise Schottroff and Marie-Theres Wacker; Grand Rapids: Eerdmans, 2012), 178–91; Antje Labahn and Ehud Ben Zvi, "Observations on Women in the Genealogies of 1 Chronicles 1–9," *Bib* 84 (2003): 457–78; Sara Japhet, *The Ideology of the Book of Chronicles and Its Place in Biblical Thought* (ET, Frankfurt: Lang, 1989; 3rd ed. Winona Lake, Ind.: Eisenbrauns, 2009), 271–74; Japhet, "The Israelite Legal and Social Reality as Reflected in Chronicles: A Case Study," now in *From the Rivers of Babylon to the Highlands of Judah: Collected Studies on the Restoration Period* (Winona Lake, Ind.: Eisenbrauns, 2006), 233–44; Japhet, "The Prohibition of the Habitation of Women: The *Temple Scroll*'s Attitude toward Sexual Impurity and Its Biblical Precedents," now in *From the Rivers of Babylon*, 268–88; Gary N. Knoppers, "Intermarriage, Social Complexity and Ethnic Diversity in the Genealogy of Judah," *JBL* 120 (2001): 19–23. See also the commentaries on Chronicles on the relevant passages. The recent book by Julie Kelso, with the promising title *O Mother, Where Art Thou? An Irigarayan Reading of the Book of Chronicles* (London: Equinox, 2007) is a psychoanalytic discussion of Chronicles from the particular perspective of Luce Irigaray's psychoanalytic feminist theory. It is described by the author as "a charitable mode of reading which enables a therapeutic encounter with the past *for the purpose of change in the future*" (xii, emphasis original).

women and gender is quite complex, so a few words of introduction seem to be necessary before the actual discussion of the book's evidence.

1. Introduction to Chronicles: Mode of Composition and Genres

The book of Chronicles was composed most probably in the second half of the fourth century BCE, at the beginning of the Hellenistic period,[2] and is the product of this social and cultural milieu. The book is a history, narrating the history of Israel from the first man, Adam (1 Chr 1:1), to the end of the first commonwealth with the conquest of Judah by the Babylonians; it concludes with a short passage from the beginning of the declaration of Cyrus (2 Chr 36:22–23). Chronicles is thus a "parallel history," repeating the history of a period that has already been described in the Pentateuch and the Former Prophets.

The greater part of Chronicles consists of texts taken from preexisting sources. These sources are either earlier biblical works—for the most part Samuel–Kings but also the Pentateuch, Prophets, Psalms, and Ezra-Nehemiah—or nonbiblical texts and traditions, the scope and origin of which are less self-evident.[3] Some of these texts are repeated in Chronicles almost literally or with minor changes, while others are more thoroughly reworked and reformulated. The remainder of the book consists of passages written by the Chronicler himself. Much of this material may be recognized by its use of the Chronicler's peculiar style and vocabulary, but again, no certainty may be reached here either. Thus from the point of view of origin, Chronicles is composed of three components: material taken from known sources, presented literally or with different degrees of change and reworking; material taken from unknown sources, their existence verifiable by their contents and style; and material written by the Chronicler himself.

This mode of composition has multiple consequences for the perception of the Chronicler's work and message. The Chronicler's views may of course be observed in the passages that he wrote himself. However, no less significant for understanding his views is the borrowed material, which he reworked and reformulated to suit his purposes. The fact that so much of the Chronicler's material is available in other biblical works encourages comparison and

---

2. See, among others, Sara Japhet, *1 and 2 Chronicles: A Commentary* (OTL; London: SCM, 1993), 3–7, 23–28. The topic is discussed in all the introductions to the commentaries on the book.

3. There should be no confusion between the sources the Chronicler mentions in his book by name—some of them quite fictional—and the sources he actually used. For the distinction between the two see ibid., 14–23.

enables the reader to see clearly how the Chronicler's own understanding of history is reflected in his work: in the selection of the materials, in the omissions of and additions to the material taken from sources, and in the changes he introduced. However, the study and use of the borrowed material may be quite complex, and the analysis should be done with caution and with constant methodological awareness.[4]

As a whole, Chronicles is a history, relating the history of Israel in a continuum, as an ongoing chain of causes and effects. However, similar to all biblical historical compositions (and historiography in general), it contains other literary genres as well: lists of various kinds, speeches, psalms, prayers, and more. For the perspective of the present discussion, one should distinguish between two parts of the book, which also represent two modes of historical presentation: the historical narrative (1 Chr 10–2 Chr 36) and the introduction (1 Chr 1–9).

The literary features of Chronicles—its mode of composition and its division into two distinguished literary parts—have determined the structure and course of my essay. I will develop the discussion of "women and gender" in three sections, in which the Chronicles data will be presented and analyzed: (1) the evidence of the historical narrative (1 Chr 10–2 Chr 36); (2) the evidence of the introduction (1 Chr 1–9); (3) the Chronicler's remarks on some legal issues pertaining to women. The analysis of the data will be followed by a synthesis and conclusions.

2. The Historical Narrative (1 Chr 10–2 Chr 36)

The greater part of Chronicles is taken up by a "parallel history" of Israel from David to the end of the kingdom of Judah, which is told in two parts: the history of David and Solomon (1 Chr 11–2 Chr 9) and the history of the kingdom of Judah (2 Chr 10–36). Even a cursory review of the historical narrative discloses that women play only a minor role in the story, but this literary fact is first and foremost a corollary of the genre of biblical historiography—determined in turn by its *Sitz im Leben*, the nature of Israelite society at the time. The historical account as such focuses on the events and deeds of the people's leaders, and in Israelite patriarchal society these were almost exclusively men. Yet a comparison of the Chronicler's historical narrative with the earlier histories discloses that the place of women in Chronicles is differently balanced.

---

4. The comparative methodology is the prevalent approach in the study of Chronicles. For a different position in the context of our topic, which regards the book at face value, with no consideration of its sources, see Labahn and Ben Zvi, "Observations on Women," 463 n. 18, and throughout the article.

Some of the changes are a by-product of other features in the Chronicler's narrative, unconnected with the women/gender perspective, while others are the result of his own goals and views.

Among the general features of Chronicles that bear on the Chronicler's presentation of women are first of all his general historical interests and decisions. As mentioned above, the Chronicler begins the historical narrative with the death of Saul (1 Chr 10) and moves directly to the history of David and his enthronement over all Israel (1 Chr 11) so that the early history of Israel, as described in the Pentateuch, Joshua, Judges, and 1 Samuel, is not included in the narrative. This historiographical decision results, among other things, in the omission of quite a few women who played a part—positive or negative—in the earlier period of Israel's history. Figures like the matriarchs (Sarah, Rebecca, and Rachel); Rahab; Deborah, Jael, Delilah, and the other women in Samson's life; Jephthah's mother and daughter; Hannah; and Saul's wives and daughters are not included in his story. Furthermore, the Chronicler's description of David's reign skips most of the negative aspects of his reign, such as the circumstances of his marriage to Bathsheba, the problems in his household, and the troubles revolving around the inheritance of the kingship. The women involved in these events, like Bathsheba (2 Sam 12), Absalom's sister, Tamar (2 Sam 13), the wise women of Tekoa and Abel (2 Sam 14; 20), and others, are thus also excluded from his story. The Chronicler also omits the negative aspects of Solomon's reign, such as the troubles at the beginning of his reign and those at its end; nor does he repeat 1 Kgs 11, so that no mention is made of Solomon's enormous harem (1 Kgs 11:3) or his foreign wives and idolatry (1 Kgs 11:1–10).

Another well-known historiographic feature of the Chronicler's work is the avoidance of a systematic history of the northern kingdom;[5] the women that played a role in the history of the kingdom of Israel are consequently absent from the Chronicler's narrative.[6]

An additional feature of the Chronicler's work is his selectivity in the use of genres, most conspicuously his avoidance of novella-like stories.[7] The Chronicler does not repeat the prophetic stories of Kings, where women play quite an important role (1 Kgs 17:8–24; 2 Kgs 4:1–37), nor the story of Solomon's judgment of the two prostitutes (1 Kgs 3:16–27). From the perspective of either

---

5. The Chronicler limited the account of the history of the northern kingdom to its relationship with Judah; for the details, see Japhet, *Ideology*, 241–53.

6. Among them, Jeroboam's wife (1 Kgs 14) and Jezebel, Ahab's Phoenician wife (1 Kgs 16:31).

7. See Japhet, *From the Rivers of Babylon*, 176–78, and 410–11 with n. 57.

topic or genre, many female figures present in the Chronicler's sources are absent from his historical account.

2.1. Female Figures Mentioned in the Chronicler's Sources

The Deuteronomistic frameworks of the histories of the Judean kings in the book of Kings include, among others, references to the king's mother, הגבירה, who enjoyed a special status in the kingdom of Judah.[8] The Chronicler regularly borrowed these Deuteronomistic frameworks from the book of Kings—with various changes as he saw fit—in his portrayal of the Judean kings. Among these changes is his treatment of the names of the kings' mothers. The Chronicler preserved the names of the kings' mothers for the early kings of Judah—from Rehoboam to Hezekiah—essentially as they are given in the book of Kings.[9] For the later kings of Judah, from Manasseh on, the Chronicler systematically omits the names of the kings' mothers.[10] It seems that the references to the kings' mothers fell victim to the Chronicler's more

---

8. On her title and status, see P. J. Berlyn, "The Great Ladies," *JBQ* 24 (1996): 26–35. For different interpretations of the term הגבירה and the position of the king's mother in the kingdom of Judah, see Zafrira Ben-Barak, "The Status and Right of the *Gĕbîrâ*," *JBL* 110 (1991): 23–34; Nancy R. Bowen, "The Quest for the Historical *Gĕbîrâ*," *CBQ* 63 (2001): 597–618.

9. The names themselves are the same, except for the name of Abijah's/Abijam's mother. She is called Maacah the daughter of Abishalom in 1 Kgs 15:2, but presented in Chronicles as both Maacah, daughter of Absalom (2 Chr 11:21–22), and Micaiah, daughter of Uriel from Gibeah (13:2). On this famous crux see Japhet, *1 and 2 Chronicles*, 670–71. Two of the names appear in variant forms: Jehoaddan of Jerusalem, Amaziah's mother (2 Chr 25:1//2 Kgs 14:2), is called Jehoaddin/Jehoaddan in Kings; Abijah the daughter of Zechariah, Hezekiah's mother (2 Chr 29:1//2 Kgs 18:2), is called Abi in Kings. The other names are Naamah the Ammonitess, Rehoboam's mother (2 Chr 12:13//1 Kgs 14:21); Maacah, Asa's mother, mentioned in reference to her "abominable thing" (2 Chr 15:16//1 Kgs 15:13); Azubah the daughter of Shilhi, Jehoshaphat's mother (2 Chr 20:31//1 Kgs 22:42); Athaliah the daughter of Omri, Ahaziah's mother (2 Chr 22:2//2 Kgs 8:26); Zibiah of Beer-Sheba, Jehoash's/Joash's mother (2 Chr 24:1//2 Kgs 12:2); Jecoliah of Jerusalem, Azariah/Uzziahu's mother (2 Chr 26:3//2 Kgs 15:2); Jerusha/h the daughter of Zadok, Jotham's mother (2 Chr 27:1//2 Kgs 15:33); altogether, ten names. Two of the mothers from this group are not named in Kings and consequently are not named in Chronicles: the name of Jehoram's mother is replaced by that of his wife; she, the daughter of Ahab (2 Chr 21:6//2 Kgs 8:18), is identified as Athaliah, the daughter of Omri, and mother of Ahaziah in 2 Kgs 8:26//2 Chr 22:2; the name of Ahaz's mother is simply missing.

10. Six names are thus omitted: Hephzibah, Manasseh's mother (2 Kgs 21:1); Meshullemeth the daughter of Haruz of Jotbah, Amon's mother (2 Kgs 21:19); Jedidah the daughter of Adaiah of Bozkath, Josiah's mother (2 Kgs 22:1); Hamutal the daughter of Jeremiahu of Libnah, the mother of Jehoahaz and Zedekiah (2 Kgs 23:31; 24:18); Zebudah the daugh-

general historiographic decision to abbreviate the account of the late years of the Judean kingdom;[11] it is nevertheless of some significance that the Chronicler regarded the names of the kings' mothers as appropriate for omission.

The stories of several women who play a relatively significant role in the book of Kings are taken over by the Chronicler in their entirety, with only small linguistic changes and adaptations: the story of the queen of Sheba (2 Chr 9:1–9, 12//1 Kgs 10:1–10, 13), the story of Queen Athaliah (2 Chr 22:10–23:15//2 Kgs 11:1–16), and the story about the prophetess Huldah (2 Chr 34:22–28//2 Kgs 22:14–20). The only change that is of any interest is a phrase that the Chronicler added to the Deuteronomistic framework of King Ahaziah: "For his mother [Athaliah] counseled him to do evil" (2 Chr 22:3).

Less significant female figures are also taken from the Chronicler's sources. Their inclusion in the historical account thus demonstrates the Chronicler's interest: Zeruiah, the mother of Joab and Abshai; the anonymous mother of the artisan Huram, who made the copper vessels for the temple in Jerusalem; and Jehoshabeath, the sister of King Ahaziah. Zeruiah is referred to in Chronicles several times, either in texts parallel to 2 Samuel (2 Sam 8:16//1 Chr 18:15) or in texts peculiar to Chronicles (1 Chr 11:6 [as mother of Joab]; 18:12 [as mother of Abshai]). Her name is omitted from one parallel text (1 Chr 11:20//2 Sam 23:18). Moreover, the Chronicler presents Zeruiah's pedigree in detail in the context of the genealogies (1 Chr 2:16).[12]

The mother of the master Huram is mentioned in Chronicles in a somewhat different context than in 1 Kings and described as of a different origin. In 1 Kings, Huram/Hiram is presented as the artist who created the copper vessels for Solomon's temple, and this is how his pedigree is recorded: "He was the son of a widow of the tribe of Naphtali, and his father had been a Tyrian" (1 Kgs 7:14). In Chronicles he is mentioned earlier, lent as a special favor to Solomon by the Tyrian king Huram, and his pedigree is recorded thus: "the son of a Danite woman, his father a Tyrian" (2 Chr 2:13). There is no way to decide which of the two pedigrees is correct, but the interest of the Chronicler in this detail is obvious.

Finally, the Chronicler preserves the names of two more women, but their role is diminished: Michal, Saul's daughter and David's wife, and the anonymous daughter of Pharaoh, Solomon's wife. The encounter between David and Michal is recorded in detail in 2 Sam 6:20–23 but is only alluded to in a short sentence in 1 Chr 15:29. The avoidance of Michal's story is no doubt

---

ter of Pedaiah of Rumah, Jehoiakim's mother (2 Kgs 23:36); Nehushta the daughter of Elnathan of Jerusalem, Jehoiachin's mother (2 Kgs 24:8).

11. See Japhet, *Ideology*, 284–90.
12. See also below, p. 42 n. 20 and p. 47.

a corollary of the Chronicler's policy of omitting the earlier history of David and his relationships with the house of Saul. In fact, even the survival of this single verse seems like a result of unsystematic editing.

The daughter of Pharaoh, Solomon's wife, is mentioned in 1 Kings five times, in different contexts (1 Kgs 3:1; 7:8; 9:16, 24; 11:1), but four of them are included in passages the Chronicler did not repeat in his presentation. Only one reference is included in Chronicles, and this is somewhat elaborated (2 Chr 8:11//1 Kgs 9:24).[13]

2.2. Women Peculiar to the Chronicler's Own Account

One of the features of the Chronicler's work, expressed in both the introduction and the historical narrative, is the increase of information regarding David's family and descendants, including women. In the historical narrative the interest in the families of the Davidic kings is attested in materials that the Chronicler added to the accounts found in his sources. The most elaborate information is provided for Rehoboam, the third king in the Davidic line. The passage relating to his family reads as follows:

> Rehoboam married Mahalath, daughter of Jerimoth son of David and Abihail daughter of Eliab son of Jesse. She bore him sons. … He then took Maacah daughter of Absalom; she bore him Abjiah. … Rehoboam loved Maacah … more than his other wives and concubines (for he took eighteen wives and sixty concubines; he begot twenty-eight sons and sixty daughters). Rehoboam designated Abijah son of Maacah as chief and leader among his brothers, for he intended him to be his successor. (2 Chr 11:18–22)

This passage includes some interesting points in relation to our topic. (1) Two of Rehoboam's wives are mentioned by name: Mahalath, unknown from any other source, and Maacah. (2) The impressive pedigree of Mahalath is recorded for three generations, including the unusual mention of her mother, Abihail.[14] Since both her parents belonged to the house of David, she was Rehoboam's second cousin. (3) One of the common biblical expressions of God's blessing is a man's prosperity, expressed, among other ways, in terms of a great number of children. This blessing is more commonly expressed by

---

13. For the significance of this matter for the Chronicler's views, see below, pp. 49–50.

14. While the practice of presenting the names of the male protagonists' mothers is quite common, the names of women's mothers are extremely rare. Another mention of a woman's mother, and perhaps also her grandmother—in this case without mention of fathers—is that of the Edomite king's wife, Mehetabel the daughter of Matred, the daughter of Me-zahab (Gen 36:39//1 Chr 1:50).

the number of sons; but Rehoboam's prosperity is described both in terms of his big harem, with its huge number of wives and concubines, and in terms of his numerous children—including not only sons but also daughters. (4) Rehoboam is the only one among the kings whose love for his wife is mentioned. The practical expression of this love is the election of her son Abijah as his successor to the throne—a fact that illuminates the role of the king's wife in the palace policy.

The Chronicler provides some details about the families of two more kings.[15] He states about Abijah: "Abijah grew powerful; he married fourteen wives and begot twenty-two sons and sixteen daughters" (2 Chr 13:21). Concerning King Joash, the Chronicler adds to the Deuteronomistic introduction taken from Kings (2 Kgs 12:1–2//2 Chr 24:1–2) that Jehoiada the priest "took two wives for him, by whom he had sons and daughters" (2 Chr 24:3). The Chronicler also provides an additional detail regarding Jehoshabeath, Joash's sister, who saved Joash during the massacre of the royal family by Athaliah. Already from 2 Kgs 11:2 we learn that Jehosheba/th was the daughter of King Joram and the sister of Ahaziah, but Chronicles adds that she was the wife of the priest Jehoiada (2 Chr 22:11–12), a detail that explains well how she was able to hide Joash for seven years in the house of the Lord.

The Chronicler also provides some additional information about the families of the Levites. In discussing the procedure for the distribution of the holy offerings, the Chronicler mentions the enrollment of the priests and Levites (2 Chr 31:16–18), and dwells on the enrollment of the Levites. In contrast to the enrollment of the priests, the registration of the Levites (NRSV: wrongly "the priests") included "the dependents of their whole company—wives, sons, and daughters" (31:18 NJPS). Thus, according to Chronicles, the portions accorded to the temple's servants were distributed "to every male of the priests and to every registered Levite" (31:19), that is, also to the women.

Another detail regarding the Levitical families is the note concerning the singer Heman who—like some of the kings—was blessed with a large family: "All these were sons of Heman, the seer of the king, [who uttered] prophecies of God for His greater glory. God gave Heman fourteen sons and three daughters" (1 Chr 25:5).

Two feminine names are included in Chronicles in the narrative of the assassination of King Joash. According to the data of 2 Kgs 12:22 (NRSV: v. 21), "The courtiers who assassinated him were Jozacar son of Shimeath and Jehozabad son of Shomer." Chronicles presents the names of the assassins'

---

15. For the daughters of Zerubbabel, the postexilic offspring of Jehoiachin, see below, p. 43 n. 22 and p. 47.

parents as feminine, and adds their ethnic origin: "These were the men who conspired against him: Zabad son of Shimeath the Ammonitess and Jehozabad son of Shimrith the Moabitess" (2 Chr 24:26). There is no way to determine which is more accurate, but I would conjecture that the Chronicler found this information in his sources, and that it was later censored and suppressed in the book of Kings. Contrary to the censor of Kings, the Chronicler did not see the need to suppress this information.[16]

The Chronicler included several references to women as a group in events and narratives peculiar to his story. In a letter sent to King Jehoram, the prophet Elijah reproves the king for his misdeeds and prophesies to him a series of punishments to be inflicted by God, among them: "The Lord will inflict a great blow upon your people, your sons, your wives, and all your possessions" (2 Chr 21:14). The prophecy is later fulfilled: "The Lord stirred up the spirit of the Philistines and the Arabs … against Jehoram. They marched against Judah … and carried off all the property that was found in the king's palace, as well as his sons and wives" (21:16–17).

In 2 Chr 28, the Chronicler records the war between northern Israel and Judah that ended with a crushing victory for the north; 120,000 Judean fighters are killed and many Judeans are taken captive: "The Israelites captured 200,000 of their kinsmen, women, boys, and girls" (2 Chr 28:8). In his address, the prophet Oded rebukes the Israelites: "Do you now intend to subjugate the men and women of Judah and Jerusalem to be your slaves?" (28:10); under his influence, the Israelites release them and bring them back to Jericho (28:15). This event is referred to later in the exhortation of Hezekiah: "Our fathers died by the sword and our sons and daughters and wives are in captivity on account of this" (2 Chr 29:9).

Women are included in Asa's oath: "Whoever would not worship the Lord God of Israel would be put to death, whether small or great, whether man or woman" (2 Chr 15:13). Women are included among the mourners for Josiah: "Jeremiah composed laments for Josiah, that all the singers, male and female, recited in their laments for Josiah, as is done to this day" (2 Chr 35:25). Finally, women are mentioned among those killed by the Babylonians: "He therefore brought the king of the Chaldeans upon them, who killed their youths by the sword. … He did not spare youth, maiden, elder, or graybeard" (2 Chr

---

16. For similar practices of censorship in the text of Samuel, see the changes in relation to Jether (Ishmaelite in 1 Chr 2:17, Israelite in 2 Sam 17:25); Eshbaal, Saul's son (1 Chr 8:33; 9:39; called Ish-bosheth in, e.g., 2 Sam 2:8); Merib-baal, Jonathan's son (1 Chr 8:34; 9:40; called Mephibosheth in, e.g., 2 Sam 4:4); Beelyada, David's son (1 Chr 14:7; called Eliada in 2 Sam 5:16; 1 Chr 3:8).

36:17).[17] Unlike the longer description of the Babylonian conquest in 2 Kgs 25, the Chronicler presents the effects of the calamity on all the segments of the Judean society, including young and old, male and female.

3. The Introduction (1 Chr 1–9)

The introduction forms a special unit in Chronicles: Its purpose is to present the ethnographic and geographic background against which the ensuing historical narrative unfolds, and its literary genres are different from those of the historical narrative. The introduction consists of lists of various kinds, speckled here and there with short anecdotes and brief records.

The introduction abounds in feminine names. Among them are twenty-one individuals and one collective group of women taken from parallel biblical sources, while the others—forty-three in all—are peculiar to Chronicles. The names taken from earlier sources are integrated into the Chronicler's presentation in three different ways: Twelve names are taken from parallel lists and presented in Chronicles without change or comment.[18] Two names are taken from the narrative sections of the sources but are added to lists, which are also taken from the sources, but from different contexts.[19] And the rest of the parallel names are taken from narrative sources and added to the Chronicler's own lists, which have no prior parallel.[20]

---

17. One may hear in this concise verse the echoes of Lamentations, such as 1:18; 2:11, 21; 4:16; 5:11–14.

18. These are (1) Keturah, Abraham's concubine (1 Chr 1:32//Gen 25:1); (2) Timna, Lotan's sister (1 Chr 1:39//Gen 36:22); (3–5) Mehetabel the daughter of Matred the daughter of Me-zahab (1 Chr 1:50//Gen 36:39); (6–11) six of David's wives, whom he married in Hebron—Ahinoam the Jezreelite, Abigail the Carmelite, Maacah the daughter of Talmai the king of Geshur, Haggith, Abital, Eglah (1 Chr 3:1–3//2 Sam 3:2–5); and (12) Serah, the daughter of Asher (1 Chr 7:30//Num 26:46, with some changes).

19. These are (13) Bath-shua the daughter of Ammiel, David's wife (1 Chr 3:5)—her name learned from the story of 2 Sam 12 and added to the list taken from 2 Sam 5:14; and (14) Tamar, David's daughter (1 Chr 3:9)—her name taken from the narrative of 2 Sam 13 and added to the list taken from 2 Sam 3:2–5.

20. These are (15) Bath-Shua the Canaanite, Judah's wife (1 Chr 2:3; referred to in Gen 38:2); (16) Tamar, Judah's daughter-in-law (1 Chr 2:4), the protagonist in Gen 38:6, 11–30; (17) Zeruiah, Jesse's daughter and the mother of Joab and Abshai (1 Chr 2:16), mentioned several times as Joab's mother (e.g., 2 Sam 2:13, 18; 3:39); (18) Abigail, mother of Amasa and sister of Zeruiah, her name taken from 2 Sam 17:25 and added to the list of Jesse's offspring (1 Chr 2:17); (19) Achsah, Caleb's daughter (1 Chr 2:49), the protagonist of Judg 1:12–15, her name added to the genealogy of Caleb; (20) Miriam, Moses' sister (1 Chr 5:29)—her name learned from Exod 2 and added to the genealogy of Levi, abridged from Exod 6:16–25; (21) Bilhah, Jacob's wife (1 Chr 7:13), her name taken from Gen 30:3–8;

A review of these names and the procedures employed to include them in the Chronicler's account creates the initial impression that the Chronicler made an effort to include in his work as many as possible of the names found in his sources. This impression, however, is misleading, in relation to both men and women. In his reconstruction of the basic genealogical structure of the people of Israel, the Chronicler draws selected passages from the Pentateuch, omits most of the names that appear in either the narratives or the lists, and replaces them with his own data. Quite a few female names in the parallel sources were not included in his work.[21]

As already mentioned, a total of forty-three women are peculiar to the Chronicler's work and do not appear anywhere else in the Bible. Twenty-eight of them are mentioned by name,[22] while fifteen are presented in relation to men: "the wife/concubine of *x*," "the daughter of *y*," or "the sister of *z*."[23] The total number of women mentioned in the introduction is thus over sixty, with some references to women in general. Since the genealogies were more sus-

---

35:25, and included in the genealogy of Dan and Naphtali; (22) one may perhaps add the daughters of Zelophehad (see Num 26:33; 27:1-11) included as a group, without their names, in the genealogy of Manasseh (1 Chr 7:15).

21. For instance Eve, the primeval mother, three of the four matriarchs (Sarah, Rebecca, and Leah), Hagar and Zilpah, Asenath, Joseph's wife, and Dinah, Jacob's daughter.

22. These are (1) Azubah (the daughter of Jerioth?), the wife of Caleb, son of Hezron (2:18–19); (2) Ephrath/ah, the wife of Caleb and the mother of Hur (2:19, 50; 4:4); (3) Abijah, the wife of Hezron (2:24—unless the text is corrupt); (4) Atarah, the "other wife" of Jerahmeel and the mother of Onam (2:26); (5) Abihail, the wife of Abishur (2:29); (6) Ephah, Caleb's concubine (2:46); (7) Maacah, Caleb's concubine (2:48); (8) Shaaph (2:49)—Caleb's wife or concubine? A masculine name? (BH); (9) Shelomith, the daughter of Zerubbabel (3:19); (10–14) Hashubah, Ohel, Berechiah, Hasadiah, Jusab-Hesed (3:19), the daughters of Zerubbabel; they are identified as female by the numeral five, which is given in the feminine form (see also below, p. 47); (15) Hazlelponi, the sister of Ishma and Iedbash (4:3); (16) Helah, the wife of Ashhur the father of Tekoa (4:5, 7); (17) Naarah, Ashhur's wife (4:5, 6); (18) Miriam? known elsewhere as a feminine name but might here be the name of a man (or is the text corrupt? 4:17); (19) Bithiah, Pharaoh's daughter (4:18); (20) Maacah, the sister of Machir (or of his son; 7:15); (21) Maacah, Machir's wife (7:16); (22) Hammolecheth, the sister of Gilead (7:18); (23) Sheerah, Ephraim's daughter (7:24); (24) Shua, the sister of Japhlet and others, the daughter of Heber (7:32); (25) Hushim, the wife of Shaharaim (8:8); (26) Baara, the wife of Shaharaim (8:8); (27) Hodesh, the wife of Shaharaim (8:9); (28) Maacah, the wife of the father of Gibeon (8:29; 9:35).

23. (1) The daughter of Machir the father of Gilead, the wife of Hezron (2:21); (2) the daughter of Sheshan (2:35; see below); (3) the mother of Jabez (4:9); (4) the Judahite wife of ? (4:18); (5) the wife of Hodiah, and sister of Naham (4:19); (6–11) six unnamed daughters of Shimei (4:27); (12) many "wives and sons" of the tribe of Issachar (7:4); (13) the Aramean concubine of Manasseh (7:14); (14) the wife taken by Machir for his son (7:15); (15) Ephraim's wife (7:23).

ceptible to textual corruptions, introduced in the process of transmission, than other parts of Chronicles, the gender of some of the registered persons may be suspect, but the general picture is not really affected.

The most important feature of the female names peculiar to Chronicles is their primary function as eponyms rather than as actual persons.[24] As such they are terminological abstractions, representing mostly ethnic but sometimes geographic entities.[25] Before going further into this matter a few explanatory remarks seem necessary.[26]

As mentioned above, the major component of the introduction is lists, most of them genealogical, which may be classified into two groups: vertical genealogies, presenting genealogical trees of individual persons; and horizontal genealogies, commonly termed segmented genealogies, which map the branching off of families for several generations.[27] These segmented genealogies serve to represent social units, be they clans, tribes, or peoples. They are thus abstract literary structures reflecting social and ethnic situations, with the names serving as eponymic terms for ethnic units. The eponymic function of the names may be illustrated by the segmented genealogies of Genesis, such as the comprehensive map of the world's peoples (Gen 10); the more limited maps of the Keturites and Hagarites (Gen 25:1–4, 12–16); parts of the Edomite genealogies (Gen 36); and more. The Chronicler's introduction may thus be seen as a "map"—a rather uneven map—of the Israelite tribes and their composition. While some of the tribes are described in great detail, others are presented in only sketchy lines. The most elaborate structures are those of the tribes of Judah and Manasseh.

The majority of the female names and figures appear in these segmented genealogies[28] and should be interpreted in this literary and sociological context. Unfortunately, not all the names in the genealogies—whether male or female—are identifiable; many of them are unique, some seem corrupt, and

---

24. It is rather surprising that Labahn and Ben Zvi ("Observations on Women"), who present their research as a sociological investigation of the roles of women in the genealogies, ignore the role of the female names as eponyms.

25. The term *eponym* is Greek, and its meaning is "a real or mythical person from whose name the name of a nation, an institution etc. is derived, or is supposed to have been derived" (*Webster's New World Dictionary* [Cleveland: Collins, 1974], 472).

26. See also Yigal Levin, "Understanding Biblical Genealogies," *CurBS* 9 (2001): 11–46.

27. For the definitions, see Marshall D. Johnson, *The Purpose of the Biblical Genealogies* (2nd ed.; Cambridge: Cambridge University Press, 1989), xi–xii.

28. The exceptions include the names of females in the house of David (1 Chr 2:16–17; 3:1–9, 19–20), and prior to David in the tribe of Judah (2:3–4) (see below), along with a few others. Among them, two are the protagonists of short anecdotes: the daughter of Sheshan (2:35; see below) and the mother of Jabez (4:9–10).

their origins cannot always be ascertained. Nevertheless, their careful analysis from this perspective proves very profitable.

The most important aspect of the female names is their definitions: "wife," "concubine," "sister," or "daughter." The definitions "wife" or "concubine" denote a secondary component within the primary social group.[29] Thus the reference to the marriage of the Judean Hezron with "the daughter of Machir" (1 Chr 2:21) signifies that the Judean clan Hezron had mixed with Transjordanian elements, described as "the daughter of Machir, the father of Gilead" (1 Chr 2:21). Their offspring are then described as "the sons of Machir" (2:23), which means that from the perspective of Judah they are a secondary element, the children of a "wife," whereas from the perspective of Manasseh they are a primary element, the children of a son, Machir. Ephrath/Ephrathah is described as the wife of Caleb (2:19); in the terminological code of the genealogies this would mean that the northern Judean clan of the Calebites had mixed with Ephraimite elements represented by the female eponym Ephrath.[30] The descendants of this bond inhabited some of the major towns in Judah, such as Kiriath-jearim, Bethlehem, and more (2:50–54; 4:2–4). The same Judean clan had also mixed with other ethnic elements—Arameans, probably Midianites, and more—represented by the feminine eponymic names Ephah (the Midianite), Maacah (the Aramean), and Bithiah (the Egyptian), described as either "concubines" (2:46, 48) or "wife" (4:18). Similarly, we learn that the tribe of Manasseh, which settled in Transjordan, had mixed with Aramean elements; Machir, the major Manassite clan, is presented as the son of Manasseh and his "Aramean concubine" (7:14), while Machir's wife bears the Aramean name Maacah (7:16). As we saw above, these Transjordanian clans mixed in turn with Judean clans, through the marriage of the Judean Hezron and "the daughter of Machir" (2:21). The mixture of ethnic elements could represent inner-Israelite connections, like those between Judah and Manasseh or Judah and Ephraim, or Israelite and non-Israelite intermingling, for example, with Aram, Midian, and others.

Some of these "wives" are presented in the genealogies as important ethnic elements in the overall structure of the social unit, and their offspring

---

29. See in particular Abraham Malamat, "Tribal Societies: Biblical Genealogies and African Lineage Systems," *Archives Européennes de Sociologie* 14 (1973): 126–36; 132–34; Malamat, "Origins and the Formation Period," in *A History of the Jewish People* (ed. Hayim H. Ben-Sasson; Cambridge: Harvard University Press, 1976), 1:63–66.

30. For a discussion of this matter and its historical consequences, see Sara Japhet, "Was David a Judean or an Ephraimite? Light from the Genealogies," in *Let Us Go Up to Zion: Essays in Honour of H. G. M. Williamson on the Occasion of His Sixty-Fifth Birthday* (ed. Mark Boda and Iain Provan; VTSup 153; Leiden: Brill, 2012), 297–306.

are registered as their mothers' sons, rather than their fathers'. A case in point is that of Ephrath/ah, a component of the Calebites, whose offspring are related to her rather than to their "father": "The sons of Hur the firstborn of Ephrathah" (4:4).[31] The significance of the eponym Ephrath is illustrated also by her appearance outside of the Chronicler's genealogies, for example, in the prophecy of Mic 5:1.[32] Another case is that of Keturah, whose offspring are described as "the sons of Keturah" rather than the sons of Abraham, in both Genesis (25:4) and Chronicles (1 Chr 1:32).

The eponymic role of "daughters" and "sisters" differs from that of "wives/concubines." Within the broader tribal framework, they represent social units—clans, families, or inhabitants of towns—that are regarded as offspring of women rather than men. The motives for this change of convention are not always clear, and neither are its consequences. This lineage is sometimes explained by the claim that the "father" had no sons, as is the case of the daughters of Zelophehad: "Zelophehad … had no sons, only daughters. The names of Zelophehad's daughters were Mahlah, Noah, Hoglah, Milcah, and Tirzah" (Num 26:33). The records of the book of Joshua specify that "Manasseh's daughters inherited a portion in these together with his sons" (Josh 17:6), and some of their names appear as place names in Ephraimite territory: Tirzah as the first capital of the northern kingdom (e.g., 1 Kgs 15:33; 16:6), Hoglah and Noah in the Samarian ostraca.[33]

Two similar cases, in which cities are called by the names of "daughters" rather than "sons," are not explained by the claim that the father had no sons. The first is Sheerah, Ephraim's daughter, who "built both Lower and Upper Beth-horon and Uzzen-sheerah" (1 Chr 7:24). This would imply that the inhabitants of these towns affiliated themselves to Ephraim through his daughter Sheerah, rather than through any of his sons, although only one of the three towns is called by her name.[34] The second case is that of Serah,

---

31. The description of a man's lineage through his mother rather than his father is found in the Bible in a few other cases, such as the sons of Zeruiah mentioned above: the daughters of Barzillai (Ezra 2:61//Neh 7:63); the assassins of Joash (2 Chr 24:26); and some more.

32. See Japhet, "Was David a Judean or an Ephraimite?"

33. See Shmuel Ahituv, *Echoes from the Past: Hebrew and Cognate Inscriptions from the Biblical Period* (Jerusalem: Carta, 2008), 298–300, 302.

34. For the affiliation of towns—that is, their inhabitants or families—to "fathers," see for instance "Shobal the father of Kiriath-jearim, Salma the father of Bethlehem, Hareph the father of Beth-gader" (1 Chr 2:50–52), and more (e.g., 1 Chr 2:24, 42, 44–45, 49). In this context, a certain person could be the "father" of "half" a town (1 Chr 2:52–54). Also specific to such contexts is the presentation of "sons" in a gentilic or plural form, such as 1 Chr 1:11–12, 14–16, and more.

"Asher's daughter" (Num 26:46), and her brothers' "sister" (1 Chr 7:30), whose name may be reflected in another city of Ephraim, Timnath-Serah (Josh 19:50; 24:30); this implies that the inhabitants of this city related themselves to Asher through a "sister/daughter" rather than to Ephraim.

The eponymic terms "sister" or "daughter" seem to imply that the social units presented as the offspring of "daughters" enjoyed a status equal to those presented as the offspring of sons, and may perhaps represent a survival of a matrilineal rather than patrilineal system; however, in the absence of further information, no definite conclusions may be reached.

Another feature of the introduction—which is common to both parts of Chronicles—is the special interest in the house of David, expressed in the detailed genealogies of 1 Chr 3. These genealogies include the names of ten women: two form part of the pre-Davidic genealogy of the tribe of Judah, two are related to David himself, and six belong to a much later phase of the Davidic house. The earlier figures of the Canaanite Bath-shua, Judah's wife, and Tamar his daughter-in-law are part of the segmented genealogies of the tribe of Judah and serve as "mothers" of the Judean clans (1 Chr 2:3–4//Gen 38). They are both taken from the Chronicler's sources. I have already mentioned Zeruiah, known from earlier sources as the mother of Joab, Abshai, and Asahel; she is presented in the Chronicler's genealogical introduction as Jesse's daughter, that is, David's sister (1 Chr 2:16). Also included is Abigail, Zeruiah's sister, who is presented as another daughter of Jesse, that is, another sister of David. She is described as the mother of Amasa and the wife of Jether the Ishmaelite (2:17).[35] The Chronicler also provides the only genealogy of the Davidic house after the destruction, presented as "the sons of Jeconia" (that is, Jehoiachin) in 1 Chr 3:17–24. This genealogy includes the names of six daughters of Zerubbabel: Shelomith,[36] who is specified as the sister of her male brothers, and five more daughters mentioned by name: Hashubah, Ohel, Berechiah, Hasadiah, Jusab-hesed (3:19–20). They may be identified as female figures not by their names but by the concluding numeral five, given in the feminine form חמש.[37]

---

35. Abigail is presented as the sister of Zeruiah already in 2 Sam 17:25, but there her father's name is given as Nahash. The name of Zeruiah's father is not recorded in 2 Sam 17:25, but he would be Nahash by implication. Thomas Willi, *Chronik: Vol 1: 1 Chr 1–10* (BKAT 24.1; Neukirchen-Vluyn: Neukirchener, 2009), 89–90, tries to harmonize these conflicting data by suggesting that Abigail's mother married twice, and Abigail was only half sister of Jesse's sons. It is difficult to decide which identification is the correct one.

36. See Eric M. Meyers, "The Shelomit Seal and the Judean Restoration—Some Additional Considerations," *ErIsr* 18 (1985): 33*–38*.

37. Quite a few scholars try to "overcome" this unusual reference by different strategies,

4. Some Legal Issues Pertaining to Women

The Chronicler's work contains texts that deal with or reflect on matters of a legal nature and sporadic anecdotes and casual remarks that may illuminate this sphere of Israel's social life. These texts shed valuable light on the Chronicler's views and positions, and I will touch briefly on four such matters relating to our topic.

4.1. The Daughter of Sheshan

The concise report about Sheshan serves as an introduction to a long vertical genealogy: "Sheshan had no sons, only daughters; but Sheshan had an Egyptian slave whose name was Jarha. So Sheshan gave his daughter in marriage to Jarha his slave and she bore him Attai" (1 Chr 2:34–35).[38] The problem facing Sheshan is attested in other biblical contexts as well: how, in the absence of sons, does one secure the continuation of his "name," that is, his inheritance rights and position within his clan, and thus within the community at large?[39] Sheshan's solution is based on the legal instructions of the slave laws, particularly Exod 21:4: "If his [the slave's] master gives him a wife and she bears him sons or daughters, the wife and her children shall be the master's." The law in Exod 21:2–6 deals with a Hebrew slave, who is let free in the seventh year of his servitude (v. 2). The law prescribes, however, that if the slave is given a wife by his master, after the slave's manumission the wife and her children remain the property of the master. This is of course all the more true for a non-Hebrew slave, who is by definition a slave for life. A wife given to him by his master and her children would all be his master's.[40] Thus the child born of the marriage of the Egyptian slave and Sheshan's daughter is born to

---

like regarding the feminine form of the numeral as an "irregular form" of the masculine (e.g., Willi, *Chronik*, 117) or regarding the numeral as a later gloss (Edward L. Curtis, *The Book of Chronicles* [ICC; Edinburgh: T&T Clark, 1952], 104). The BH simply instructs: "read חמשה" (not repeated by *BHS*). I see no reason to follow this track.

38. For a detailed discussion of this passage see Japhet, "Israelite Legal and Social Reality."

39. See, e.g., the levirate law in Deut 25:5–10.

40. For a possible yet very different use of this law as the legal basis for the decision to expel the foreign women and their children during the period of the restoration and under the leadership of Ezra, see Sara Japhet, "The Expulsion of the Foreign Women: The Legal Basis, Precedents and Consequences for the Definition of Jewish Identity," in *"Sieben Augen auf einem Stein" (Sach 3,9): Studien zur Literatur des Zweiten Tempels. Festschrift für Ina Willi-Plein* (ed. Friedhelm Hartenstein and Michael Pietsch; Neukirchen-Vluyn: Neukirchener, 2007), 149–50.

"him," that is, to Sheshan; the long genealogy that follows presents the line of Sheshan for thirteen generations, a fact that testifies to the distinguished position of the family for many generations.[41]

This short episode illustrates well certain aspects of the patriarchal system, in which a daughter is not, and cannot be, an heiress to her father's name or estate. She may, however, serve as an instrument through which the family's "name" is secured. The episode sheds light also on the Chronicler's view regarding the issue of mixed marriage, for which see below.

4.2. The Daughters of Eleazar

First Chronicles 23 contains detailed information about the Levitical families and functions and includes, among others, a short remark about the line of Merari, Levi's third son: "The sons of Merari: Mahli and Mushi. The sons of Mahli: Eleazar and Kish. Eleazar died having no sons but only daughters; the sons of Kish, their kinsmen, married them" (1 Chr 23:21–22). The short note about the marriage of Eleazar's daughters illustrates the implementation of the laws of inheritance as outlined in Num 27 and 36, apropos the case of the daughters of Zelophehad. "If a man dies without leaving a son, you shall transfer his property to his daughter" (Num 27:8). Then, "Every daughter among the Israelite tribes who inherits a share must marry someone from the clan of her father's tribe" (Num 36:8). This is precisely the procedure the daughters of Eleazar followed: Since their father had no sons, they married their cousins (1 Chr 23:22). This legal arrangement would secure the continuation of Eleazar's name among the Levites, and thus the family's continued right to the Levitical portions, as determined by registration.

4.3. The Daughter of Pharaoh

The book of Kings extols Solomon's marriage to Pharaoh's daughter and highlights the fact that Solomon built for her a special residence. During the period of construction she stayed in "the city of David" (1 Kgs 3:1) but moved to her own lodging when the works were completed (1 Kgs 9:24). The Chronicler refers to Pharaoh's daughter only once, regarding her move from the city of David to her special residence. However, to the laconic statement of the book of Kings the Chronicler adds an explanation of this move, presented as

---

41. There is no way to discover who the personages are, listed in this vertical genealogy. A person by the name of Zabud the son of Nathan—similar to the second and third generations in this genealogy—is mentioned among Solomon's high officials as a priest and the king's "friend" (1 Kgs 4:5), but this could be merely a coincidence.

a quotation of Solomon's considerations: "For he said: No wife of mine shall dwell in the house of King David of Israel for [the area] is sacred since the ark of the Lord has entered it" (2 Chr 8:11).

From the remarks of the book of Kings one might conclude that the move of Pharaoh's daughter to her own residence emphasized her special position among Solomon's wives; in Chronicles, by contrast, the move is viewed as a legal act, based on religious considerations.[42] The daughter of Pharaoh, according to the Chronicler's account, is actually removed from "the house of David," a matter of necessity not because she is a foreigner—an Egyptian princess—but because she is a woman! Her dwelling "in the house of David" is incompatible with the holiness of the area, incurred by the presence of the ark. Although the ark itself is no longer there—having been transferred from the city of David to its permanent abode in the temple (2 Chr 5:2–14//1 Kgs 8:1–10)—the holiness it incurred persisted even in its absence.

The issue at hand is the need to safeguard the sacred precincts from any kind of impurity—a matter of great significance in both biblical and postbiblical laws. The Chronicler's view illustrates the attempt to set rigorous boundaries in regard to sexual impurity, caused by the very presence of women.[43]

4.4. Mixed Marriages

The issue of mixed marriage, pertaining in particular to the marriage of Judean men and foreign women, was one of the most troubling issues during the Restoration period, as demonstrated by the book of Ezra-Nehemiah.[44] The decision made by the Judean community during the time of Ezra was clear and sharp—to expel both the women and their children: "Let us make a covenant with our God to expel all these women and those who have been born to them" (Ezra 10:3). Scholars are still debating whether this decision was ever implemented,[45] but the attitude of Ezra, Nehemiah, and their fol-

---

42. For a similar structure and formulation, see 2 Chr 23:6; 2 Chr 23:14//2 Kgs 11:15.

43. See in more detail, and in comparison to the regulations of the *Temple Scroll*, Japhet, "Prohibition of Habitation." Also see Shaye J. D. Cohen, "Solomon and the Daughter of Pharaoh: Intermarriage, Conversion and the Impurity of Women," *JANES* 16–17 (1984–85): 23–37; Tarja S. Philip, *Menstruation and Childbirth in the Bible: Fertility and Impurity* (New York: Lang, 2006).

44. See in particular Ezra 9–10; Neh 10:31; 13:23–27; Mal 2:10–16. This issue has attracted much scholarly attention. See, among others, Japhet, "Israelite Legal and Social Reality"; Ina Willi-Plein, "Problems of Intermarriage in Postexilic Times," in *Shai le-Sara Japhet: Studies in the Bible, Its Exegesis and Its Language* (ed. Moshe Bar-Asher et al.; Jerusalem: Mosad Bialik, 2007), 177*–89*, with further bibliography.

45. See in particular Yonina Dor, *Have the "Foreign Women" Really Been Expelled?*

lowers is unequivocal: There is no place in the Israelite community for foreign women of any origin, or their children.[46]

The Chronicler's position regarding this matter is diametrically opposed to that of Ezra-Nehemiah. On the one hand, he does not present the issue of mixed marriages as a problem, at any period of Israel's history. Therefore he does not repeat the record of 1 Kgs 11, which blames Solomon for this practice, and which served Nehemiah in his rebuke (Neh 13:26). On the other hand, his own presentation of Israel's origins and history demonstrates that he is fully aware of the phenomenon of mixed marriages in Israelite society along its history. According to his presentation—expressed in remarks taken from his sources and material peculiar to his work—there is nothing wrong in mixed marriages, because the spouses and offspring of such marriages are part of Israel, a welcome component of Israelite society.[47] As far as the composition of the Israelite society goes, this is the most inclusivist position attested in biblical literature.

5. Synthesis and Conclusion

The Chronicler's evidence regarding the topics of women and gender demonstrates very clearly that he is in every way a spokesman of his social milieu. His basic social framework, from which all his positions regarding social and legal issues are derived, is the patriarchal social system of his time, which is reflected in both parts of his work.

In the historical narrative the main protagonists of the story are men, while women play only a minor part in the historical process. The Chronicler did not add any active female participants to the storyline taken from his sources, which is very much in contrast to his procedure regarding male protagonists, where additional figures and names of prophets, army commanders, temple servants, and more are added to the story.

The patriarchal social system is clearly expressed in the Chronicler's structure of Israelite origins, as presented in the genealogical introduction; however, the conceptual structure of Israelite ethnic identity, formulated

---

Separation and Exclusion in the Restoration Period (Jerusalem: Hebrew University Magnes Press, 2006) (in Hebrew). For the opposite claim, that the separation did take place, as described in 1 Esd 9:36, see Zipora Talshir, *1 Esdras: A Text Critical Commentary* (Atlanta: Society of Biblical Literature, 2001), 482.

46. See Ezra 9–10; Neh 9:1–2; Neh 10:31; Neh 13:1–3, 23–28 and the article of Tamara Cohn Eskenazi in this volume.

47. Several of these cases were mentioned above, p. 45. For more detail, see Japhet, *Ideology*, 261–74.

through the construct of eponyms, employs both male and female names. While the meaning of these eponyms is not the same, as determined by the different status of males and females in the contemporary society, their epistemological function as eponyms is the same for both genders. Moreover, in the actual genealogical "maps" sketched by these genealogies, some remnants of the matrilineal system may still be observed.

The patriarchal setting is also expressed, among other ways, in the care for the continuation of the family's "name" through male progeny, and the application of the inheritance laws. A special aspect of this position is the Chronicler's attention to purity laws, with its concomitant view of the incompatibility of women and the holy precincts.

Within the confines of this basic social framework, however, the Chronicler displays a great interest in matters concerning women, and presents them as essential components of the social structure. He preserves in full all the parallel narratives from the book of Kings in which women played a significant role—the queen of Sheba, the queen Athaliah, and the prophetess Huldah—and includes other parallel data referring to women. Moreover, the presence of women in the public domain, and as a component of the social fabric, is emphasized in the Chronicler's own descriptions.[48]

Another feature of the Chronicler's handling of the "women" motif is his use of it in the enhancement of his general historical and theological goals. One of the major foci of the Chronicler's work is the centrality of the house of David in the history of Israel, and its theological significance. An important aspect of this interest is the detailed data about the Davidic families—concerning David himself and some of the Davidic kings. This additional data contains quite a few details about the women (and the children) of the family. Chronicles is also the only biblical work that contains the genealogy of the house of David after the Babylonian conquest, including some data about women.

To a lesser degree, women serve as a component of the Chronicler's interest in the Levites, which is illustrated throughout his book.

One of the major goals of the Chronicler's history is the enhancement of the concept of "all Israel," a concept developed throughout the entire work and emphasized in different ways. The role of women in this context is of the greatest significance, promoting the Chronicler's most inclusive definition of Israelite identity. The Chronicler's liberal attitude toward mixed marriages is a

---

48. The book of Kings does not refer to women as participants—or as of any significance—in its description of public events: the dedication of the temple (1 Kgs 8), the covenant of Josiah (2 Kgs 23), or the effects of the Babylonian conquest (2 Kgs 25).

major aspect of this definition of identity—according to his view, mixed marriages were practiced in Israel throughout its history, and the foreign spouses and their descendants form an integral part of the people of Israel.

In sum, the Chronicler's positions regarding women and gender may be seen as vacillating between two poles: At one pole is the traditional patriarchal system, which forms his basic social presuppositions and dominates his social views and values, and at the other, his interest in matters female, and his view of women as an integral part of the social fabric. It is up to the reader to judge how successful he was in navigating between these two poles and transmitting this delicate balance in his historical composition.

Part 2
"Good" and "Bad" Women? Images of Women in Israel's Wisdom Tradition

Personified Wisdom: Contexts, Meanings, Theology

Gerlinde Baumann

1. Introduction

Wisdom appears in three Old Testament writings in a personified manner: in Prov 1–9, in Sirach (Ecclesiasticus), and in the book of Wisdom (Wisdom of Solomon).[1] In these texts, Wisdom is portrayed as a person who can speak and act. The word "wisdom" is feminine in Hebrew (Proverbs) and in Greek (Sirach; Wisdom). The personification of Wisdom is also feminine; she is therefore often called "Lady Wisdom." The expansion of an earlier image of God, dominated by masculine aspects, to include the missing feminine side may help account for this feminine portrayal of Wisdom.[2] Personified

---

1. For recent overviews of the biblical wisdom figure, see Christl M. Maier, "Weisheit (Personifikation) (AT)," in *Das wissenschaftliche Bibellexikon im Internet* (2007): http://www.wibilex.de; Ilse Müllner, *Das hörende Herz: Weisheit in der hebräischen Bibel* (Stuttgart: Kohlhammer, 2006), 96–121 (esp. regarding Proverbs); Irmtraud Fischer, *Gotteslehrerinnen: Weise Frauen und Frau Weisheit im Alten Testament* (Stuttgart: Kohlhammer, 2006), 173–209; Alice M. Sinnott, *The Personification of Wisdom* (SOTSMS; Aldershot: Ashgate, 2005); Martin Neher, *Wesen und Wirken der Weisheit in der Sapientia Salomonis* (BZAW 333; Berlin: de Gruyter, 2004), 18–154; Peter Schäfer, *Mirror of His Beauty: Feminine Images of God from the Bible to the Early Kabbalah* (Princeton: Princeton University Press, 2002), 23–38 (incl. Job 28); as well as the articles by Silvia Schroer, *Wisdom Has Built Her House: Studies in the Figure of Sophia in the Bible* (trans. Linda Maloney; Collegeville, Minn.: Liturgical Press, 2000). Older, but still relevant and readable, are especially Bernhard Lang, *Frau Weisheit: Deutung einer biblischen Gestalt* (Düsseldorf: Patmos, 1975) (almost only Proverbs); as well as Gerhard von Rad, *Wisdom in Israel* (Nashville: Abingdon, 1972), 189–228 (also for wisdom theology as a whole).

2. According to Fischer, *Gotteslehrerinnen*, 171, the portrayal of Wisdom next to God demonstrates that postexilic monotheism is forced to be open to nonmasculine images of God: "If there is only one single deity, it must unite everything within itself and integrate all functions of all deities, masculine and feminine, into the image of God."

Wisdom appears in different social and literary contexts and can be viewed as one of the most fascinating literary creations of the Bible,[3] especially in relation to the question of a feminine image of God.

This essay does not include wisdom in Job 28 and in Bar 3:9–4:4 because in these texts wisdom is not personified, but appears as an entity without personal characteristics.[4] Likewise, this is not the place for more detailed remarks about the image of wisdom outside the Old Testament writings—in other words, in Jewish and Christian postbiblical texts.[5]

In biblical exegesis the consensus is that the image of Wisdom is a poetic personification.[6] Personification is a subgenre of the poetic form of the metaphor and originates through an interaction between a "source" and a "target."[7] The target is personified Wisdom herself. The source cannot be so clearly identified. Theoretically, concrete women (those of flesh and blood) or even God, gods, or goddesses could be sources. Since personified Wisdom is a figure of the divine sphere, she should also be analyzed as such.[8] For personified Wisdom, however—as with the imagery of God—the reference to the concrete world is a broken one. Therefore, actual women as a source[9]

---

3. See Sinnott, *Personification*, 177: "Indisputably, Wisdom is the Bible's most fascinating literary figure."

4. See, e.g., Marie-Theres Wacker, "Baruch: Mail from Distant Shores," in *Feminist Biblical Interpretation: A Compendium of Critical Commentary on the Books of the Bible and Related Literature* (ed. Luise Schottroff and Marie-Theres Wacker; Grand Rapids: Eerdmans, 2012), 531–38, here 533. She also points out that wisdom in Job 28 and in Baruch is confusing, unapproachable, and remains "in terms of syntax and semantics the object of God." A similar opinion is held by Sinnott, *Personification*, 173–74; she nevertheless treats the texts in her monograph.

5. See, e.g., Maier, "Weisheit," §§1.1.5. and 2.2.1, with references to further texts and literature.

6. Lang, *Frau Weisheit*, 168–71, was the first to formulate this theory clearly. For recent German feminist-theological studies, see, e.g., Maier, "Weisheit," §1.1.; Susanne Gorges-Braunwarth, *Frauenbilder—Weisheitsbilder—Gottesbilder in Spr 1–9: Die personifizierte Weisheit im Gottesbild der nachexilischen Zeit* (Exegese in unserer Zeit 9; Münster: LIT, 2002), 92–97; Gerlinde Baumann, *Die Weisheitsgestalt in Proverbien 1–9: Traditionsgeschichtliche und theologische Studien* (FAT 16; Tübingen: Mohr Siebeck, 1996), 27–37; as well as Schroer, *Wisdom Has Built Her House*, 26–68, esp. 26–30.

7. Schroer, *Wisdom Has Built Her House*, 26; important impulses from the English discussion were provided primarily by Claudia Camp, *Wisdom and the Feminine in the Book of Proverbs* (Bible and Literature 11; Sheffield: Sheffield Academic, 1985), 73.

8. See also Gerlinde Baumann, *Love and Violence: Marriage as Metaphor for the Relationship between YHWH and Israel in the Prophetic Books* (Collegeville, Minn.: Liturgical Press, 2003), 31.

9. This position is held primarily by Schroer, *Wisdom Has Built Her House*, 52–68, as

are less likely; instead, we must look to already existing images of the God of Israel as well as those goddesses known in Israel at the time. In order to trace the meaning of personified Wisdom more exactly, these ideas should also be examined.

2. Personified Wisdom in Proverbs 1–9

2.1. Text and Content

In the book of Proverbs, we find probably the oldest wisdom texts in the Bible; chapters 10–29 likely originate for the most part from the time of the monarchy. They contain mostly wisdom sayings gained from experience about appropriate behavior in different life situations. Chapters 1–9 introduce the book. "Wisdom" is mentioned in almost all of these nine chapters. But not all verses denote *personified* Wisdom. Most important are the texts in which she herself speaks: Prov 1:20–33; Prov 8; and Prov 9:1–9; as a person, she also appears in Prov 3:16–17; 4:6, 8–9; 7:4; 9:11.[10]

In her first-person speeches, personified Wisdom is positioned at the city gate (Prov 1:20–21; 8:1–3) and thus in a public location in which trading is done and where the local court holds its sessions. In the first speech (Prov 1:22–33) personified Wisdom resembles a prophetess. However, she declares her own message and not the word of YHWH. She warns her audience to heed her words and not to remain in a situation of inexperience. In the second and longest speech in Prov 8, personified Wisdom primarily praises herself. Here she appears at first (Prov 8:4–11) as the bringer of wisdom and knowledge. In Prov 8:12–21, she is described more closely from a number of different aspects: She is the counselor of the powerful; she loves those who love her, and she allows herself to be found by those who seek her; she promises her followers material wealth, and she walks on the path of law and justice. Probably the most well-known passage is the third part of this chapter: In

---

well as by Christine Roy Yoder, *Wisdom as a Woman of Substance: A Socioeconomic Reading of Proverbs 1–9 and 31:10–31* (BZAW 304; Berlin: de Gruyter, 2001).

10. Regarding personified Wisdom in Prov 1–9, see Christl M. Maier, "Proverbs: How Feminine Wisdom Comes into Being," in Schottroff and Wacker, *Feminist Biblical Interpretation*, 255–72; Baumann, *Weisheitsgestalt*, as well as the English summary of her monograph, "A Figure with Many Facets: The Literary and Theological Functions of Personified Wisdom in Proverbs 1–9," in *Wisdom and Psalms* (ed. Athalya Brenner and Carole R. Fontaine; FCB 2/2; Sheffield: Sheffield Academic, 1998), 44–78; Carole R. Fontaine, "Proverbs," in *Women's Bible Commentary* (ed. Carol A. Newsom and Sharon H. Ringe; 2nd ed.; Louisville: Westminster John Knox, 1998), 153–60; Bernhard Lang, *Wisdom in the Book of Proverbs: A Hebrew Goddess Redefined* (New York: Pilgrim, 1986); Camp, *Wisdom*.

Prov 8:22–31 personified Wisdom introduces herself as the one who was born before God's creation, and plays as his "favorite" (Heb. אָמוֹן)[11] in the presence of God. The book of Proverbs is not any clearer in its description of the relationship between personified Wisdom and God. In the following verses (Prov 8:32–36), personified Wisdom praises those who follow her and threatens those who do not. In Prov 9:1–9, she finally appears as a lady who invites all those who pass by to her banquet in her palace. This text passage corresponds to Prov 9:13–18, a section in which her antagonist, the "strange woman" or "Lady Folly" (see below §2.2.), speaks.

2.2. Context and Meaning

Feminist-exegetical research on personified Wisdom still focuses on the book of Proverbs. Most researchers argue that personified Wisdom in Prov 1–9 is to be seen as a poetic personification and not as a hypostasis of God or as an allusion or "citation" of an ancient Near Eastern or ancient Egyptian goddess.[12] There is little disagreement about the argument that the introduction to the book of Proverbs (Prov 1–9), including personified Wisdom, is a creation of members of the urban upper class of the postexilic era (fifth/fourth century BCE). Their situation is not mainly characterized by economic problems, but rather by religious or ideological questions: Who is really Israelite and who is not? Which behavior is proper for this community? Answers to these questions are given with regard to the figure of the "strange woman" in Prov 1–9.[13] She is the negative antagonist of personified Wisdom. The "strange woman" more strongly exhibits characteristics of concrete women of flesh and blood than personified Wisdom does. Thus in Prov 1–9 there is a constellation in which the negatively classified behavior of actual women in the form of the "strange woman" is juxtaposed with the positive figure of personified Wisdom, who exhibits very few characteristics of concrete women. As a result, some feminist exegetes warn against evaluating personified Wisdom in Prov 1–9 only as positive, perhaps as an important "symbol of connectedness" or even

---

11. For this interpretation, see Othmar Keel, *Die Weisheit spielt vor Gott: Ein ikonographischer Beitrag zur Bedeutung des mᵉsaḥäqät in Sprüche 8,30f.* (Fribourg: Universitätsverlag; Göttingen: Vandenhoeck & Ruprecht, 1974); cf. Baumann, *Weisheitsgestalt*, 4–41.

12. See the research overview of Gorges-Braunwarth, *Frauenbilder*, 4–64; and Baumann, *Weisheitsgestalt*, 4–41.

13. See especially Christl Maier, *Die "fremde Frau" in Proverbien 1–9: Eine exegetische und sozialgeschichtliche Studie* (OBO 144; Fribourg: Universitätsverlag; Göttingen: Vandenhoeck & Ruprecht, 1995); see as well her essay in the current volume.

the "future of feminist spirituality"[14]—as this is only one side of the coin, the other side of which devaluates the behavior of actual women.[15] Likewise, personified wisdom may also be interpreted as the "advertiser for the dominant male culture":[16] she served to press women and men into patriarchal societal structures that made women heavily dependent on their husbands and forced them to adjust to rigid patriarchal standards and morals.

The other question connected to personified Wisdom is whether or how she could have been derived from one of the numerous contemporary goddesses in Israel and its environment.[17]

> Aspects of goddesses which may have contributed to the image of personified wisdom are: the first-person speech of personified wisdom in Prov 1:22–33 that resembles the first-person speech of the Egyptian Isis; wisdom as giver of life and protection in Prov 3:16–18 as close to the Egyptian goddess Maʿat; wisdom as the tree of life in Prov 3:18 takes up a Mesopotamian motif; Prov 4:6 with wisdom as a lover resembles Maʿat; the first-person speech of personified wisdom in Prov 8:4–36 has parallels in speeches of Isis, the Egyptian deities Heqet and Shu as well as the speech of Pharaoh Ramesses II; wisdom's portrayal as the power behind the throne in Prov 8:15–16 resembles Maʿat or a Syrian-Canaanite goddess; the motif of wisdom as a lover and loved one in Prov 8:17, 20–21, 30 and 7:4 parallels again Maʿat; the fruit of wisdom in Prov 8:19 takes up Mesopotamian notions; the pre-existence of wisdom in Prov 8:22 can be compared to Maʿat as well as to the Baʿal epic; the creation of the world in Prov 8:24–25 comes close to Ugaritic texts; the playful wisdom in Prov 8:30 has parallels in the Syrian-Canaanite region, as well

---

14. According to the title and headings in Susan Cady et al., eds., *Sophia: The Future of Feminist Spirituality* (New York: Harper & Row, 1986).

15. See Gerlinde Baumann, "'Zukunft feministischer Spiritualität' oder 'Werbefigur des Patriarchats'? Die Bedeutung der Weisheitsgestalt in Prov 1–9 für die feministisch-theologische Diskussion," in *Von der Wurzel getragen: Christlich-feministische Exegese in Auseinandersetzung mit Antijudaismus* (ed. Luise Schottroff and Marie-Theres Wacker; BibIntS 17; Leiden: Brill, 1996), 135–52.

16. So Fokkelien van Dijk-Hemmes, *On Gendering Texts: Female and Male Voices in the Hebrew Bible* (BibIntS 1; Leiden: Brill, 1993), 58–62, 54; for a similar tone, see Carol A. Newsom, "Woman and the Discourse of Patriarchal Wisdom: A Study of Proverbs 1–9," in *Gender and Difference in Ancient Israel* (ed. Peggy L. Day; Minneapolis: Fortress, 1989), 142–60; Mieke Korenhof, "Spr. 8,22–31: Die 'Weisheit' scherzt vor Gott," in *Feministisch gelesen* (ed. Eva R. Schmidt et al.; Stuttgart: Kreuz, 1988), 1:118–26.

17. Sinnott lists further goddesses discussed in current research (*Personification*, 171). Lang, *Wisdom*, 129, sees parallels between personified wisdom and the Sumerian Nisaba as well as the Egyptian Seshat, two scribal goddesses. For an overview of the discussion (until 1994) and the methodical problems of the results to date in religious-historical research, see also Baumann, *Weisheitsgestalt*, 13–27.

as Ma'at, Hathor and the "goddess of play;" Prov 8:31 with wisdom close to humanity again resembles Ma'at.[18]

As this list demonstrates, it is Ma'at, the Egyptian goddess of justice and world order who is primarily discussed as a prototype for personified Wisdom.[19] There are, however, a number of reasons that speak against Ma'at as the only "model": For one, the content-based connection between personified wisdom and Ma'at is not close enough to assume that the image of personified wisdom is based on Ma'at; for another, Ma'at has no myth and does not speak herself.[20] In addition, there are a number of other goddesses as possible prototypes in the world surrounding Israel.[21] Therefore it is questionable whether personified Wisdom in Prov 1–9 was derived only from Ma'at and whether Ma'at has to be seen in the strict sense as a "model" for personified Wisdom.

2.3. Personified Wisdom and God in Proverbs

In Proverbs, the depiction of personified Wisdom is fed primarily by two sources: That Wisdom can be imagined as a feminine figure at all undoubtedly has to do with the fact that in the ancient Near Eastern world of ancient Israel there were a large number of goddesses, to some of whom an enormous amount of power was attributed. As a figure of the heavenly sphere, personified Wisdom certainly integrates facets of ancient Near Eastern goddesses; it is not possible, however, to explicitly identify them.[22] It is possible, though, to precisely identify a number of references to religious traditions of ancient Israel that can be found in the image of personified Wisdom as regards content. Primarily, these are references to prophetic texts (mostly Jeremiah) as well as the Priestly creation narrative (Gen 1:1–2:4a).[23] Based on these traditions, a figure is formed that is closely linked to the image of God in postexilic

---

18. For the source references, see Baumann, *Weisheitsgestalt*, 26–27.

19. For this thesis based on texts, see Christa Kayatz, *Studien zu Prov. 1–9: Eine form- und motivgeschichtliche Untersuchung unter Einbeziehung ägyptischen Vergleichsmaterials* (WMANT 22; Neukirchen-Vluyn: Neukirchener, 1966), based on iconographic sources, see Keel, "Weisheit." For the Egyptian Ma'at (without reference to biblical wisdom), see Jan Assmann, *Ma'at: Gerechtigkeit und Unsterblichkeit im Alten Ägypten* (Munich: Beck, 1990).

20. For this argument, see Burton L. Mack, *Logos und Sophia: Untersuchungen zur Weisheitstheologie im hellenistischen Judentum* (SUNT 10; Göttingen: Vandenhoeck & Ruprecht, 1973), 38.

21. See Baumann, *Weisheitsgestalt*, 24–25.

22. In contrast to Silvia Schroer; see her essay in the present volume.

23. See, among others, Baumann, *Weisheitsgestalt*, 145–46; Michaela Bauks and Gerlinde Baumann, "Im Anfang war…? Gen 1,1ff und Prov 8,22–31 im Vergleich," *Biblische*

Israel.²⁴ Personified Wisdom was already present before the creation of the world; she was created by God and is therefore a figure of the divine sphere.²⁵ A number of aspects contribute to the image of God in postexilic Israel: First, the Wisdom figure adds femininity to the divine, not only because *she herself* is a feminine personification but also due to the fact that she was given birth by *God* (Prov 8:24–25). Second, she is a mediator between God and humanity; she delivers to humanity the knowledge of the divine idea of inherent order in creation.²⁶ In this way, personified Wisdom in Proverbs is an extension of or even a breakthrough in ancient Israelite monotheism: When personified Wisdom enters the divine sphere, God is no longer the only being in this sphere. In a more subtle way, personified Wisdom transmits concepts of feminine and masculine behavior, primarily in her comparison to the "strange woman" or "Lady Folly" in Prov 1–9.

Personified Wisdom in Proverbs is also a figure through which the knowledge of the divine as well as human wisdom is to be passed on to the next generation. In the Old Testament, she is the first more-developed feminine figure of the divine sphere that is positively connoted and finds her origins (in parts) in Israel itself. As she was already with God before creation, she knows the deepest secrets of the world. Based on her connection to the "strange woman," it is questionable whether she could be received as a liberating figure for women in the respective time period.

3. Personified Wisdom in the Book of Sirach (Ecclesiasticus)

3.1. Text and Content

The book of Sirach (Jesus Ben Sira, Ecclesiasticus) like the book of Proverbs contains individual sayings or groups of sayings with teachings about actual life situations. Other than Proverbs—and for the first time in Israelite wisdom tradition—the book also refers explicitly to historical traditions

---

Notizen 71 (1994): 24–52; Scott L. Harris, *Proverbs 1–9: A Study of Inner-Biblical Interpretation* (SBLDS 150; Atlanta: Scholars Press, 1995), 67–109.

24. Contrary to Yoder's thesis in *Wisdom*, 111. For her, the "woman of strength" in Prov 31:10–31 and personified Wisdom in Prov 1–9 are one and the same figure, based on genuine descriptions of women's life. Yoder does not fully consider the characteristics of personified Wisdom, which bring the figure very close to God.

25. The texts are intentionally vague about the relationship between God and Wisdom. Marie-Theres Wacker formulates rightly that "wisdom literature throughout leaves a certain 'free space' between God and wisdom (cf. Prov 8:30!)" (Wacker, "Baruch," 534).

26. This is especially emphasized by von Rad, *Wisdom*, 144–76, esp. 175, in his formulation of personified Wisdom as a "self-revelation of creation."

of Israel (primarily in Sir 44:1–50:24).²⁷ Personified Wisdom appears in all parts of Sirach and therefore plays an important role for the entire writing.²⁸ Conspicuously, larger text passages at the beginning, middle, and end of the book are dedicated to her. She appears right in the introduction in Sir 1:1–27. In Sir 24:3–22 (with vv. 1–2 as introduction) she gives a long speech in which she praises herself. This chapter forms the book's center and connects the two halves. In an appendix, personified Wisdom is again praised by the wisdom teacher and author of the book (Sir 51:13–26). Additionally, there are three wisdom poems in the book (Sir 4:11–19; 6:18–37; 14:20–15:10).

In Sir 1:1–27 the author introduces personified Wisdom: As in Prov 8:22–31, she was created before the world, and as in Job 28 she can be perceived through the order of the world. Beyond and before all wisdom, however, is God, and only God is truly wise; he created and conceived Wisdom and confers her to God-fearing men and women. Primarily in Sir 1:10–20, personified Wisdom is closely connected to the "fear of God" (similar to Prov 1:7; 8:13; 9:10; Ps 111:10; Job 28:28). In Sir 1:26, the connection of (personified) Wisdom with divine instruction (Heb., תורה; Gk., νόμος) is clearly pronounced: "If you desire wisdom, keep the commandments, and the Lord will lavish her upon you" (NRSV).²⁹ This statement is emphasized by the identification of wisdom and torah in Sir 24:23.

Sirach 4:11–19 highlights the love for personified Wisdom: serving her is equivalent to serving God, and whoever loves her will be loved by God (v. 14). In this section (according to the Hebrew text tradition), personified Wisdom herself speaks in five verses. In 4:19, she even warns her followers and threat-

---

27. See Nuria Calduch-Benages, "The Absence of Named Women from Ben Sira's Praise of the Ancestors," in *Rewriting Biblical History: Essays on Chronicles and Ben Sira in Honor of Pancratius C. Beentjes* (ed. Jeremy Corley and Harm van Grol; Deuterocanonical and Cognate Literature Studies 7; Berlin: de Gruyter, 2011), 301–17.

28. As far as I know, there is no feminist-theological study dedicated only to personified Wisdom in Sirach. Still recommendable is the monograph by Johannes Marböck, *Weisheit im Wandel: Untersuchungen zur Weisheitstheologie bei Ben Sira* (2nd ed.; BZAW 272; Berlin: de Gruyter, 1999). See also Nuria Calduch-Benages, ed., *El Libro de Ben Sira (Sirácida o Eclesiástico)* (Reseña Bíblica 41; Estella: Verbo Divino, 2004), esp. 27–36. In feminist exegesis, personified Wisdom in Sirach is treated in overview articles; see Angelika Strotmann, "Sirach (Ecclesiasticus): On the Difficult Relations between Divine Wisdom and Real Women in an Androcentric Document," in Schottroff and Wacker, *Feminist Biblical Interpretation*, 539–54; Schroer, *Wisdom Has Built Her House*, 84–97; see also Ibolya Balla, *Ben Sira on Family, Gender, and Sexuality* (Deuterocanonical and Cognate Literature Studies 8; Berlin: de Gruyter, 2011).

29. A similar statement can be found in Sir 6:37; see Strotmann, "Sirach (Ecclesiasticus)," 549.

ens them (cf. Prov 1:22–33). On the other hand, Sir 6:18–37 emphasizes the relationship between personified Wisdom and education, that is, the teacher's judgment or advice. Such instruction is highly praised and is described, among other things, as a precious crown (6:31), which, like wisdom, must be achieved. In Sir 14:20–15:10, personified Wisdom acts like a rich woman who lives in a house, and to whom one should try to be near; in Sir 15, she is compared to a mother, a young bride, or a wife. Whoever approaches her finds happiness and a crown of rejoicing (Sir 15:6). Personified Wisdom is thus portrayed like the girlfriend of a young man, and his approach to her is described in erotic or sexual metaphors.[30]

In another way, personified Wisdom in Sir 24:1–22 speaks of herself in a style similar to the Hellenistic genre of aretalogy, a form of sacred biography.[31] Similar to Sir 1, she emphasizes that she was created by God, but then underlines her connections to Israelite history. Like a queen, she wanders through the world and seeks for a place to live, which she then finds with God's help in Jacob or Israel. She lives in Jerusalem and serves before God like a priestess in the holy tent. She compares herself to different trees that offer their fruits to those who approach them. Sirach 24 is a text in which numerous allusions to Old Testament traditions are found and which proves the high, almost divine position of personified Wisdom. She remains, however, clearly subordinated to God: He created her, he allows her to live in Jerusalem, and she serves him in the cult.

At the end of the book of Sirach, the wisdom teacher once again praises personified Wisdom in Sir 51:13–26. In this passage, the teacher looks back on his life with Wisdom as a companion and also uses erotic metaphors: As a young man, he sought her as he would search for a girlfriend or wife, and he found her. Finally, this hymn to Wisdom aims at elating the students for the wisdom teacher's "house of instruction" (51:23).

3.2. CONTEXT AND MEANING

The book of Sirach was presumably written in the second century BCE by an educated wise man named Jesus ben Sira who lived in Jerusalem and may have been a priest. His grandson translated the text into Greek. The Greek

---

30. For the erotic and sexually explicit language in Sirach and the wise man's relationship to personified Wisdom, see the summary in Balla, *Ben Sira*, 226–28; Balla often notes that the Greek translation of Sirach weakens the erotic content (230).

31. For the aretalogies of Isis, see Silke Petersen, *Brot, Licht und Weinstock: Intertextuelle Analysen johanneischer Ich-bin-Worte* (NovTSup 127; Leiden: Brill, 2008), esp. 184–99.

version[32] is the basis for most of the exegetical work on the book of Sirach, although the Hebrew text is older (though it only has survived in fragments).

Compared to the time when Proverbs was written, the overall situation has changed significantly: On the one hand, the issue of "foreignness" in Israel is apparently not so important anymore; on the other hand, Hellenism now significantly influences the culture of Israel. In his book of wisdom, Sirach attempts to connect Israelite and Hellenistic traditions with each other.

Relevant for the interpretation of personified Wisdom are Sirach's androcentrism and his hostility toward women, as Silvia Schroer points out.[33] The positive representation of personified Wisdom contrasts with the negative representation of actual women; here Sirach partially reiterates the contrast between personified Wisdom and the "strange woman" in Prov 1–9. While Wisdom praises herself in Sir 24, there are numerous verses immediately following in Sir 25–26 that speak quite negatively about women. Here as well, the description of the extremely positive figure of personified Wisdom is coupled with a degradation of concrete women. Other than at the end of Proverbs (31:10–31),[34] there is no figure in Sirach that integrates both aspects.

In her interpretation, Angelika Strotmann emphasizes that personified Wisdom in Sirach is based to a large extent on personified Wisdom from Proverbs.[35] Both extend an invitation to a meal (Prov 9:1–6; Sir 15:2–3; 24:19–21), speak like a prophetess (Prov 1:20–33; Sir 4:19), and talk about their "fruits" (Prov 8:19; Sir 24:19–21).[36] In addition, both are closely bound to the fear of God (Prov 8:13; Sir 1:10–20); they are filled with love for humanity and are loved in return (Prov 8:17, 21; Sir 24:18; 51:19–20). Strotmann also takes a position in the frequently discussed question of whether personified Wisdom in Sirach, in comparison to Proverbs, has a less universalistic profile (i.e., directed toward humanity). Personified Wisdom in Sirach is much more closely connected to Israel, with the fear of God, the torah, and the commandments.[37] Strotmann points out (in my opinion correctly)

---

32. There are two Greek versions, a longer (G II) and a shorter one (G I). In most cases, the shorter one is the basis for modern Bible translations, which is why the reference point in the following is the shorter version.

33. Schroer, *Wisdom Has Built Her House*, 85–89; see also Nuria Calduch-Benages's essay in this volume.

34. Regarding the "woman of strength," see in addition to the work of Yoder, *Wisdom*, also Katrin Brockmöller, "*Eine Frau der Stärke—wer findet sie?*" *Exegetische Analysen und intertextuelle Lektüren zu Spr 31,10–31* (BBB 147; Berlin: Philo, 2004), as well as Tamara Cohn Eskenazi's essay in this volume, §3.4.

35. Strotmann, "Sirach (Ecclesiasticus)," 539–54, 548.

36. Ibid.

37. Ibid., 548 and 551–52.

that personified Wisdom in Sirach—compared with Proverbs—is linked to additional aspects of Israelite theology, which are embedded in a larger context, because Sirach strives for a synthesis between Israelite and Hellenistic thought. In some respects, Sirach adopts Hellenistic concepts, while he rejects them in other areas. He writes against a universalistic background in which the message of Israel's God is directed to all peoples. Therefore, the identification with the torah does not represent any limitations for personified Wisdom, but exactly the opposite, namely an expansion. Moreover, the representation of personified Wisdom oscillates between Hellenistic thinking and the closeness to the aretalogies of Egyptian-Hellenistic Isis[38] on the one side and—compared to Proverbs—the connection to a larger breadth of Israelite tradition on the other side: Personified Wisdom in the book of Sirach seems to be both—she is unquestionably Israelite, but at the same time connected to Hellenistic thinking.

The latter is due to parallels between personified wisdom, primarily in Sir 24, and the Hellenistic Isis, not only based on the joint literary genre of the aretalogy but also through the polymorphism[39] of both figures. The parallels also stretch across individual aspects of her representation. The proposition of Hans Conzelmann that Sir 24:3–6(7) is "nothing other than a practically literal copy of a song to Isis, which is only retouched in one or two places"[40] has been widely approved in research. According to Conzelmann, personified Wisdom and Isis share many aspects: they both emerge from the mouth of God, wander around the earth in an act of creation, and rule the cosmos. Both figures serve as overseer of the world, goddess of the seas, and ruler of destiny. For other passages from Sir 24, Conzelmann also names the closeness to the law (Sir 24:23) and to the cult (Sir 24:10).[41] Burton L. Mack specifies the parallels between Isis and personified Wisdom with regard to the motif "circulation, descent and search for a dwelling place," the close

---

38. For the parallels between Isis and personified Wisdom in Sirach (and in the Wisdom of Solomon), Mack, *Logos*, 38, has already pointed out: "Maat is a mythical figure, but does not have a myth herself; she never speaks in monologues and lacks the sexual characteristics of wisdom. All these features apply to the goddess Isis. ... Because Isis has a myth, she is closely related to the word, and probably also lended wisdom the sexual characteristics." See also John S. Kloppenborg, "Isis and Sophia in the Book of Wisdom," *HTR* 75 (1982): 57–84.

39. Maier, "Weisheit," refers to this feature in §1.2.4.

40. Hans Conzelmann, "Die Mutter der Weisheit," in *Zeit und Geschichte: Dankesgabe an Rudolf Bultmann zum 80. Geburtstag* (ed. Erich Dinkler; Tübingen: Mohr Siebeck, 1964), 225–34, here 228; Mack, *Logos*, 40, shares this opinion.

41. Conzelmann, "Mutter," 232–33.

relationship to the word, the sexual characteristics, and the overall mythological representation.[42]

An argument against the close relationship between Isis and personified Wisdom seemed for a long time to be the dating of the Isis aretalogies and texts on the Hellenistic Isis to the post-Christian era.[43] If one assumes, however, that these texts only mark the end point of a longer development, then the close relationship between personified Wisdom and Isis is quite possible.[44] In addition, personified Wisdom, with her invitation to refresh her follower with her fruits (Sir 24:19–21), to nourish, and to provide shade (Sir 24:13–22), could have been inspired, according to Schroer, by a Near Eastern tree goddess.[45] In the tree metaphor in Sir 24:13–22, one can also discern—as with a number of other previously observed aspects—an Israelite tradition, which Schäfer refers to in the following: "Wisdom is like everything beautiful and delightful that has ever been promised in the Bible, like all the famous trees and fragrances, not least like the odor of incense in the Temple."[46]

3.3. Personified Wisdom and God in Sirach

Compared to the introduction of Proverbs, how has the relationship between personified Wisdom and God changed two or three centuries later in the book of Sirach? Schroer and Strotmann stake out two opposing positions in German exegesis. In Schroer's view, personified Wisdom in Sirach, in comparison to Proverbs, is more strongly limited; she is clearly subordinated to the God of Israel and a kind of priestly mediator. The love of Wisdom is limited in two ways: First, it consists mainly of keeping the commandments; second, Wisdom acts only in Israel and in the Jerusalem temple.[47]

Strotmann considers the relationship between personified Wisdom and God in a somewhat different light. She emphasizes texts such as Sir 4:14, in

---

42. According to Mack, *Logos*, 38–42; the last-named aspect is already noticed by Conzelmann, "Mutter," 234.
43. According to Lang, *Frau Weisheit*, 152–54.
44. See also Schäfer, *Mirror of His Beauty*, 38.
45. Schroer, *Wisdom Has Built Her House*, 91–92, points to the Canaanite tree goddess as well as to the Egyptian tree goddess. See her more detailed discussion in "Die Zweiggöttin in Palästina/Israel: Von der Mittelbronze II B-Zeit bis zu Jesus Sirach," in *Jerusalem: Texte—Bilder—Steine: Zum 100. Geburtstag von Hildi und Othmar Keel-Leu* (ed. Max Küchler and Christoph Uehlinger; NTOA 6; Fribourg: Universitätsverlag; Göttingen: Vandenhoeck & Ruprecht, 1987), 201–25, esp. 218–21, and her article in the present volume (§3.1).
46. Schäfer, *Mirror of His Beauty*, 31.
47. According to Schroer, *Wisdom Has Built Her House*, 94–95.

which personified Wisdom and God almost merge with each other. She also discovers parallels between the search for God according to Deut 6:5 and the search for wisdom according to Sir 6:26; in the end, both grant the seekers peace (Sir 6:28; Deut 12:9-10).[48] Gottfried Schimanowski points to further parallels between personified Wisdom in Sirach and God: The "high places" (Sir 24:4a) are not only the residence of Wisdom but also the residence of God; the "throne on a pillar of cloud" (Sir 24:4b) is, according to Exod 13:21; 14:19, also the place where God appears.[49] The areas of the world named in Sir 24:5-6 are not accessible to humans, but rather only to God—and Wisdom.[50] When Wisdom in Sir 24:8 lives in Zion and in Sir 24:9 stays there for all eternity, she takes God's dwelling place in Old Testament tradition.[51] Besides this near identification or equal status of God and personified Wisdom,[52] there are also texts in Sirach in which personified Wisdom is clearly subordinated to God. For the latter, Strotmann refers to the creation of personified Wisdom by God (Sir 1:1-27; cf. Sir 24:3), Wisdom's obedience to God's commands (Sir 24:8-9), and her service before God in the temple (Sir 24:10).[53]

Personified Wisdom in Sirach thus appears on the one hand as a figure who exhibits characteristics of great independence and high authority and on the other hand as one who is partially subordinated to God. Schäfer summarizes this ambiguity in arguing that personified Wisdom, as a creation of God, is not God, but is "nevertheless God's representative on earth."[54] Her activities in Israel and in the temple do not limit her outreach since Jerusalem is now seen as the center of the world, to which all peoples relate in their faith. Personified Wisdom in Sirach and in Proverbs have in common that they are based on Old Testament traditions and ancient Near Eastern goddesses. In Sirach, however, the links to the Egyptian-Hellenistic Isis are much clearer than those to Maʿat in Prov 1-9. Personified Wisdom in Sirach differs from personified Wisdom in Prov 1-9 through her identification with the torah as well. In addition, there is a stronger polarization in Sirach than in Proverbs between the positive Wisdom figure on the one side, with which the

---

48. Strotmann, "Sirach (Ecclesiasticus)," 549.
49. See Gottfried Schimanowski, *Weisheit und Messias: Die jüdischen Voraussetzungen der urchristlichen Präexistenzchristologie* (WUNT 17; Tübingen: Mohr Siebeck, 1985), 50.
50. Ibid., 51-52.
51. Ibid., 54.
52. Strotmann, "Sirach (Ecclesiasticus)," 550, regarding Sir 14-15: "Wisdom seems to be YHWH himself."
53. Ibid., 551.
54. Schäfer, *Mirror of His Beauty*, 30.

addressees should cultivate a close relationship, and the negatively depicted concrete women on the other.

4. Personified Wisdom in the Book of Wisdom (Wisdom of Solomon)

4.1. Text and Content

The book of Wisdom (Sapientia; Wisdom of Solomon) attempts—like the book of Sirach—to create a synthesis of Israelite and Hellenistic thought. The reader is instructed or courted by a single person to turn toward the wisdom of Israel. The book's speaker is clothed, however, not only in Israelite but also in Hellenistic robes; in Wis 9:7–8 he claims to be King Solomon.

In the book of Wisdom, personified Wisdom plays an even more important role than in Proverbs or in Sirach.[55] Wisdom is the dominant figure in the first part (Wis 1:1–11:1) and appears at least implicitly in all other parts. The "encomium," or hymn, on wisdom in Wis 6:22–11:1 with the transitional section 6:12–21 talk explicitly about her.[56] "Solomon" praises the advantages of wisdom in life, and even asks God for the gift of wisdom (7:7–22a; cf. 8:21–18). This song of praise culminates in a hymn to wisdom, her being, and her works (7:22b–8:1). Wisdom was also at work in Israel's history (10:1–11:1). Because of these qualities, "Solomon" wants to win her as a bride and spend his life with her (8:2–20).

In these passages, wisdom entails a large variety of aspects, many of which we have already seen in Proverbs and in Sirach. The topic of justice is important in the book of Wisdom (Wis 1:1–15); in addition, personified Wisdom is identified with the power behind the throne (Wis 6:20–21): She is the one who rules and guides the rulers (cf. Prov 8:15–16). Personified Wisdom was already present at the beginning of creation (Wis 6:22), at the creation of the world (Wis 9:9), and knows all of creation, because she is the "master craftswoman" or "creator" (Gk. τεχνῖτις; Wis 7:21) of all things. Thus personified Wisdom appears as God's co-creator. In Wis 9:4, she can be designated as πάρεδρος, as the one enthroned beside God. At this point, the book of Wisdom

---

55. As far as I know, there is no feminist-theological study that focuses only on personified Wisdom in the book of Wisdom. Yet Silvia Schroer dedicates some space to her in "Wisdom: An Example of Jewish Intercultural Theology," in Schottroff and Wacker, *Feminist Biblical Interpretation*, 555–65. The detailed study by Neher, *Wesen*, limits itself to the question of the function and essence of personified Wisdom in the book of Wisdom.

56. See, e.g., Helmut Engel, "Weisheit Salomos," in *Das wissenschaftliche Bibellexikon im Internet* (2005): §2.2.3, http://www.wibilex.de; Schroer, "Wisdom," 556–58.

goes one step further than Proverbs and Sirach. However, there are also verses in which personified Wisdom is subordinated to God, who leads her (7:15).

Different from Sirach, personified Wisdom is no longer *compared* to the partner of the person seeking her (Sir 15:2); she *is* now the life partner of "Solomon" (Wis 6:12–21; 8:2, 18). Only those who live with Wisdom will be loved by God (Wis 7:28); as such, the role as mediator between God and humans is even more strongly emphasized. The relationship of personified Wisdom to God and to humans, as Martin Neher has elaborated, is often conveyed by the spirit of God (esp. Wis 1:6; 7:7, 22–23; 9:17).[57]

Personified Wisdom in Wisdom of Solomon differs in some points from Proverbs and Sirach: First, she is portrayed as a historically powerful being who intervenes on behalf of the people (Wis 10:1–11:1). In this role, personified Wisdom can serve as the key to older traditions of Israel.[58] Second, personified Wisdom is connected to immortality, which "Solomon" hopes to attain through his life partner by making the right decisions and acting properly (Wis 8:13, 17). Third, the profile of personified Wisdom has changed, especially in comparison to Sirach, insofar as the erotic and sexual imagery—even if personified Wisdom is the bride and life partner of "Solomon"— is missing in her description.[59] Fourth, personified Wisdom does not have her own voice: the book does not present any first-person speeches, and she instead appears only in the speeches of "Solomon."

4.2. Context and Meaning

The book of Wisdom was designed with the help of Hellenistic literary forms and genres, namely in Egyptian Alexandria, probably in the century before or after the beginning of the Common Era. The book presents a fictitious speech of King Solomon that focuses on justice and wisdom. Its author is probably a scribe or wise person who is extremely well-informed about the traditions of Israel and trained in Hellenistic rhetoric.[60]

In contrast to her representation in Proverbs and in Sirach, personified Wisdom in the book of Wisdom has no negative antagonist, neither on a concrete nor a metaphorical level. There are no texts in the book of Wisdom in which women are devalued or negatively portrayed; in any case, the book mentions real women and men only once (Wis 3:12–14). Similar to other

---

57. See, e.g., Neher, *Wesen*, 233.
58. Ibid., 236.
59. This feature has been pointed out by Jane S. Webster, "Sophia: Engendering Wisdom in Proverbs, Ben Sira and the Wisdom of Solomon," *JSOT* 78 (1998): 74–77.
60. For more detail, see Engel, "Weisheit Salomos," §4.

topics discussed in the book of Wisdom, personified Wisdom also appears indeterminate and vague.

The book of Wisdom was strongly influenced by the Hellenistic context in which it was written. The book attempts to express Israelite wisdom in the rhetorical forms of Hellenistic literature.[61] It is probably addressed to young, Jewish people (more likely men than women) and seeks to offer a synthesis of Old Testament and Hellenistic wisdom.[62] The book assumes a nonpolemical and fearless stance toward Hellenism, and therefore offers an extended image of God; it does not seem to be a problem that personified Wisdom is placed on God's side as a co-creator sharing God's throne.

As Mack has pointed out, there is further overlapping between the portrayal of personified Wisdom in the book of Wisdom and Isis—in contrast to personified Wisdom in Sirach and in addition to the polymorphism and the genre of aretalogy: The aspect of light (Wis 6:12; 7:10, 29) like Isis's aspect of the sun goddess; Wisdom is the universal goddess who fills the world (Wis 7:23), a "breath" of God and his purity (Wis 7:25), and the principle of the cosmos, which she renews (Wis 7:27). Further results of Mack are summarized by Schäfer.

> Isis is the spouse and sister of the sun god Osiris; even the term *parhedros* is used in her relationship to Serapis, the Hellenistic Osiris. Isis is the goddess of earth and nature, the "female principle of nature" (*to tēs physeōs thēly*), the mother of the cosmos (*mētēr tou kosmou*).[63]

Schäfer concludes: "It is this peculiar mixture of Platonic, Stoic and Egyptian elements that gives Wisdom/Spirit in Sapientia Salomonis her distinctive tinge."[64]

At the time the book of Wisdom was written, Israel's cult in the Jewish communities in Egypt was in competition with the worship of the goddess Isis. It is possible that the book of Wisdom attempts to again bind those Jews who tended toward the worship of Isis or even turned away from Judaism more strongly to the Jewish faith.[65] In this context, it makes sense that personified Wisdom was portrayed in the image of Isis. With personified

---

61. For the Greek literary style and its variations, see ibid., §2.2.
62. See ibid., §4; similarly also Neher, *Wesen*, 240.
63. Schäfer, *Mirror of His Beauty*, 37 with reference to Mack, *Logos*, 66–72.
64. Schäfer, *Mirror of His Beauty*, 38; from a different perspective, Neher, *Wesen*, 239–40, comes to a similar result: The writer of the Sapientia had "no specific philosophical basis," but rather "made use of the philosophical terms common among all educated persons in Alexandria, in order to systematically integrate them into his theological argumentation."
65. Engel, "Weisheit Salomos," §4, emphasizes that the book of Wisdom is a piece of

Wisdom, who resembles Isis and is also closely tied to the God of Israel, Judaism would become more attractive.

4.3. Personified Wisdom and God in the Wisdom of Solomon

The relationship between personified Wisdom and God in the book of Wisdom is constructed similarly to that in Sirach. On the one hand, she is almost placed on equal terms with God: "She rules all things full of goodness" (Wis 8:1); she "is the beginning of it all" (7:12); she lives with God, who loves her (8:3); whoever loves her will be loved by God (7:28); she knows his whole creation in all of his works (8:4); she is God's co-creator (7:21) and is enthroned as πάρεδρος at the side of God (9:4). On the other hand, she is also called the "pure effluence from the glory of God" (7:25), and everything that she is comes from God; he is the one who shows the way to wisdom (7:15),[66] and "Solomon" asks him for the gift of wisdom (7:7; 8:21; 9:4, 10). Sometimes she appears as a personification; for example, when "Solomon" wishes to bring her home as a bride and live together with her (8:2–20). In other passages, by contrast (such as 7:22b–8:1), she is more of an abstract—although very powerful—"being" (cf. Job 28; Bar 3–4). Thus she has the same two sides as personified Wisdom in Sirach: On the one hand, she is placed on the same level as God; on the other hand, she is subordinated to him. Seemingly, the aspect of subordination more likely applies to wisdom as a "being" or "creation," whereas personified Wisdom more likely has the same position as God. A new aspect here is not only that humans love personified Wisdom but also that God loves her (8:3).[67] God and personified Wisdom share a number of aspects: They allow themselves to be found; they rescue; they love—especially the people.[68] In the retrospection to Israelite history in 10:15–21, personified

---

internal Jewish promotional literature that is designed not to convince or argue, but to win over.

66. According to ibid., in §2.2.3, with reference to Wis 8:2–9 (italics in original): "Not even the shadow of a doubt remains, whether she (like Isis) is also a 'goddess.' There is only *one* God and creator of everything, who also gives wisdom, which as his creation (Prov 8:22; Sir 1:4, 9) shares in *his* characteristics and titles."

67. Schroer, "Wisdom," 557–58, speaks of Sophia as "the beloved and the companion of God."

68. Engel, "Weisheit Salomos," in §2.2.3 (italics in original): "Through the *literary personification* of wisdom, one recognizes that a one-sided or predominantly 'masculine' image of God is erroneous.… In the figure of 'wisdom,' the author reflects in an original way the loving, personal presence of God with humans and expresses it in the philosophical and educated language of his present time."

Wisdom acts—compared with the older texts, which are revised here—in the place of God.

Therefore, Isis was a model for personified Wisdom in the book of Wisdom, at least in some aspects and with regard to her authority. Again, personified Wisdom takes on many elements from her forerunners in Proverbs and in Sirach. Her relationship to God vacillates between subordination and equality.[69]

5. Summary

Personified Wisdom in Prov 1–9 is born into the world as a figure who is to lead the reader into the older wisdom of the book of Proverbs (Prov 10–29). She warns the young people to whom she is speaking to turn toward her and not to the "strange woman" who wants to lead them to inappropriate social behavior. But not only with the threats of a prophetess does personified wisdom speak to her public; she also woos them with the information that she was already with God before he created the world and therefore has intimate knowledge of the interrelations of creation and the proper behavior. In Sirach, personified Wisdom is expanded and receives new competencies; she now comes close to the fear of God and is identified with the torah. At the same time, she receives strong erotic-sexual characteristics. In her portrayal, the influence of the Egyptian-Hellenistic Isis is noticeable, which underlines the extent of the power of personified Wisdom. Occasionally she has the same ranking as God. Since God's sphere of influence now extends to the entire world, this also applies to personified wisdom—she is now also a figure based in Israel and its history but shining out over the entire world, confidently speaking to her listeners. The position of personified Wisdom in the book of Wisdom is even higher: Now she is at the side of God and is partly made equal to him; she is the basis of just actions and was already active in the history of Israel. Yet she does not speak herself anymore. She has become the life partner of the exemplary wise man "King Solomon," who praises her highly. They have a close relationship that, however, has lost its erotic aspects. In close cohabitation with Wisdom, it is now possible for people like "Solomon" to act justly according to the commandments and thus attain immortality.

---

69. In my opinion, Schroer neglects the independence of God as well as the passages of the subordination of personified wisdom under God when she says: "Sophia in the book of Wisdom is Israel's God imaged as woman and goddess" (Schroer, "Wisdom," 564). On the other hand, Engel in "Weisheit Salomos," §2.2.3, overlooks the divine characteristics of Wisdom when he completely disputes the aspect of a goddess.

But the joy over this figure, who at least in some instances can be considered a female image of God in the Bible, is not unclouded, because some aspects of personified wisdom have given way to feminist criticism: In all three books, she turns primarily to young men, who are warned about interacting with certain women (Proverbs). The young man should pay more—also sexual-erotic—attention to Wisdom than to problematic, concrete women (Sirach), or they should see their ideal life partner in Wisdom, who can help them to act justly or even attain immortality (Wisdom). Today's female readers of these androcentric texts should not allow themselves to be pushed into the less attractive alternative of either identifying themselves with the male addressees or with the devalued and even demonized women in the texts. Instead they could try to appreciate personified Wisdom mainly by way of her numerous connections to ancient Israelite traditions and her power, which is borrowed from Isis.

Translated from German by Dale J. Provost; revised by Christl M. Maier

Good and Evil Women in Proverbs and Job: The Emergence of Cultural Stereotypes

Christl M. Maier

In the last decades, the numerous female figures in Proverbs, Job, and other wisdom books of the Hebrew and Greek Bible have been widely interpreted. The present volume also offers many insights into this discussion. In particular, feminist scholars have analyzed these female characters with regard to their social status in ancient Israel as well as their symbolic role in a patriarchal society. In this article, I deal with the tendency in Wisdom literature to generate types of human characters. I name them "cultural stereotypes" and will first demonstrate their dangerous potential in consolidating a bias toward women (and men). Second, I will analyze some characterizations of women in Proverbs and Job by treating these portrayals not as timeless truth but as cultural stereotypes that serve a particular purpose. Methodologically, I combine the perspectives of ideology criticism and feminist criticism, adopting a reading of wisdom sayings that reveals androcentrism and forms of gender bias. In some instances, I will broaden my feminist-critical approach with a social-historical reconstruction of the text's setting. The combination of synchronic and diachronic approaches helps to carve out the authors' interests and intentions to educate their intended audience in a specific way. My thesis is that cultural stereotypes for women do not, for the most part, adequately describe women's lives and, in the end, have a negative effect on the overall evaluation of women's roles in society. Last, I will assess the significance of cultural stereotypes for audiences and readers past and present, and point out why a deconstructive reading is necessary.

1. Definition and Function of a Stereotype

The wisdom books of the Hebrew Bible are part of an old and enduring cultural tradition of the ancient Near East that aims at ordering the world. Starting from Sumerian item lists to collections of proverbs and elaborate exhortations, the so-called wisdom texts served as material for learning how to read and write in Mesopotamia and Egypt. In ancient Israel, the sayings, exhortations, and poems that now form the book of Proverbs stemmed from different sources: an oral clan tradition, an urban school tradition, and postexilic scribal circles.[1] The process of collecting and writing down these sayings can be attributed to learned men (and perhaps some women) at the royal court (Prov 25:1 mentions the "men of Hezekiah, king of Judah"). They aim at educating their readers through proverbial sayings and admonitions, which are often rhythmic or poetic and thus easy to memorize.[2] A peculiar feature of these proverbs is binary pairing such as "wise" and "fool" (10:8; 11:29), "lazy" and "diligent" (13:4; 26:14–16), "righteous" and "wicked" (10:3, 6, 11; 11:23).[3] In describing certain deeds and thoughts of a "wise" or a "foolish" person, the proverbial sayings characterize them as types, or rather, stereotypes.

The term *stereotype* was introduced into the discourse on social life by the journalist Walter Lippmann (1898–1974), who defined it as "an ordered, more or less consistent picture of the world, to which our habits, our tastes, our capacities, our comforts and our hopes have adjusted themselves."[4] Lippmann further argues that in order to cope with their complex world people need stereotypes. From a psychological point of view, building stereotypes seems to be a coping strategy, with the help of which, in light of conflicting perceptions and complex anxieties, humans are able to orientate themselves in their world. Johnny Miles rightly points out that stereotyping individuals or groups always runs the risk of "othering," that is, distinguishing individuals or a group from oneself through negative assessments.[5] Such stereotyping reduces particularity and distinctiveness by fusing the behavior or habits of individuals into a homogenous evaluation. In other words,

---

1. For an overview of the material, see Christl Maier, "Proverbs: How Feminine Wisdom Comes into Being," in *Feminist Biblical Interpretation: A Compendium of Critical Commentary on the Books of the Bible and Related Literature* (ed. Luise Schottroff and Marie-Theres Wacker; Grand Rapids: Eerdmans, 2012), 255–72; 255–56. Proverbs 22:17–23:11 has direct parallels in the Egyptian Instruction of Amenemope.

2. For this setting, see Roger N. Whybray, *The Book of Proverbs: A Survey of Modern Studies* (Leiden: Brill, 1995), 19–21.

3. In Egyptian wisdom literature, another binary pair besides "wise" and "fool" is "hot" and "hush"; see Hellmut Brunner, *Altägyptische Weisheit: Lehren für das Leben* (Darmstadt: Wissenschaftliche Buchgesellschaft, 1988), 24–27.

4. Walter Lippmann, *Public Opinion* (1922; repr., New York: Macmillan, 1949), 95.

5. Johnny Miles, *Constructing the Other in Ancient Israel and the USA* (The Bible in the Modern World 32; Sheffield: Sheffield Phoenix, 2011), 30–33.

a stereotype fixates on a few, simple, essential characteristics (behavior, disposition, physical qualities) and reduces people to those characteristics. These characteristics are taken out of context and attributed to everyone associated with that characteristic. ... Such a process where projection fuels the stereotype that reduces, essentializes, naturalizes, and fixes does serve several functions, not least of which are to establish identity and boundaries.[6]

A cultural stereotype is one that has become permanent, that is, a standard image in a certain culture.

The negative depiction of the "wicked" (Heb. רשעים) may serve as an example: they speak violent words, and their mouth pours out evil (Prov 10:6, 11, 32; 11:9, 11; 12:6; 15:28; cf. Ps 73:8–9), their actions are deceptive or evil (Prov 11:18; 12:2, 10; 13:5; 21:7; cf. Job 10:3; Ps 37:14, 32), they bribe other people (Prov 17:23), they give treacherous counsel (Prov 12:5), and their ways lead others astray (Prov 12:26; 15:9). The aim of this dismissive characterization of the "wicked" is twofold. First, the sages try to reveal violent actions and deceitful speech as detrimental to human relations. In contrasting such behavior with the positive characterization of the "righteous," they intend to instruct their audience about socially accepted behavior. Second, the stigmatization of the "wicked" and especially the recurrent announcement of their well-deserved doom aim at consoling the "righteous" that the obvious thriving of the wicked will end soon (see Ps 37; 73). Acknowledging the sages' urge to define desirable behavior, one has to be aware that they promote a certain ideology. Stereotyping becomes problematic if it is used to denigrate certain persons or if it leads to a reduced perception of reality. If cultural stereotypes are taken as real and gain the status of undisputed truth, they exclude others and lose their potential to bring order to the complexity of life.

The problem of "othering" individuals or groups when using stereotypical characterization arises especially if modern readers perceive the statements of the biblical wisdom tradition as time-invariant and cross-cultural truth without acknowledging the differences in societal values and gender relations between then and now. In order to ward off such interpretations, the ideology inherent in cultural stereotypes has to be critically assessed. From a feminist perspective, such ideology criticism requires a reading that deconstructs the cultural stereotypes and analyzes their function for the society of the texts' authors.

---

6. Ibid., 31.

2. Cultural Stereotypes of Women

In the maxims of proverbial wisdom, that is, the thematically unsorted sayings in Prov 10–30, women are portrayed as mothers, spouses, widows, and prostitutes—thus by reference to their relationship with men. The proverbs constantly speak *about* women, not from their own perspective, and when they mention women, they primarily name problems in relations between men and women. The book of Job focuses so much on the male protagonist and his dispute with his male friends that it appears as a world almost without women.[7] Women are only mentioned in passing as mother, widow, the wife of the neighbor, and servant—again always in relation to men. In the following, I analyze four major types of women characterized in Proverbs and Job: the diligent wife, the seductress, the female counselor, and the poor widow.

2.1. The Diligent Wife

In proverbial wisdom, the married woman is viewed with regard to her usefulness to her husband: "A strong wife is the crown of her husband, but like rottenness in his bones is the one who brings shame" (Prov 12:4).[8] The crown as a visible symbol of royal power (see 2 Sam 12:30) is here used metaphorically for the high value of a diligent woman as companion in life. Similar value is attributed to the wife in the saying "a prudent wife is from YHWH" (Prov 19:14; cf. 18:22). While a woman's beauty is praiseworthy (Job 42:15), beauty is not sufficient for a marriage partner if it is not paired with discretion, as stated in Prov 11:22: "a gold ring in a pig's snout [is] a beautiful woman without good sense." The "good" spouse is thus beautiful, bright, diligent, and subjects herself to the paterfamilias, the master of the family. Summarizing the significance of the diligent wife, Prov 14:1 states, "The wisdom of women builds her house, but foolishness tears it down with her own hands."

These proverbs articulate common knowledge of an agricultural clan culture with households that are largely oriented toward producing their own food and basic handicraft, which were widespread in Israel in premonarchic times and even until the seventh century BCE.[9] Israelite women were responsible for the daily meals and crafts like spinning and weaving as well as for their children's early education. Thus, in Prov 10–30, the partnership of men

---

7. See Christl Maier and Silvia Schroer, "Job: Questioning the Book of the Righteous Sufferer," in Schottroff and Wacker, *Feminist Biblical Interpretation*, 221–39.

8. All translations of biblical passages are mine unless otherwise noted.

9. See Carol Meyers, *Discovering Eve: Ancient Israelite Women in Context* (New York: Oxford University Press, 1988).

and women is economically based; love between the marriage partners is not mentioned at all.

A predominant theme, however, is the potential failure of such domestic partnership. Five proverbs mention a belligerent spouse who aggravates the life of her husband: "A persistent dripping on a day of continual rain and a contentious wife are alike" (27:15). "Dwelling in a corner of the roof is better than in a house shared with a contentious wife" (21:9; cf. also 19:13; 21:19; 25:24). This negative counterpart of the diligent wife also emerges from focusing on the welfare of the male family head and serves as a means to blame the woman for any conflict that may occur.

The postexilic frame of the book of Proverbs (chs. 1–9; 31) deepens the stereotype of the ideal wife through a personification of Wisdom and the strong woman.[10] While Lady Wisdom integrates different roles of women and even goddesses,[11] Prov 9:1-6 underlines her particular role as principal of the house: She builds her spacious house, prepares a copious meal, and invites young men in order to nourish them with food and wisdom teaching.

The acrostic poem in Prov 31:10-31 summarizes all positive aspects of the diligent wife in characterizing her as an industrious household manager: she works day and night, spins, weaves, and tailors clothing; she produces food in fields and vineyards. She even buys a field and a vineyard (v. 16) and contacts foreign traders (v. 24). She is called אשת־חיל, "woman of valor" (v. 10), a title that is otherwise only used for Ruth the Moabite (Ruth 3:11). Since the term חיל expresses physical and mental strength as well as courage, I name her the "strong" woman.[12] Like Lady Wisdom, the strong woman builds her house, feeds, and educates the members of her household (vv. 15, 26–27).[13] Both female figures enhance the wealth and honor of the men around them and are therefore praised as "more worthy than corals" (8:11; 31:10). An assessment of the ideology of this stereotype reveals that the characterization of the diligent wife in Prov 31:10-31 bears some ambivalence.

As Christine Yoder has demonstrated, the activities of the strong woman in Prov 31 are documented in extrabiblical sources as workings, sometimes

---

10. For the role and dating of the frame, see Claudia V. Camp, *Wisdom and the Feminine in the Book of Proverbs* (Bible and Literature 11; Sheffield: Almond, 1985), 282–90.

11. See the article of Gerlinde Baumann in this volume.

12. In her dissertation, Karin Brockmöller, *"Eine Frau der Stärke—wer findet sie?": Exegetische Analysen und intertextuelle Lektüren zu Spr 31,10-31* (BBB 147; Berlin: Philo, 2004), offers a detailed literary analysis of the poem.

13. For an evaluation of the parallels, see Silvia Schroer, *Wisdom Has Built Her House: Studies in the Figure of Sophia in the Bible* (trans. Linda Maloney; Collegeville, Minn.: Liturgical, 2000), 18–25.

even professions, of women in the Persian period.[14] Yoder, Karin Brockmöller, Irmtraud Fischer, and I thus read the poem as a condensed portrayal of women's authority and self-reliance in the Persian period.[15] Considering the initial question, "Who can find a woman of valor?" as rhetorical in the sense that its answer is no, Jutta Hausmann cautions against reading the poem as an affirmative image of women's life and sees in the figure the unattainable Lady Wisdom.[16] Alternatively, the poem may be interpreted as a means to restrict the influence of women to the house, while it asserts the public role of the husband (31:23).[17] In my view, the modern distinction between private and public is not valid for Israelite society in the Persian Period since the household of Prov 31 includes an extended family and serves as the basic economic unit. Thus its management is not just private, but of communal significance. Indeed, the text states that the skills of the strong woman are publicly praised (vv. 28–31).[18]

In sum, the literary figure of the strong woman offers a summary of women's roles and skills that emerges as an ideal, a cultural stereotype, especially because of its exaggeration and elaboration. The most striking feature of the strong woman is that she incorporates aspects not only of Lady Wisdom but also of the "strange" woman, who belongs to the stereotype of the seductive woman (see below §2.2). Her comparison with merchant ships (v. 14) and her possession of imported linen and purple fabric (v. 22) refers to Phoenician trade; she has contacts with traders (v. 24), who in most cases were foreigners like the associates of the strange woman in Prov 5:9–10. The coverings the strong woman makes for herself (v. 22) are named with the same term as those in the house of the "strange" woman (7:16).[19] With perfumes and fine fabrics,

---

14. Christine R. Yoder, *Wisdom as a Woman of Substance: A Socioeconomic Reading of Proverbs 1-9 and 31:10–31* (BZAW 304; Berlin: de Gruyter, 2001), 75–91. See also Ina Willi-Plein, "'Eschet Chajil': Weisheit und Lebensart Israels in der Perserzeit," in *Exegese vor Ort: Festschrift für Peter Welten zum 65. Geburtstag* (ed. Christl M. Maier et al.; Leipzig: Evangelische, 2001), 411–25.

15. Yoder, *Wisdom*, 91, calls her a "composite figure of real—albeit exceptional—women in the Persian period"; see also Brockmöller, *Frau der Stärke*, 232–35; Irmtraud Fischer, *Gotteslehrerinnen: Weise Frauen und Frau Weisheit im Alten Testament* (Stuttgart: Kohlhammer, 2006), 169–72.

16. See Jutta Hausmann, "Beobachtungen zu Spr 31,10–31," in *Alttestamentlicher Glaube und biblische Theologie: Festschrift für H.D. Preuß zum 65. Geburtstag* (ed. Jutta Hausmann and Hans Jürgen Zobel; Stuttgart: Kohlhammer, 1992), 261–66.

17. This reading is mentioned and then refuted by Fischer, *Gotteslehrerinnen*, 169.

18. Similarly Brockmöller, *Frau der Stärke*, 164–65, who also lists a range of traditional interpretations of this feature.

19. See Yoder, *Wisdom*, 92–93.

both women possess imported luxury goods, which refer to the Persian era, when trade in such wares was blossoming. Whereas this association with foreigners, trade, and imported supplies is judged positively with regard to the strong woman, it is rendered negatively in reference to the strange woman. This contrast demonstrates that stereotypes are not logical but often related to emotive and sensational judgments.

While unfolding this ideal, however, the portrayal of the strong woman "reinforces the values and customs of a context that is patriarchal in structure and androcentric in bias."[20] The speaker of the poem may be male or female like in Prov 1–9. Moreover, the preceding instruction of King Lemuel's mother to her son in 31:1–9 offers a context in which a female advisor is plausible.[21]

Finally, the characterization of the diligent wife has a long tradition in Israelite wisdom. As a cultural stereotype, the depiction clearly influences the expectations of young men, who are the primary addresses of the admonitions and poems in the book of Proverbs. Yet, as a written text and especially through their mnemonic and acrostic forms, the sayings, instructions, and poems also influence the assessment and self-image of real women from the monarchic to the Persian period and beyond. Whether women in ancient Israel were encouraged or confined by this stereotype cannot be reconstructed, yet modern readers should be aware of the portrayal's ambivalent message.

2.2. The Seductress

The integrity of the family and its property, which are targeted by the Hebrew sages, may be endangered by sexual relations between the male family head and other women. Instead of scolding the man for such relations, however, proverbial wisdom blames the women.

> For a prostitute [זונה] is a deep pit
> and an alien woman [נכריה] is a narrow well.
> She also lies in wait like a robber and increases the unfaithful among men.
> (Prov 23:27–28)

> The mouth of strange women [זרות] is a deep pit;
> he with whom YHWH is angry falls into it. (Prov 22:14)

---

20. Ibid., 109.
21. Fischer, *Gotteslehrerinnen*, 150, 167–68, argues that if one sees the king's mother as speaker also of Prov 31:10–31, the addressee in v. 29 could even be her royal daughter.

The prostitute is paralleled with the "alien" woman, who may not be a foreigner but who is "extraneous" to the family. Proverbs 23:27–28 deems both women dangerous to the man who encounters them since the locations "deep pit" and "narrow well" connote darkness, danger, and even death. Both sayings underline that meeting such women are a sign that the man's relation to God is impaired.

This pointed image of the prostitute is amplified by an antagonist figure to Lady Wisdom in Prov 1–9, who is alternatively named "foreign," "alien" (נכריה), or "strange" (זרה) and serves as a stereotyped outsider to the community. While the Hebrew and English have various terms to denote otherness or foreignness, the German word *fremd* comprises all of these meanings. In Prov 6:24, this figure is called "the evil woman" (אשת רע), while Prov 6:26 names her "the wife of another man" (אשת איש) and judges her as more harmful than a prostitute (אשה זונה). In direct contrast to Lady Wisdom, the figure is called "Lady Folly" (אשת כסילות) in Prov 9:13. Four admonition speeches in Prov 1–9 (2:16–20; 5:1–23; 6:20–35; 7:1–27) warn a young man, called "my son," of this mysterious woman whose characterization is showered with negative attributes. According to Prov 2:17 she is unfaithful to her human companion (cf. 7:19) and to her God. From the perspective of the instruction's speaker, only a man who is inclined to wisdom and thus knows righteousness and justice can resist this woman (2:6, 9, 16).

The admonition in Prov 5 warns the son against the smooth words of this adulterous woman and threatens him in the case of disobedience with the loss of possessions and good reputation in the community (vv. 9–14). Instead of embracing the strange woman, the teaching person recommends that he discover his own wife as the source of satisfying sexuality (vv. 15–19).

Another warning in Prov 6:20–35 has strong intertextual links to the prohibitions of the Decalogue against stealing, committing adultery, and coveting one's neighbor's wife.[22] The teaching person argues that this woman who can fan the flames of passion with a single alluring gaze will lead the ensnared young man to dishonor or even legal proceedings—in short, social death.

Finally, Prov 7 describes a scene intended to unmask the dangerous pretense of the strange woman who resembles Potiphar's wife (Gen 39:7–12). While the husband and master of the house is away (v. 19), she wanders the streets under the protection of the dusk to ensnare her victim (vv. 9, 12). She persuades a spineless man with flattery and deceptive words (vv. 14–20) and

---

22. See Christl M. Maier, "'Begehre nicht ihre Schönheit in deinem Herzen' (Prov 6,25): Eine Aktualisierung des Ehebruchsverbots aus persischer Zeit," *BibInt* 5 (1997): 46–63.

entices him into her house and onto her bed, which has been arranged with fine quilts and perfumes. The warning is reinforced by drastic metaphors, representing the strange woman's house as antechamber to the underworld and the woman as a murderous warrior (vv. 26–27; cf. 2:18-19; 5:4-6; 9:18).

Although this imagery is reminiscent of Ishtar, the ancient Near Eastern goddess of love and war, the strange woman in Prov 7 neither has the qualities of a deity nor, it seems, worship a goddess. An association with cultic apostasy arises only implicitly based on the idea that foreign women worship foreign deities, which is also found in Num 25:1-3; Ezra 9–10; and Neh 13:26.

Claudia Camp detects implicit connotations with foreign worship in similarities of the woman's portrayal in Prov 2:17 and 7:14 with prophetic texts that use the metaphor of adultery to criticize the worship of foreign deities (Jer 3:3-5; 13:21, 25; Isa 57:7; Zech 5:5-11).[23]

The naming of the woman as foreign or strange carries different connotations and also alludes to the rejection of marriages with "foreign women" (נשים נכריות) mentioned in Ezra 9–10 and Neh 13:23-31.[24] The overt focus on her sexual behavior, however, is based on the stereotype of the dangerous prostitute in the older wisdom tradition. Characterizing her as sexually promiscuous denigrates and dismisses her as a potential marriage partner. Instead, she becomes the antagonist of both the "good" wife and Lady Wisdom. In this figure, connotations of ethnic, cultic, and ethical deviation are condensed into a rhetorical construct that renders all strangeness feminine.

> The shifting metonymic associations of woman with strangeness—women's blood standing for all pollution, foreign wives standing for all things foreign,

---

23. See Claudia V. Camp, *Wise, Strange and Holy: The Strange Woman and the Making of the Bible* (JSOTSup 320; Sheffield: Sheffield Academic, 2000), 42–53.

24. Nancy Nam Hoon Tan, *The "Foreignness" of the Foreign Woman in Proverbs 1–9: A Study of the Origin and the Development of a Biblical Motif* (BZAW 381; Berlin: de Gruyter, 2008), analyzes the figure of Prov 1–9 basically with regard to other texts about the "foreign wives" (Deuteronomistic History; Ezra-Nehemiah). She posits that the "foreign" woman in Prov 1–9 designates apostasy (104), which in my view is rather the idea of the Greek translation of Proverbs. For the topic of intermarriage, see the essays of Tamara Cohn Eskenazi and Sara Japhet in this volume. See also Tamara Cohn Eskenazi and Eleanore P. Judd, "Marriage to a Stranger in Ezra 9–10," in *Temple and Community in the Persian Period* (vol. 2 of *Second Temple Studies*; ed. Tamara Cohn Eskenazi and Kent H. Richards; JSOTSup 175; Sheffield: JSOT Press, 1994), 266–85; Christl M. Maier, "Der Diskurs um interkulturelle Ehen in Jehud als antikes Beispiel von Intersektionalität," in *Doing Gender—Doing Religion: Fallstudien zur Intersektionalität im frühen Judentum, Christentum und Islam* (ed. Ute E. Eisen et al.; WUNT 302; Tübingen: Mohr Siebeck, 2013), 129–53.

adulterous women standing for idolatrous Israel—have reified into an "ontological metaphor": Strangeness is a Woman.[25]

The portrayal of the seductress—named strange in Prov 1–9—thus offers a clear case of othering that merges physical, behavioral, ethnic, and social aspects into a cultural stereotype.[26] Viewed against the Persian-period background and its supposed challenges to the reestablishment of an Israelite community in the province of Yehud, the portrayal of the seductress highlights the ideological message to the young men not to seek a marriage partner on their own but to rely on their parents' and teacher's insight and counsel to find a "good" wife.[27] Although the warnings explicitly address only a son, the negative stereotype of the strange woman offers a role model also for daughters, albeit in reverse, that is, in the sense that daughters are seriously warned not to become a strange woman or a prostitute. For a society challenged by economical and political constraints, the education of the next generation in "conservative" ethics, that is, an ethics that retains values, may seem appropriate. Interpreters, however, should be aware of possible harmful effects that such texts may exert on readers today if taken at face value. In my view, the denigrating characterization of the seductive woman is both androcentric and prejudicial to the general perception of women.

2.3. THE FEMALE COUNSELOR

Proverbs 1:8 and 6:20 explicitly affirm that a father or a mother could take the role of the wisdom teacher. This idea is also present in the earlier proverbial wisdom, although more indirectly stated (Prov 10:1; cf. 15:20; 20:20; 23:22; 29:15). In Prov 31:1, the mother of Lemuel, king of Massa, appears as a personal and political advisor to her son. Like the speaker in Prov 7:1 she warns him against sexual misconduct and drinking bouts. This foreign mother serves as a positive role model: she repeats the ethical admonitions of

---

25. Camp, *Wise, Strange and Holy*, 59.

26. Therefore, the strangeness of the figure includes different facets, deduced from "reality" and with metaphorical meaning; it cannot be restricted to just one meaning as Michael V. Fox, *Proverbs 1–9* (AB 18A; New York: Doubleday, 2000), 134–41, and Daniel J. Estes, "What Makes the Strange Woman of Proverbs 1–9 Strange?" in *Ethical and Unethical in the Old Testament: God and Humans in Dialogue* (ed. Katherine Dell; LHBOTS 528; New York: T&T Clark, 2010), 151–69, try to argue.

27. For a fuller assessment of the sociohistorical background of Prov 1–9 see my *Die "fremde Frau" in Proverbien 1–9: Eine exegetische und sozialgeschichtliche Studie* (OBO 144; Fribourg: Universitätsverlag; Göttingen: Vandenhoeck & Ruprecht, 1995), 25–68, 264–69.

personified Wisdom to judge rightly (cf. Prov 1:3; 8:15–16 with 31:9) and to help the destitute and poor (cf. Prov 8:27–31 with 31:8–9).

Lady Wisdom and the strong woman are the most prominent examples of female counselors. Wisdom lauds her own good council (8:14–16) and scolds those who would not heed her advice (1:23–25, 30). The strong woman opens her mouth with wisdom and gives good instruction (31:26). As Silvia Schroer has demonstrated with regard to Hebrew Bible narratives, the task of being a good counselor to her husband is part of the ideal characterization of the female spouse.[28]

Only Job does not follow his wife's counsel and even rejects her advice, which leads commentators to assess her role controversially. Job's wife also experiences the loss of their children and their property, but she is neither fully elaborated as a character nor granted a name. Although she seems to have accompanied him until his recovery, the epilogue does not mention her or any other woman as mother of Job's ten children born to him after his restitution (42:13). In the prologue, she only utters two short sentences: "You still hold on to your integrity. Bless God, and die!" (2:9). The Hebrew leaves open whether the first sentence is a comment or a question and whether she asks Job to bless or curse God. In case of the latter, the Hebrew verb ברך, "to bless," would serve as a euphemism. Traditionally, the suggestion of Job's wife has been interpreted as an expression of incomprehension and mockery, because it echoes the prediction of the adversary ("the Satan") that Job would bless/curse God to the face (2:5). The church father Augustine, for instance, calls the wife a *diaboli adiutrix*, "Satan's helper," who was to tempt Job—and thus uses the stereotype of the belligerent wife. Yet the woman's speech adopts not only the adversary's words but also God's announcement that Job will persist in his integrity (2:3).[29] The text deliberately leaves the meaning of ברך undecided: as a curse in the sense of fending off disaster or a blessing in the sense of praising what is worthy of praise.[30] It may be read as a suggestion that Job bless God once more as long as he holds on or is able to hold on to his integrity and then die at peace with God after his farewell.[31] Alternatively, the words of Job's wife

---

28. Schroer, *Wisdom Has Built Her House*, 52–68.

29. For this interpretation, see Jürgen Ebach, *Hiobs Post: Gesammelte Aufsätze zum Hiobbuch, zu Themen biblischer Theologie und zur Methodik der Exegese* (Neukirchen-Vluyn: Neukirchener, 1995), 68–70.

30. See Tod Linafelt, "The Undecidability of *brk* in the Prologue of Job and Beyond," *BibInt* 4 (1996): 165–72; Magdalene L. Frettlöh, *Theologie des Segens: Biblische und dogmatische Wahrnehmungen* (2nd ed.; Gütersloh: Kaiser/Gütersloher, 1998), 308–14.

31. Thus a midrash on Job 2:9; see Solomon A. Wertheimer, ed., *Batei Midrashot* (2nd ed.; Jerusalem: Mosad ha-Rav Kuk, 1968), 2:165.

may be interpreted as pointing out the absurdity of Job's holding on to God and proposing that he curse and turn away from this God who has forsaken him and then die, since blasphemy would incur the death penalty (see Lev 24:16). Both cases could involve compassion or, at any rate, common sense instead of mockery or sarcasm. Thus Job's wife is portrayed as recommending a way out of hopelessness even if it means death. But Job rejects her as "one of the foolish women" (אחת הנבלות;[32] 2:10). Although Job rebuffs his wife's counsel, it is through her that the plot moves on and Job reaches a point where he even considers the possibility of not accepting evil from God.[33]

The lacuna in the Hebrew text has been filled in subsequent rereadings of Job's story. The Greek text tradition has preserved a much longer version of the couple's dialogue, in which Job's wife talks about her suffering to find work and sustain her sick husband and herself:

> Then after a long time had passed, his wife said to him, "How long will you persist and say, 'Look, I will hang on a little longer while I wait for the hope of my deliverance?' For look, your legacy has vanished from the earth—sons and daughters, my womb's birth pangs and labors, for whom I wearied myself with hardships in vain. And you? You sit in the refuse of worms as you spend the night in the open air. As for me, I am one that wanders about and a hired servant—from place to place and house to house, waiting for when the sun will set, so I can rest from the distresses and griefs that now beset me. Now, say some word to the Lord and die!'" (Job 2:9 LXX)[34]

While the origin of this longer text is disputed, it is usually dated later than the Septuagint and thus represents an expanded interpretation.[35] The woman's speech emphasizes Job's steadfastness but also envisions her affliction and grief, rendering her more sympathetic.

The Testament of Job, written probably in the second century CE, is based in its description of Job's wife on this Greek text. In this writing, Job's wife is

---

32. Besides the idea of foolishness, the equivalent Hebrew masculine term נבל represents a socially inferior person (Prov 30:8) but also one who denies God (Ps 14:1).

33. This reading is suggested by Ellen van Wolde, "The Development of Job: Mrs Job as Catalyst," in *A Feminist Companion to Wisdom Literature* (ed. Athalya Brenner; FCB 9; Sheffield: Sheffield Academic, 1995), 201–21.

34. Translation by Claude E. Cox in Albert Pietersma and Benjamin G. Wright, eds., *A New English Translation of the Septuagint and the Other Greek Translations Traditionally Included under That Title* (Oxford: Oxford University Press, 2007), 671.

35. See Martina Kepper and Markus Witte, "Job/Das Buch Ijob/Hiob," in *Septuaginta Deutsch: Erläuterungen und Kommentare* (Stuttgart: Deutsche Bibelgesellschaft, 2011), 2:2047–48; David J. A. Clines, *Job 1–20* (WBC 17; Dallas, Tex.: Word, 1989), 53.

sympathetically portrayed as full of compassion and loyal to her husband, caring for him, feeding him, and even giving her hair to buy bread (*T. Job* 23:2–10).³⁶ She even receives a name, Σιτίς, which is evocative of Αυσίτις, the Greek translation of Job's homeland Uz, or Σιτίδος, an allusion to Greek σιτίζειν, "to give bread." Eventually she dies and Job has a second wife, called Dinah, with whom he has more children, among them three daughters who also inherit part of Job's property with a special spiritual significance (cf. Job 42:14-15 with *T. Job* 46).³⁷

These later narrative traditions and the controversial interpretations of Job 2:9 demonstrate that it depends on the reader's imagination whether Job's wife is seen as belligerent or diligent, an evil or a good wife. Since in the book of Job her character is not developed and she is only briefly mentioned, one may interpret her according to the stereotype of the nagging wife or the helpful counselor.

Although the stereotype of the female counselor offers, like the one of the diligent wife, a positive evaluation of women's contribution to marriage and family, it is similarly embedded in a patriarchal context and a gender hierarchy of which the husband is at the center.

2.4. The Poor Widow

From the androcentric perspective of the "good" wife, widows and orphans, whose status is defined by the absence of a husband and father, appear as marginalized and in danger of being deprived of their property. Proverbs 23:10 conveys the prohibition against violating the borders of the field of orphans, which is well known from the Egyptian Instruction of Amenemope (7:11–14),³⁸ to Israelite wisdom. When Prov 15:25 describes YHWH as maintaining the boundary for the widow, it indicates that any violation of her land property is considered an offense against God (see also Prov 22:28). Both sayings underline that in ancient Israel women and children had minor legal rights and would not be able to defend themselves in court.³⁹

---

36. See Pieter W. van der Horst, "Images of Women in the Testament of Job," in *Studies on the Testament of Job* (ed. Michael A. Knibb and Pieter W. van der Horst; SNTSMS 66; Cambridge: Cambridge University Press, 1989), 93–116.

37. For a feminist interpretation of this writing, see Luzia Sutter Rehmann, "Testament of Job: Job, Dinah and Their Daughters," in Schottroff and Wacker, *Feminist Biblical Interpretation*, 586–95.

38. See Brunner, *Weisheit*, 241.

39. For the status of widows, see Christl M. Maier and Karin Lehmeier, "Witwe," in

In the book of Job, the existence of the poor widow and the orphans is especially indicative of the distorted world order (Job 24:3, 21). The description of communal misery in Job 24 mentions infertile, childless women and widows whose infants were used as pawns because their mothers were in debt. While Eliphaz accuses Job that he has sent away widows empty-handed (22:9), Job defends himself arguing that he always supported both widow and orphans (29:12–13; 31:16–17) and as a wealthy landowner upheld the principles of solidarity with the poor laid down in the Torah (Deut 24:17, 19–22).

While the stereotype of the poor and oppressed widow was certainly based on the experience of numerous women, especially in times of political or economic crises, it also reveals the androcentric viewpoint that women and children would not survive without a male guardian. The poem praising the strong woman in Prov 31, however, contradicts the idea that women are economically dependent on their husbands, although one has to acknowledge that her husband is still alive. Even if many widows were actually poor, the cultural stereotype of the "poor widow" unduly constricts the reality.

3. The Function and Significance of Cultural Stereotypes in Wisdom Literature

Cultural stereotypes, I have argued, are necessary to order one's world, to deal with one's anxieties and instabilities of perception. The series of cultural stereotypes of women in Proverbs and Job presented here establishes clear distinctions between the "evil" and the "good" woman. The rather fixed characteristics and clear negative or positive evaluations of the diligent wife, the seductive woman, the female counselor, and the poor widow encourage the intended audience to choose the "right" way, to find a "good" wife. For young men this meant following their parents' religious tradition and especially their suggestions for a spouse instead of endangering their property and reputation by contacts with a "strange" woman. The book of Proverbs, especially its postexilic frame, aims at educating sons of the wealthy and landowning class to choose a way of life that may be called "conservative" in the best sense of the word, namely, preserving established values. The instructions and poems demonstrate an outright didactic purpose to instruct a male addressee about how to live a successful life. In reverse, the story of Job demonstrates the loss of such a life and the breakdown of the male protagonist's relationships with his wife, children, friends, and other persons.

Sozialgeschichtliches Wörterbuch zur Bibel (ed. Frank Crüsemann et al.; Gütersloh: Gütersloher, 2009), 667–68.

Beyond a mere individual level, both writings instruct their audience about socially accepted behavior. Job's statements that he cared for his household, fed the poor, and never cast an eye on his neighbor's wife (Job 29:12–16; 31:9–10) reflects the ideal behavior of a male family head. The poem about the strong woman (Prov 31:10–31) concisely develops the ideal of a wife and household manager. These stereotypical characterizations of both women and men serve to reduce the complexity of life.

I argue that all traditions preserved in Proverbs and Job demonstrate the influence of women on men and women's significance for the functioning of family and household. Recent studies about the social organization and economic situation of Judeans in the Persian province of Yehud show that the contribution of women to the family's sustenance, their role as wise counselors to their husbands, and their education of small children was significant, because the household formed the basic unit of society.[40] Their role and influence, however, did not mean that the patriarchal structure of the family was shattered. Only some women of the upper class could establish inheritance rights or marriage contracts that preserved their individual property and rendered them economically autonomous. Moreover, women were involved in the production of cultural stereotypes like the strange woman and the diligent wife as the figure of the mother as teacher underlines (Prov 1:8; 6:20; 31:1). Thus one has to acknowledge that women in ancient Israel shared this androcentric perspective.

While such stereotyping can be explained in relation to the social-historical background of the texts, it is in no way innocent but rather has a direct effect on the evaluation of women and their roles. This effect can be seen in the different interpretations of Job's wife, who may be seen as a "good counselor" or a belligerent and thus "bad" wife, depending on which stereotype a specific interpreter favors. From a feminist point of view, the othering of the strange woman and the negative assessment of Job's wife cannot be accepted without objection, even if Lady Wisdom, the strong woman, and the foreign king's mother are praised and positively characterized. That the female stereotypes in Proverbs and Job had a detrimental effect on the overall assessment of women can be seen in the later wisdom writings: Sirach repeats and deepens the distinction between good (Sir 26:1–4, 13–18) and bad women (Sir 25:15–26; 26:7–12, 22–27) and calls daughters a source of constant anxiety for a man (Sir 7:24–25; 42:9–10).[41] Both Ecclesiastes/Qoheleth and Sirach even discuss whether "the woman" is the cause of all

---

40. See Yoder, *Wisdom*; Maier, "Der Diskurs um interkulturelle Ehen," 141–46.
41. See Nuria Calduch-Benages's essay in this volume.

evil (Qoh 7:26; Sir 25:24).[42] In wording similar to the characterization of the strange woman of Prov 1–9, a text from Qumran, originally named "the Wiles of the Wicked Woman" (4Q184), describes a seductive woman who brings about destruction.[43] In the reception history of female characters, this binary stereotyping eventually led to the polarization of the "whore" and the "holy one," the sexually promiscuous seductress, and the faithful, almost asexual mother—stereotypes that exert some influence even today.

My effort to highlight the complexity and variety of portrayals of women in the books of Proverbs and Job intends to make today's readers aware of their dangerous potential in consolidating a bias towards all women. With regard to the denigrating effect of stereotyping women as "wise" or "strange," "good" or "bad," I plead for a deconstructive reading that brings out the ambivalence of such an androcentric perspective on women. Thus, beyond all stereotypes, new images of women (and men) may arise.

---

42. For an assessment of Qoh 7:26, see Vittoria D'Alario's essay in this volume.
43. See Tan, *Foreign Woman*, 112–21. However, it is not clear whether 4Q184 typifies real women or personifies apostasy in a female figure.

Between Misogyny and Valorization: Perspectives on Women in Qoheleth

Vittoria D'Alario

1. Introduction

In the book of Qoheleth, the subject of women has to be framed in the context of a more general reflection about humans (אדם), in connection to their condition of frailty (הבל). The book of Qoheleth is primarily concerned with an anthropological question, as can be inferred from the opening of the text itself: What do people gain from all their toil under the sun? (1:3).[1] In his search, Qoheleth[2] questions human experience, presenting it in its many facets. His observations range from social phenomena of injustice and oppression (3:16; 4:1–3; 8:9; 9:3) to everyday issues, such as the meaning of work (2:11, 17–22; 5:12–17; 6,1, 12) and the value of interpersonal relationships (4:8–12), as well as the political sphere (4:13–16; 5:7–8; 10:5–7). The human being, with the multiplicity of its experiences, as well as with its demands and limits, is the main object of Qoheleth's reflection.

In the first six chapters of the book, Qoheleth, through reflections and exemplifications, endeavors to prove the uselessness of human strivings, especially when they are aimed at self-affirmation and omnipotence. In the second part of the work (7:1–11:6), he takes into account humans' potential for knowledge and consequently the limits of wisdom. In Qoh 6:10–12 he poses some questions challenging one of the fundamental principles on which the quest for wisdom is based, that is, a human person's capability of finding his or her own way in the present and making plans for the future: "Whatever

---

[1]. For citations of biblical verses, the translation of this essay uses the New Revised Standard Version (NRSV). In cases where the author provided her own translation into Italian, the translator translated this text into English.

[2]. For the meaning of the Hebrew word "Qoheleth," see below, §2.4. The author understands Qoheleth as a male wisdom teacher.

has come to be has already been named, and it is known what human beings are, and that they are not able to dispute with those who are stronger. The more words, the more vanity, so how is one the better? For who knows what is good for mortals while they live the few days of their vain life, which they pass like a shadow? For who can tell them what will be after them under the sun?" The texts concerning women in Qoheleth are included in the second part of the book and, though rare, are particularly relevant to our theme: 7:26–28 and 9:9.

On a first reading, the texts on women seem to contradict each other, as is often the case with different topics in the whole book. In 7:26–28 Qoheleth gives the impression of aligning his negative judgment on women with that of all the antifeminist writers of the ancient world,[3] while in 9:9 there is a positive exhortation to enjoy the relationship with one's own wife. Thus there is a shift from a pessimistic view, which emphasizes the vulnerability of the female person, to her subsequent valorization.

2. Women and the Mystery of God's Work (Qoh 7:23–27)

In order to provide a correct interpretation of Qoheleth's thought, it is important to start by analyzing his remarks first in their immediate context and then in the whole work. The analysis should never be limited to single verses, since it is crucial to consider Qoheleth's arguments in the section comprising the texts on women and to respect its logic, even though it might often be different from ours.[4]

---

3. It is no wonder feminist literature has never appreciated this passage of the Qoheleth, in which the personal experience of the author can allegedly be found. See Athalya Brenner, "Figurations of Women in Wisdom Literature," in *A Feminist Companion to Wisdom Literature* (ed. Athalya Brenner; FCB 9; Sheffield: Sheffield Academic Press, 1995), 50–66, 59–60; Carole R. Fontaine, "Ecclesiastes," in *Women's Bible Commentary* (ed. Carol A. Newsom and Sharon H. Ringe; 2nd ed.; Louisville: Westminster John Knox, 1998), 161–63. For a critical evaluation that takes into account different interpretations of Qoheleth, see Jennifer L. Koosed, *(Per)mutations of Qohelet: Reading the Body in the Book* (LHBOTS 429; New York: T&T Clark, 2006), 77–87.

4. On the relationship between logic and rhetoric in the book of Qoheleth, see Vittoria D'Alario, *Il libro del Qohelet: Struttura letteraria e retorica* (RivBSup 27; Bologna: Dehoniane, 1993), 185–231.

2.1. An Antifeminist Qoheleth? (Qoh 7:26–28)

The first text I will analyze is Qoh 7:26–28,[5] which is presented here in its immediate context, 7:25–29.

> I turned my mind to know and to search out,
> and to seek wisdom and the reason of things [חשבון],
> and to know that evil is folly and foolishness madness.
> And I *find* that more bitter than death is woman, if [since]
> she is all laces: her heart a net, shackles
> her arms. He who pleases God escapes her,
> but the sinner is taken by her.
> See, *this I found*, says Qoheleth, adding
> one thing to another to *arrive* [מצא]
> at a final sum, *which I still seek and not find*.
> One man among a thousand I *found*:
> but a woman among all I have not *found*.
> See, *only this I found*,
> that God made man upright,
> but they seek out many devices [חשבנות].

We are in the presence of one of the most controversial passages of Qoheleth, one that can be translated and interpreted in many different ways. The first difficulty is that of identifying the mysterious female character described in verse 26. Is it the portrait of women in general or of a particular kind of woman? Some scholars have propounded the hypothesis that Qoheleth is here referring to the metaphor of "Woman Wisdom," frequently attested in the book of Proverbs. If these verses are isolated, they would retain their cryptic character forever; examined, however, in the light of the context in which they are included, they can be understood more adequately.

There is no doubt about the immediate context: verses 25–29, presented as a finite unity, both in the theme (the sage's continuous and passionate quest) and in the literary clues, allow for a precise delimitation of the pericope.[6] First, we have to notice the *inclusio* between חשבון in verse 25 and חשבנות in verse 29; it certainly is one of the text's keywords (on which more later). In addition, there is frequent use of the first person singular, the "I" of the sage, which

---

5. I am proposing my own translation of the text, which will be justified throughout the analysis.
6. For this delimitation of the pericope, I share the arguments of José Vílchez Líndez, *Eclesiastés o Qohelet* (Nueva Biblia Española; Sapienciales 3; Estella: Verbo Divino, 1994), 322–33.

addresses the issue of women. Women become the object of a persistent quest, as evident in the fact that the verb מצא ("to find") recurs seven times in these verses. Qoheleth's reflection on women, though, finds its place in an even wider section beginning at 7:23 and ending at 8:1, in which Qoheleth investigates the matter of the quest for wisdom and evaluates its results.

First of all, let us consider verses 23–24, which show the inaccessibility of wisdom, shrouding with mystery all that Qoheleth has sought and found.

> All this I have tested with wisdom and I have said:
> "I will be wise!"
> But wisdom was far from me,
> That which was is far and deep, very deep,
> who can find it out [מצא]?

He states that he has examined everything "with wisdom": בחכמה defines wisdom as an instrument for research, a means to achieve wisdom. Nonetheless, the results obtained by Qoheleth are unsatisfactory, because wisdom is ultimately unattainable. Qoheleth has to stop before the unfathomable abyss that presents itself to him, a reality that in many ways remains incomprehensible and mysterious. Verse 24 ends with a rhetorical question: "Who can reach it?" Here the verb מצא, one of the text's key words, appears for the first time. This verb has several different meanings and must be explained each time it is used.[7] In 7:24 it means "to grasp," and reality itself cannot be grasped. The answer to the question posed by Qoheleth cannot but be negative. Nobody, no matter how hard they try, is actually able to grasp the essence of things and to understand the deep meaning of reality.[8] The issue of women is framed within this reflection about the mystery of being, where Qoheleth questions the ability of the human mind to attain a comprehensive understanding of reality. The discourse on women becomes, then, an exemplification, as is often the case with Qoheleth's frequent resorting to "typical" figures of the literature and experience of his time in order to substantiate his arguments.

---

7. In using the verb מצא, Qoheleth utilizes the rhetorical device of antanaclasis. See Anthony R. Ceresko, "The Function of Antanaclasis (*mṣ'* 'to find'//*mṣ'* 'to reach, overtake, grasp') in Hebrew Poetry, Especially in the Book of Qoheleth," *CBQ* 44 (1982): 551–69; see also the more recent study by Luca Mazzinghi, "The Verbs מצא 'to Find' and בקש 'to Search' in the Language of Qohelet: An Exegetical Study," in *The Language of Qohelet in Its Context: Essays in Honour of Prof. A. Schoors on the Occasion of His Seventieth Birthday* (ed. Angelika Berlejung and Pierre van Hecke; OLA 164; Leuven: Peeters, 2007), 91–120.

8. The phrase מה־שהיה (7:24) might mean both being ("what has happened") and becoming ("what will happen"). See Antoon Schoors, "Words Typical of Qohelet," in *Qohelet in the Context of Wisdom* (ed. Antoon Schoors; BETL 136; Leuven: Peeters, 1998), 17–39, esp. 23–24.

2.2. The Mystery of the Fatal Woman (Qoh 7:25–26)

Despite having concluded that wisdom is unattainable (v. 24), Qoheleth carries on his quest. The verb סבב is also used in the introductory poem to describe the rotatory movement of wind twirling on itself. This is a metaphor for the human mind occupied, according to God's will, with a pitiful but unavoidable quest, which forces it to return repeatedly to the same topics. There seems to be a circularity of the spirit, which some authors claim to be reflected in the structure of the book.[9] At this point, Qoheleth's commitment is so intense that verse 25 is rich in verbs pertaining to the field of research: ידע ("to know"), תור ("to explore"), בקש ("to search")—three verbs that have two nouns as their objects, namely, חכמה ("wisdom") and חשבון, a term that indicates the outcomes of research.[10] Qoheleth aims to investigate and explore the whole tradition of Jewish wisdom in order to verify its conclusions. For this reason, he focuses on one of the fundamental theses of the tradition: that evil is folly and foolishness is madness. His reflection on women is produced in this context.

Verse 26 begins with the participle of מצא, "I find." Is this a personal experience Qoheleth himself has gone through, an experience that has brought him to the conclusion that women are bitterer than death? Is he actually stating his own opinion about women, or rather was the proverb inserted by a later redactor, struck by the disparaging tone of Qoheleth's arguments?[11] Another hypothesis is that Qoheleth might have encountered in his search the commonplace association of women with evil and foolishness.[12]

---

9. On the circular structure of the book of Qoheleth, see D'Alario, *Il libro del Qohelet*, 227–29.

10. The term מה־שהיה is used in Qoheleth and Sirach, especially meaning "quantifiable, concrete result," "final, practical result," or "final sum and point of arrival," which can be reached only by adding facts to one another. See Klaus Seybold, "חָשַׁב ḥāšab," *TDOT* 5:228–45, esp. 235.

11. This is the interpretation according to Maria Claustre Solé i Auguets, *Déu, una paraula sempre oberta: El concepte de Déu en el Qohèlet* (Collectània Sant Pacià 65; Barcelona: Facultat de Teologia de Catalunya, 1999), 141–46. She believes that the text would remain coherent even without v. 26. Such a negative judgment of women cannot be found anywhere else in this book, while Qoheleth often repeats the same concepts. All other references to women (Qoh 2:8b; 9:9) relate to those texts that suggest to live joyfully in the present (2:24; 3:12, 22; 5:18b; 8:15; 11:5).

12. See Prov 1:7–33; 8:1–9, 18. On the dualism wisdom/foolishness, see Armin Lange, *Weisheit und Torheit bei Kohelet und in seiner Umwelt: Eine Untersuchung ihrer theologischen Implikationen* (EHS 23; Theologie 433; Frankfurt am Main: Lang, 1991), 7–48.

This last hypothesis is the most plausible, especially because of the use of the participle,[13] which Qoheleth usually employs to introduce ideas belonging to tradition.[14] The participle introduces what Qoheleth finds during his quest. Nevertheless, it is difficult to determine which sources inspired him to portray women in such a negative way. It might have been rabbinical Jewish thought, where the power of women is associated with the theme of death,[15] or, more simply, Wisdom literature warning young men not to associate with the "foreign" woman, because her paths lead to death.[16] However, it remains clear that verse 26 highlights the lethal power of women, because they are able to imprison men in a mortal trap.[17] The same words are used to refer to time and accident in 9:12: "For no one can anticipate the time of disaster. Like fish taken in a cruel net, and like birds caught in a snare, so mortals are snared at a time of calamity, when it suddenly falls upon them." Basing his conclusions on these elements, Dominic Rudman goes so far as to define the woman as the agent of some inescapable deterministic force.[18] The woman would thus be the symbol of the arbitrary nature of divine intervention in the life of a man, a topic dealt with in 9:11–12.[19] In this text, Qoheleth delineates a deterministic approach to

---

13. See Diethelm Michel, *Untersuchungen zur Eigenart des Buches Qohelet* (BZAW 183; Berlin: de Gruyter, 1989), 235–37; Luca Mazzinghi, "The Verbs מצא and בקש in Qohelet," 110–11.

14. Norbert Lohfink, "War Kohelet ein Frauenfeind? Ein Versuch, die Logik und den Gegenstand von Koh. 7,23–8,1a herauszufinden," in *La Sagesse de l'Ancien Testament* (ed. Maurice Gilbert; BETL 51; Gembloux-Leuven: Leuven University Press, 1979), 259–87, esp. 277–87. According to him, Qoheleth doesn't state his own experience in v. 26, but rather a perception of women widely shared in Wisdom literature. Lohfink goes on to suggest switching Qoheleth's words from direct to indirect speech: "I find that bitterer than death is woman," interpreting the relative pronoun אשר as causal: "since, in fact."

15. Lohfink, "War Kohelet ein Frauenfeind?" 278–83. In v. 26 woman would thus be presented as a terrible power, even more so than death, especially because of her ability to generate new life. Consequently, Lohfink translates the adjective מר as "strong" instead of "bitter," because Qoheleth's language was deeply influenced by Aramaic, where מר might also mean "strong." He finds a close relationship between Qoh 7:26 and Song 8:6, in which love is said to be stronger than death.

16. A showcase of the different female figures associated to Qoh 7:26 can be found in Jean-Jacques Lavoie, *La pensée du Qohélet: Étude exégétique et intertextuelle* (Héritage et projet 49; Québec: Fides, 1992), 129.

17. See Yohan Y.-S. Pahk, "The Significance of אשר in Qoh 7,26: More Bitter Than Death Is the Woman, if She Is a Snare," in Schoors, *Qohelet in the Context of Wisdom*, 373–83.

18. Dominic Rudman, "Woman as Divine Agent in Ecclesiastes," *JBL* 116 (1997): 411–27.

19. Ibid., 420.

time, which can be seen in 3:1–15 as well. According to Rudman, Qoheleth's portrayal of women in 7:26 might be confirmed in 3:8, where "a time for love" is mentioned. Moreover, women's role as an instrument for divine judgment on humankind is highlighted: "He who pleases God escapes her, but the sinner is taken by her" (7:26). Rudman concludes that "escape from the woman is therefore a mark of divine favor. Though one who falls victim to 'time' (עת) may not find the work of God, he may find contentment. Qoheleth's advice to the 'sinner'—the vast majority, if not all, of his audience—is to accept the decision of God with equanimity."[20] Taking into account these similarities in terminology, is it possible to hypothesize a relationship between the two passages in which Qoheleth mentions women (7:26–29 and 9:9)? Such a possibility cannot be discarded, given Qoheleth's insistence on some topics that are presented under a different light, thus also implying a reinterpretation, as we will see in the analysis of the second text on women: Qoh 9:9.

As for Qoh 7:26–28, going so far as to consider women as the means of some deterministic force is perhaps far-fetched, but still it cannot be denied that the female figure acquires here a symbolic value far beyond its factual historicity. We are now in a place to better understand the scope of this symbolic transposition.

2.3. Qoheleth and the "Woman Wisdom" Metaphor

Some interpreters, drawing on the similarities between Qoh 7:26 and some passages in the book of Proverbs, have suggested that Qoheleth might be referring to the "Woman Wisdom" metaphor.[21] There is no doubt that the portrayal of the woman in Qoh 7:26 might evoke the negative image depicted in Prov 5:3–5; 7:25–27. Both of these texts deal with a "foreign" woman who is able to lead men to death by means of her seducing power. The adjective מר is linked by assonance to the bitterness of absinthe in Prov 5:3–5: "For the lips of the foreign woman drip honey, and her speech is smoother than oil; but in the end she is bitter as absinthe, sharp as a double-edged sword. Her feet go down to death; her steps lead straight to the hell." The other images in Qoh 7:26 evoke Prov 7:21–27, the latter sketching a portrait of the foreign woman, which seems an illustration of the former. Net and lace (Prov 7:22) suggest the woman's ability to imprison men in a lethal grip. However, as is well known, the foreign woman in the book of Proverbs represents an unknown wisdom,

---

20. Ibid., 421.
21. On this topic, see Thomas Krüger, "'Frau Weisheit' in Koh 7,26?," *Bib* 73 (1992): 394–402.

simultaneously dangerous and fatal to young Jews.[22] Two attitudes can be taken in the presence of female seduction skills: that of the wise man, who is good before God, and that of the sinner, who becomes a victim because of his foolishness. In verse 26c there is in fact a summary of the fundamental options provided by traditional ethics.

Is Qoheleth alluding to Woman Wisdom? This is a fascinating hypothesis, which could be justified by the context in which the reflection on women is placed. This suggests, I propose, that Qoheleth is developing a discourse on wisdom and on metaphors focusing on the female figure, widely employed in the wisdom tradition; this would be consistent with the whole context.

In 6:12 Qoheleth questions the capacity of human wisdom to understand what is good for humankind.

> For who knows what is good for mortals
> while they live the few days of their vain life, which they pass like a shadow?

To this he adds another query, concerning human ability to project oneself toward the future.

> For who can tell them what will be after them under the sun?

These are two rhetorical questions, both implying a negative answer: no one, not even the savant, can really understand what is good for humanity, because human existence is not only characterized by its brevity but also and especially by הבל, "vanity, futility." This makes a human's image itself evanescent: he or she lives his or her life like a shadow.

In the following chapters—from 7:1 to 11:6—Qoheleth proceeds to develop this idea through various arguments, ranging from the question of the connection between deed and consequence (7:15–22) to that of knowledge of past and future (8:7–8). He particularly insists on the latter point, arguing that humans cannot know their future, let alone the time of their own death. The conclusion of this reflection can be found in 8:16–17.

> When I applied my mind to know wisdom,
> and to see the business that is done on earth,
> —how one's eyes see sleep neither day nor night—

---

22. On the feminine metaphor in the book of Proverbs, see Christl M. Maier, *Die "fremde Frau" in Proverbien 1–9: Eine exegetische und sozialgeschichtliche Studie* (OBO 144; Fribourg: Universitätsverlag; Göttingen: Vandenhoeck & Ruprecht, 1995), 184–214; Irmtraud Fischer, *Gotteslehrerinnen: Weise Frauen und Frau Weisheit im Alten Testament* (Stuttgart: Kohlhammer, 2006), 174–203.

then I saw all the work of God,
that no one can find out what is happening under the sun.
However much they may toil in seeking, they will not find it out;
even though those who are wise claim to know, they cannot find it out.

Qoheleth here states his conviction that true wisdom is unattainable, and that we cannot fully understand the meaning of things (8:1). This is proved by the unfathomable mystery of woman and of her relationship to men. The female figure in Qoh 7:26–28 becomes the measure of the obscurity of reality, in its many contradictions.

In chapters 7–8, Qoheleth formulates a critical discourse on wisdom. Consequently, the metaphorical use of the female figure, widely accepted in traditional thought, becomes here a tangible exemplification of the impossibility of adopting absolute criteria to understand reality.

Qoheleth started on a quest that brought him to evaluate the traditional negative image of women, which is interpreted as a metaphor for foreign wisdom. This metaphor is used in the book of Proverbs as a warning to young students against the allure of foreign culture, which leads to idolatry and thus to death. At this point, it is necessary to point out that Qoheleth himself is a teacher, as attested in the epilogue of the book (12:9–10). However, he is not a traditional instructor who teaches at school. On the contrary, his figure is reminiscent of that of the wandering philosophers of the Hellenistic era, for example, the cynics and skeptics of Socratic inspiration. "Other than being wise, Qoheleth also taught people knowledge; he listened to, searched for, and composed many proverbs. Qoheleth sought to find pleasing words, and wrote accurately words of truth" (Qoh 12:9–10).

The characteristic element of his teachings is to question "everything," and even the metaphorical use of the female figure might be included in this critical research. Moreover, Qoheleth's mind is open to any inspiration the culture of his time has to offer: his work frequently alludes to terms and categories taken from Greek philosophy, as well as from apocalyptic Jewish thought, with which he establishes a dialectical relationship. His research covers every field of knowledge, focusing on themes and problems of traditional faith and everyday life. Therefore, it is no surprise that this pericope on women once again shows Qoheleth's intention to deliver to his disciples—and to all of us—a different take on those clichés so popular at the time.

2.4. Human Wisdom and God's Design (Qoh 7:27–29)

Verse 27 begins with "see, this I found," and it is of particular importance because it also contains the expression אמרה קהלת, "Qoheleth said." This formula was probably used by the editor to highlight the relevance of Qoheleth's statements, but in this context his use of the feminine form might relate to a personification of Wisdom different from the traditional one.²³

The object of the expression "see, this I found" is verse 28a: "which I still seek and do not find." Qoheleth, like Socrates, is convinced that human knowledge cannot reach the truth: he knows that he knows nothing.²⁴ The opening statement in verse 28a is perfectly suited to the specific kind of research Qoheleth is carrying on, a kind that never reaches definite conclusions. Each stage of his quest leads to further research, an inescapable endeavor that God bestowed on humans so that they would keep struggling for it (3:10).²⁵

In the book of Qoheleth there is a frequent use of the opposition "search/not find," an example of which can be found in verse 28b, where it is constructed around a highly enigmatic statement.²⁶

> One man among a thousand I found:
> but a woman among all I have not found.

What is then the meaning of verse 28b? Is Qoheleth like Diogenes, who equipped with a lamp set out to search for a human being? The answer to this depends heavily on how we decide to translate אדם. Is it the word for "human being" or for "man"? Some have interpreted אדם as a synonym for איש,²⁷ thus emphasizing the opposition man/woman. However, in Qoheleth the term אדם always refers universally to humankind.²⁸ Even if this is the case, the proverb nonetheless sounds misogynistic: in searching the totality of humankind it is possible to find at least one righteous person, but not even one will be found if we take into account women only. This interpretation,

---

23. Some authors have argued that Qoheleth was a woman. See Amos Luzzato, *Chi era Qohelet?* (Brescia: Morcelliana, 2011), 7.

24. For a thorough examination of knowledge in Qoheleth, see Annette Schellenberg, *Erkenntnis als Problem: Qohelet und die alttestamentliche Diskussion um das menschliche Erkennen* (OBO 188; Fribourg: Universitätsverlag; Göttingen: Vandenhoeck & Ruprecht, 2002), 150–59.

25. Agnès Gueuret, "Observations sur Qohélet," *Sémiotique et Bible* 127 (2007): 25–39, 30: "not stopping to search, knowing that one cannot find her."

26. On the importance of the verb מצא in the structure of Qoh 7:26–29, see Ingrid Riesener, "Frauenfeindschaft im Alten Testament? Zum Verständnis von Qoh 7,25–29," in *"Jedes Ding hat seine Zeit...": Studien zur israelitischen und altorientalischen Weisheit. Diethelm Michel zum 65. Geburtstag* (ed. Anja A. Diesel et al.; BZAW 241; Berlin: de Gruyter, 1996), 193–207.

27. See Mitchell Dahood, "Qohelet and Recent Discoveries," *Bib* 39 (1958): 302–18, 310.

28. Anton Schoors, "Words Typical of Qoheleth," 17–20.

quite popular among exegetes, can be countered by referring to verse 28b, in which Qoheleth is not dealing with justice, but with humankind and with that portion of it constituted by women. The opposition between אדם and אשה could be intentional: so, what could its meaning be?

Keeping in mind what has been said about the general context, I believe that the text might be interpreted as follows: If we carry out an investigation of man meant as human being, we might obtain a result—however modest (one man in a thousand!)—but if we were to investigate a woman, we would not find anything! A woman will always be a mystery, as mysterious as the very essence of humankind, which, being a creation of God, cannot be grasped by man. The maxim in verse 28b, exactly because of its general character, cannot be interpreted as misogynistic: it does not deal with men and women in moral terms. It is indeed moralism, with its overzealousness, that Qoheleth criticizes in 7:16: "Be not overly righteous; neither make yourself overly wise: why should you destroy yourself?" In the book of Qoheleth, women become a "cipher" of an unfathomable reality, a mystery leading to a deeper mystery: the work of God.

Verse 29 concludes this complex pericope by finally stating Qoheleth's position: "see, only this I found." His quest does not end in complete skepticism. Faced with human opinions about the woman, which is traditionally conceived as a metaphor for Wisdom, Qoheleth has not come to any conclusion (I still seek and I don't find). Hence, he falls back on God's original plan. The fact that the verb מצא ("to find") appears seven times in this pericope should not be overlooked. It is, I believe, a relevant number because of its implicit reference to the perfection of creation, exhorting the reader to transcend the realm of experience so as to frame the theme of women within a wider discourse that refers to the beginning of creation. In the beginning, God created man as a righteous being. ישר, a term referring to moral righteousness, defines what is straight in opposition to what is twisted. In verse 29b, the idea of tortuousness is conveyed by the term חשבנות ("machinations"). They (arguably Qoheleth's interlocutors) elaborate complicated theories, and end up clouding God's design with their convoluted conjectures, exactly like Job's friends. God's wisdom is instead simple and straight: He created אדם, male and female.

3. Woman and the Joy of Living (Qoh 9:9)

The second passage we are going to analyze (Qoh 9:9) opens up a completely different perspective on women, because here Qoheleth clearly gives a positive evaluation of the female figure, albeit within the context of an even more miserable and more dismal reflection on human existence (9:1–12). Once again, context might prove crucial to understand the meaning of Qoheleth's words. Chapter 9 opens with an important statement: the just and the wise, and their works, are in the hands of God (9:1). However, such a reassuring assertion seems to be undermined by the following words: "whether it is love or hate one does not know" (9:1b). No one can claim knowledge of God's judgment over men's actions, because divine logic is unfathomable. In order to prove this theory, Qoheleth investigates the question of deed and its consequence in 9:2–3, arguing that the same fate awaits the just and the wicked alike, the good and the bad, the pure and the impure, those who offer sacrifices and those who do not, who vow and who fear vowing. Death is everyone's destination, irrespective of one's behavior. It is on the basis of this indisputable assumption that Qoheleth proves the inadequacy of the traditional doctrine on the firm connection between deeds and fate.

The final verses of this chapter (9:11–12) insist on this reflection, mentioning five other categories of humans: the swift, the strong, the wise, the cautious, the clever. Society does not take into account people's skills and, if said skills are not rewarded during life, they are much less so after death. Time and chance do not spare anyone.[29] It is within such a complex context that we can find the invitation to joy, which is elaborated to great extent (see 2:24; 3:12; 3:22; 5:17; 8:15).

3.1. COMPANION OR WIFE? (QOH 9:9)

The following passage, although easier to penetrate, still retains some difficulties.

> Enjoy [ראה] life with the woman you love,
> all the days of your vain life,
> which God has given you under the sun,
> because that is your fate
> in life and in your toil at which you toil under the sun.

Let us start by analyzing the verb ראה, which is usually translated as "to enjoy." This verb is usually accompanied by the noun טוב, with the meaning of "to enjoy what is good" (see 2:1; 3:13; 5:17; 6:6). Horacio Simian-Yofre argues instead that "to enjoy" is not an evident translation of ראה in this passage, and that the meaning here might be closer to the concept of knowledge: "to behold" or "to contemplate." In addition, he connects the relative clause

---

29. See Vittoria D'Alario, "Liberté de Dieu ou destin? Un autre dilemme dans l'interprétation du Qohélet," in Schoors, *Qohelet in the Context of Wisdom*, 457–63.

"which God has given you under the sun" to the woman rather than to "all the days of your vain life." Consequently, he proposes a translation that differs considerably from the one commonly known.[30]

> Contemplate life with [the] woman you love,
> that God gave you under the sun,
> for all the days of your vain life,
> (for all of them, your vain days);
> for this is your portion in life,
> and in your toil which you suffer under the sun.

Although appealing, this interpretation is not consistent with the context in which we find Qoheleth's exhortation. In fact, verse 8 does not invite to contemplation, but to joy, and to make use of all those possessions, such as clothes and perfumes, which make life more acceptable.

Verses 7–10 constitute a well-defined unit,[31] in which Qoheleth develops his exhortation to enjoy life, once again in unconventional terms, to the point of eliciting charges of hedonism or Epicureanism.[32]

Verse 7 includes an invitation to eat and drink, already expressed in other passages in which Qoheleth elevates the joy of living to a principle. In 9:7 the double clause is given by the expression "your bread and your wine," which clearly evokes the celebration of a happy event in everyday life. The expressions "with joy" and "with cheerful heart" insist on the positive feelings that should inspire everyday life. At this point, it is important to clarify the reason for this invitation, stated in verse 7b "for God has cherished your works." There is no certainty about God's future judgment over the actions of man (cf. 3:17; 9:1b), but there is no doubt about divine favor in the present, as explicitly stated in 2:25 and 3:13. Happiness is a right of humans and at the same time a gift from God, and cannot derive from extraordinary events, despite what might be inferred from 3:4–7. In fact, it is important to show the marks

---

30. Horacio Simian-Yofre, "Conoscere la sapienza: Qohelet e Gen 2–3," in *Il libro del Qohelet: Tradizione, redazione, teologia* (ed. Giuseppe Bellia and Angelo Passaro; Cammini nello Spirito; Biblica 44; Milano: Paoline, 2001), 314–36, esp. 333.

31. On the definition of this unit, see Pedro R. Anaya Luengo, *El hombre, destinatario de los dones de Dios en el Qohélet* (Bibliotheca Salmanticensis; Estudios 296; Salamanca: Publicaciones Universidad Pontificia, 2007), 211–21.

32. See Ernest Horton, "Koheleth's Concept of Opposites as Compared to Samples of Greek Philosophy and Near and Far Eastern Wisdom Classics," *Numen* 19 (1972): 1–21, esp. 14–18. On the theme of *carpe diem* in Qoheleth, see Ludger Schwienhorst-Schönberger, *Nicht im Menschen gründet das Glück (Koh 2,24): Kohelet im Spannungsfeld jüdischer Weisheit und hellenistischer Philosophie* (HBS 2; Freiburg: Herder, 1994), 204–7.

of one's joy at any time, such as white clothes and perfume on one's head (v. 8). It is essential to enjoy everyday life thoroughly and in simplicity, without struggling to reach futile chimeras and dreams of grandeur leading only to disappointment. This joyful existence has to be lived with one's wife.

In 9:9 the term אשה is not accompanied by the article. The omission would suggest that the reference here is to "any woman," rather than the wife, who is introduced with the definite article.[33] Based on the hypothesis that the reference here is not to the "wife" but to "any woman" one is in love with, the text would further confirm Qoheleth's nonconformity. He would not be thinking of marriage, but rather of love free from all ties, which would thus become a source of joy and delight, following the principle of carpe diem.

Other scholars maintain that the absence of the article is not that important in the language of Qoheleth, which might be influenced by Aramaic[34] or Phoenician; in this case, אשה would still refer to the "wife" even with no article. Johan Yeong-Sik Pahk supported this interpretation by connecting the relative clause "that God gave you" to the woman, on the basis of parallelism between this passage and other biblical texts (Exod 21:4; Judg 21:18; 1 Kgs 11:19) as well as ancient Near Eastern texts such as the Epic of Gilgamesh (3.12–13), which promote the idea of an institutional family.[35]

As we have seen, the question of the female figure once again involves the interpretation of the figure of Qoheleth as a savant. A nonconformist or a traditionalist? A hopeless pessimist or a preacher of joy? Whatever the answer to this dilemma—which goes beyond the scope of this essay—it has to be acknowledged that, as far as our discourse on women is concerned, in Qoh 9:9 the female figure is definitely valorized. In this regard, we must stress the importance of the particle עם, "together with," which suggests an equal relationship between a man and his woman.

---

33. Keeping this in mind, Schoors translates "Enjoy life with a woman you love all of the days in the absurd life God gives you under the sun." See Antoon Schoors, "L'ambiguità della gioia in Qohelet," in Bellia and Passaro, Il libro del Qohelet, 278–80.

34. See the bibliography on this subject in Johan Y.-S. Pahk, Il canto della gioia in Dio: L'itinerario sapienziale espresso dall'unità letteraria in Qohelet 8,16–9,10 e il parallelo di Gilgameš Me. iii. (Dipartimento di Studi Asiatici, series minor 52; Naples: Istituto Universitario Orientale, 1996), 248–58.

35. Johan Y.-S. Pahk, "A Syntactical and Contextual Consideration of 'iš in Qoh. IX 9," VT 51 (2001): 370–80.

3.2. Qoheleth and the Gift of Love

Qoheleth counters the disruptive power of death with love, although it is not explicitly stated whether this love is to be experienced freely or in the context of marriage. It is a love relationship that closely resembles the one in the Song of Songs, with which the book of Qoheleth shares peculiar aspects. In Qoh 7:28 the opposition search/not find actually brings to mind Song 3:1–2; 5:6, where there is an allusion to the tormented search for God, which usually takes place during the darkness, as in the book of Job or in the Psalms. The book of Qoheleth and the Song of Songs share a common sense of mystery: the Song looks into the enigma of love, which contains the mystery of creation,[36] whereas Qoheleth insists on the mystery of divine wisdom, impenetrable to the human mind, allowing for a reflection on God's greatness, who omniscient and omnipotent rules the world. The theme of women is a part of Qoheleth's arguments on the mystery of divine works and the limits of human wisdom.

Human life is הבל—everything suddenly might vanish like smoke—but God does not leave humans alone in the abyss. He manifests his presence, bestowing gifts of joy in everyday life. Love also is one of God's gifts, a gift that men and women can share, thus rendering their transitory existence more joyful. Can these joys totally compensate the sense of vanity and the uncertainty of life? This question is difficult to answer.

Certainly, man and woman are united in a common destiny of a life marked by sorrow as well as joy. Maybe the answer to our questions can be found in Qoheleth's exhortation: "In the day of prosperity be joyful, and in the day of adversity consider; God has made the one as well as the other" (7:14).

The duty of any human being is to conform to God's will, serenely accepting both sad and happy moments. Life is a gift from God, and it has to be thoroughly experienced together with one's companion. However, what matters above all is to revere God and to observe his commandments (12:13).

Translated from Italian by Fiorenzo Iuliano

---

36. See Gianfranco Ravasi, *Il Cantico dei Cantici* (Bologna: Dehoniane, 1992), 69.

GOOD AND BAD WIVES IN THE BOOK OF BEN SIRA: A HARMLESS CLASSIFICATION?

Nuria Calduch-Benages

1. Introduction

The book of Ben Sira (also known as Sirach or Ecclesiasticus) was written between 200 and 180 BCE in Jerusalem, where its author, a professional scribe, ruled some sort of school or academy of wisdom.

The crisis provoked by the attempted hellenization of the Jewish people under the Seleucid king Antiochus IV Epiphanes (175–163 BCE) was already latent in the time of Ben Sira. In the first decades of the second century BCE, the confrontation between the new Hellenistic ideas and the traditional religious values of the Jews had already begun. Nevertheless, Ben Sira wrote his book not to oppose or defend against Hellenism but rather to strengthen the faith and confidence of his people. In other words, his main purpose was to encourage the Jews to stay attached to the religion, wisdom, and traditions of their ancestors.[1]

Compared with Proverbs, Job, Qoheleth, and the Wisdom of Solomon, the book of Ben Sira dedicates the largest space to women. In fact, 10 percent of this sage's teachings from Jerusalem refer to particular women or, from time to time, present typically feminine images such as those relating to motherhood ("the maternal bosom/womb," 1:14; 40:1; 46:13Hb; 49:7; 50:22) or to birth ("born of woman," 10:18). Mothers, wives, widows, daughters, virgins, maids, singers, courtesans, prostitutes, and adulteresses always appear in relation to men: son, husband, father, a eunuch, master, or client/victim. Moreover, they all move in the shadows of anonymity, without an identity, faceless members of a generic and undefined group. Even in the "Praise of the Ancestors" (Sir 44–50), a real parade of famous personalities in Israel's history, no

---

1. For a good introduction to the book, see Richard J. Coggins, *Sirach* (Guides to the Apocrypha and Pseudepigrapha 6; Sheffield: Sheffield Academic Press, 1998).

woman is named. On that occasion, Ben Sira could well have included the matriarchs or the heroines of his people, among others, but he chose to silence them, thus also silencing their stories and memories.[2]

Now, my goal is not to make a general survey of women in the book of Ben Sira[3]—that would exceed the scope of this essay—but rather to consider one category of women: the wives, and their classification into "good" and "bad" on the basis of the Hebrew text (not always available) and the Greek version.[4] What does this classification correspond to? What are its criteria? For what purpose does the sage use it? What are its implications? None of these questions seem to exceedingly preoccupy A. B. Davidson, the author of the first article on Ben Sira and women, written in the late nineteenth century.

---

2. Nuria Calduch-Benages, "The Absence of Named Women from Ben Sira's Praise of the Ancestors," in *Rewriting Biblical History: Essays on Chronicles and Ben Sira in Honour of Pancratius C. Beentjes* (ed. Jeremy Corley and Harm van Grol; Deuterocanonical and Cognate Literature Studies 7; Berlin: de Gruyter, 2011), 301–17.

3. See especially the following monographs: Warren C. Trenchard, *Ben Sira's View of Women: A Literary Analysis* (BJS 38; Chico, Calif.: Scholars Press, 1982); and Ibolya Balla, *Ben Sira on Family, Gender and Sexuality* (Deuterocanonical and Cognate Literature Studies 8; Berlin: de Gruyter, 2011). See also Judith E. McKinlay, *Gendering Wisdom the Host: Biblical Invitations to Eat and Drink* (JSOTSup 216; Gender, Culture, Theory 4; Sheffield: Sheffield Academic, 1996), 160–78; Angelika Strotmann, "Sirach (Ecclesiasticus): On the Difficult Relation between Divine Wisdom and Real Women in an Androcentric Document," in *Feminist Biblical Interpretation: A Compendium of Critical Commentary on the Books of the Bible and Related Literature* (ed. Luise Schottroff and Marie-Theres Wacker; Grand Rapids: Eerdmans, 2012), 539–54; and Nuria Calduch-Benages, "Ben Sira y las mujeres," *Reseña Bíblica* 41 (2004): 37–44. For the Syriac version, see Nuria Calduch-Benages, "La mujer en la versión siríaca (Peshitta) de Ben Sira: ¿Sesgos de género?" in *Congreso Internacional "Biblia, memoria histórica y encrucijada de culturas"* (ed. Jesús Campos Santiago and Víctor Pastor Julián; Zamora: Asociación Bíblica Española, 2004), 686–93.

4. The evolution of the text of Ben Sira is undoubtedly the most complicated of all the books of the Old Testament. Ben Sira wrote in Hebrew (Hb), but his work was mainly preserved in Greek (Gr), Syriac (Syr), and Latin (Lat). Since 1896 the Hebrew text has been gradually recovered, and we now have about two-thirds of it. Notwithstanding many unresolved problems, most scholars now agree on the existence of two text forms, a shorter and a longer one, both in the Hebrew (HbI and HbII) and Greek textual tradition (GrI and GrII). On this question, see Patrick W. Skehan and Alexander A. Di Lella, *The Wisdom of Ben Sira: A New Translation with Notes by Patrick W. Skehan, Introduction and Commentary by Alexander A. Di Lella* (AB 39; New York: Doubleday, 1987), 51–62; Maurice Gilbert, "Siracide," *DBSup* 12 (1996): 1390–402; and Nuria Calduch-Benages, *En el crisol de la prueba. Estudio exegético de Sir 2,1–18* (Asociación Bíblica Española 32; Estella: Verbo Divino, 1997), 113–21.

> The judgment of Jesus-ben-Sira ... regarding women is popularly supposed to be very damnatory. This opinion is scarcely justified. Sirach believes that there are bad women and good women, and if the badness of a bad woman be something as bad as can be, the goodness of a good woman is something superlatively good. ... They pretty well balance one another.[5]

I will delve into this supposed balance between good and evil to discover the meaning of this classification, its role in the sage's teaching, and the ideological assumptions that support it. My general approach will focus on the literary dimension of the selected texts, paying special attention to the communicative strategies used by the author as well as to the influence of the sociohistorical context on his work and teaching.

Before embarking on this study, I want to make an important observation. Ben Sira is the heir of an ancient wisdom tradition, in which women (motherhood, marriage, adultery, and prostitution) constitute one of the main themes. Its authors tend to separate them into "good" and "bad," and they often refer to them ironically or even satirically. Some notable examples are the demotic Instruction of Ankhsheshonqy (24–25),[6] Papyrus Insinger (the ninth instruction),[7] the Anthology of Stobaeus (22–23)[8] as an example of the gnomic Hellenistic wisdom, or the monostiches of the playwright Menander (83–87).[9] In this sense, then, the texts of Sirach presented below merely perpetuate a line of thought that persists in the time of the sage.

2. Two Main Categories of Wives

Along with daughters (7:24–25; 22:3–5; 42:9–14) and dangerous women (9:1–9; 23:22–26), wives receive special attention from Ben Sira. As already indicated, the sage places them in the two basic ethical categories of good and evil, the same categories he also uses to refer to people in general. Among these, the

---

5. Andrew B. Davidson, "Sirach's Judgment of Women," *ExpTim* 6 (1894–95): 402–4, 402.

6. Miriam Lichtheim, *Late Egyptian Wisdom Literature in the International Context: A Study of Demotic Instructions* (OBO 52; Fribourg: Universitätsverlag; Göttingen: Vandenhoeck & Ruprecht, 1983), 88–90.

7. Ibid., 203–5.

8. Curt Wachsmith and Otto Hense, eds., *Ioannis Stobaei Anthologium* (vol. 4 of *Anthologii libri quarti partem priorem ab Ottone Hense editam continens*; Berlin: Weidman, 1909), 494–99 (chaps. 22–23 = chaps. 67–74 in the edition by A. Meinecke). See specifically the *Poem on Women* by Semonides of Amorgos in 22.193 (pp. 561–66), the first misogynist work of Western literature (sixth century BCE).

9. Lichtheim, *Late Egyptian Wisdom Literature*, 50.

servants stand out as the only ones who, like wives, are explicitly characterized as good/wise/intelligent (7:20–21; 10:25) or bad (33:27; 42:5).[10] We must not forget that, at the time, wives and servants, as well as sons, daughters, and cattle, were considered true possessions of the paterfamilias (see 7:18–28).

The most significant texts on wives are concentrated in chapters 25–26, immediately after the self-praise of Lady Wisdom. If, in chapter 24, the protagonist was the mysterious figure of personified Wisdom, now concrete and real women from everyday life occupy center stage. If the first is distinguished by the excellence of her speech, the latter seem to be voiceless. They do not utter a single word, but are constantly the subject of discussion. They are subject to the sage's teaching. The instructions on the wives alternate in the following order: 25:13–26 (bad wives);[11] 26:1–4 (good wives); 26:5–12 (bad wives); 26:13–18 (good wives).[12] To these passages we must add 36:21–26 Hebrew (26–31 Greek) on the good wife, situated inside a section on discernment (36:18–37:31). Finally, many verses scattered throughout the book complete the portrait of the good wife (7:19, 26a; 9:1; 25:1, 8; 28:15; 40:19.23) and of the bad wife (7:26b; 9:2; 33:19ab; 37:11a; 42:6; 47:19).

All these texts presuppose a male audience, and especially young men who attended Ben Sira's school in Jerusalem. They belonged to wealthy families of the city and were preparing themselves to occupy positions of responsibility in the future. The sage directed his teachings about the wives specifically to them. Consequently, all the advice reflects the mentality and perspective of a husband—everything in the book suggests that Ben Sira was married—who wants to instruct the future husbands about the virtues they should look for in a wife and about the dangers they must avoid. Hence, the division between good and bad wives, emerging from a totally male-centered perspective, contemplates only the husband's happiness, desire, convenience, honor, and authority. For this reason, some of the sage's statements about marital harmony, in which husband and wife are placed on the same level, are truly sur-

---

10. Woman and servant appear together in the Instruction of Ankhsheshonqy: "Do not open your heart to your wife or to your servant" (13:17) (Lichtheim, *Late Egyptian Wisdom Literature*, 78).

11. On this passage, see Renate Egger-Wenzel, "'Denn harte Knechtschaft und Schande ist es, wenn eine Frau ihren Mann ernährt' (Sir 25,22)," in *Der Einzelne und seine Gemeinschaft* (ed. Renate Egger-Wenzel and Ingrid Krammer; BZAW 270; Berlin: de Gruyter, 1998), 23–49.

12. The next passage (26:19–27) only exists in the Syriac and in the long form of the Greek version (GrII); consequently, it does not seem to come originally from Ben Sira (*pace* Skehan and Di Lella, *The Wisdom of Ben Sira*, 351). Verses 19–21 talk about the choice of the spouse, and vv. 22–27 give both positive and negative maxims about women and marriage. See on this subject Balla, *Ben Sira on Family*, 107–110.

prising; he says, for example, "With three things I am delighted, for they are pleasing to the Lord and to men: Harmony among brethren, friendship among neighbors, and the mutual love of husband and wife [συμπεριφερόμενοι]"[13] (25:1); or "Friend and companion are encountered at the right time, but especially the woman with the husband" (40:23 Gr).[14] In these verses, we should note the order in which the spouses are cited: husband and wife, wife and husband, as well as the absence of possessive adjectives to indicate the relationship between them.

2.1. Bad Wives

In texts on bad wives, the Hebrew expression רע[ת] אשה, "evil woman," appears three times (25:13, 17, 19), and the Greek one, γυνὴ πονηρά, "the bad/evil woman," is repeated four times (25:6, 25, 26:7; 42:6).[15] At first glance, it is unclear what this feminine evil is, since both the noun and the adjective are used in a rather broad sense. Only in the light of context, and in some cases with the help of the different versions, is it possible to discover meanings, nuances, and specific allusions. It is, however, clear that the women's wickedness is worse than any other evil (25:13.19a), and so the evil woman deserves the fate of the sinner (25:19b), that is, to marry a sinner and not a just man, so that she will serve as punishment for her husband.[16] The same view, although without explicit mention of sin and punishment, is shared by Hesiod: "For a man ... there is nothing else more chilling than an evil one [wife], a meal-ambusher who scorches her husband without a firebrand, even though he be strong, and gives him over to raw old age" (*Works and Days*, 695).[17] Similarly, Euripides writes: "Terrible is the violence of the ocean waves, terrible the impetuosity of rivers and burning breath of fire, terrible poverty and a thousand other things, but of all calamities the worst is a bad woman"

---

13. On this term, see Balla, *Ben Sira on Family*, 58–60.
14. See, on the contrary, the Hebrew text of MsB in the second hemistich (the first one is damaged): "but better than both is a sensible woman [אשה משכלת]."
15. See manuscript Bmg: טפשה, "crazy."
16. John J. Collins, *Jewish Wisdom in the Hellenistic Age* (OTL; Louisville: Westminster John Knox, 1997), 67; and Charles Mopsik, *La Sagesse de ben Sira: Traduction de l'hébreu, introduction et annotation par Charles Mopsik* (Collection "Les Dix Paroles"; Paris: Verdier, 2003), 173n2.
17. Martin L. West, ed., *Hesiod, Works and Days: Edited with Prolegomena and Commentary by M. L. West* (Oxford: Clarendon, 1978), 129.

(*Uncertain Fragments*, 1059).[18] Much later, the midrash on Ps 59 points out: "If she [a woman] is a bad wife, there is no end to her badness."[19]

2.1.1. Communicative Strategies

As a skilled master and teacher, Ben Sira employs various communicative strategies to convey his teachings and to convince the audience. In the two longer passages on bad wives, 25:13-26 and 26:5-12, two strategies are worth mentioning: the ingenious use of grammatical persons and the concentration of images (the latter will be discussed in the next section).

Both passages abound in general as well as specific judgments, expressed in the third person in a marked proverbial style: "Worst of all wounds is that of the heart, worst of all evils is that of a woman" (25:13); "A bad wife is a chafing yoke; he who marries her seizes a scorpion" (26:7). Among the sayings, there are interspersed pieces of advice given directly to the disciple in the second person, and formulated negatively: "Stumble not upon woman's beauty, nor be greedy for her wealth" (25:21); "Allow water no outlet, and do not trust an evil woman" (25:25);[20] and positively: "Keep a strict watch over an unruly daughter/wife" (26:10); "Follow close if her eyes are bold" (26:11). One of these pieces of advice is the climax of the first composition, in which Ben Sira unhesitatingly recommends divorce to the husband if his wife refuses to submit to his will: "If she walks not according to your wishes [lit., "if she does not walk according to your hand"], cut her away from you (25:26)."[21]

In my view, however, the rhetorical power lies in the use of the first-person singular: "With a dragon or a lion I would rather dwell than live with an evil woman" (25:16). With this rhetorical device, frequent throughout the book,[22] the sage not only expresses his opinion (which appears muted at 25:19b) but also imposes himself as an authority on his disciples, for whom

---

18. August Nauck, *Tragicorum Graecorum Fragmenta: Supplementum adiecit Bruno Snell* (Hildesheim: Olms, 1964), 695 (translation mine).

19. William G. Braude, trans., *The Midrash on Psalms* (3rd ed.; Yale Judaica Series 13; New Haven: Yale University Press, 1976), 1:509. See also Papyrus Insinger 8:10 (Lichtheim, *Late Egyptian Wisdom Literature*, 204).

20. Other examples are found in 7:26; 9:2; 33:20ab; 37:11a.

21. Nuria Calduch-Benages, "'Cut Her Away from Your Flesh': Divorce in Ben Sira," in *Studies in the Book of Ben Sira: Papers of the Third International Conference on the Deuterocanonical Books, Shime'on Centre, Pápa, Hungary, 18–20 May, 2006* (Géza G. Xeravits and József Zsengellér; JSJSup 127; Leiden: Brill, 2008), 90–92.

22. See Jan Liesen, "Stratregical Self-references in Ben Sira," in *Treasures of Wisdom: Studies in Ben Sira and the Book of Wisdom: Festschrift M. Gilbert* (ed. Nuria Calduch-Benages and Jacques Vermeylen; BETL 143; Leuven: Peeters, 1999), 63–74.

the master's words take on special meaning. His teaching is based not only on the legacy of tradition or wisdom but also on personal experience. This is the special way in which he confers credibility to his words. Moreover, in 25:24, this time using the first-person plural, Ben Sira speaks as an authorized teacher and also apparently as spokesman for all husbands. Now, if we accept the interpretation proposed by Jack Levison, instead of seeing in the text a reference to Eve's sin (see Gen 3:6), this is to be understood in direct relation to the context: "From the woman [implying "wicked"] [is] the beginning of sin, and because of it we all [implying husbands] die."[23]

2.1.2. Description of the Bad Wife

In 25:13–26 and 26:5–12, Ben Sira attributes to the "bad" wife other epithets that render a more detailed portrait of our protagonist. She is described as talkative (25:20: אשת לשון, γλωσσώδης), jealous of other women (26:6: ἀντίζηλος ἐπὶ γυναικί), a drunkard (26:8: μέθυσος), sensual/an adulteress (26:9: πορνεία γυναικός), stubborn (26:10: ἐπὶ θυγατρὶ ἀδιατρέπτῳ),[24] and shameless (26:11: ἀναιδοῦς ὀφθαλμοῦ). These qualifiers, with the exception of the first one, are in the sexual sphere or are related to it by the context. For example, jealousy between wives may be motivated by sex; drunkenness is associated with indecent conduct and illicit relationships (26:8b; cf. 9:9; 19:2); and the wife's stubbornness is related to an offense of a sexual nature against the husband (see 26:11a). This is how Alonso Schökel understands 26:10 when he translates: "Keep a close eye on the shameless [rather than stubborn] girl [i.e., wife], so that she does not take the opportunity to fornicate."[25] Finally, the evil wife is the one who financially supports her husband (25:22) and does not make him happy (25:23). In this category we also find the "hated" or "hateful" (שנואה, μισουμένη) wife, that is, the less beloved wife, possibly in a bigamous marriage, or the abhorrent and undesirable wife who, finally, ends up being

---

23. Jack Levison, "Is Eve to Blame? A Contextual Analysis of Sirach 25:24," *CBQ* 47 (1985): 617–23. For a different view see the recent study of Teresa Ann Ellis, "Is Eve the 'Woman' in Sirach 25:24?" *CBQ* 73 (2011): 723–42.

24. Although the Greek text speaks about the daughter, according to Semitic custom (see Gen 30:13; Prov 31:29), this designation can also refer to the wife; see A. Minissale, *Siracide (Ecclesiastico)* (Nuovissima versione della Bibbia dai testi originali 23; Rome: Paoline, 1980), 135.

25. L. Alonso Schökel, *Proverbios y Eclesiástico* (Los Libros Sagrados 8.1; Madrid: Cristiandad, 1968), 238.

divorced by her husband. In any case, the sage's advice to the husband is blunt: "Do not trust her" (7:26).[26]

As previously indicated, the use of images is characteristic of the text. Ben Sira employs them to make an impact on his young audience and prepare them for when the time comes to choose a wife. There is a notable abundance of images taken from the animal world.[27] Except for the ox, the animals mentioned in connection with the bad wife are all extremely dangerous: serpent, lion, dragon, bear, and scorpion.[28] In two daring hyperboles, Ben Sira compares the snake's venom with the hatred of women (25:15) and confesses that he prefers to live with lions and dragons rather than with a wicked woman (25:16).[29] This last text reminds us of the aphorisms, certainly more gentle, in Prov 21:9, 19 and Prov 25:24. Although "living in a desert" (Prov 21:19) or "on a corner of a roof" (Prov 21:9, 25:24) is tiring but feasible, the comparison used in Sir 25:16 states that the time spent with an evil woman is absolutely intolerable. The image of the bear, associated with its proverbial ferocity (see 1 Sam 17:34; 2 Sam 17:8), is reflected in the somber face of the evil woman (25:17). Later, in 26:7, the maladjusted (chafing) yoke of oxen seems to evoke 25:8, which refers to incompatibility between the spouses. Here, however, the difficulty lies only in the woman, who is a constant source of irritation for the husband. Wanting to control an evil woman is like trying to catch a scorpion. It is an arduous and risky enterprise, because this little animal is constantly moving and its sting contains a deadly poison (cf. Deut 8:15).

Other metaphors refer to the human body. A woman's wickedness not only appears in her countenance (25:17) but also affects the husband's health: inert hands make him incapable of working, and quaking knees prevent him from moving with agility and security (25:23). Due to a wicked wife, his life is painful, like walking on shaky ground ("Like a sandy hill to aged feet," 25:20), in other words a project lacking firmness[30] without prospects for the future and always dependent on circumstances.

The sage's instruction in 26:12 concludes with a series of suggestive images on the double meaning of the immoderate sexual appetite of the wicked wife; these images are reminiscent of Jerusalem's promiscuous behavior in Ezek

---

26. On this verse, see Calduch-Benages, "Cut Her Away from Your Flesh," 86–88.

27. Cf. the Instruction of Ankhsheshonqy: "When a man smells of myrrh his wife is a monkey before him. When a man is suffering his wife is a lion before him" (15:11–12) (Lichtheim, *Late Egyptian Wisdom Literature*, 80).

28. See also 26:25, only in Syr and GrII: "A shameless woman is regarded as a dog."

29. See Egger-Wenzel, "'Denn harte Knechtschaft und Schande ist es,'" 29–30.

30. Víctor Morla Asensio, *Eclesiástico: Texto y Comentario* (El Mensaje del Antiguo Testamento 20; Estella: Verbo Divino, 1992), 134.

16:25. Like the whoring city, the bad wife offers herself to any man who comes along: "As a thirsty traveler with eager mouth drinks from any water that he finds, so she settles down before every tent peg and opens her quiver for every arrow" (26:12).

2.1.3. The Husband of the Bad Wife

The evil woman's husband is always present. Indeed, his presence in the text is constant, and even overwhelming in the text. He is everywhere, either explicitly ("her husband," 3x; "peaceful husband," 1x) or implicitly. Let us recall that the instructions are given by a husband (I, we) and directed to other men, who are already married or have not yet chosen a wife (you).

Ben Sira emphasizes the physical and psychological consequences that living with a wicked wife has for her husband: his strength fails and sadness fills his heart when he is with his friends (25:18, 23 Hb and Gr). By her irritating behavior and sharp tongue (25:20; 26:6-7), the wife takes away his happiness. Hence, the sage recommends avoiding infatuation with the evil women, especially if she is beautiful or rich (25:21),[31] since in this case the husband sees his honor sullied when he is forced to rely on her assets (25:22).[32] Such a situation was inconceivable for the mentality of the time, so that the sage sees it as "hard bondage"[33] and "great shame." The husband's honor will also be seriously threatened if his wife falls into the vice of drunkenness (26:8) or, even worse, maintains illicit relations with other men to satisfy her sexual desire (26:9-12).

Clearly, then, the husband should keep the evil woman in check. Just remember what happened to Solomon and the shame that came over him for having succumbed to women, losing his authority over them and, worst of all, being controlled by them (47:19). In other words, the sage describes "a man 'unmanned' by women."[34] To prevent this shameful history from repeating itself, Ben Sira gives the husband the following recommendations: Do not trust an evil woman (25:25; 7:26; 9:2), do not give her power (33:20ab),

---

31. Rudolph Smend, *Die Weisheit Jesus Sirach* (Berlin: Reimer, 1906), 231: "The rich woman is both a bait and a trap."

32. See Claudia V. Camp, "Understanding Patriarchy: Women in Second Century Jerusalem through the Eyes of Ben Sira," in *"Women Like This": New Perspectives on Jewish Women in the Greco-Roman World* (ed. Amy-Jill Levine; Atlanta: Scholars Press, 1991), 1-40, here 29.

33. Possibly an allusion to the oppression suffered by the Israelites in Egypt (Exod 1:14; 6:9; Deut 26:6).

34. Balla, *Ben Sira on Family*, 150.

mistrust her (42:6), or, in extreme situations, give her a certificate of divorce (25:26). For Judith E. McKinlay, divorce is the only alternative for the husband who wants "to remain in control, and presumably to be seen to be in control for the sake of his honor and reputation."[35]

2.2. Good Wives

In the passages about good wives, the Hebrew expression אשה טובה, "good wife," appears twice (26:1, 3), corresponding to the Greek γυνὴ ἀγαθή (26:1, 3, 16;[36] 7:19[37]). The goodness of the wife, as noted by Burkard Zapff in his commentary, is not so much a moral quality but rather "the idea that the woman will turn out to support the life of her husband."[38] Ben Sira is certainly not the first to point out how beneficial the good wife is to her husband (see Prov 31:11–12, 23). The same idea is found in the demotic Instruction of Ankhsheshonqy: "A good woman of noble character is food that comes in time of hunger" (24:21);[39] in Hesiod: "For a man carries off nothing better than a good wife" (*Works and Days*, 702);[40] and Theognis: "Nothing, Cyrnus, is more delightful than a good wife" (1225).[41]

2.2.1. Communicative Strategies

The communicative strategies that stand out in the texts about the good wives are the presence of a macarism, or beatitude, in 26:1–4; the exclusive use of the third person; and the novelty of some images in 26:13–18 and 36:21–26 Hebrew (26–31 Greek) (see the following section).

It is surprising that, in a poem dedicated to the good wife, the first verse contains a statement referring to the happiness of her husband.[42] Instead of "Happy is the husband of a good woman" (the usual translation of 26:1Gr;

---

35. McKinlay, *Gendering Wisdom the Host*, 171.
36. MsC: [שה]א יפי, a "beautiful wife."
37. Gr: γυναικὸς σοφῆς καὶ ἀγαθῆς; MsA: אשה משכלת, "a prudent wife" (also in 25:8; 40:23).
38. Burkard M. Zapff, *Jesus Sirach 25–51* (NEchtB 39; Würzburg: Echter, 2010), 150.
39. Lichtheim, *Late Egyptian Wisdom*, 89.
40. West, *Hesiod, Works and Days*, 129.
41. Martin L. West, ed., *Archilochus, Hipponax, Theognidea* (vol. 1 of *Iambi et elegi graeci ante Alexandrum cantati*; 2nd ed.; Oxford: Oxford University Press, 1989), 233 (translation mine).
42. For Claudia V. Camp, on the other hand, "the point is not that he feels internally happy but that he has attained an honor worthy of social notice" (Camp, "Understanding a Patriarchy," 24).

cf. 25:8c), one would expect something like: "Blessed is the good woman because ..." Thus the accent would fall on the alleged protagonist and not on her husband. We need to note that the Hebrew text of manuscript C (also Syr) adopts an emphatic position: "Good wife, happy husband." Be that as it may, the important thing is that this initial macarism sets the tone of 26:1–4, which after being interrupted in 26:5–12 (on the bad wife) is taken up again at 26:13–18.

We have seen that the texts on bad wives are characterized by the alternate use of grammatical persons, in particular, the presence of the sage's "I" (we). This is not so in the passages about good wives, since most are formulated in an impersonal style based on statements in the third person with a rhetorical question, for example, in 36:26 Gr. The only exceptions are the recommendations given directly to the husband/disciple in 7:19: "Do not dismiss a sensible wife" (Hb); "do not separate yourself from a wise and good woman" (Gr); and 9:1: "Do not be jealous of the wife of your bosom" (Hb, Gr). In other words, the personal tone and highly incisive insistence with respect to the bad wife has disappeared and left room for a reflection of a proverbial character, which is more objective and therefore less striking for the audience. Here, too, we would have liked to hear the sage's voice directly. However, for whatever reason, he chose to express himself indirectly and impassively.

2.2.2. The Description of the Good Wife

In 26:1–4, 13–18 and 36:21–26 Hebrew (26–31 Greek), other adjectives are attributed to the good wife: "strong, brave" (26:2: אשה חיל, γυνὴ ἀνδρεία),[43] "charming/graceful" (26:13: אשה [חן], χάρις γυναικός), "prudent" (26:13b: שכלה, ἡ ἐπιστήμη αὐτῆς), "silent" (26:14: γυνὴ σιγηρά), "beautiful" (26:15: אשה יפה; cf. "beauty of a woman," אשה יפה, in 36:22, "beautiful face," κάλλος προσώπου, in 26:17, and "beautiful feet/legs," πόδες ὡραῖοι, in 26:18), "modest" (26:15: γυνὴ αἰσχυντηρά), "chaste soul" or "capable of self-control" (ἐγκρατοῦς ψυχῆς), "peaceful or curative language" (36:23: מרפא לשון), and "compassionate and gentle/sweet" (36:23: ἐπὶ γλώσσης αὐτῆς ἔλεος καὶ πραΰτης). If we take into consideration the rest of the book, the good wife is also described as "sensible" (25:8: γυναικὶ συνετῇ; 40:23: אשה משכלת), "wise" (7:19: γυναικὶ σοφῆς), "devoted" (40:19: אשה נחשקת), and "irreproachable/without fault or defect" (40:19: γυνὴ ἄμωμος).

This brief review of the vocabulary renders it obvious that beauty is the quality most appreciated in the good wife. In 36:21–26 (26–31), for example,

---

43. Also in 28:15 (in plural).

beauty not only is the first of the qualities listed but also is described with a superlative ("it surpasses everything desirable"). If, in these texts, Ben Sira exclusively presents the positive side of female beauty (see also 7:19), on other occasions he also warns of its dangers (9:8; 25:21; 42:12). Of course, in both cases this is always seen from the perspective of the man/husband. Along with beauty, the virtue of silence, traditionally praised by the sages, deserves special attention. Surprisingly, this is the only quality that is accompanied by explicit mention of the Lord: "A silent woman is a gift from the Lord" (26:14; cf. 26:3). For Syriac Menander, the control of the tongue is a decisive criterion for the choice of wife: "And if you want to take a wife, make first inquiries about her tongue, and take her [only] then. For a talkative woman is a hell and … a bad man a deadly plague" (*Sentences*, 118–22);[44] and a monostich of Menander, the foremost representative of the New Comedy, says: "Silence is any woman's ornament" (83).[45]

In addition to specific words, images give much information about the good wife. Inspired by Prov 19:14 ("House and estate are an inheritance from parents, but a sensible woman is granted by the Lord"), Ben Sira equates the good wife with a "generous gift" (good lot or portion) that the Lord bestows on the man who fears him, that is, a good and pious husband (26:3). A very different aspect is the image of the "sealed mouth" found in 26:15. In fact, this is an ambivalent image that can refer either to the control of the tongue or to the chastity of the wife, who should not exercise her sexuality outside of marriage.[46] The latter meaning can be glimpsed in the Greek version that replaces this image with the expression "self-controlled person or character," which refers to the "modest woman" of the first hemistich. The good and beautiful wife is so attractive that, in 26:15a, she is compared to the glorious spectacle of the sun when it rises to the heights.[47]

However, the most innovative images are, without doubt, those that appear in 26:17–18. As C. Mopsik puts it: "La comparaison de la beauté et de la grâce de l'épouse *de celui qui craint Dieu* avec les objets sacrés du temple

---

44. Tjitze Baarda, "The Sentences of the Syriac Menander (Third Century A.D.): A New Translation and Introduction," in *Expansions of the "Old Testament" and Legends, Wisdom and Philosophical Literature, Prayers, Psalms and Odes, Fragments of Lost Judeo-Hellenistic Works* (vol. 2 of *The Old Testament Pseudepigrapha*; ed. James H. Charlesworth; Garden City, N.Y.: Doubleday, 1985), 583–606, 595.

45. Lichtheim, *Late Egyptian Wisdom Literature*, 50.

46. According to Di Lella, "(restricted, shut up of) mouth" is a euphemism for "closed vagina" (Skehan and Di Lella, *The Wisdom of Ben Sira*, 350). This opinion is shared by Mopsik (*La Sagesse de Ben Sira*, 175).

47. In the second hemistich, the Hebrew text and the Greek notably differ. See on this matter Balla, *Ben Sira on Family*, 66–67.

de Jérusalem est tout à fait exceptionelle dans la littérature hébraïque de l'Antiquité."[48] Let us consider the text in the Greek version.

> A lamp shining upon a holy candlestick
> face upon[49] a slender body.
> Golden columns on silver pedestals
> are [her] pretty legs on firm heels.[50]

If, in the previous verse, the sage has compared the good wife to the noblest and most luminous star of nature (26:16; cf. 43:1–5), now he compares her to the noblest and brightest elements of the cult. Thus, from the cosmic order we pass to the religious and cultic order. The wife's beautiful face, sustained by a well-formed body, shines like a lamp on the holy lampstand, and her pretty legs are supported by firm heels that evoke the majestic columns of gold and silver plinths of the temple. These comparisons raise many questions; for example: Is there, then, "something sacred" about the figure of the good wife described in 26:17–18?[51] Is she able to give dignity to "the liturgy of the home"?[52] Why so much emphasis on physical beauty? Or where are the wife's human, moral, and religious values (cf. Prov 31:10–31)? Are these verses a real compliment to the woman, or do they transmit another, less flattering message?[53]

In my view, the close relationship established between women and liturgical sacred space refers to the discourse of Lady Wisdom, more precisely in 24:10–11, 15, where by means of a series of very suggestive expressions and images the sage describes the liturgical function of the protagonist.[54] In 24:10 she declares her active participation in the worship service: "I officiated in the holy tent before Him, and so I settled in Zion." However, as Judith E. McKinlay rightly indicates in reference to 26:17–18, "this is a static picture; in these verses the wife is very much an object that is being evaluated, in contrast to the Picture of Wisdom and Simon actively taking part in liturgical services."[55] In fact, what Ben Sira exalts is the beauty of the bride, her face, her body, and implicitly her sex appeal. Reading between the lines, we can see something

---

48. Mopsik, *La Sagesse de ben Sira*, 176 (italics mine).
49. MsC has "the splendor of a face."
50. All of v. 18 is missing in MsC.
51. Alonso Schökel, *Proverbios y Eclesiástico*, 238.
52. Morla Asensio, *Eclesiástico*, 136.
53. Skehan and Di Lella, *The Wisdom of Ben Sira*, 351.
54. See Nuria Calduch-Benages, "Aromas, fragancias y perfumes en el Sirácida," in Calduch-Benages and Vermeylen, *Treasures of Wisdom*, 15–30.
55. McKinlay, *Gendering Wisdom the Host*, 172.

that the sage does not say openly: the more beautiful the wife is, the more her husband wants her (see 36:22 in manuscript B: "The beauty of a woman lights up the face and surpasses any human desire [lit., "eye"].")

Finally, in 36:24–25 (29–30), the sage describes the good wife with two images of married life, referencing the urban world and the rural world: as a column (vertical dimension) and a fence (horizontal dimension), respectively. If, on the one hand, the image of the column suggests the idea of support (foundation, rest), on the other hand, the fence suggests the notion of protection (safety, surveillance).[56] It is difficult to say what specifically constitutes this support or protection, as the author does not offer any details. In any case, since the main objective of 36:21–26 (26–31) is to provide criteria for choosing a wife, we can understand that those pictures are simply intended to highlight the crucial importance of the woman in a man's life. The rabbis taught, "He who has no wife dwells without good, without help, without joy, without blessing, and without atonement" (midrash on Gen 2:18).[57]

2.2.3. Her Relationship with Her Husband

An attentive reader soon realizes that the good wife is praised not for her intrinsic value as a person but in relation to what she is, does, and means for her husband. As in the texts about the bad wife, here the husband's presence is strongly felt, either explicitly ("[her] husband" four times; "man" twice) or implicitly by means of masculine pronouns and adjectives.

In fact, the central theme of the texts studied here is not so much the good wife but rather her husband receiving benefits from her. Not all men are worthy of her; therefore, the Lord gives her to the husband who fears him (26:3, 14). She is a priceless gift, more precious than coral and gold (7:19; 26:14–15; cf. Prov 31:10). She is a blessing that brings a long, peaceful, and joyful life (26:1–2). The wife's goodness is a value that transcends the economic status of the husband, whether he is rich or poor, with positive effects for his body and soul: joy fills his heart, and it lights up his face (26:2, 4; 36:22 [27]). In a different order, the good wife delights her husband with her physical charms (or kindness) and makes him prosper economically with her prudence or skill (26:13; cf. 40:19cd). It is impossible not to recall the poem of the strong woman in Prov 31, especially verses 11–12: "The heart of her husband

---

56. Morla Asensio, *Eclesiástico*, 180.

57. *Midrash Rabbah Translated into English with Notes, Glossary and Indices under the Editorship of Rabbi Dr. M. Freedman and Maurice Simon* (3rd ed.; London: Soncino, 1961), 1:132.

trusts in her, and he will have no lack of gain. She does him good, and not harm, all the days of her life."

Dazzled by her beauty, her modesty, her sweet and friendly talk[58] or silence, the husband becomes an exceptional being, unlike other mortals, a kind of angel on earth (36:23 [28]). Thus Ben Sira formulates the sentence: "He who acquires a wife [presumably a good one] gets his best possession, a helper fit for him and a pillar of support" (36:24 [29]). A man needs to build a home, a family, have offspring; but above all, he needs social recognition, because as Gilbert rightly noted, the wife is the "principle of social integration."[59] The husband of the strong woman of Proverbs certainly received social recognition through her. The text says about him, "he is respected in the town square when he sits among the elders of the city" (Prov 31:23). The sage describes the other side of the coin in Sir 36:25-26 (30-31), three verses that could be summarized as follows: Who will trust a vagabond, without a wife, without a family, and without a home? Few words are enough for a wise man, and the young disciple, presumably, has got the message.

3. Conclusion

A brief comparison between the passages on the bad wife and the good wife leads to the following results. In my opinion, Ben Sira seems to be more interested in the bad wife than in the good one. Indeed, he gives her not only a special place in his instruction (the first of the series, see 25:13-26) but also far more attention (see the number of verses dedicated to each). Moreover, the sage speaks about her in a very personal, vivid, and incisive style. The same is true for the advice and recommendations he gives to the disciples about her, which contrasts sharply with the impersonal and dispassionate tone used to describe the good wife. Is the sage speaking from experience? Does his wife belong to the category of "bad wives"? Of course, we do not know, but the texts may seem to indicate this.

On the other hand, the sage presents both good and bad wives in the same way, that is, in terms of physical appearance, control of language, and behavior in the sexual sphere (more pronounced in the case of the bad wife), as these three aspects affect, positively or negatively, the personal and social life of her husband. Hence, the reference point of all the texts is not, as we might expect, the figure of the wife, whether good or bad, but her husband in his role as

---

58. According to Schökel, the good wife is a woman "who caresses as she speaks"; see *Proverbios y Eclesiástico*, 274.

59. Maurice Gilbert, "Ben Sira et la femme," *RTL* 7 (1976): 426-42, 438.

paterfamilias for all intents and purposes. The classification proposed by Ben Sira works then as follows: the wife is good when she is good for her husband, and she is bad when she is bad for her husband. This same androcentric perspective is perceptible in the introduction to the commentary of Hilaire Duesberg and Irenée Fransen: "It would be good to know whether Ben Sira was happy in his family or not." And immediately they add: "He told us about both cases with almost the same vivacity. From his eloquence, it is not possible to make any conclusion neither in one sense nor in the other"[60]—which incidentally is not entirely accurate. The two cases to which the authors refer are, of course, the happily married husband and the unhappy one.

Ben Sira stresses the patriarchal control of women, especially of the wife. Described with cross-cultural topics relating to women (beauty, modesty, silence, and sweetness), the good wife is called to obey meekly the authority of the husband, to please him in everything, and above all not to compromise his honor by her words, gestures, or behavior. In other words, she is regarded as an effective aide who, however, must be kept under control. The one who is in control has the power.

How can the sage's ideas and teaching about wives be judged? How is their apparently harmless classification as "good and bad wives" to be assessed? In my opinion, the answer should not be sought solely in the sage's exacerbated misogyny, possibly associated with a negative family experience, or in the mentality and customs of a society and a culture in which women had almost no rights and were completely subordinated to men, or in the influence that ancient wisdom exercised in his work.[61] Could it be that Ben Sira was interested in maintaining this position and therefore instilled this attitude in his young disciples? In the end, they would be responsible for transmitting it to new generations, that is, perpetuating it among their people. Ben Sira was not the only Jewish sage in second-century-BCE Jerusalem. In fact, he represents a collective, a group or school of wisdom that was confronted with others who advocated different and even contradictory ideas, such as the Enochic circles. He was also confronted with the progress of Hellenism and proposed his alternative.[62] As I mentioned in the introduction, Ben Sira did not adopt a polemical approach against Hellenistic culture and philosophy but a concilia-

---

60. Hilaire Duesberg and Irenée Fransen, eds., *Ecclesiastico* (La Sacra Bibbia volgata latina e traduzione italiana dai testi originali illustrate con note critiche e commentate a cura di Mons. Salvatore Garofalo. Antico Testamento sotto la direzione di P. Giovanni Rinaldi C.R.S.; Torino/Rome: Marietti, 1966), 50.

61. See Silvia Schroer, *Wisdom Has Built Her House: Studies on the Figure of Sophia in the Bible* (trans. Linda Maloney; Collegeville, Minn.: Liturgical, 2000), 84–97, 85–86.

62. Calduch-Benages, "Absence of Named Women," 312–13.

tory one. From the beginning to the end of his book, he maintains an impressive balance through the use of pondered expressions, opportune omissions, implicit allusions, and fine irony. His main aim is to transmit the true wisdom (fear of the Lord, love for the law, and the tradition) to the new generations in such a way that the young disciples recognize themselves in the shared past and assume it as part of their identity. With respect to women (wives), the sage does not make any concession. A change, however small, in favor of women would have shaken the patriarchal system that protected him, and that would have been too dangerous. One who loses control loses his power.

Part 3
Women's Voices and Female Metaphors in Poetic Texts

Ancient Near Eastern Pictures as Keys to Biblical Metaphors

Silvia Schroer

Relations between ancient Near Eastern art and biblical texts are not only of interest for gender research. It is generally illuminative to analyze such interrelations in order to precisely locate a literary motif or theme with regard to the history of religion or theology and to better understand the proposition of the biblical text. Gender research in theology and exegesis particularly requires extrabiblical sources that provide information about women's history or the development of religious ideas and help to identify androcentric perspectives of biblical texts. This essay does not aim at illustrating the reality behind biblical texts, so-called *Realienkunde*, although it may be legitimate and important, for instance, to relate the scenes on the field in the book of Ruth with Egyptian depictions of impoverished women who collect corn stalks behind the mowers (fig. 1).[1] This image from Egypt illustrates a social reality similar to the one in the book of Ruth. Registering such depictions enhances our knowledge of actual life in ancient cultures. Yet there is no inner or closer relationship between the book of Ruth and the Egyptian image. For the themes selected in this essay, however, there are interrelations between textual and iconographic traditions, which result from a shared cultural treasure trove of motifs and thus are similar to a citation: A given text may cite an iconographic tradition. Within the כתובים, the Writings, such interrelations especially exist for the poetic books such as Psalms, wisdom books, and the Song of Songs; their metaphors open a window to the iconographic traditions of Palestine/Israel and its neighboring cultures at every turn; or rather, these metaphors are more comprehensible if viewed in light of iconographic motifs.[2] In contrast to the

---

1. All illustrations of this essay are reproduced by courtesy of the Bibel + Orient Museum Fribourg, Switzerland.

2. The interrelations between iconography and biblical texts are summarized in each volume of the standard work of Silvia Schroer and Othmar Keel, *Die Ikonographie Palästi-*

Fig. 1. Wall painting of the tomb of Menna (ca. 1400 BCE). During the harvest of barley in the fields, Menna, who sits in a hut, supervises the workers. Poor, naked women, who glean, get into a fight (Staubli, *Begleiter*, fig. 12).

books of the Torah, the Writings more often reveal relations between texts and pictures along a broader range of themes and motif sets.

Metaphors in the Psalms at large, for instance, constitute a reception and actualization of ancient Near Eastern iconography since the Psalter as a corpus is a repository of this tradition's iconographic symbolism.[3] Many metaphors that are used in Israel's language of prayer are hardly comprehensible without this background. In many cases, gender issues are implied with regard to images of both humanity and divinity.[4] And in terms of creation theology, the Psalms offer many astonishing impulses that are also relevant for gender issues (Ps 8; 104).[5] Ancient Israel's attitude toward mortality and

nas/Israels und der Alte Orient: Eine Religionsgeschichte in Bildern (*IPIAO*), vol. 1, *Vom ausgehenden Mesolithikum bis zur Frühbronzezeit*, 2005; Silvia Schroer, vol. 2, *Mittelbronzezeit* (2008); Silvia Schroer, vol. 3, *Spätbronzezeit* (2011) (Fribourg: Academic Press); in the following cited as *IPIAO* 1, 2, 3.

3. See the standard work by Othmar Keel, *The Symbolism of the Biblical World: Ancient Near Eastern Iconography and the Book of Psalms* (trans. Timothy J. Hallett; Winona Lake, Ind.: Eisenbrauns, 1997).

4. For obvious and hidden feminine images of the divine, see Othmar Keel, *Gott weiblich: Eine verborgene Seite des biblischen Gottes* (Liebefeld: Bibel + Orient Museum, 2008).

5. See Othmar Keel and Silvia Schroer, *Schöpfung: Biblische Theologien im Kontext altorientalischer Religionen* (2nd ed.; Fribourg: Universitätsverlag; Göttingen: Vandenhoeck & Ruprecht, 2008). The entire topic of animals in the biblical tradition opens

death, recorded throughout the Hebrew Bible, and especially in the Psalms as well as in Qoheleth (3:19–21), offers a truly tangible challenge for feminist theology. However, not only the Psalms are rich in iconographic concepts.

The divine speeches in the book of Job are based on iconographic motifs such as the "master of animals" or the battle of Horus against hippopotamus (Behemoth) and crocodile (Leviathan). At first sight, the significance of creation theology linked to these motifs for feminist issues seems hardly evident. Closer inspection, however, reveals how critical this model is to the concepts of creation in Gen 1 and 2, because it does not define humans as the rule or as all creation's crowning glory.[6] The Song of Songs enriches the experience and portrayals of the two lovers with images that convey divine beauty and agency; these icons are fed by venerable images of gods and goddesses both of the Near East and Egypt.[7] This book was originally a collection of songs of longing and love from Palestine/Israel. In terms of genre, these songs are closely linked to love lyrics of the Egyptian New Kingdom. Although these songs may have been cheerfully sung at weddings, they are not proper wedding songs. The relationship between the man and the woman is situated beyond or at the margin of societal norms and to some extent only in wishful fantasy. Thus it comes close to the initial relation of man and woman in paradise, described in Gen 2 beyond or before the liabilities of reality like the founding of a family, the raising of children, and matrimonial norms. In Gen 2, man and woman have a relationship as equal partners. There are images of a human pair in ancient art from the Middle Bronze Age, which demonstrate that there was the experience of equality between the sexes besides and despite a patriarchal and hierarchical social order.

The themes and motifs of Hebrew love songs are saturated with images and metaphors that are partly of Egyptian origin and partly based on the treasure of Near Eastern motifs. Especially the beloved woman in the songs often mirrors the goddesses of Palestine/Israel, as well as Syria, Anatolia, and—less frequently—Egypt. The oscillating form of the divine appears to

---

fresh approaches to the perception of humanity and the world with interesting gender aspects; see Silvia Schroer, *Die Tiere in der Bibel: Eine kulturgeschichtliche Reise* (Freiburg: Herder, 2010).

6. Christl M. Maier und Silvia Schroer, "Job: Questioning the Book of the Righteous Sufferer," in *Feminist Biblical Interpretation: A Compendium of Critical Commentary on the Books of the Bible and Related Literature* (ed. Luise Schottroff and Marie-Theres Wacker; Grand Rapids: Eerdmans, 2012), 221–39.

7. Othmar Keel, *Deine Blicke sind Tauben: Zur Metaphorik des Hohen Liedes* (SBS 114/115; Stuttgart: Katholisches Bibelwerk, 1984); Keel, *The Song of Songs: A Continental Commentary* (trans. Frederick J. Gaiser; Minneapolis: Fortress, 1994).

have motivated early on an understanding of the texts in terms of an encounter between heaven and earth, transcendence and immanence. Eroticism encompasses a cosmic and a religious dimension that is fed by anterior ideas manifest in ancient art.[8]

The Writings date partly to the postexilic and even the early Hellenistic era. Thus in particular cases, the time lag between the mythological traditions and the actual art, to which the metaphors revert, may be immense. The "master of animals," a figure of ancient Near Eastern iconography attested constantly as early as the third millennium BCE certainly constitutes the backdrop of the divine imagery in Job 39. In this specific case it is evident that the motif was still in use in contemporary, that is, Persian-period, glyptic and that it is also attested in the glyptic of Palestine/Israel. It is therefore safe to assume that the authors of the book of Job knew this image and actual artifacts from their own experience. One cannot reconstruct such a complete "chain" of a motif in all cases, however. The "playful" wisdom figure in Prov 8:22–31, for instance, traces back to "role models" in Syrian and Egyptian art. Yet exactly which depictions the authors of this text had in mind and whether they knew them from their own experience cannot be reconstructed anymore. In the ancient Near East, traditions of art were shaped by handcraft tradition and thus were stable not only for centuries but also for millennia. Sometimes we only have two loose ends in hand, an icon and a biblical motif or a metaphor without really knowing the way of transmission from one to the other. Nevertheless, it would be nonsensical to rule out any relation just because some elements are lacking in the chain of tradition. Similarly, literary connections, such as the one between the book of Job and the Mesopotamian precursors of the "suffering servant" or the one between Prov 22:17–23:11 and the Egyptian Instruction of Amenemope cannot be disputed categorically even if the way of transmission cannot always be reconstructed satisfactorily.[9] Constellations of motifs like the "master of animals" or the "woman at the window" are generally more suitable to secure the way of tradition than one isolated icon like a sole branch. The idea that the scribes or groups of authors to which we owe particular psalms or the Song of Songs or the book of Proverbs would sit at their desks and understand a metaphorical statement such as "the persons who pray take refuge in the shadow

---

8. Martti Nissinen, "Song of Songs and Sacred Marriage," in *Sacred Marriages: The Divine-Human Sexual Metaphor from Sumer to Early Christianity* (ed. Martti Nissinen and Risto Uro; Winona Lake, Ind.: Eisenbrauns, 2008), 173–218.

9. Bernd U. Schipper, "Die Lehre des Amenemope und Prov 22,17–24,22—eine Neubestimmung des literarischen Verhältnisses (Part 1)," *ZAW* 117 (2005): 53–72; Part 2, *ZAW* 117 (2005): 232–48.

of God's wings" (see Ps 38:7) *only* metaphorically, that is, that they would neither know the mythological or iconographic reference nor aim at evoking it in their audience, projects modern notions of text production onto the ancient world and does not sufficiently accommodate the Hebrew language's closeness to images. Each metaphor in a psalm—for instance, "God is a midwife" (Ps 22:10–11)—evoked a world of ideas that was sustained by myths, cult, mental images, and literary metaphors. It is anachronistic to postulate "pure" metaphors, namely, figures of speech that would not reactivate the mythological-imaginary background.

The following selection of examples is oriented toward groups of motifs and metaphors with iconological backgrounds which are either central or used repeatedly in the כתובים, the Writings, and which are relevant to feminist or gender issues. To a large extent, we will deal with perceptions of the divine and images of gods or goddesses respectively.

1. Images of Confidence: God's Caring Qualities

1.1. Pregnancy, Birth, and Mother-Child Relationship

Hebrew anthropology devotes much attention to the fact that humans are born.[10] To be born of a woman is a basic datum of being human. In manifold ways, being born is related to the presence and acting of the divine. Israel's God participates in the development of the embryo in the womb, assists the child's coming to light in the birthing process, and places the newborn at its mother's breast. For women in ancient cultures, such divine assistance during pregnancy and birth was essential. Their pleas for a smooth birth and life for the mother, the newborns, and infants have been perpetuated in myriads of votive figurines (figs. 2–3).

> Yet it was you who drew me from the womb;
> you kept me safe on my mother's breast.

---

10. [Translator's note: The author uses the German term *Geburtlichkeit*, which can hardly be translated into English.] See also Silvia Schroer, "Ancient Near Eastern Pictures as Keys to Biblical Texts," in *Torah* (ed. Irmtraud Fischer et al.; The Bible and Women: An Encyclopaedia of Exegesis and Cultural History 1.1; Atlanta: Society of Biblical Literature, 2011), 31–60; 44–46. For the topic of birth in the Hebrew Bible, see Detlef Dieckmann and Dorothea Erbele-Küster, eds., *Du hast mich aus meiner Mutter Leib gezogen: Beiträge zur Geburt im Alten Testament* (Neukirchen-Vluyn: Neukirchener, 2006); Marianne Grohmann, *Fruchtbarkeit und Geburt in den Psalmen* (FAT 53; Tübingen: Mohr Siebeck, 2007).

> On you I was cast from the womb,
> and from my mother's belly you have been my God. (Ps 22:10–11)[11]

In Ps 131, the praying person compares the existential orientation of the child, which she carries in her arms, with her own mental state with regard to YHWH.[12] The image of an infant at its mother's breast symbolizes satiation, peace, and security.

> Like a weaned child on/with its mother;
> like the weaned child on/with me—is my נפש. (Ps 131:2)

Psalm 139:15 suggests that an individual is "woven" in the earth and born by mother Earth. At the same time, however, it is YHWH, Israel's God, who creates the human being in the womb. According to ancient Israelite imagination, a mother's womb is associated with the womb of the earth, and thus the human being will return naked "there," that is, into the motherly earth (Job 1:21; Sir 40:1). This set of metaphors is distinctive insofar as Israelite cosmology and theology of creation are generally reluctant to deal with biological ideas of development and becoming.[13] In Ps 90:2 the birth imagery is transferred even to the mountains and earth, which are said to be born by God (cf. Prov 8:22–23). Deuteronomy 32:18 commemorates God's labor pains during the birth of an individual.[14]

In Palestine/Israel, depictions of mother and child are attested only since the early Iron period (ca. 1100 BCE), more frequently in the Persian period (sixth–fifth century BCE; see figs. 4–6). The "mother and child" icon has an almost divine aura—similar to the "cow and calf" motif that also symbolizes divine care[15]—and replaces an icon attested in the polytheistic religions since the third millennium, namely, the image of the royal child sucking at his

---

11. [Translator's note: Because the author translated the biblical passages herself, the English wording of the NRSV has been adapted accordingly. The verse numbers always follow the Masoretic Text; sometimes NRSV differs by one number.]

12. Erich Zenger, "'Wie das Kind bei mir...': Das weibliche Gottesbild von Ps 131," in *"Gott bin ich, kein Mann": Beiträge zur Hermeneutik der biblischen Gottesrede: FS für Helen Schüngel-Straumann zum 65. Geburtstag* (ed. Ilona Riedel-Spangenberger and Erich Zenger; Paderborn: Schöningh, 2006), 177–95.

13. See Keel and Schroer, *Schöpfung*, 108–21.

14. A woman's womb receives special dignity because God himself is struck with רחמים, "compassion," which is situated in the uterus. From the womb emerge life and the ability for empathy, which protects and preserves everything that is alive. See Silvia Schroer and Thomas Staubli, *Body Symbolism in the Bible* (trans. Linda M. Maloney; Collegeville, Minn.: Liturgical, 2001), 68–82.

15. See Schroer, "Ancient Near Eastern Pictures," 53, figs. 26–27.

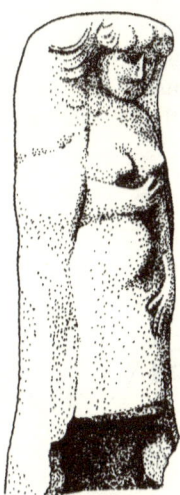

Fig. 2. Terracotta figure from northern Israel or Phoenicia (six–fifth century BCE). From the Persian period on, women were depicted as pregnant, naked, or clothed with a wrap, or as nursing a child. In earlier periods, pregnancy is denoted, if at all, only discretely (Keel and Schroer, *Schöpfung*, fig. 76).

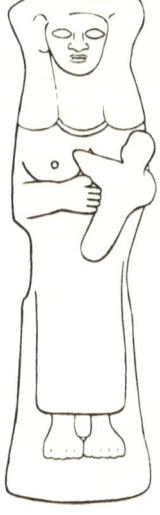

Fig. 3. Cypriot terracotta of a woman with a child, from Kition/Larnaca (probably sixth century BCE) (Winter, *Frau und Göttin*, fig. 385).

Fig. 4. Fragmentary terracotta figure from Beth Shean (early Iron Age, 1100–1000 BCE). A woman adorned with bracelet, belt, crossband over the chest, and necklace holds a child in her arm, who faces the viewer. Due to its composure the child is a toddler rather than a baby or newborn (Winter, *Frau und Göttin*, fig. 57).

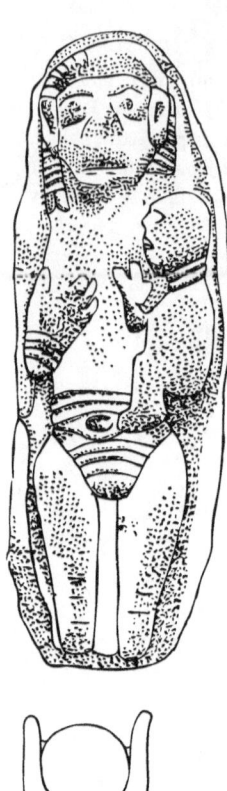

Fig. 5. Terracotta figure of a woman with dressed hair, clothed only with a belt, who holds a child on her arm, from Pella in Jordan (ninth century BCE) (sketch by Ulrike Zurkinden-Kolberg after Potts et al., "Preliminary Report," 141, with pl. 22.3).

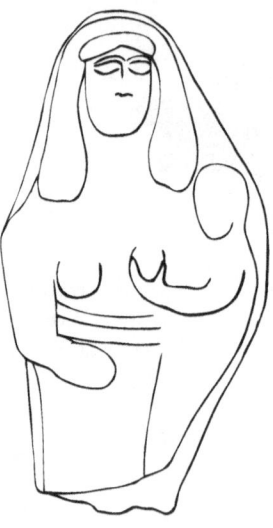

Fig. 6. Phoenician terracotta of a woman with child from Tell Zippor (fifth century BCE) (Urs Winter, *Frau und Göttin*, fig. 60).

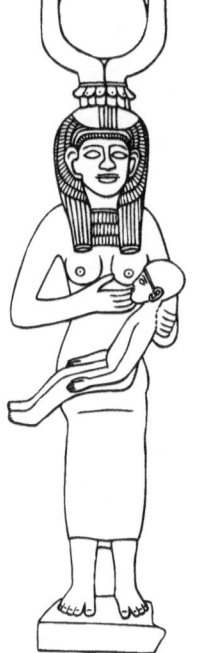

Fig. 7. Egyptian bronze figure of Isis with a child (sixth–fifth century BCE). The goddess here is crowned, as often, with cow horns and sun disk, which is rather typical for the goddess Hathor (Winter, *Frau und Göttin*, fig. 405).

ANCIENT NEAR EASTERN PICTURES

Fig. 8. Amulet from Megiddo (ca. 1000 BCE). The amulet depicts the goddess Isis nursing the Horus child. Connected to this image is the entire mythological story of Horus, begotten by the reanimated Osiris, conceived and born by Isis, chased by Seth, saved and protected by Isis. From this image of a protective and powerful goddess, women expect assistance for themselves and their child (Hermann, *Ägyptische Amulette*, no. 42).

Fig. 9. Silver pendant from Ugarit (fourteenth–thirteenth century BCE). In this heavily schematized picture of a goddess, the vulva, connected to fertility by a twig, small breasts, and the face are emphasized. The beautiful, Hathor-like goddess is kindly facing the viewer; hairstyle and necklace are especially accentuated as well as the ears that are almost oversized and not hidden by the big curls (Schroer, *IPIAO* 3, no. 839)

divine mother's breast.[16] In Egyptian iconography, the image of Isis breastfeeding Horus on her lap occurs since the Third Intermediate period (from 1070 BCE); the icon enjoyed great popularity also in Palestine/Israel (figs. 7–8). Although this mother and child are mythic and royal figures, Isis and her child play an important role also in the piety of the common population.

As essential as being fed at a mother's breast is the experience of being viewed, or facing someone kindly.[17] In the Psalms, the benevolent face of God is a recurrent motif of prayer language (Ps 17:15; 31:17; 41:13; 104:29). The metaphor is based on images of goddesses, more rarely gods, who face their

---

16. See ibid., 51, fig. 23.
17. See ibid., 55, figs. 32–33.

followers kindly. In Palestine/Israel, it is the indigenous earth and vegetation goddess who faces her devotees benevolently. Moreover, she has big ears in order to hear their concerns (see Ps 130:2) and to answer their prayers (see fig. 9 above). Thus in the gender-neutral metaphors of biblical texts, sometimes gendered signs of the history of religion are supplied.

1.2. "In the Shadow of your Wings"

> How precious is your steadfast love, O God!
> All people take refuge in the shadow of your wings. (Ps 36:8)

> You who live in the shelter of the Most High,
> who abide in the shadow of the Almighty,
> will say to YHWH:
> My refuge and my fortress;
> my God, in whom I trust!
> For he will deliver you from the snare of the fowler,
> from the deadly pestilence;
> with his pinions he will cover you,
> and under his wings you will find refuge ...
> You need not fear.... (Ps 91:1–5*)

The yearning of the psalmists to take refuge in the shadow of God's wings is attested several times and belongs to the metaphors of security (see also Ps 17:7–9; 57:2; 61:4–5; 63:8–9).[18] In the ancient Near East, wings are associated with virility,[19] but often also with protection. First and foremost, ornithomorphic gods and goddesses have wings, for instance, in Egypt since the third millennium BCE: Horus, but also the vulture goddesses Mut and Nechbet (figs. 10–11). The goddess Maat in her feminine form often wears a vulture's wings (fig. 12). In principle, almost every goddess or god may be furnished with wings in specific roles.[20] The protégé of Egyptian winged gods

---

18. Silvia Schroer, "'Im Schatten deiner Flügel': Religionsgeschichtliche und feministische Blicke auf die Metaphorik der Flügel Gottes in den Psalmen, in Ex 19,4; Dtn 32,11 und in Mal 3,20," in *"Ihr Völker alle, klatscht in die Hände!": FS für Erhard S. Gerstenberger zum 65. Geburtstag* (ed. Rainer Kessler et al.; Münster: LIT, 1997), 296–316.

19. Wings grow *ad libitum*, e.g., to the "master of animals," which in ancient Near Eastern glyptic appears alternately without or with wings, even with four wings. In this case, the wings express numinosity, i.e., superhuman capabilities of the depicted figure. In the Middle East, Ishtar appears winged already on seals of the third millennium, although the aspect of protection is missing.

20. On scarabs of the fifth and fourth century BCE, even Isis enthroned with a child occasionally appears winged; see Othmar Keel and Christoph Uehlinger, *Gods, Goddesses,*

Fig. 10. Granite statue from Tanis (time of Ramses II, 1279–1213 BCE). In the Egyptian delta, the god Horon, originally a Canaanite god of the netherworld, is portrayed as a falcon, like Horus. Here, he protects Pharaoh Ramses II, who is depicted as a child (Schroer, *IPIAO* 3, no. 689).

Fig. 11. Golden pectoral (breast decoration) with inlays of lapis lazuli and glass, from the mummy of Tutankhamun, Valley of the Kings (1333–1323 BCE). From the Old Kingdom on the griffon vulture represents the goddesses Nechbet and Mut, sometimes also Nut. The vulture goddess with the two Shen-rings, symbols of protection, accompanied the kings during life and death (Schroer, *IPIAO* 3, no. 732).

Fig. 12. Counterweight of a pectoral, made of gold, silver, and colored glass inlays, from the tomb of Tutankh-amun, Valley of the Kings (1333–1323 BCE). Exceptionally, the goddess Maat here stands not behind but before the enthroned king in order to protect him with her wings (Schroer, *IPIAO* 3, no. 699).

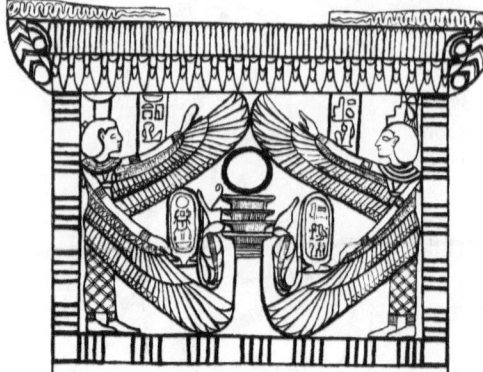

Fig. 13. Pectoral of quartz, with inlays of glass and gold, from the tomb of Tutankhamun, Valley of the Kings (1333–1323 BCE). Osiris's sisters Isis and Nephthys protect with their wings the djed-pillar that represents Osiris (Schroer, *IPIAO* 3, no. 795).

Fig. 14. Carved ivory plaque from Samaria (ninth–eighth century BCE). The kneeling goddesses at the djed-pillar of Osiris are no longer marked by their traditional symbols as Isis and Nephthys, but wear sun-disks on their heads (Keel and Uehlinger, *Gods, Goddesses, and Images of God*, fig. 243).

is initially the king, or with regard to Isis, the god Osiris. As the deceased identify with Osiris, the idea that one may find refuge under the wings of goddesses like Isis, Nephthys, or Nut, becomes popular (figs. 13–14). Also the protective deity Bes is often depicted as winged. Scholars discuss whether the image of God's wings in the Psalms is based on zoomorphic images of the divine, namely, ornithomorphic ones, or whether it refers to the rather vivid view of a big bird's wings in relation to an anthropomorphic, perhaps even gynomorphic, figure.[21] A further possibility of association pertains to the sphere of winged sun-disks, which have a long tradition in Egypt and Middle Asia. It is hardly feasible to fully prescind from these original vehicles of images. In Exod 19:4 and Deut 32:11, too, YHWH introduces himself as a vulture that cares for his offspring.[22]

---

and Images of God in Ancient Israel (trans. Allan W. Mahnke; Minneapolis: Fortress, 1996), fig. 363b.

21. Joel M. LeMon, *Yahweh's Winged Form in the Psalms: Exploring Congruent Iconography and Texts* (OBO 242; Fribourg: Academic Press; Göttingen: Vandenhoeck & Ruprecht, 2010).

22. See Schroer, "Ancient Near Eastern Pictures," 50–53.

2. Theology of Creation:
God as "Master of Animals"

Reading the book of Job from a feminist perspective poses many challenges.[23] The main protagonists of this book are male; women have only supporting roles, even if these are significant. In the frame narrative, God and Satan, one of the divine sons, appear on stage. In the dialogue sections, Job and his three, later four, friends alternate as speakers, and finally, God appears. The interpretation of God's speeches is highly significant for the exegesis of the entire book. Othmar Keel offered a groundbreaking interpretation of these chapters through his analysis of the motifs of the "master of animals" and *Chaoskampf* ("the struggle against chaos"), against Behemoth and Leviathan in Job 39–41.[24] After introducing himself by traditional motifs such as the creator of the cosmos in chapter 38, God presents himself as shepherd and master of animals of the wilderness in Job 38:39–39:30. Five pairs of animals are listed here as examples of divine care and sovereignty: lion and raven, wild goat and deer, wild ass and wild bull, ostrich and war horse, a bird of prey and the griffin vulture. God cares for the wild animals;[25] he controls them and their world, which is not subjugated to and uninhabitable for humans. The same ten animals that are mentioned in the second part of the first divine speech are attested in ancient Near Eastern iconography in connection with a male figure. In a dominant gesture, a nude hero, a winged, numinous figure or a (Persian) king seize in their right and left hand lions, goats, ostriches, and so forth on the neck or the hind legs (figs. 15–16). The animals, too, may be winged, a feature that clearly emphasizes the scene's mythical dimension. The master of animals is a quasi-divine figure that represents supremacy over chaos. Judean stamp seals showing a "master of ostriches" and "master of wild goats" (figs. 17–18) attest that these local variants of the figure were venerated in the region as favorites, which may even represent an authentic divine image linked to the deity YHWH.[26] The book of Job unfolds this icon, which is attested from the third millennium for almost two thousand years in both the Near East and the Aegean, in a narrative way. In contrast to the creation

---

23. See Maier and Schroer, "Job."

24. Othmar Keel, *Jahwes Entgegnung an Ijob: Eine Deutung von Ijob 38–41 vor dem Hintergrund der zeitgenössischen Bildkunst* (FRLANT 121; Göttingen: Vandenhoeck & Ruprecht, 1978).

25. Only the horse does not represent the chaotic antiworld that accompanies creation, but a hostile world of war and dominance created by humans.

26. Othmar Keel, *Die Geschichte Jerusalems und die Entstehung des Monotheismus* (OLB 4/1; Göttingen: Vandenhoeck & Ruprecht, 2007), 205–11.

Fig. 15. Middle Assyrian cylinder seal (fourteenth–eleventh century BCE). A "master of animals," with face and upper part of the body in frontal position, seizes with his left and right hand two wild goats or ibexes at their horns, thus pulling them off the stylized tree, on which they straighten up to eat its leaves. The animal world, the wilderness, is thus kept in check in favor of the ordered world (Keel and Schroer, *Schöpfung*, fig. 156).

Fig. 16. Neo-Assyrian cylinder seal (ninth–seventh century BCE). A four-winged "master of animals" seizes two erect wild bulls at one front leg each. The wings underline the potency of the divine hero. He, too, seems to pull the wild animals off a stylized palm tree that symbolizes the ordered world (Keel and Schroer, *Schöpfung*, fig. 157).

story in Gen 1–2, the theology of creation in these divine speeches does not focus on humanity. God turns out to be the master and shepherd of the entire creation. The wild animals accomplish nothing for humans and are said to have an independent existence, similar to Ps 104. God also feeds the wild goats and other animals that have their own habitats and a right to live independently of and without being exposed to human domination. Even if at first sight the image of a hero who dominates the animals may hardly be attractive for a feminist approach, it offers some important clues for the specific understanding of creation and Creator in the wisdom writings.

Fig. 17. Scaraboid from Beth Shemesh (ca. 1000 BCE). A strongly schematized Judean "master of animals" seizes two ostriches (Keel and Schroer, *Schöpfung*, fig. 162).

Fig. 18. Stamp seal impression from Dan (early Iron Age, 980–840 BCE). A "master of animals" seizes two wild goats by the neck and pulls them backward (Keel, *Corpus*, Dan no. 6).

3. Images of Women—Images of Goddesses

The suppression of the goddesses in the religious symbol system of the southern Levant sets in already under Egyptian hegemony in the Late Bronze Age, that is, in the second half of the second millennium BCE.[27] Fighting, bellicose, mostly male gods dominate the repertoire of images. The presence of goddesses is more frequently only hinted at by "representatives" such as the branch, the goats at the tree, the dove, and so forth. The goddesses are no longer represented in full figures and less often on precious material. This trend continued during the following centuries, when the states Israel and Judah, later on Judah alone, existed. In the eighth to the sixth century BCE, however, there was a revival of full-figured goddesses in terracotta art.

Apparently, the veneration of a local goddess did not cease until the exilic period. By polemical renunciation the biblical texts attest to cults for Asherah or the Queen of Heaven and demonstrate that these were not marginal phenomena. At the same time, the worship of YHWH was able to copiously absorb and integrate important traditions of the goddesses' heritage. Part of this legacy was integrated into ideas about Israel's God and the divine wisdom figure. Another part remained alive when experience of the divine in creation and love was expressed by the venerable images of the cults for goddesses. A third part was taken up in images and roles of women in Israel. As Urs Winter has demonstrated,[28] images of women and images of goddesses often come

---

27. For more details, see Keel and Uehlinger, *Gods, Goddesses, and Images of God*.
28. Urs Winter, *Frau und Göttin: Exegetische und ikonographische Studien zum weibli-*

very close to each other. Every woman could try to resemble the goddess by imitating her (*imitatio deae*).

In ancient art, the goddesses of the Levant are not labeled by crowns, scepters, clothing, or symbols as goddesses like the Egyptian or Mesopotamian deities. The tendency of similarity thus is effective in both directions, a phenomenon that may be related to the idea of humans being created in the likeness of God (Gen 1:28). In the biblical text, such likeness is stated for both sexes.

Clay figurines from Mesopotamia, Syria, and Palestine/Israel emphasize the same body parts as the description of the woman in the Song of Songs, for instance, the navel (Song 7:3), the proudly cherished breasts (8:8–10), or the proud, towering neck adorned by necklaces (4:4; 7:5) and beautiful hair (fig. 19).

3.1. The Long Life of the Twig and Tree Goddesses

The earth and vegetation goddess of Middle Bronze Age Palestine/Israel (1750–1550 BCE) is characterized by twigs. This main attribute would play a role in the country's iconography and history of religion for centuries. The mighty tree is named in Hebrew אלה, "goddess" (fig. 20). In the books of Proverbs and Psalms, the tree of life often appears, to which also divine wisdom is compared.

> She is a tree of life to those who grasp her;
> whoever holds on to her can be called happy. (Prov 3:18)

Grasping and holding onto a palm tree or a stylized tree is a frequent motif in glyptic art (figs. 21–22). Whoever holds on to twigs or branches grasps the life that they symbolize. In Sirach one finds the phrase:

> To fear YHWH is the root of wisdom, and her branches are long life. (Sir 1:20)

Not only the Levantine tradition of the goddess's twigs and mighty trees, but also the palm tree, which is widespread and popular in Mesopotamia and Egypt, has left traces in biblical metaphors.

> How fair you are, how beautiful!
> O Love, with all its rapture!

---

chen Gottesbild im Alten Israel und in dessen Umwelt (2nd ed.; OBO 53; Fribourg: Universitätsverlag; Göttingen: Vandenhoeck & Ruprecht, 1987).

Your stately form is like the palm;
your breasts are like clusters of dates.
I say: I will climb the palm, take hold of its branches;
Then your breasts will be like clusters of grapes,
your breath like the fragrance of apples,
and your palate like choicest wine
that goes down smoothly to my caresses,
gliding over the lips of sleepers. (Song 7:7–10)

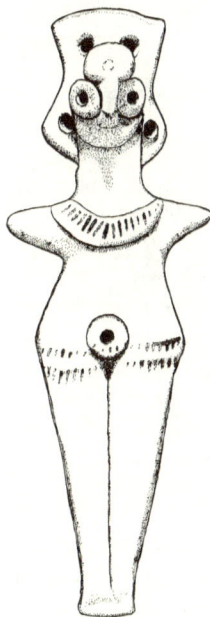

Fig. 19. Terracotta from the Levant (1900–1600 BCE). Peculiar of this small figurine are the skillful headdress, necklace and hips, accentuated eyes, and the big navel, whereas breasts, face, and arms were not modeled. The ears may originally have carried rings (Schroer, *IPIAO* 2, no. 395).

Fig. 20. Fragmentary clay pitcher from Lachish (end of thirteenth century BCE). The inscription reads "donation, a gift for my mistress ʾelat [i.e., the goddess]"; the word ʾelat is written directly above a tree that is flanked by horned animals (Schroer, *IPIAO* 3, no. 852).

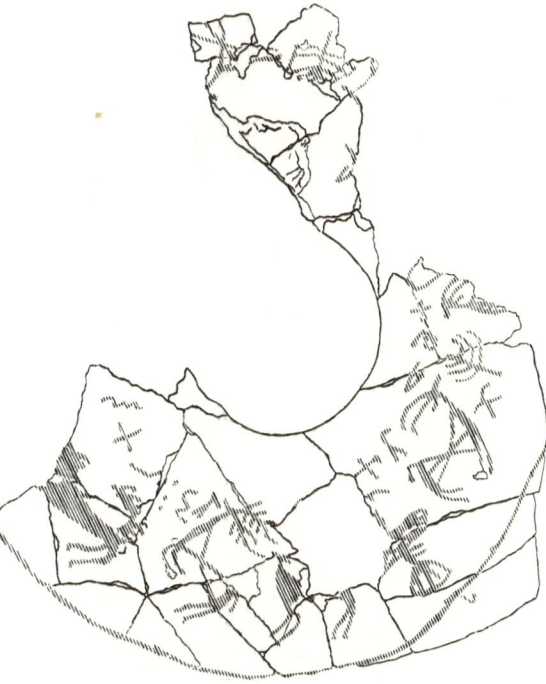

Fig. 21. Scarab from Sichem (seventeenth–sixteenth century BCE). Two kneeling female worshipers hold or touch a big branch or little tree; above them a goddess fetish that represents the twig goddess of Palestine/Israel, but here is shown in the Egyptian context of the veneration of Hathor with uraei, Horus falcon, and the hieroglyphic sign for "gold." (Schroer, *IPIAO* 2, no. 418).

Fig. 22. Scaraboid from Ekron (seventh century BCE). A worshiper, clothed in a long robe, touches a tree with one hand while he seems to carry a donation in his other hand (Keel, *Corpus* 2, no. 51).

The comparison of the woman with a palm that nourishes and brings forth delicious fruits traces back to primarily Mesopotamian iconographic traditions in which the goddess Ishtar was associated with date palms already in the third millennium (fig. 23). Centuries later, big date palms stood in the courtyard of the Ishtar temple at Mari (fig. 24). The association of the date palm with breasts is found, even if rarely, in the glyptic art of the first millennium BCE (fig. 25).

In the book of Ben Sira (Sirach) wisdom is influenced less by the idea of the tree of life,[29] but is characterized as tree goddess who offers food and drink. The person who seeks wisdom's company is praised.

---

29. For this topic see Urs Winter, "Der 'Lebensbaum' in der altorientalischen Bildsymbolik," in … *Bäume braucht man doch: Das Symbol des Baumes zwischen Hoffnung und Zerstörung* (ed. Harald Schweizer; Sigmaringen: Thorbecke, 1986), 57–88; Winter, "Der stilisierte Baum: Zu einem auffälligen Aspekt altorientalischer Baumsymbolik und seiner Rezeption im Alten Testament," *Bibel und Kirche* 41 (1986): 171–77.

Fig. 23. Cylinder seal of the Akkadian period (ca. 2300–2200 BCE). A praying person is lead in front of the enthroned goddess Ishtar. Left of this "initiation scene" are two women plucking dates from a palm. While the goddess is depicted in her warrior robe, the date palm refers to her nourishing aspects (Schroer and Keel, *IPIAO* 1, no. 260).

Fig. 24. Colored wall painting from the palace of Mari (1800 BCE). The image is located to the right of the entrance to the throne room and shows the temple of Ishtar, in which the ruler of Mari and the goddess Ishtar meet. The temple is located in a huge park with stylized trees and date palms. Two men climb each of the palms' slim trunks (for harvesting or fertilizing?). In the preserved crown of the palm to the right a white dove starts to fly off (Schroer, *IPIAO* 2, no. 434).

Fig. 25. Relief from Karatepe (ca. 700 BCE). Under a date palm, a woman, either queen, royal wet nurse, or goddess, presents her breast to a child, probably a prince. As on older Egyptian pictures of this type, the heir to the throne sucks while standing (Winter, *Frau und Göttin*, fig. 411).

> Happy is the person who meditates on wisdom and reasons intelligently, ...
> who builds his nest in her leaves,
> and lodges under her boughs;
> who is covered by her shade from the heat,
> and dwells in her shelters.
> Whoever fears YHWH will do this,
> and whoever holds to the law will obtain wisdom.
> She will come to meet him like a mother,
> and like a young bride she will welcome him.
> She will feed him with the bread of learning,
> and give him the water of wisdom to drink. (Sir 14:20, 26–15:3)

Divine Wisdom, who manifests herself in an abundance of trees in the book of Ben Sira, extends an invitation.

> Come to me, you who desire me,
> and eat your fill of my fruits.
> For the memory of me is sweeter than honey,
> and the possession of me sweeter than the honeycomb.
> Those who eat of me will hunger for more,
> and those who drink of me will thirst for more. (Sir 24:19–21)

While the Canaanite tradition of the goddesses of the earth and vegetation may be in the background of this invitation, the mention of feeding and giving

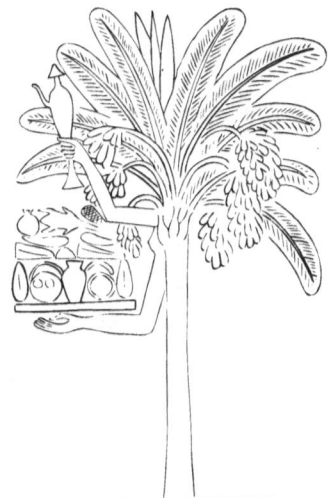

Fig. 26 (left). Relief from Abusir in Egypt (thirteenth century BCE). In this case the date palm is presented with only human arms and hands that hold a tablet with food and a jug. In most images of this type, also the upper part of the body and the head of the goddess are visible in the treetop (Winter, *Frau und Göttin*, fig. 464).

Fig. 27 (right). Painting from the tomb of Pashedu in Der el-Medineh (ca. 1100 BCE). The deceased kneels in the shade of a treetop, from which a goddess leans over to him offering water and bread (Winter, *Frau und Göttin*, fig. 462).

to drink explicitly refers to an Egyptian tradition. In tomb paintings of the New Kingdom starting with Thutmosis III, various goddesses appear as tree goddesses that nourish and offer shade and recreation. They lean out of the treetops in order to feed the dead. In the oldest paintings, they even present their breast; yet a dominant later variant has them offering food and drink and, as the epigrams reveal, words of invitation. Tree goddesses are often depicted as sycamores or date palms (figs. 26–27). Palms do not grow everywhere in the Levant; thus people valued them as something special and admired their impressive form. The sweet dates were extremely popular back then, especially because people neither had nor were able to produce goodies besides honey and fruit sugar. While Ben Sira probably refers to the Egyptian icon of the tree goddess, he transposes her from the context of the world of the dead to the world of the living.[30]

---

30. Silvia Schroer, "Die Zweiggöttin in Palästina/Israel: Von der Mittelbronze IIB-Zeit bis zu Jesus Sirach," in *Jerusalem: Texte—Bilder—Steine* (ed. Max Küchler and Christoph Uehlinger; NTOA 6; Göttingen: Vandenhoeck & Ruprecht, 1987), 201–25. For the continuing significance of the twigs or branches in the history of religion of Palestine/Israel, see also Thomas Staubli, "Land der sprießenden Zweige," *Bibel und Kirche* 60 (2005): 16–22.

In the Song of Songs (2:1–2, 16; 4:5; 5:13; 6:2; 7:3), the Egyptian background of the imagery of love is retrieved when the lips of the lovers or the woman's bosom are compared to a refreshing lotus plant (fig. 28). Twigs and lotus flowers are often exchangeable in Levantine art, especially in stylized presentations (figs. 29–30).

Fig. 28 (right). Egyptian faience bowl (1350–1300 BCE). Lotus flowers surround the face of the goddess Hathor. This goddess was often linked to the biotope marsh and its corresponding plants, papyrus and lotus, as well as animals, for example, ducks. The lotus is a symbol of freshness and renewed life because its flowers open up each morning in new purity (Schroer, *IPIAO* 3, no 748).

Fig. 29 (below). Drawing on a pitcher from Kuntillet Ajrud (ca. 800 BCE). Two wild goats (or ibex) straighten up to a stylized tree with lotus buds. Goats at a tree are a long-attested motif that is strongly connected to the Levantine goddesses. Here, the icon appears above a striding lion, so that the parallel to the same constellation with a full-fledged goddess (see the next figure) is obvious (Keel, *Deine Blicke sind Tauben*, fig. 107).

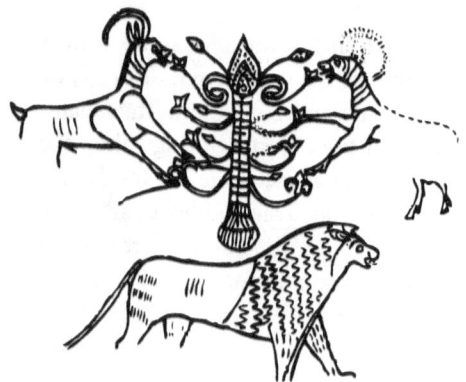

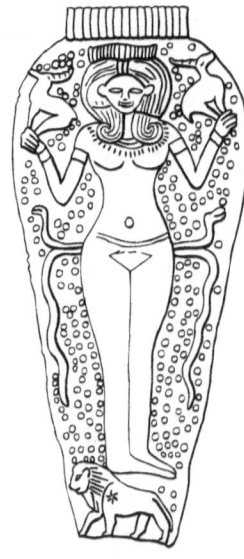

Fig. 30 (right). Golden pendant from Minet el-Beida, the port of Ugarit (ca. 1400 BCE). The nude goddess, adorned with necklaces, bracelets around arms and hips, as well as a beautiful Hathor headdress, is standing on a striding lion. Besides the wild goats that she lifts up by the hind legs, the serpents that cross behind her belong to her sphere of influence (Schroer, *IPIAO* 3, no. 859).

3.2. The Goddesses and Their Animals

Starting in the second millennium BCE, doves appear in the context of the erotic goddesses of Syria and Palestine/Israel. They stand for the love and sex appeal of the goddess; they fly as envoys to her partner, the weather-god or prince of the city, and become an emblem of love (figs. 31–33). In the poetry of the Song, the lovers' eyes with their passionate gaze are compared

Fig. 31. Classical Syrian cylinder seal (eighteenth century BCE). The Syrian goddess takes off her dress in front of an enthroned ruler of the city. Doves fly from her to her partner to underline the erotic aura of the scene, to which also the reclined hares and horned animals belong (Schroer, *IPIAO* 2, no. 439).

Fig. 32. Etruscan mirror (fifth century BCE). The dove flies from the enthroned goddess Aphrodite to her lover Adonis (Keel, *Deine Blicke sind Tauben*, fig. 53).

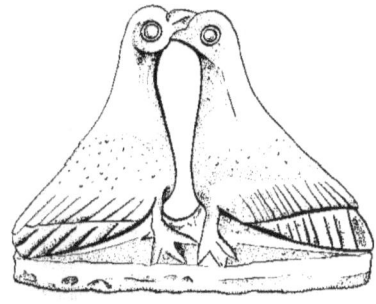

Fig. 33. Cypriot limestone figure (probably Hellenistic, third–first century BCE). Already in antiquity, the billing of the doves, which is interpreted as enamored whispering sweet nothings until today, has brought the birds close to the goddesses of love or love itself (Keel, *Deine Blicke sind Tauben*, fig. 39).

to doves—not with regard to their form or appearance but in terms of the message they deliver.

> Ah, you are beautiful, my love; ah, you are beautiful;
> your eyes are doves. (Song 1:15; cf. 4:1; 5:12)

In another verse, the beloved is addressed and named a dove.

> O my dove, in the clefts of the rock, in the covert of the cliff,
> let me see your face, let me hear your voice;
> for your voice is sweet, and your face is lovely. (Song 2:14)

Further animals that typically accompany the goddesses are gazelles, does, and wild goats (figs. 34–35). For the protection of the lovers in the Song of Songs one would swear by them—not by YHWH:

> I adjure you, O daughters of Jerusalem,
> by the gazelles or the wild does:
> do not stir up or awaken love until it pleases! (Song 2:7; cf. 3:5; 8:4)

Fig. 34. Middle Assyrian cylinder seal (thirteenth century BCE). The light-footed deer and gazelles were admired for their delicate and agile mobility. As shy animals of the wilderness, they were associated with the goddesses of love (Keel, *Deine Blicke sind Tauben*, fig. 80).

Fig. 35. Scarab of the end of the Middle or Late Bronze Age (fifteenth–fourteenth century BCE) from Tell Beit Mirsim. Reclined wild goats, in later periods very often suckling goats or ibex, evoke the sphere of the goddesses. The twigs underline this association (Schroer, *IPIAO* 2, no. 843).

ANCIENT NEAR EASTERN PICTURES

Fig. 36. Fragment of a stone vessel from southern Iraq (2400–2250 BCE). The goddess with opulent hair and a crown of horns, in which grain spikes or twigs seem to stuck, carries a date risp in her hand (Schroer and Keel, *IPIAO* 1, no. 212).

Fig. 37. Terracotta plaque from Mari (ca. 1800 BCE). The goddess Ishtar with a crossband on her chest and weapons in her hands in a classical pose places one foot on a lying lion. She is accompanied by two gods or rulers armed with axes. The entire group is standing in frontal pose on a mountain marked by a scales pattern (Schroer, *IPIAO* 2, no. 449).

The earliest types of goddesses in the Near East depict the female figure with a gorgeous tuft of curls (fig. 36). For the lover in the Song, her black hair is evocative of lively goats.

> Your hair is like a flock of goats,
> moving down the slopes of Gilead. (Song 4:1)

Like the Neolithic female figurines or the goddess Ishtar (fig. 37), the beloved woman in the Song appears in the company of lions and panthers (see §2 above), which withdraw to barren mountain regions.

> You will come with me from Lebanon, my bride;
> with me from Lebanon;
> you will depart from the peak of Amana,
> from the peak of Senir and Hermon,
> from the dens of lions,
> from the mountains of panthers. (Song 4:8)

3.3. Images of Women and Goddesses as Elements of Temple and Palace Architecture

In its description of the blessing Israel's God offers, Ps 144 compares the country's young men with well-grown trees and the young women with special elements of the splendid buildings of its time, the hall of a palace or temple.[31] It is striking that in these metaphors women are associated with architectural forms and men with plants.

> May our sons be like saplings, well-tended in their youth,
> our daughters like cornerstones trimmed to give shape to a palace. (Ps 144:12)

Equating young men or righteous persons with ever-growing trees is a frequent motif in the Hebrew Bible (Deut 20:19; Ps 1; Jer 17:8; cf. Ps 128:4; Sir 50:12). The connection between a woman and a building or the activity of building is already presupposed in Gen 2:21–22, when YHWH "builds" (Heb. בנה) the woman from the man's rib.[32] Particularly temple models from the Levant suggest a relation between female bodies and architecture. In windows and entrances of such small temples, nude women appear often like columns and seem to play, sometimes paired with lions, a role as guards (figs. 38–39). The nude female bodies at the entrance that needs to be protected may have had a "disarming" effect. They are replaced by columns or pilasters in other models (fig. 40). The hoard of clay temple models from Yavneh near Tel Aviv contains many exemplars that depict small naked female figures or stylized trees or columns/pilasters, but also goats at the tree of life or cherubim.[33]

A motif not only attested in the Writings but also in the Prophets, which corresponds with a relevant icon of ivory carving, is the "woman at the window" (Prov 7:6). In Prov 7, the seductress of a young Judean, of whom the frame of the book of Proverbs warns unrelentingly, is a married foreign woman. She is portrayed as a woman who, during her husband's absence, is up to nothing else than alluring young men into her house for a sexual adventure.

---

31. See Silvia Schroer, "Frauenkörper als architektonische Elemente: Zum Hintergrund von Ps 144,12," in *Bilder als Quellen/Images as Sources: Studies on Ancient Near Eastern Artefacts and the Bible Inspired by the Work of Othmar Keel* (OBO special edition; ed. Susanne Bickel et al.; Fribourg: Academic Press; Göttingen: Vandenhoeck & Ruprecht, 2007), 425–50.

32. In Prov 9:1, divine Wisdom "builds" her house and carves out its seven columns herself.

33. See Raz Kletter et al., *Yavneh I: The Excavation of the "Temple Hill" Repository Pit and the Cult Stands* (OBOSA 30; Fribourg: Academic Press, 2010).

Fig. 38. Fragmentary terracotta stand from Pella in Jordan (eleventh–tenth century BCE). Two nude women are flanking a window-like opening, both originally standing above a lion head, of which only one is preserved. This kind of ceramic stands evokes, like the temple models, the façade of a sanctuary (Schroer, *Images and Sources*, fig. 9).

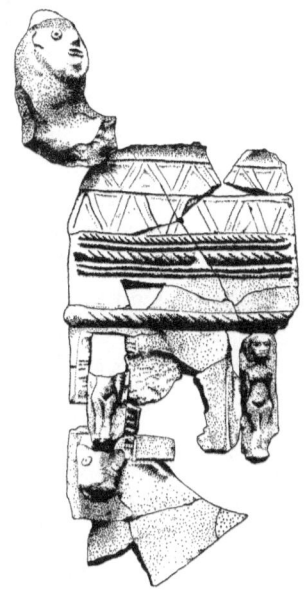

Fig. 39. Terracotta model from Kerak in Jordan (eleventh–tenth century BCE). Two nude women, adorned with rings and necklaces as well as with a beautiful headscarf, flank the entrance to the temple model. Probably they hold a tympanum in front of their left breast (Schroer, *Images and Sources*, fig. 8).

Fig. 40. Terracotta model from Tell el-Fara North (end of tenth century BCE). Instead of female figures, the model has only pilasters with volute capitals, between which a crescent moon appears (Schroer, *Images and Sources*, fig. 11).

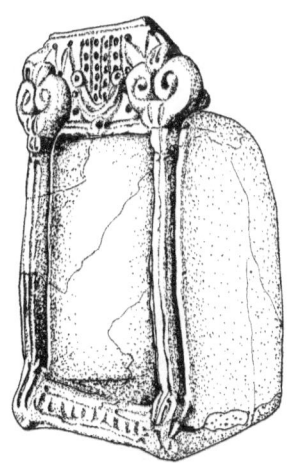

She starts her slick raid by looking out for prey at the window of her house.[34] Such an upper-class woman at the window is, however, a famous motif, especially in Phoenician ivory art of the first millennium BCE (fig. 41), but also in monumental art (fig. 42). Ivory plates with a woman, finely adorned and with dressed hair, in a frontal posture at the palace window decorate furniture and walls in the courts or the sleeping rooms of officers. It is, however, difficult to locate in detail the identity of the woman and thus the meaning of the motif. Is the woman a goddess or rather a woman who seeks to look proud and attractive like the goddess? Does the motif allude to erotic encounters, or even love for sale, or do these faces represent mainly powerful women, whose appearance at the window implies a different kind of message? The location of the window suggests a situation of spying out. Other biblical texts like the stories of Sisera's mother (Judg 5:28–30), Michal (2 Sam 6:16), and Jezebel (2 Kgs 9:30–34) reveal that their looking out is connected to situations of crisis, issues of power, and decisive words. Although the setting in Prov 7:6 is not political, the woman's appearance at the window entails a twist of fate, at least for the man. The woman at the window exerts an almost magic attraction on him, which also extends to the bed that she has prepared for him and herself. Starting with Early Bronze Age art in Palestine/Israel (third millennium BCE), the bed with a pair of lovers stands pars pro toto for the pleasures and anticipation of love between a man and a woman (fig. 43). In a less problematic context, such scenes of love's encampment are described in the Song of Songs.

> … his left hand is under my head, his right arm embraces me. (Song 2:6)

3.4. (The Goddess of) Love as Mythical Antagonist of Death's Power

Song 8:6 conveys a programmatic statement about the relationship between death and love. The woman assures her beloved:

> for [my] love is fierce as death,
> [my] passion relentless as the netherworld.

In the Hebrew text, mythological, impressive words without article are used: מוֹת or rather מָוֶת, "death"; שְׁאוֹל, "netherworld"; אהבה, "love"; and קנאה, "passion"; continued by images of fiery arrows, flashes, and cosmic forces like floods of water. Both מות, "death," and רשפים, "arrows," are etymologically

---

34. See also Christl M. Maier's essay in the present volume.

Fig. 41. Ivory plaque from Arslan Tash (eighth century BCE). A woman with fine hairstyle and diadem or headdress looks out of a window that seems to be placed above a palace balustrade; her ears are accentuated. The cross on her headdress may mark her affiliation with the goddess (Winter, *Frau und Göttin*, fig. 308).

 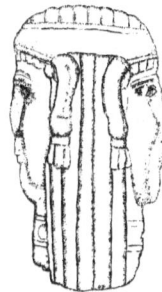

Fig. 42. Double-sided carved stone head from Amman (seventh century BCE). The head with a height of thirty centimeters was part of a balustrade that could be viewed from both sides (Schroer, *Images and Sources*, fig. 20).

Fig. 43. Old Babylonian terracotta plaque (eighteenth–seventeenth BCE). A woman and a man lie naked on a bed in an embracing posture. The bed seems to be covered with a nice blanket (Winter, *Frau und Göttin*, Fig. 360).

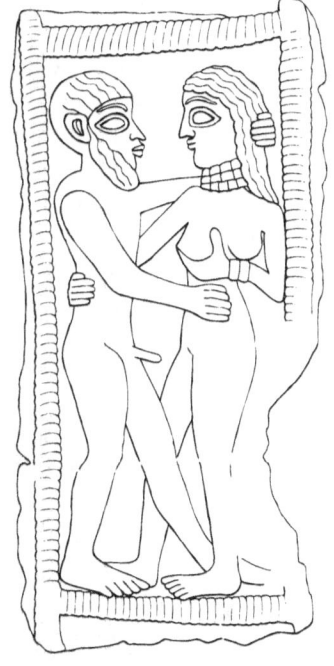

connected to Semitic deities. In Ugarit, Mot is the deity of deadly drought.[35] Reshef is a dreaded god armed with spear and lance who brings but also wards off plagues.[36] Behind such abstract "love" there is the loving woman; it is her love that is fierce like death and therefore effective as an amulet worn at the beloved's arm. This role, however, is incomprehensible without the actual goddesses of love in the ancient Near East who revolted against the death of their brother or husband.[37] This mythology and veneration of goddesses who subdue death is not only documented by images. The images, however, often reveal the core type—for instance, the woman "wailing" over the death of her brother or beloved—more clearly than the narratively unfolded myths.

In Ugarit, Mot, the deity of deadly drought, and the weather-god Baal fight against each other. Baal succumbs, but before he is drawn to the netherworld by Mot, the fierce goddess Anat, who here includes aspects of the goddess of love, conceives from him a bull, the new Baal. Thus, in the cycle of seasons, Baal revives once and again due to Anat, who defies Mot. In the eastern Mediterranean region, this tradition has been merged with the fate of Adonis, the beloved of Aphrodite, by Hellenistic times at the latest; yet the female part, as far as the sources account, was limited to the wailing.

Bewailing the dead and resisting death play a central role also in the Egyptian myths of Osiris and Isis. Osiris is slain by his brother Seth; his sister and spouse Isis collects the parts of his corpse and yet conceives with the dead a son and avenger, Horus, who restores life against Seth's force and destructive power. From the thirteenth century BCE until the first century CE, this conception of Horus is depicted in chapels of Osiris, such as in the famous representation of the funerary temple of Sethos I in Abydos (fig. 44). Thus life prevails over death, thanks to Isis. Iconographic sources from Lachish and Samaria attest that the wailing women Isis and Nephthys were known in Palestine/Israel (see above). The idea that female eroticism is able to infect even the dead with life has probably been generally known in the Middle East for a very long time. Erotic nude female figures are documented from Neolithic times and in much greater quantity than male figures. Sometimes, especially

---

35. See John F. Healey, "Mot," in *Dictionary of Deities and Demons in the Bible* (ed. Karel van der Toorn et al.; 2nd ed.; Leiden: Brill, 1999), 598–603.

36. See Izak Cornelius, *The Iconography of the Canaanite Gods Reshef and Ba'al: Late Bronze and Iron Age I Periods (c 1500–1000 BCE)* (OBO 140; Fribourg: University Press; Göttingen: Vandenhoeck & Ruprecht, 1994).

37. See Silvia Schroer, "Liebe und Tod im Ersten (Alten) Testament," in *Liebe und Tod: Gegensätze—Abhängigkeiten—Wechselwirkungen* (ed. Peter Rusterholz and Sara M. Zwahlen; Bern: Haupt, 2006), 35–52.

Fig. 44. Painted limestone relief from Abydos. Isis in female form is standing at the head of the deceased Osiris, who lies on the bier. In the shape of a female falcon sitting on Osiris's phallus, she conceives Horus. The falcon-headed figure standing at Osiris's feet represents the grown-up Horus. The goddesses Isis and Nepthys are also depicted to the left and right in a falcon's shape (Schroer, *IPIAO* 3, no. 801).

---

clay figurines are found in tombs, that is, near the dead, to which they may convey a breath of pulsating life.[38]

In the narratives of ancient Israel, the loving goddesses who defy death are replaced by mundane women who fight death in its different variations. Women fight, sometimes in a rather risky and even provocative manner, for the dissemination of life, such as Lot's daughters (Gen 19:30–38), the childless widow Tamar (Gen 38), or Ruth and Naomi (in the book of Ruth). Besides, there are ample stories in which women distinguish themselves as protectors and saviors of life: Michal (1 Sam 19:8–17), Abigail (1 Sam 25), the wise woman of Abel-beth-Maacha (2 Sam 20:14–22). The midwives Shiphrah and Puah (Exod 1:15–22), too, and, much later, Esther and Judith defy death and save the entire people. Silent but impressive and effective is the attestation of Rizpah's love; by day and night she dispels the wild animals from the unburied corpses of her sons, who became victims in a politically motivated murder case (2 Sam 21:8–14).

---

38. See Othmar Keel and Silvia Schroer, *Eva—Mutter alles Lebendigen: Frauen- und Göttinnenidole aus dem Alten Orient* (3rd ed.; Fribourg: Academic Press, 2011).

4. Goddesses as Models of (Personified) Wisdom

In the wisdom writings of the postexilic period, wisdom (חכמה in Hebrew, σοφία in Greek, *sapientia* in Latin) is often personified.[39] She assumes different roles, for instance in the frame of the book of Proverbs, in central chapters of the book of Ben Sira and in later writings such as Baruch or the Wisdom of Solomon.[40] Wisdom (חכמה) is not a goddess; neither veneration nor cult is attested for her. She is part of a monotheistic—not polytheistic—symbol system. Nevertheless, she receives her significance, also her clarity, her colors, and her contours from the goddesses of Israel's neighboring polytheistic regions. The relationship between the Egyptian Maat theology and the Israelite wisdom theology is particularly constitutive. The Egyptian concept of Maat, the "righteous order," is comprehensively attested in texts and images.[41] Like the Egyptian goddess Maat, the wisdom figure of the Hebrew Bible cannot be separated from a comprehensive objective order and righteous behavior. Wisdom (חכמה) is a prophet and a teacher of righteousness; studying her leads to righteousness (צדקה) since wisdom is something like the inner side of justice. The introduction to the book of Proverbs starts with verses that demonstrate the close connection between wisdom, righteousness, justice, and equity (Prov 1:2–3). In the speech of personified Wisdom (Prov 8:1–21), the Hebrew root צדק, "to be righteous," is used five times (vv. 8, 15, 16, 18, 20). The Wisdom of Solomon, too, begins with a programmatic call to righteousness (Wis 1:1). The Hebrew term צדקה, "righteousness, justice," accentuates the social aspects of justice. The Egyptian idea of Maat, however, is broader and also implies the cosmic and natural order; thus her image can be found in the context of music, judicial office, the funerary court, and the cult. In her calls, Wisdom addresses especially the powerful:

> By me kings reign, and rulers decree what is just;
> by me rulers rule, and nobles, all who govern rightly. (Prov 8:15–16)

Although all humans are called to act righteously, the king has the particular task to support justice and righteous order (fig. 45), to sustain and defend it, and thus to prove himself to be the son of God who created this world order (in Hebrew חכמה, "wisdom," or עצה, "counsel"). According to Job 28, God

---

39. See Silvia Schroer, *Wisdom Has Built Her House: Studies on the Figure of Sophia in the Bible* (Collegeville, Minn.: Liturgical, 2000).

40. See also Gerlinde Baumann's essay in this volume.

41. See the essential work by Jan Assmann, *Ma'at: Gerechtigkeit und Unsterblichkeit im Alten Ägypten* (Munich: Beck, 1990).

Fig. 45. Scarab from Tell el-Ajjul (1390–1353 BCE). The throne name Amenophis' III, the father of Echnaton, constitutes the image of the sitting goddess Maat with a feather on her head and an ankh-sign (for life) on her knees. The pharaoh's name "the master of Maat is the sun-god" is a programmatic affirmation that the king will respect and implement the righteous order (Maat) of the sun-god Re in his government (Schroer, *IPIAO* 2, no. 693).

Fig. 46. Pectoral (breast decoration) of Pharaoh Sheshonq II from Tanis (tenth century BCE). Together with the goddess Hathor, Maat (to the right with the feather of an ostrich on her head) protects the sun-disk in its bark. At the same time, Maat stands within the sun-disk in a worshiping pose before the enthroned sun-god Amun-Re (Keel and Schroer, *Schöpfung*, fig. 167).

alone knows the way to wisdom, which is hidden. The biblical idea of righteousness that goes before YHWH (Ps 85:14) corresponds to Maat, who sits or stands before Re-Harachte in the sun-bark (fig. 46).

Whereas in Egypt the cultic offering of Maat by the king counts as an effective ritual to secure justice and order (fig. 47), the biblical traditions, both in prophetical and wisdom texts (e.g., Ps 50), devalue such cultic-magical "offering" of righteousness in favor of a religious ethics (Ps 40:7–11; 50:14–15; 51:18–19; 69:31–32). According to biblical authors neither king nor humans generally are able to increase YHWH's righteousness, because he already owns it completely (Ps 36:7, 11; 48:11–12; 85:11, 14; 89:17). The king rather receives righteousness from YHWH (Ps 72:1–2) and swears to hold on to divine righteousness (Ps 101).

The passage that most clearly reveals the mythological remnants of personified wisdom is Prov 8:22–31. In order to legitimize her divine author-

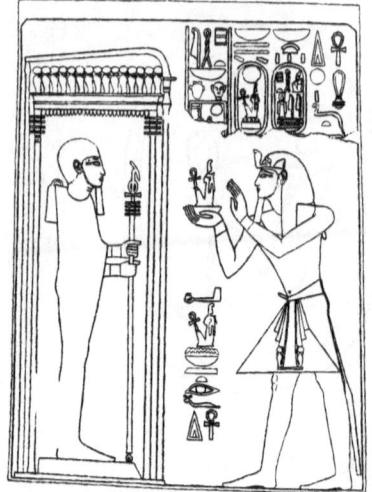

Fig. 47. Scene of a relief on a sandstone column from the temple of Sethos I in Abydos (1290–1279 BCE). The king dedicates the sitting Maat figure on his hand to the god Ptah, who stands in a chapel (Schroer, *IPIAO* 3, no. 720).

ity, Wisdom talks about her beginnings, when the world was created and she delighted the Creator God with her presence. As a literary genre, wisdom's first-person speech is mainly influenced by Egyptian divine speeches; it also resembles in tone later Hellenistic aretalogies. Othmar Keel has been the first to discern and describe the iconographic background of personified Wisdom, who banters and jokes before YHWH.[42] Life-affirming and attentive divine female figures like the Egyptian Hathor, but also earlier Syrian goddesses, have been an inspiration for the Wisdom figure (fig. 48). The biblical text paints Wisdom (חכמה) in the colors of these goddesses as a counterpart to Israel's Creator God. Creation here happens, in contrast to Gen 1–2, in relationship. When Wisdom in the book of Wisdom is named with the specific Greek word πάρεδρος, "the one enthroned beside" the God of Israel, this title evokes polytheistic images of divine pairs (fig. 49).

> By your wisdom you have formed humankind. …
> Give me the wisdom that sits by your throne [τὴν πάρεδρον]
> and do not reject me from among your children. (Wis 9:2, 4)

---

[42]. Othmar Keel, *Die Weisheit spielt vor Gott: Ein ikonographischer Beitrag zur Deutung des mesaḥäqät in Sprüche 8,30f.* (Fribourg: Universitätsverlag; Göttingen: Vandenhoeck & Ruprecht, 1974). The Hebrew word *mĕśaḥeqet* (משחקת) relates to bantering and joking, which makes somebody laugh or just rejoice. The same word is used for David's cultic dance in front of the ark of the covenant in 2 Sam 6:5, 21. The verb שחק does not mean "to play" as a child would do, but rather "to banter or flirt with someone" and "to jump, dance." Michal's reaction in 2 Sam 6:20 proves that the verb has erotic overtones, because Michal finds David's dancing embarrassing.

Fig. 48. Classical Syrian cylinder seal (1850–1750 BCE). A nude goddess unveils herself, probably while dancing in front of the weather-god. He strides over hilltops while the goddess meets him on his attributive animal, the bull. A procession of worshipers accompanies the sacred encounter that guarantees the thriving of plants, animals, and humans. In contrast to the Egyptian goddesses, who are not depicted dancing, the older Syrian goddesses, who in the iconography of Palestine/Israel develop into the special type of twig goddesses, have a strong sex appeal; they are portrayed in action, while unveiling or perhaps dancing in front of a ruler or god (Keel and Schroer, *Schöpfung*, fig. 89). While in Egyptian art the flirting goddess is not represented, the Egyptian myth "Conflict between Horus and Seth" (*TUAT* 3:938) narrates that Hathor, by her erotic dance, helped the ailing and aging creator god Re to recover.

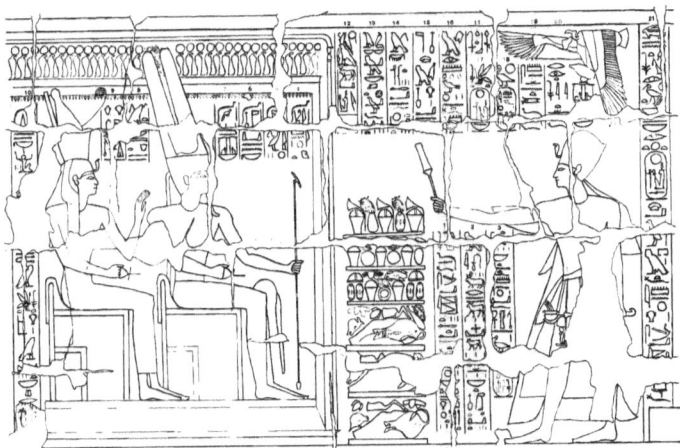

Fig. 49. Relief at the western wall of the great hypostyle hall of the Amun temple in Karnak. The deities Mut and Amun-Re are jointly enthroned in a chapel; in front of them stands Ramses II (1279–1213 BCE) (Nelson, *The Great Hypostyle Hall*, pl. 39).

As many scholars have demonstrated, the book of Wisdom literally refers to the veneration of Isis in Hellenistic Egypt, which had been influenced by Greek thought until the beginning of the Roman period. With regard to iconography, however, Isis is much better known in her role as mother (see the references to Isis and Horus above) than in her role as spouse of the ruling god. Thus she is hardly the model for the πάρεδρος mentioned in Wis 9:4.

Translated from German by Christl M. Maier

Feminine Symbols and Metaphors in the Psalter

Donatella Scaiola

1. Introduction

There are many feminine metaphors and symbols throughout the Old Testament, particularly in the Psalter. Important symbols—for example, the bride (Pss 45; 128:3) and childbirth—are not considered in this essay, but they could be studied at some future date. The working hypothesis of this essay is as follows: In the Psalter, feminine symbolism is, generally speaking, positive; we do not find equivocal or problematic figures as in other wisdom books—for example, Proverbs, which features the adulteress, the idolatress, the foreigner, the seductress—or any other misogynist descriptions such as those found in Job 2:9–10 and Qoh 7:28.[1] Due to the vast number of feminine metaphors in the Psalms, I can only deal in this essay with some specific texts in the Psalter. The approach I take here is canonical and therefore synchronic. I analyze the last stage of the Psalter; the textual corrections and redactional history of the Masoretic Text are not taken into consideration. This study is not exhaustive but is intended to be emblematic. In order to substantiate my working hypothesis, the essay is presented in two parts. In the first, I analyze the metaphor of the mother; in the second, the metaphor of the city. These two metaphors are connected to each other and in fact overlap in the psalms taken into consideration. Thus in the Psalter one can find interesting feminine symbols and metaphors from which, of course, theological consequences result.

---

1. For different interpretations of Job 2:9–10, see the essay by Christl M. Maier (§2.3); for Qoh 7:28, the essay by Vittoria D'Alario (§2) in this volume. One could add Tob 2:14, even though this book is not present in the Hebrew canon.

2. The Motherly Metaphor: "From the Womb of My Mother, You Are My God"

In Pss 22, 139, and 131, among others, God is described as a mother[2] or is connected with the birth of a person and with his or her growth. In this section, I will first consider the metaphors of pregnancy and creation in Ps 139:13–16, which describes the life of a child before birth. Second, I will examine the metaphor of childbirth as it is presented in Ps 22:10–12. Third, I discuss the weaning stage as portrayed in Ps 131:1–2. The fourth aspect regarding motherhood to be explored is in retrospection of life during old age, as found in Ps 71:5–9, 17–18. In considering these metaphors as a portrait of God, new insights in theological study can be gained.

2.1. Psalm 139:13–16: Pregnancy and Creation[3]

In many texts,[4] the authors of Scripture consider the antenatal moment, the time before birth, and suggest the idea that there is a relationship between the acceptance of oneself as a creature shaped by God and as a son or daughter in the mother's womb. This experience is universal, an anthropological and spiritual experience, the peculiar characteristic of which consists of recognizing indebtedness to God for a life that we did not give to ourselves, that we did not produce autonomously, and that, perhaps, we would not necessarily wish to have. To recognize ourselves and to accept ourselves as creatures and as sons or daughters, therefore, are not different experiences, but the expression of a singular awareness. This consciousness could lead to the bearing of a grudge against God, which can be overcome by a process leading to a trustful abandon. In Ps 139 we find a process that begins with the discovery of God as all-knowing (vv. 1–6) and omnipresent (vv. 7–12) Creator, from whom the psalmist tries to escape even by attempting to destroy himself,[5] but comes in

---

2. For more details, see Marianne Grohmann, *Fruchtbarkeit und Geburt in den Psalmen* (FAT 53; Tübingen: Mohr Siebeck, 2007), who analyzes many psalms that deal with this topic.

3. Ibid., 27–50.

4. For the insights in this paragraph, I am indebted to Roberto Vignolo, "Il legame più complesso: Luci e ombre delle relazioni parentali nella Bibbia," in *Genitori e figli nella famiglia affettiva* (ed. Giuseppe Angelini; Disputatio; Milan: Glossa, 2002), 147–215. See also Roberto Vignolo and Laura Giangreco, "Paternità e maternità," in *Temi teologici della Bibbia* (ed. Romano Penna et al.; Dizionari San Paolo; Cinisello Balsamo: Edizioni San Paolo, 2010), 980–85.

5. Ps 139:11 ("And if I say: 'Surely the darkness shall envelop me, and the light about me shall be night'") describes an attempt to regress to the original chaos, upsetting the

the end to receive him and at the same time, in so doing, to receive his original creatural condition.

> For you have made[6] my reins;
> You have knit[7] me together in my mother's womb.
> I praise you because I am fearfully and wonderfully made;
> your works are wonderful,
> I know that full well.[8]
> My bones were not hidden from you
> when I was being made in secret
> sewed together[9] in the depths of the earth.
> Your eyes saw my unformed[10] body;
> all the days ordained for me were written in your book,
> when as yet there was none of them.[11] (Ps 139:13–16)

As in Job 10:8–11 and Jer 1:5, life in the womb is described with a sense of admiration and is recognized as a wonderful action of God, realized in the secret of the womb, which is associated with mother earth (v. 15). In order to describe God's deed, the psalmist uses a metaphor that comes from the world

---

creation's order, by removing the separation between light and darkness (Gen 1:2–3). In Ps 139:11 there are also terms similar to the experience narrated in Job 3.

6. In the Hebrew text, the verb קנה means "to buy, to own" and "to form, to create, to give birth to" (e.g., Gen 4:1; 14:19, 22; Exod 15:16; Deut 32:6; Prov 8:22; Ps 78:54). The verb can have different subjects: God, a human person, and also a woman, Eve, e.g., in Gen 4:1.

7. The verb סכך means "to weave" and "to protect"; this double meaning creates a wordplay that cannot be translated into English (or into Italian), but is theologically very telling, because it inextricably connects creation and providence. This relationship comes from the mother's womb (the preposition ב, meaning "from," is given).

8. This verse can also be translated slightly differently. For example, we can read it this way: "I will thank you, for I am fearfully and wonderfully made; wonderful are your works; and that my soul knows right well."

9. The verb רקם, here in *pual* (a *hapax legomenon*), is very suggestive because it refers to a multicolored brocade textile. The verb is found eight times in the book of Exodus (26:36; 27:16; 28:39; 35:35; 36:37; 38:18.23; 39:29), and is always used in a sacral context. It also refers to the ark of the covenant's veils.

10. The *hapax* term גלמי, has been translated in many different ways. It can be connected to something rolled up (see the use of the verb גלם in 2 Kgs 2:8). The meaning "embryo" may come from this root. In another text, Job 10:8–11, we find another metaphor used to speak of the human body's formation. Ps 139:6 could also be translated in this way: "My embryo saw your eyes."

11. This part of v. 16 is difficult. Literally it can be read: "On your book all of them [i.e., "the days"] are written, the days are formed and no one in them." Several textual corrections have been proposed. The image of the book of God is rather frequent in the Hebrew Bible; see Ps 56:9; 69:29, 87:6.

of craftsmanship. He speaks of the weaving of a cloth (vv. 13, 15) and of God's book, the book of life (v. 16). God "weaves" the psalmist's internal organs—the loins,[12] the bones—and then embroiders them. It is interesting to note that only here the verb has God as its subject. From this metaphor, the idea emerges of the care God gives to each particular human being—although one could also think of a mass production line—attributing absolute value to the individual characteristics of everybody (see the many colors of the woven textile suggested in v. 15). Being Creator, God "knows" (vv. 14–16) his creature even before his or her first moments of life (Isa 44:2, 24; 49:1, 5; Jer 1:5). As a consequence, to be conceived, to be begotten in the mother's womb, means to be known by God even before one can know him. This original experience, of which we have no memory, is nevertheless written in our genes, and we need to return to it at painful moments that seem to question the original goodness of human life or, less dramatically, during the different seasons of life. Therefore, our life consists of a part that is invisible to us and very short, but it is nonetheless a fact that the psalmist chooses to describe. Its main characteristic is the provident and creative care of God. The other part of our life, which is accessible to us, is longer and often painful, as described in our second example, Ps 22.

2.2. Psalm 22:10–11: The Birth, Initiation to Trust

We here discuss only a few lines of Ps 22, taken from its first part (22:1–12), which opens (vv. 2–3) and finishes (vv. 11b–12a) by repeating the invocation to God, "my God" (אלי), and the root רחק "to be far" (vv. 2, 12). In this prayer, the psalmist, who feels himself abandoned by God and excommunicated by the community, tries to reestablish contact with the Lord by recovering the original experience of confidence described in the previous example. In order to overcome the present situation, in which God seems to be far from the psalmist and insensitive to his cry (22:2–3), the psalmist tries first to reappropriate the collective confidence experienced by the ancestors during the exodus (22:5–6).[13] At that time, the ancestors had faith in God, appealed to him, and were saved (22:5–6). The psalmist does not speak of "my father"; instead, he remembers "my mother" (vv. 10–11).[14] Mentioning

---

12. According to biblical anthropology, the loins are connected with the affections and the passions and are often joined to the heart (Ps 7:10; 26:2; 73:21).

13. Almost all of the fifty-one references to "our ancestors" point to the patriarchs and matriarchs as well as to the exodus generation, with particular emphasis on the land's promise and on the alliance (e.g., Deut 5:23; 6:23; 26:3, 7, 15; Num 36:3–4).

14. Grohmann, *Fruchtbarkeit und Geburt*, 52–69.

"our ancestors," the psalmist roots his plea in the community and in the history of the people of Israel. But his attempt seems to be unsuccessful because he is considered a "worm," not a human being (22:7–9). In order to regain a standard of confidence even more primordial than that of his people, the psalmist moves from God as Savior to God as mother.

> You are the one who brought me out[15] from the womb
> and made me feel trust[16] on my mother's breast.
> On you was I cast from my birth,[17]
> and from my mother's womb you have been my God.

The relationship between the psalmist and his God is rooted not only in the history of the ancestors, in a distant time, but also in what God did when the psalmist was born.[18] In verses 10–11, God is the subject of four verbs that all relate to the mother and her child. As stated in note 15 above, the word גחי is a *hapax legomenon*, a term only used once; it may refer to the waters coming from the womb during childbirth. The emphatic repetition of the personal pronoun "you" (אתה) at the beginning of verse 10 and at the end of verse 11 is unnecessary from a grammatical point of view; it seems to assign to God a parental function even more radical than a human one, which is at the same time both paternal and motherly.[19] This idea is suggested in verse 11, which opens with the syntagma "on you" (עליך) and closes with the psalmist's profession of faith: "you are my God" (אתה אלי). The confidence that the newborn child learns in its mother's arms is paralleled in this text with the experience of the ancestors during the exodus. The same verb, בטח, "to trust," is repeated in verses 5–6, 11. God is therefore the main character of the psalmist's begetting because he saved Israel's ancestors from death in the past and then was the actor of the psalmist's own childbirth. After having been able

---

15. The word גחי is a *hapax legomenon* and can derive either from the root גחה, "draw forth," or from גיח, "burst forth, bring forth." The few references of the second root (Judg 20:33; 2 Sam 2:24; Job 38:8; 40:23; Ezek 32:2; Mic 4:10) seem to refer to the flow of waters, sometimes even violent, thus evoking childbirth.

16. The *hiphil* participle of the root בטח may have an ingressive meaning in the current context.

17. Literally the line can be translated: "On you was I cast from the womb."

18. To deepen this point, I refer to Alessandro Cavicchia, *Le sorti e le vesti: La "Scrittura" alle radici del messianismo giovanneo tra re-interpretazione e adempimento: Sal 22 (21) a Qumran e in Giovanni* (Tesi Gregoriana: Serie Teologia 81; Rome: Editrice Pontificia Università Gregoriana, 2010).

19. Of course not all scholars agree with this interpretation; Alonso-Schökel and Vignolo, for example, think that in this text God is described not as a mother but as a midwife.

to recuperate the original experience of confidence, the psalmist feels himself inwardly sustained by the relationship with God, which allows him to face and to overcome the painful situation he is living in.

2.3. Psalm 131:1–2: Weaning

The phase after pregnancy in the womb and childbirth is weaning, described in Ps 131:1–2. Here, the child is no longer entirely dependent on the mother and on her breast, but able to choose her as interlocutor.

> O Lord, my heart is not lifted up and my eyes are not haughty;
> I do not concern myself with great matters or things too marvelous for me.
> I have calmed and quieted my soul, like a weaned child with its mother,
> like a weaned child is my soul within me.

Psalm 131 uses the metaphor of a person who has completed the way of inner unification. This journey not only is theoretical but also involves the whole body. The starting point is the heart, which thinks, since in biblical anthropology the heart is like the mind in modern terms. Then it is the moment for the eyes, by which a person evaluates reality. The eyes are connected with desire. The next step is related to the choices, the way of life; and the last step, the center of everything, is desire.[20] In verse 2, the psalmist uses the metaphor of a baby that after completing the weaning phase, at approximately three years of age, rests in his mother's arms. The child is held by his mother not because of a necessity, but because he finds in the mother a kind of stillness. The baby has become quite independent, but looks for peace, care, and calm and finds all these in the mother. God is compared with the mother, who has directed the search and the way of the psalmist's inner unification.

2.4. Psalm 71:5–9, 17–18: Retrospection of Life During Old Age

Psalm 71 belongs to a group of texts (Pss 70–72) in which Pss 70–71 form a single anthological composition.[21] To confirm this hypothesis, we notice the

---

20. This translation of the word נפשׁ seems more appropriate than "soul." The first meaning of the term is concrete: "breath, throat, jaws." Moreover, the term often refers to the whole person, considered as a living, breathing being; the phrase "my נפשׁ" then simply means "I." Additionally, the term can be metaphorically used in the sense of "eagerness, lust." In some cases it can be translated by "desire." See Claus Westermann, "נֶפֶשׁ naéfaeš anima," *TLOT* 2:743–59; Horst Seebass, "נֶפֶשׁ nefeš," *TDOT* 9:497–519.

21. Jean-Marie Auwers, *La composition littéraire du Psautier: Un état de la question* (Paris: Gabalda, 2000), 103, 136.

presence of a refrain that is repeated three times, with slight variations: "Let them be put to shame and confusion who seek my life! Let them be turned back and brought to dishonor who delight in my hurt!" (70:3; 71:13, 24b).

The originality of Ps 71 consists in giving voice to an elderly person.

> You, O Lord, are my hope,
> my trust, O Lord, from my youth.
> Upon you I have leaned from birth,
> it was you who took me from my mother's womb;
> my praise is continually of you. ...
> Do not cast me off in the time of old age,
> do not forsake me when my strength is spent. ...
> From my youth, O God, you have taught me,
> and I still proclaim your marvelous deeds.
> Even when I am old and gray,
> O God, do not abandon me,
> until I have declared your might,
> to all who are to come. (Ps 71:5–9, 17–18)

In these verses we can hear an echo of Ps 22, where, as we have seen, the reminder of birth was the point of departure. In Ps 71, instead, memory becomes a complete rereading of life, departing from a perspective acquired during old age. Ps 71 is less anguished when compared to Ps 22, but it is interesting because it is the only example of a prayer of an aged person in the Psalter. The psalmist, who has arrived at the end of his life, can witness that God has been his lifelong shelter. God has been the basic reference point, which is even more important than the original relationship with his parents.

2.5. Conclusion

The texts considered here have given us the opportunity to outline a route through the themes of generation, birth, and growth in which God is represented by means of maternal or at least generative metaphors. In this human and spiritual way, God as mother favors the progressive emancipation of the child without binding it in a narcissistic and fusing way, but on the contrary encouraging human freedom and autonomy (Ps 131:1–2). This route does not consist in being thrown into a vacuum; instead, it is rooted in an original experience of which we have no real awareness, but the experience of being known by God even before we are generated in the mother's womb is a real one. This experience is the foundation of the psalmist's trust; it gives rise to prayer and remains effective even if the parents were to forsake their creature (Ps 27:10). The memory of birth and the care connected to it can offer support for the entirety of one's life, as witnessed by the elderly psalmist in Ps 71.

3. The Mother City: "All of Them Are Born There"

The second part of this essay deals with a metaphor that differs from the previous one but is nevertheless related to it. The discourse shifts from the personal to the universal experience of generation, which is connected to the "metropolis," the mother city of all people. This symbol is common both in the Psalter and in the Old Testament[22] as a whole. In this second part, only one example will be considered, Ps 87, which is taken as an original and unusual example of this symbol. Unfortunately, the psalm contains many textual problems and is therefore difficult to understand.

3.1. Text[23] and Structure

> [1] A Psalm or Song for the sons of Korah.
> His foundation[24] in the holy mountains.[25]
> [2] The Lord *loveth*[26] the gates of Zion
> more than all the dwellings of Jacob.

---

22. See, e.g., Isa 49:22; 51:18; 54:1; and Christl M. Maier, *Daughter Zion, Mother Zion: Gender, Space, and the Sacred in Ancient Israel* (Minneapolis: Fortress, 2008).

23. This is the KJV translation, slightly modified. I also add some textual notes that I consider relevant for the topic of this essay. Moreover, to deepen the interpretation of the psalm, I refer to some articles: Gianni Barbiero, "'Di Sion si dirà ognuno è stato generato in essa': Studio esemplare del Sal 87," in *Biblical Exegesis in Progress: Old and New Testament Essays* (ed. Jean-Noël Aletti and Jean-Louis Ska; AnBib 176; Rome: Pontifical Biblical Institute, 2009), 209–64; Stanisław Bazyliński, "Psalm 87: Motivation for Pilgrimage," in *Nova et Vetera: Miscellanea in onore di padre Tiziano Lorenzin* (ed. Luciano Fanin; Studi religiosi; Padova: Edizioni Messaggero, 2011), 71–90; Thijs Booij, "Some Observations on Psalm LXXXVII," *VT* 37 (1987): 16–25; John A. Emerton, "The Problem of Psalm LXXXVII," *VT* 50 (2000): 183–99.

24. The Hebrew word יסודתו is a *hapax legomenon*; it probably means "foundation" either as an act of founding or as the building structure. It is a feminine word with a third-person masculine singular suffix. In order to explain the apparent contradiction, some authors change the masculine suffix into a feminine one and thus link the word to the city. The MT is maintained here and, as many other scholars argue, is considered as referring to God.

25. The term is plural and can be explained as plural of excellence; see Gianfranco Ravasi, *Il Libro dei Salmi: Commento e attualizzazione* (Lettura pastorale della Bibbia 14; Bologna: EDB, 1983), 2:794. The psalmist may also refer to the two hills on which Jerusalem is built, i.e., Mount Zion and the Mishneh.

26. All italicized verbs are participles in the MT. While this does not come through in the translation, it is significant for the structure of the psalm.

FEMININE SYMBOLS AND METAPHORS IN THE PSALTER 173

³ Glorious things *are spoken*[27] of thee,[28] O city of God. *Selāh.*

⁴ "I will make mention[29] of Rahab and Babylon to them that *know me*: behold Philistia, and Tyre, with Ethiopia; this man was born there."
⁵ And of Zion[30] it shall be said, "This and that man[31] was born in her": and "the Highest himself shall establish her."
⁶ The LORD shall count,[32] when he writeth up[33] the people, "This man was born there." *Selāh*

⁷ As well *the singers as the players on instruments*[34] shall be there: "All my springs are in thee."

As indicated above, the psalm can be divided into three strophes: verses 1–3, 4–6, and 7.[35] The word סלה (*selâ*) at the end of verses 3 and 6 probably means

---

27. The Hebrew verb is a participle *pual*. It may be understood as an impersonal form and therefore is maintained here, even if many scholars suggested that it should be changed into *piel*. See Paul Joüon and Takamitsu Muraoka, *A Grammar of Biblical Hebrew* (2nd ed.; SubBi 27; Rome: Gregorian and Biblical Press, 2009), §128b.

28. The MT reads בך, which can have a locative meaning and thus been translated "(spoken) in you," as John Goldingay suggests, *Psalms* (Baker Commentary on the Old Testament Wisdom and Psalms; Grand Rapids: Baker Academic, 2006), 2:635: "Honorable things are spoken in you, city of God." Because the LXX translated περὶ σοῦ, "about you," I suggest that the preposition refers to the theme of the discourse. Other biblical examples are 1 Sam 19:3–4; Ps 119:46.

29. Some scholars, e.g., Barbiero ("Di Sion si dirà," 4) translate in this way. However, the *hiphil* of זכר means "to register," as is suggested by Franciscus Zorell, *Lexicon Hebraicum Veteris Testamenti* (Rome: Pontifical Biblical Institute, 1984), 209.

30. The LXX (followed by the Vulgate) translates "mother Zion": μήτηρ Σιων ἐρεῖ ἄνθρωπος, "A man will say: 'Zion is mother.'" See Christl M. Maier, "'Zion wird man Mutter nennen': Die Zionstradition in Psalm 87 und ihre Rezeption in der Septuaginta," *ZAW* 118 (2006): 582–96, 592–97.

31. The rather literal Hebrew phrase means "each one"; cf. Exod 36:4; Lev 15:2; Esth 1:8.

32. The verb ספר means "to count, to register, to list."

33. Some ancient versions (LXX, Targum, Theodotion) and many scholars change the Hebrew infinitive with preposition בכתוב "while writing" or "in writing" into a noun with preposition: בכתב "in the book." I prefer to maintain the MT.

34. At the beginning of the verse there are two participles that are sometimes translated as nouns, e.g., KJV and, among other scholars, David Kimchi, *Commento ai Salmi* (ed. Luigi Cattani; Tradizione d'Israele 6; Rome: Città Nuova, 1995), 2:394: "the singers and the flute players." For a detailed discussion, see Booij, "Some Observations," 21–22; Emerton, "The Problem," 186. With other scholars (Barbiero, "Di Sion si dirà," 220–221) I read the preposition ב in a temporal sense: "They sing while dancing."

35. As a matter of course, many other divisions have been proposed depending on the translation and interpretation of the Hebrew text, which is so difficult that some schol-

"pause"; even if some interpreters disagree with this structuring, I argue that this repetition could confirm the division proposed.

The first and the third strophe present some similarities: both of them use participle verb forms and speak about Zion in the third person (vv. 3, 7). Moreover, in both of them the Tetragrammaton, YHWH, is found (vv. 2.6). In comparison, in the middle strophe, Zion is referred to indirectly (v. 5), the verb "to give birth" is repeated three times, and there are no participle forms. In verses 4 and 6, the same phrase "this man was born there" appears, and in both cases YHWH is the subject.

The first strophe focuses on the relationship between YHWH and Zion, whereas the second strophe presents three characters: YHWH, Zion, and foreign (enemy) nations. The third strophe has again two subjects, Zion and the people.

3.2. Motherhood without Boundaries

3.2.1. YHWH and Zion (First Strophe, vv. 1–3)

Psalm 87 refers to some texts of the Old Testament in which Jerusalem is compared to a woman, a mother, or a wife. The particular condition of Jerusalem related to other "dwellings of Jacob" does not depend on her merits, but is due to God's love for her (v. 2). As a confirmation of this relation, in verse 3 the expression "city of God" is found. In verse 2, the psalmist refers to the city by means of a synecdoche, "Zion's gates," which indicates several aspects. Ancient cities were commonly surrounded by walls; in this way the cities were made more secure, protected from external enemies. Only through the gates was it possible to enter the city. These gates were closed in the evening in order to protect the citizens living inside, and were opened in the morning so that people could go to work in the fields located outside the city walls.

Because the gate was the weakest point of the city, there was often an open space at its inner side in which defense systems could be built in case of war. In times of peace, however, this open space was generally used as a marketplace, a space for conversation or meeting (Ps 69:13; 127:5) and also as a place where public trials were held (Deut 25:7; Prov 22:22; 31:23).

> The free space that opened in front of the gate between the city's walls comprised the center of public life. Here, judicial issues were discussed and legal

---

ars even consider it incomprehensible. Other factors that influence the structuring of the psalm are the determination of the *Sitz im Leben* and the significance scholars assign to structural clues.

decisions made (cf. Ruth 4:1–11; 2 Sam 15:2; Job 31:21). Being in charge of the gate meant to be in charge of the whole city; therefore, the gates of Zion are mentioned pars pro toto for the whole city of God.[36]

Finally, the expression "Zion's gates" could also refer to the temple (Ps 24:7, 9; 118:19–20), that is, to the religious experience of the city.

3.2.2. YHWH, Zion, and the Nations (Second Strophe, vv. 4–6)

The idea of the closed space of the city resemble a womb that, on the one hand, protects and takes care of the people who are inside the gates and, on the other hand, keeps out people who are outside. This idea is found in different cultures and describes the motherly link between the city and her residents. The innovation of Ps 87 is, however, to describe Zion as an open city, whose motherhood reaches beyond common experience; in fact, it extends even to people traditionally considered enemies.[37]

There is a relationship between the first two strophes of the Psalm. In verses 1–3, the verb "to love" is used to describe the marriage between the city-woman Jerusalem and God (cf. Deut 21:15–17). In the second strophe, however, as Gianni Barbiero rightly says, "the text leads from the metaphor of the spouse (vv. 1–3) to the mother metaphor, through which the act of reproduction is emphasized.[38]

Jerusalem is compared to a mother in other texts like Isa 54:1–10 and 66:7–14. In Ps 87, the metaphor refers to Zion, which is considered the

---

36. Translated to English from Manfred Lurker, *Wörterbuch biblischer Bilder und Symbole* (2nd ed.; Munich: Kösel, 1978), 327.

37. This interpretation is proposed by some scholars, among them Gianfranco Ravasi, "A Sion tutti sono nati! L'universalismo del salmo 87," *Parola Spirito e Vita* 16 (1979): 53–63; and Erich Zenger, "Zion, als Mutter der Völker in Psalm 87," in Norbert Lohfink and Erich Zenger, *Der Gott Israels und die Völker: Untersuchungen zum Jesajabuch und zu den Psalmen* (SBS 154; Stuttgart: Katholisches Bibelwerk, 1994), 117–50. Other exegetes, however, disagree and argue that Ps 87 only refers to Jews in the Diaspora who probably lived in the countries mentioned in vv. 4–5; see, e.g., Bernard Duhm, *Die Psalmen erklärt* (KHC 14; Freiburg im Breisgau: Mohr Siebeck, 1899), 218–19. A third group of scholars suggests that the psalm refers to proselytes who lived in these countries (Rudolf Kittel, *Die Psalmen* [4th ed.; KAT 13; Leipzig: Deichert, 1922], 289), or to Jews and proselytes in the Diaspora (Hermann Gunkel, *Die Psalmen übersetzt und erklärt* [4th ed.; HKAT 2/2.; Göttingen: Vandenhoeck & Ruprecht, 1926], 379–80). Another suggestion is that of Alfons Deissler, *Die Psalmen* (Die Welt der Bibel; Düsseldorf: Patmos, 1964), 338–39, for whom the psalm describes the eschatological conversion of the nations.

38. Barbiero, "Di Sion si dirà," 229.

mother not only of the sons of Israel but also of the nations.[39] They are included among the city's sons not because of a "natural" birth, but through divine election. The subject of the verbs is, in fact, YHWH, who guarantees citizenship in his city to people who come from many nations by adding them to the list of citizens in Jerusalem's register office. Rahab[40] (to the west) and Babylon (to the east), on the one hand, remind us of the great empires with whom Israel had to deal with throughout her history, from the exodus to the exile, which is often described as a second exodus by the prophets. Philistia and Tyre (to the north), on the other hand, call to mind closer enemies, that is, neighboring states, whereas Ethiopia (Cush, to the south) hints at a remote place. This list is incomplete but intends to refer to the entire world with Jerusalem at the center (see Ezek 5:5). The favored relationship between God and his city, expressed by the election of Jerusalem, does not oppose her to the world, but means that Jerusalem receives a vocation. She is indeed called to become the mother of other people, thus building a bridge between YHWH and the nations, as it is described in the psalm's central strophe (vv. 4–6): "The people in v. 4 know … YHWH, because Zion has generated them with this knowledge; this is Zion's privileged role as revelator of the true God, which is praised in the oracle."[41]

Through this list the text not only receives a universalistic tone but also expresses a prophecy, even a utopia. As it speaks of nations traditionally considered enemies, it is noteworthy that God himself, in the center of the psalm, declares them to be Zion's children. In the first strophe Zion is said to be a city-bride; in the middle strophe, the city is described as mother of the nations.[42] Since these nations are recorded in the city's register, the expression "this man was born there" could, in fact, be the quotation of a juridical formula[43] by which a person was recognized as a legal citizen of a place.[44]

---

39. I emphasize the novelty of this idea, as other scholars do: "The idea that Zion is the mother of the nations is unheeded in the rest of the Hebrew Bible because it disregards all boundaries between Israel and the nations and denies any prerequisites for joining with Israel in its faith in YHWH" (Christl M. Maier, "Psalm 87 as a Reappraisal of the Zion Tradition and Its Reception in Galatians 4:26," *CBQ* 69 [2007]: 473–86, 480–81).

40. Rahab is the name of a sea monster (e.g., Job 9:13; Ps 89:11; Isa 51:9). It often refers to Egypt (see Isa 30:7).

41. See Marina Mannati, *Psaumes 73 à 106* (vol. 3 of *Les Psaumes*; Cahiers de la Pierre-qui-Vive; Paris: Desclée de Brouwer, 1967), 140.

42. For a more thorough discussion, see Odil Steck, "Zion als Gelände und Gestalt: Überlegungen zur Wahrnehmung Jerusalems als Stadt und Frau im Alten Testament," *ZTK* 86 (1989): 261–81.

43. The symbolism may be strengthened by comparing the psalm with some extrabiblical texts and traditions. For example, Barbiero calls attention to the Assyrian verb, *manû*,

3.2.3. Zion and the Nations (Third Strophe, v. 7)

Verse 7 describes the joyful reaction of the nations who are signed up in Jerusalem's register. Although the end of the psalm poses some textual problems, it seems to be connected with its beginning, especially with verse 1b, where the mountains of God are mentioned. Some scholars have called attention to a possible mythical-cosmological reference at the beginning of the psalm that is taken up at its end: the mountains in verse 1b may refer to the primeval hill as the place where the Creator defeated the chaos, a scene that appears in some extrabiblical creation myths. It is possible that some later biblical traditions inserted this myth after purifying it from what was considered unacceptable for Hebrew orthodoxy. Such traditions can be recognized in Old Testament texts that took from the Canaanites the idea that the place of Zion was connected to the world's navel. Following this tradition, it is said that Solomon's temple was built on a stone that is right at the world's center, the cosmic mountain, the foundation rock of creation, the end of the umbilical cord that connects the three parts of the universe: sky, earth, and underworld. Later, this place was connected to the cosmic tree, the Garden of Eden,[45] and, finally, in the New Testament, identified with heavenly Jerusalem (Rev 22:1–2).[46]

The relationship between Ps 87 and these traditions, in order to be confirmed (or denied), needs to be explored in more detail than it is possible to do here. I only suggest that a link is possible. More convincing, however, is the idea that the springs mentioned in verse 7 refers to verses 3–4 of the psalm. The springs are an obvious symbol of life and thus related to creation (Gen 2:10-14), to the holy city (Ps 46:5), and to the temple (Ezek 47:1–12).

"to count"; it may also mean "to consider a person, a place, an object, belonging to a particular class, region or place." Being attested in many inscriptions, it basically means "to be assimilated (or: to be part?) to Assyrian territory." In the referred context it was considered an honor to be Assyrian, even if the conquered nations had to pay taxes and duties. Following this interpretation, Barbiero translates the Hebrew verb ספר in v. 6 as "to count"; see Barbiero, "Di Sion si dirà," 240.

44. The expression "indicates the act of registration of an individual (here, as an analogy, a collective is meant, namely, peoples) who is then formally considered as 'native' of the implied place." See Angelo Lancellotti, *I Salmi: Versione—introduzione—note* (Nuovissima versione della Bibbia dai testi originali 18/C; Rome: Paoline, 1984), 307.

45. E.g., in Sir 24.

46. Samuel Terrien, "The Omphalos Myth and the Hebrew Religion," *VT* 20 (1970): 314–38, 317. The author offers a large bibliography on the issue and also refers to the study of Brevard Childs, *Myth and Reality in the Old Testament* (SBT 27; London: SCM, 1960), 183–93.

3.3. Conclusion

The dominating symbolism of Ps 87 is motherly, which, compared to other Old Testament texts, is elaborated in an unusual way. There is also coherence between the metaphors used in the different parts of the psalm, especially between the idea of founding a city and fortifying it (cf. Ps 24:2). The latter concept is connected with the idea of fertility, as Luciano Manicardi argues: "If one talks about fortifying a city, or of securing one's own future, respectively, this necessarily implies the idea of fecundity."[47]

The universal motherhood of Zion is, ultimately, accomplished by God's performative declaration; this act underlines the idea that the inclusion of the nations in the mother-city does not require an application but is, on the contrary, an explicit fruit of God's grace.

4. Final Conclusion

Without repeating what has been said in this essay, I hope to have demonstrated the validity of my working hypothesis, namely, that in the Psalter feminine symbolism is associated essentially with a positive reality. Due to matters of space, this analysis cannot be exhaustive, and some important metaphors such as the bride or childbirth (cf. Ps 45; 128:3) are not considered and must be left to other scholars. In my view, the Psalter makes an important and original contribution to a gender-sensitive reading and also offers some interesting aspects that differ from what is found in other wisdom books of the Old Testament (Proverbs, Qoheleth, Job, and Sirach).

Translated from Italian by Donatella Scaiola and Christl M. Maier

---

47. Luciano Manicardi, "Sion, la 'città di Dio' (Sal 87)," *Parola Spirito e Vita* 50 (2004): 83–102, here 100.

On Gendering Laments:
A Gender-Oriented Reading of the
Old Testament Psalms of Lament

Ulrike Bail

1. Living the Psalms

Psalm 2: Punish My Abusers[1]

God of hope and all blessings,
I need your help and assurance.

My tormentors have walked free,
While I have been racked with pain.

Where is my freedom?
Where is their punishment?

I have worked with much difficulty,
Fear, doubt, and trepidation to recover.

Where is their punishment? Why do they walk free?
You speak of justice. Where is your wrath upon them?

This psalm comes from a collection of psalm prayers written by a survivor of sexual abuse. By updating her reading of the Old Testament Psalms, she found

---

1. Excerpt from a newly versified psalm of lament from a woman who has survived sexual abuse. The numbering of the psalm follows her collection of psalms. This psalm is published in James Leehan, *Defiant Hope: Spirituality for Survivors of Family Abuse* (Louisville: Westminster John Knox, 1993), 168–69. See also the prayers of lament by Carola Moosbach, *Gottesflamme Du Schöne: Lob- und Klagegebete* (Gütersloh: Gütersloher, 1997); Catherin J. Foote, *Survivor Prayers: Talking with God about Childhood Sexual Abuse* (Louisville: Westminster John Knox, 1994).

her experience reflected in them and wrote new psalms of her own to express and process her trauma. The supplicant has found a speech pattern in the tradition of the Old Testament psalms of lament that sustains her words and allows her to break out of her silence.

Throughout the ages, women have read the Psalms and "have translated them for themselves, so that the thoughts and images fit their lives."[2] *Living the Psalms* is the English translation of a book that was published in 2002 and included new psalms of women from around the world. *Living the Psalms* expresses, in the words of Ps 109, "but I—I am Prayer" (ואני תפלה). It is the moment of praying; existence is wholly word. The entirety of women's lives, their physical and mental wounds, finds space in the textual realm of the psalms of lament. Everything has its place, as expressed in the heading of Ps 102: "A prayer of one afflicted, when faint and pleading before YHWH."[3] One may express everything in the psalm, either softly or loudly.

My thesis is that what women around the world have always done, which is to express their life situations through the Psalms, can already be found in the Old Testament Psalms. We can read the psalms of lament as women's voices.

2. "And I": The Open Speech of the Psalms of Lament

The individual psalms of lament are prayers of a literary "I": ואני/"and I." The "I" is not grammatically differentiated according to gender.[4] However, the listener immediately identifies the gender of the person in the actual act of articulating the Psalms orally. The gender remains open in written text, and the first-person singular personal pronoun found there may therefore be either masculine or feminine.

---

2. Bärbel Fünfsinn und Carola Kienel, eds., *Psalmen leben: Frauen aus allen Kontinenten lesen biblische Psalmen neu* (Hamburg: EB, 2002), 11. The authors write that women have "done the work of translation for themselves, so that the thoughts and images fit their lives." See also Klara Butting, "'Die Töchter Judas frohlocken' (Ps 48:12): Frauen beten Psalmen," *BK* 56 (2001): 35–39.

3. [Translator's note: In her original German essay, Ulrike Bail quoted biblical verses from the *Bibel in gerechter Sprache* (Gütersloh: Gütersloher, 2011). For this English translation, the translator has relied on the New Revised Standard Version to the degree that a given translation matched the meaning of Bail's text. Where this was not the case, the NRSV translation was modified in accordance with the verse as given in Bail's original article.]

4. Ilse Müllner, "Klagend laut werden: Frauenstimmen im Alten Testament," in *Schweigen wäre gotteslästerlich: Die heilende Kraft der Klage* (ed. Georg Steins; Würzburg: Echter, 2000), 69–85, 81–82. See also Dörte Bester, *Körperbilder in den Psalmen: Studien zu Psalm 22 und verwandten Texten* (FAT 2/24; Tübingen: Mohr Siebeck, 2007), 98.

In connection with this point, it is interesting that even the body is not sexually differentiated in the Psalms. Supplicants express their own situations and their own emotional states through corporeal images. The reader cannot infer a female or male person on the basis of body parts mentioned in a particular text. Emotional, physical, and social dimensions are intertwined in the Psalms, and all aspects of human life, including fear, desire, and pleasure, are expressed by means of a body-oriented language and corporeal images.[5] The Psalms linguistically condense peoples' experiences of violence, especially those experiences that destroy a person's social, psychological, and physical integrity and identity.

The Psalms do not describe traumatic situations concretely, as in a criminological or medical diagnosis. Nor does the language of the Psalms claim to depict reality photographically or in detail, but rather it expresses the full extent of internal and external distress. They do so through certain metaphors and structures of speech that lend voice to the pain a victim experiences as speechless, making processing and communication possible.

Dorothea Erbele-Küster's *reception-aesthetics study* of the Psalms reaches the conclusion that the so-called gaps or places of indeterminacy in descriptions of distress are deliberately kept open so as to provide a space for all recipients and their respective experiences of distress.[6] This openness can be understood as an offer of substantiation: prayer transforms the open language of the Psalms into words that express quite concretely the supplicant's situation. Based on the literary "I," the Psalms are gender neutral; therefore, both men and women can equally borrow the words as if they were their own, expressing themselves and recovering through them. Only when the Psalms are read does their literary subject become gendered.

For this reason, the reconstruction of a possible female author or first female supplicant of the Psalms becomes uninteresting; rather, the female reader becomes their hermeneutical key.[7] We cannot date the Psalms with

---

5. Susanne Gillmayr-Bucher, "Body Images in the Psalms," *JSOT* 28, no. 3 (2004): 301–26; Bester, *Körperbilder*; Christl M. Maier, "Body Imagery in Psalm 139 and its Significance for a Biblical Anthropology," *lectio difficilior* 2 (2001): http://www.lectio.unibe.ch/01_2/m.htm; Susanne Gillmayr-Bucher, "Emotion und Kommunikation," in *Biblische Anthropologie: Neue Einsichten aus dem Alten Testament* (ed. Christian Frevel; Freiburg: Herder, 2010), 278–89; Gillmayr-Bucher, "Rauchende Nase, bebendes Herz: Gefühle zur Sprache bringen," *BK* 67 (2012): 21–25.

6. Dorothea Erbele-Küster, *Beten als Akt des Lesens: Eine Rezeptionsästhetik der Psalmen* (WMANT 87; Neukirchen-Vluyn: Neukirchener, 2001), 142.

7. See also Ulrike Bail, *Gegen das Schweigen klagen: Eine intertextuelle Studie zu den Klagepsalmen Ps 6 und Ps 55 und der Erzählung von der Vergewaltigung Tamars* (Gütersloh: Gütersloher, 1998), esp. 31–73; Erbele-Küster, *Beten*, 42.

certainty, and their descriptive language does not depict a single situation. Experience connects to text in complex ways, which prohibits reduction to a single situation that would be historically determinable. It is a question of the voice in the text that corresponds to the reader's voice as she prays a psalm of lament and that is audible as her own. The concept of voice in the text allows for the "gendering" of "laments."

3. The Concept of Voice in the Text

In 1993, Athalya Brenner and Fokkelien van Dijk-Hemmes published *On Gendering Texts: Female and Male Voices in the Hebrew Bible*,[8] in which they present a new concept of authorship. They no longer search for historical authors, but rather for gender-specific voices that may be heard on the textual level, that is, "voices within a text." They define voice as the sum of the speech acts that the text attributes to a fictitious person, the narrator. They refer to the women's voices they find in the primarily male discourse of the biblical books as "F voice," that is, as "female voice." Likewise, they label male-dominated voices "M voices" ("masculine/male voices"). Brenner and van Dijk-Hemmes do not attempt to identify an author as a historical person, but rather they search for the voice that holds textual authority.

They assume that biblical texts were written exclusively, or almost exclusively, by men and for men. Texts by women are, if anything, embedded in them, and male editorial activities have shaped and framed them.[9] Since primarily men have put women's oral traditions into writing because men dominate the field of literature, female voices, although often present, are hidden as traces. Whether these traces can be detected depends on the reader and his or her interest in screening biblical texts for women's voices. Texts and readers are never gender neutral, and texts often tell a different story, depending on whether the reader understands the textual voice as a male voice or as a female voice. We may therefore understand biblical texts as "dual gendered,"[10] containing two possible parallel readings. In a culture dominated by androcentrism, women themselves speak with a doubled voice. They speak with the voice of the dominant discourses, which practically drown out and override their own voices, and simultaneously with the voice of repressed, silent discourses. In their search for F voices, Brenner and van Dijk-Hemmes highlight the silent voices, the "muted voices," which especially in the psalms of lament

---

8. Athalya Brenner and Fokkelien Van Dijk-Hemmes, *On Gendering Texts: Female and Male Voices in the Hebrew Bible* (Leiden: Brill, 1993).
9. Ibid., 2–3.
10. Ibid., 9.

the reader cannot ignore. However, I want to emphasize that the voices under discussion are not abstract, inaudible, and disembodied. Rather, to pray the Psalms means to pray with the body.

4. Psalms as Corporeal Prayers and Imagining Female Bodies

The Old Testament understands the human being corporeally. It is not that a person has a body; rather, the human *is* the body. The physical dimension is interwoven with intellect, emotions, identity, and sociality; indeed, it is inseparable from moral and social dimensions. Thus devotion to God—that is, prayer—is expressed in certain bodily gestures. For example, a basalt stele from the thirteenth century BCE portrays outstretched, praying hands (see fig. 1)[11] positioned as described in Ps 28:2: "Hear the voice of my supplication, as I cry to you for help, as I lift up my hands toward the sanctuary of your heart." Outstretched hands want to reach someone; they want to reduce distance and create a relationship. The inner yearning finds expression in a physical gesture.[12]

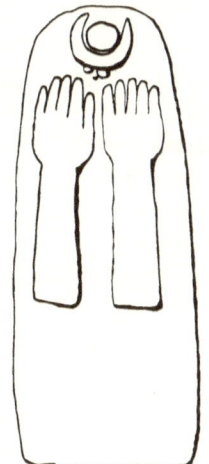

The petitioners also use body language to express themselves. One body part often stands for the whole person. Body parts that are clearly sex-specific, such as the womb, breasts, or beards, are found only in general statements.[13] For example, Ps 22:10 reads: "Yet it was you who took me from the womb." Birth in the Old Testament is generally associated with God and does not refer to the sex of the supplicant.[14]

This gender-specific vagueness regarding corporeal images allows readers to discover their own gendered bodies in the Psalms. Women do not have to ignore male body characteristics in order to read for their own bodies. The "I" of the Psalms is open to the visualization of someone with a female body. By repeating the Psalms, a woman confirms her own

---

11. From the Late Bronze Age stelae sanctuary of Hazor. Othmar Keel, *The Symbolism of the Biblical World: Ancient Near Eastern Iconography and the Book of Psalms* (trans. Timothy J. Hallett; Winona Lake, Ind.: Eisenbrauns, 1997), 321, fig. 431; reproduced by courtesy of Bible + Orient Museum Fribourg Switzerland.

12. Kneeling before God is also mentioned in Ps 29:2b; 95:6; 96:9a; 138:2.

13. See Ps 22:10, "On you I was cast from the womb."

14. For metaphors of fertility and birth see Marianne Grohmann, *Fruchtbarkeit und Geburt in den Psalmen* (FAT 53; Tübingen: Mohr Siebeck, 2007).

body, which becomes the yardstick of her life. The supplicant represents her emotions as a physical experience.[15] This is evident in Ps 102:1–8.

> A prayer of one afflicted, when faint and pleading before YHWH.
> Hear my prayer, YHWH, let my cry come to you.
> Do not hide your face from me on the day of my distress.
> Incline your ear to me; answer me speedily on the day when I call.
> For my days pass away like smoke, and my bones burn like a furnace.
> My heart is stricken and withered like grass;
> I am too wasted to eat my bread.
> Because of my loud groaning my bones cling to my skin.
> I am like an owl of the wilderness, like a little owl of the waste places.
> I lie awake; I am like a lonely bird on the housetop.

Even in the title, the emotional distress of the woman praying[16] is identified through a weighed-down posture and a weak physical condition. Her stooped posture cannot be separated from either her psychological condition or from social relations. Many translations neglect this and translate only the inner feeling of despair. Psalm 102 begins with YHWH, the name of God, whom the woman implores as she prays. In the middle of her entreaty, she requests that God no longer hide his face. The granting of the divine countenance guarantees success in life,[17] while God's turning away and becoming distant is associated with distress. The face is the part of the body that contains all that is necessary for communication, including eyes, ears, and the mouth.[18] A movement on the part of God can diminish the distance between God and the supplicant.

Verses 4b–6 describe the infirmity of the body. The bones, the body's scaffolding and powerhouse, smolder; the heart, the body's emotional and intellectual center, withers, and the bones protrude from under the skin, visually signifying vulnerability. These corporeal images do not provide a medical diagnosis, however, even if a reader can see her own illness mirrored in them. Rather, these are metaphors that express the multicausal web of emergencies that led the supplicant to lose her momentum in life. Even the life-sustaining rhythm of eating, drinking, and sleeping has been disrupted (vv. 5, 10).

---

15. Gillmayr-Bucher, "Emotion," 279–90.

16. Because I wish to demonstrate that it is possible to read the psalms of lament as prayers by women, I will henceforth speak only of a female supplicant, not a male one.

17. See Ps 31:17; 67:2; 80:4, 8, 20; Num 6:24–26.

18. This is indicated by Hans Walter Wolff, *Anthropology of the Old Testament* (trans. Margaret Kohl; London: SCM, 1974), 74.

The supplicant is socially isolated, as expressed by the images of birds. The desert bird and the owl were considered unclean animals, from which one kept one's distance. The dryness of the desert, its life-threatening aridity, corresponds to the withering heart in verse 5. Even in other psalms, dryness is associated with corporeal images of desperate longing, such as in Ps 63:2: "O God, you are my God, I seek you; my soul thirsts for you; my flesh faints for you, as in a dry and weary land where there is no water."

These passages, which express a supplicant's plight through corporeal images, are often positioned directly next to verses that reflect her social isolation. The social sphere is interwoven with corporeal images; there is a strong conjunction between physical and social integrity. In Ps 102, as well, a so-called enemy lament follows immediately on corporeal images in verse 9: "All day long my enemies taunt me; those who deride me use my name for a curse."

This passage does not use corporeal language to symbolize the enemy; however, the basic characterization here of the so-called enemy is also found in several other texts and represents the social sphere as experienced negatively. Corporeal images related to communication in particular symbolize a social sphere perverted through violence. The enemies' mouths, their lips, their tongues and teeth, are all employed to describe behavior that destroys the community.

The power of language shaped by violence is intertwined with power over life and the body. Language constructs a reality in which violence and oppression appear as an exclusive and legitimated reality.[19] It is precisely the language that in our present understanding is connected more to the spirit than to the body, which is here understood physically, in that the physical organs of speech symbolize language and are described as "weapons." This kind of representation makes almost palpable the physical effect of language; it demonstrates that language always has a physical effect.

When German youth today hurl the insult "you victim" at someone, this is not just a word. This swear word strikes and affects the whole person. The tongue becomes a weapon that throws the other to the ground—without mercy. Through the aggressive form of address of "you victim," the person who has been or will be the victim of violence is portrayed as despicable. A victim is not deserving of pity. Never! In the language of the Old Testament: "There they are, bellowing with their mouths, with sharp swords on their lips" (Ps 59:8).

In addition to "victim," I have observed that the words "gay" and "girl" are used as swear words among adolescents, who use deviations from the

---

19. Bail, *Gegen das Schweigen klagen*, esp. 31–73.

male-dominated heterosexual norm to humiliate others. Against this background, the Psalms with their gender-neutral language are quite interesting, because they reveal exactly these relationships and counter them. On the one hand, they make the power of corporeal language visible and audible, unmasking in an intense way the connection between language, power, violence, and the body. Violence that has been experienced can be expressed; the supplicants find words to share their experiences. On the other hand, perpetrators, when they read the corporeal images of the victims, change their perspective in that they become aware of the effects violence has, what corporeal experiences the victims have, what happened to them, and what they want.

The body-centered language of the Psalms may signify for readers that they find access to their feelings through their body and experience the body as an organ of knowledge. Susanne Gillmayr-Bucher explains that the corporeal language of the Psalms does not allow for a distanced reading; indeed, readers are forced to add their own corporeal experiences.[20] Self-knowledge and knowledge of others is bound to a conscious awareness of one's own body.

Through the reading of the Psalms and thus by entering into their textual space, the Psalms allow one to encounter one's own body, a needy body, a person full of yearning, an "I" with injuries and scars, with the longing for dignity and security. The possible imagining of a woman's body enables a supplicant to position her own body in the space of prayer. Her body then becomes safe, as it says in Ps 16:8–9:

> I keep Adonai always before me;
> because God is at my right hand, I shall not be moved.
> Therefore my heart is glad, and my soul rejoices;
> my body also rests secure.

5. A Psalm of Tamar? The Titles of the Psalms

With the intention of understanding the Psalms as the confirmation, strengthening, and empowering of women, Marchienne Vroon Rienstra wrote the liturgically oriented *Swallow's Nest: A Feminine Reading of the Psalms*.[21] Beginning with the Hebrew text, she paraphrased the Psalms. She is concerned less

---

20. Gillmayr-Bucher, "Body Images," 325.
21. Marchienne Vroon Rienstra, *Swallow's Nest: A Feminine Reading of the Psalms* (Grand Rapids: Eerdmans, 1992). Rienstra wrote this book in the form of a prayer book. Each day features morning, midday, and evening prayers, which cover four weeks. In addition to the Psalms, there are also traditional Bible readings and prayers.

about scholarly discourse as with the liturgical and spiritual reading of the Psalter. It is her aim to encourage readers to read the Psalms as prayers of individual women in various contexts around the world. Rienstra ascribes to the Psalms certain situations that do or can characterize the biographies of women, by which she means concrete, specific political and social contexts, as well as general experiences. To illustrate this, she provides the Psalms with new headings, for example, Ps 6: "This might be the prayer of a woman who was raped."[22] Just as with Ps 6, Rienstra puts all of her headings in the subjunctive mood, to indicate that the correlations to female-specific situations given in the heading are not the only ones possible, but are conceivable.

By giving the Psalms headings, Rienstra proceeds not unlike the early (inner-biblical) exegetes, who correlated many Psalms with the biography of David and recorded this correlation in the heading, "A Psalm of David."[23] But this information cannot be understood historically. The authors mentioned in the titles, such as David, sons of Korah, Asaph, Solomon, Ethan, or Moses, are literary and fictional. By this means, the psalm headings substantiate the Psalms as the voices of the named men and associate them with their biographies as narrated in the Old Testament. About half of the 150 psalms name David in their headings. This note is not intended as an author's statement, but as a link to David's biography, in which the situations that move people to invoke God are evident. In the biblical tradition, David is considered the ideal supplicant of the Psalms, not as the bellicose and victorious king, but rather as one persecuted, full of doubt and repentance, who prays and hopes that God will listen and draw close. That David's authorship is a literary one makes it possible to hear the Psalms not only as his voice but also as the prayers of both male and female individuals in quite different circumstances. By means of the same concept of the voice described in this essay, the psalms of lament can be read as gender-specific.

The biblical psalm headings were added secondarily to the Psalms. Thus, for example, Ps 51 is interwoven through its heading with the story of David and Bathsheba, and represents the voice of David (see 2 Sam 12). It reads: "For the musical performance. A psalm of David, when the prophet Nathan came to him, after he had gone in to Bathsheba" (Ps 51:1). David thus becomes the author of the psalm—not the historical but rather the fictional author—in the sense that David becomes the sustaining voice at the textual level. The words

---

22. Rienstra, *Swallow's Nest*, 44.

23. For details, see Bail, *Gegen das Schweigen klagen*, 83–86. See also Bail, "The Psalms: Who Is Speaking May Be All That Matters," in *Feminist Biblical Interpretation: A Compendium of Critical Commentary on the Books of the Bible and Related Literature* (ed. Luise Schottroff und Marie-Theres Wacker; Grand Rapids: Eerdmans, 2012), 180–91.

conveyed by Ps 51 are his words. David would therefore correspond to the "voice" in the text, according to Brenner and van Dijk-Hemmes. Based on the literary authorship of David, one would conclude that Ps 51 represents a male voice on the literary level, described as an M voice. But it is a fictional voice that can be present only on the literary level. Solely by means of the literary correlation of the Psalms with the biography of David can the psalm be heard as the voice of David. Precisely because it is possible to link psalm texts with other texts, however, we can use the psalms of lament as an opportunity to read the voices of women.

The psalm headings guide us to read and understand each psalm in a certain way. These added titles determine the reception of the psalms through a particular historical, sociocultural, and theological point of view. They stipulate one manner by which one should read the psalms apart from the variety of ways the psalms could be received. By providing each psalm with an interpretive title, the authors of these headings "annotated" the result of their reading.

The "I" of the psalm is substantiated by the naming of a subject that allows for correlation with other inner-biblical Old Testament texts. The combination of a poetic psalm text and a narrative-biographical (con)text via the psalm headings create the possibility of reading the psalms through a feminist lens. We can therefore modify and expand the net of inner-biblical correlations spun through the psalm headings. We can focus the net of references on the voices of women, from the perspective of women, in the sense of an intertextual reading. Hence, in addition to the psalms of David, there would be psalms of Tamar, Dinah, and other biblical women.

6. Intertextual Correlations

The Psalms' intertextual, literary-contemporizing potential for connection makes it possible to hear women's voices in the psalms of lament by linking the Psalms to narrative texts about women. I do not mean linking in the simple sense of sympathy, empathy, or identification, but rather in the sense of the literary theory of intertextuality. At this point, I can go into only the most basic commonalities of these theories.[24]

---

24. See the detailed discussion in Bail, *Gegen das Schweigen klagen*, 98–113. See also Beth LaNeel Tanner, *The Books of Psalms through the Lens of Intertextuality* (Studies in Biblical Literature 26; New York: Peter Lang, 2001); Stefan Alkier, "Intertextualität—Annäherungen an ein texttheoretisches Paradigma," in *Heiligkeit und Herrschaft: Intertextuelle Studien zu Heiligkeitsvorstellungen und zu Psalm 110* (ed. Dieter Sänger; BThS 55; Neukirchen-Vluyn: Neukirchener, 2003), 1–26; Nancy R. Bowen, "A Fairy Tale Wedding?

The starting point is a particular understanding of what a text is and how one establishes its meaning. Intertextuality refers to the relationship of texts to each other. All literary texts are "woven" out of other literary texts, not in the conventional sense as traces of other texts' influence, but rather in the sense that each text can basically enter into conversation with every other one.

This definition of "text" resists an excessive emphasis on textual boundaries. An overemphasis on this idea makes texts appear as islands, isolated from all other texts in an endless expanse of ocean, even as prison islands, where the meaning is fixed once and for all and only one perspective on how to read dominates. Texts are not islands, however, and the reader is not a castaway who numbers the psalms and places them into categories without memory or retrospection. Rather, texts are dialogical; they call to mind other texts already read and events already experienced. No text exists in isolation; each finds itself a place in a world of already existing texts. Nor is this place static; rather, the text is in motion and not fixed by a statement. Texts contain a variety of meanings in themselves; they are ambiguous and polyphonic, never unequivocal. New interpretations evoked by correlations occur during every reading of a text; thus there is not *the* text, but rather always only different interpretations of a text.

Intertextuality thus denotes the hermeneutical fact that texts are always located in interrelation with other texts. While redaction criticism diachronically analyzes the relationship between texts, an intertextual analysis describes the interrelationship between texts. In the process, new correlations of a given text with others that are not yet registered in the given text become possible. Each concrete reading brings a text into connection with other new texts. It is impossible to escape intertextuality, argues Danna Nolan Fewell, because texts talk to each other, mutually echo each other, stumble against each other, fight with each other; they are voices that are consonant with each other, voices that are in conflict and in competition with each other.[25]

The process of reading brings out a text's meaning. This meaning is determined in relation to the texts that the given text indicates as correlations, as well as those texts the reader associates with the given text. These can be both visible traces and empty spaces, both words and silence. Moreover, the interpretation can influence the connective interaction of texts, in that the reader determines not only which texts to compare but also the points of

---

A Feminist Intertextual Reading of Psalm 45," in *A God So Near: Essays on Old Testament Theology in Honor of Patrick D. Miller* (ed. Brent A. Strawn and Nancy R. Bowen; Winona Lake, Ind.: Eisenbrauns, 2003), 53–71.

25. Donna Nolan Fewell, ed., *Reading Between Texts: Intertextuality and the Hebrew Bible* (Louisville: Westminster John Knox, 1992), 12.

comparison. For the psalms of lament, this means that in the process of their reception, women become subjects of the lament; they can hear their voices in the psalms of lament.

7. Psalm 55 and the Story of the Rape of Tamar (2 Sam 13)

Second Samuel 13 narrates how Amnon, on the advice of his friend Jonadab, lures his half sister Tamar into his room with the lie that he is sick. There he rapes her, although she verbally puts up a fight. The rooms in the story become increasingly narrow, until Tamar loses the power of control over both the space and her own body. After the rape, Amnon throws her out into the street. Thereafter, she lives in the house of her other brother Absalom, silent and forgotten, after which Absalom says to her, "Has Amnon your brother been with you? Be quiet for now, my sister; he is your brother; do not take this to heart" (v. 20a). The violence takes place behind closed doors, and Tamar remains trapped behind closed doors. Violence and secrecy go hand in hand.

The last sentence concerning Tamar reads: "So Tamar remained, completely destroyed, in her brother Absalom's house" (v. 20b). The Hebrew word שׁממ, which is translated here as "completely destroyed," is usually translated as "lonely."[26] This translation, however, makes light of Tamar's state. The Hebrew word שׁממ is frequently used for lands and cities that have been devastated and destroyed. They are considered both uninhabited and uninhabitable; they are thus associated with the desert, which cannot sustain life. The book of Jeremiah clearly states this at one point: "Her cities have become an object of horror, a land of drought and a desert, a land in which no one lives, and through which no mortal passes" (Jer 51:43). Instead of "lonely," the word "homeless" more clearly describes Tamar's state.

The house of Absalom offers Tamar no refuge, but acts more like a shelter for her perpetrators, because no sound penetrates through the walls. The rape is ostracized from speech, by relegating Tamar's words to the confines of the house. By means of the concept of voice, *reception aesthetics,* and an intertextually oriented reading, we can read the psalms of lament as the voice of the raped Tamar; the "wordless cry of Tamar" can be "filled with texts of the psalms of lament."[27]

The rape of Tamar takes place in a geographically and emotionally intimate space. It is Amnon, her half brother, who rapes her. This topography of

---

26. The NRSV translates the word as "desolate."
27. Müllner, "Klagend laut werden," 83; For greater detail, see Bail, *Gegen das Schweigen klagen,* 160–78.

affinity is also visible in Ps 55. The perpetrator is addressed directly with the words "But you—my equal, my companion, my familiar friend" (v. 14). The psalm designates the abuser as one who was in a relationship of trust with the supplicant. He abuses the friendly relationship that should for all intents and purposes exclude violence, and he destroys it with his actions.

Tamar has no verbal language to refer to her trauma—she walks away screaming, as related in 2 Sam 13:19. She tears her dress and puts her hand on her head. By means of traditional acts of mourning, she expresses her traumatic experience.[28] Tamar speaks nonverbally through her body, which she changes. Her body becomes a symbol for others, conveying to them what happened. The trauma is inscribed through the socially mediated textures of grief in the body that can be read by others. After Amnon throws her out into the public space of the street, Tamar provides by means of her body information about what has happened. Tamar cannot talk about it. She is not capable of it, and her brother forbids it. This inability to express herself results in her preference for physical gestures. "Speech is preceded by corporeal language; the 'eloquence of the body' has to stand up for the lack of language."[29] The physical changes make the loss, trauma, and grief both visible and legible. In phases of a search for orientation and identity, the body can become the bearer of meaning, materializing possible deficits and concepts of meaning.

The bodies of those in whom sorrow has been inscribed are not sexually differentiated: both men and women give their grief a physical form in the same way. Men and women weep openly and thereby give expression to their pain.[30] It is nevertheless striking that, on this point—that is, at the intersection of body and speech—women, specifically professional wailing women, are assigned a prominent role. The cultural decoding of physical productions of mourning resides to a certain degree with them (Jer 9:17–21).

It would have been possible for anyone to read what befell Tamar. Nevertheless, no one counters the following silence, except the story itself, by relating what happened—and a psalm of lament such as Ps 55, which creates space for Tamar's traumatic experience, interweaving the trauma of sexual violence with the topography of violence in Ps 55.

---

28. Ulrike Bail, "Hautritzen als Körperinszenierung der Trauer und des Verlustes im Alten Testament," in *"Dies ist mein Leib:" Leibliches, Leibeigenes und Leibhaftiges bei Gott und den Menschen* (ed. Jürgen Ebach et al.; Jabboq 9; Gütersloh: Gütersloher, 2006), 54–80.

29. Gisela Ecker, "Trauer zeigen: Inszenierung und Sorge um den Anderen," in *Trauer tragen—Trauer zeigen: Inszenierungen der Geschlechter* (ed. Gisela Ecker; Munich: Fink, 1999), 9–25, 17.

30. Rainer Kessler, "Männertränen," in *Gotteserdung: Beiträge zur Hermeneutik und Exegese der Hebräischen Bibel* (Stuttgart: Kohlhammer, 2006), 30–34.

In Ps 55, the supplicant's experience of terror and violence is compared with a city, the walls of which are occupied by violence, and the center marketplace of which has been penetrated by violence (vv. 10–12). In Hebrew, the city has feminine gender and is often personified as a woman.[31] The figures "Daughter Zion," "Virgin Jerusalem," and "Whore Babylon" are just a few examples of the associations between women and cities. These points of contact between the city and "I" in Ps 55 on the one hand and between the city and women on the other hand suggests that it is possible to imagine a female subject in Ps 55. Even the verb "surround, circle" (סבב) is evidence for this. In the psalms of lament, this verb articulates the threat of violence, its frightening magnitude, and the impotence of the supplicant (see Ps 17:11). Often the verb implies extreme terror (see Jer 6:25; Ps 31:14). The meaning of "surrounded antagonistically" is found in bellicose, military contexts, for example, in the context of the siege and conquest of a city (Jer 4:17; 50:14–15). As the consequence of a city's conquest, the word "to be destroyed" (שמם) is used in the Old Testament to denote the strategy of war that leaves only scorched earth to the opponent (Jer 51:43). Interestingly, this word can also be applied to women (Isa 54:1; 62:4; Jer 50:12–13; Ezek 23:33). In this case, it is parallel with "to be unfruitful" or "to be abandoned"; it appears as the opposite of "to be married." This word also articulates the state of the raped king's daughter Tamar in 2 Sam 13:20: "So Tamar lived, homeless [שממה], in her brother Absalom's house."

In light of the use of the verb to denote devastated land and ruined cities, the word, in relation to Tamar, means the destruction of her integrity and identity through the rape. By means of the topography of violence, an intertextual correlation arises between the story of the rape of Tamar and the psalm of lament.

It becomes clear from the context of the entire psalm that the city is not only a place but also the object of violence. There is a connection between the "I" of the psalm, who verbalizes her experience of violence, and the city that is conquered and occupied (see the keyword connections, "disaster" in vv. 4, 11, and "in the middle" in vv. 5, 11, 12). Both the city and the "I" are objects of violence to which they are exposed. If one adds the verbs with which the "I" expresses her experience in verses 4b–6 to the image of the city, the total domination of the space by violence becomes clear. While in the image of the city, the pressing movements run horizontally ("surround, not to yield"), the calamity to which the "I" is exposed moves in a vertical line ("to upset,

---

31. See also the extensive study by Christl M. Maier, *Daughter Zion, Mother Zion: Gender, Space, and the Sacred in Ancient Israel* (Minneapolis: Fortress, 2008).

to be conspicuous, cover"). The topography of violence dominates the space from which there is no escape. Against this hopeless topography, however, the psalm creates alternative spaces.

The trust in God sketches a counterdiscourse that empowers the subjectivity and identity of the powerless object of violence. This takes place in the space of the desert, which is conceived as an alternative space to the city (vv. 7–9). These verses present salvation as an unrealizable possibility; still, they also reflect a survival strategy, namely, dissociation. Dissociation means that emotions are split off and the ego separates itself from the body, in order to create boundary between the ego and an unbearable pain in hopeless situations of physical and psychological distress. The image of the dove, which flees into the desert as its refuge, is not integrated by keywords into the rest of the psalm, but rather it stands alone. The dove-and-desert image is in a sense dissociated. The imagined flight of the dove into the desert therefore also performs the function of demonstrating that the ego is not destroyed as far as its innermost depths. This image helps the ego to withstand the completely overwhelming experience of violence without losing itself. The power of new images to speak in a situation of absolute powerlessness and to create new spaces corresponds to the words "but I will trust in you" at the end of the psalm. What is only implied in verses 7–9, namely, to find shelter, gains certainty by the corresponding "but I will trust in you." God is on the side of the woman who prays. By claiming God as her advocate against violence, the supplicant ties even God into the daily and nightly experiences of violence against women. To deny her grievance would be to identify God with the horror and violence. Her loud and public lament could create a real refuge for the dove, a place where not only surviving, but also living without danger, is possible, every day and every night. A grievance filed on behalf of the dove can begin the process of liberation. Hence, the title of Ps 55 could state, "The lament of a woman. To speak out against silence."[32]

---

32. Magdalene Frettlöh and Jens Herzer understand this aspect in their own way and connect it to the crucifixion of Jesus. Magdalene L. Frettlöh, "Der auferweckte Gekreuzigte und die Überlebenden sexueller Gewalt: Kreuzestheologie genderspezifisch wahr genommen," in *Das Kreuz Jesu: Gewalt—Opfer—Sühne* (ed. Rudolf Weth; Neukirchen-Vluyn: Neukirchener, 2001), 77–104; Jens Herzer, "Freund und Feind: Beobachtungen zum alttestamentlich-frühjüdischen Hintergrund und zum impliziten Handlungsmodell der Gethsemane-Perikope Mk 14,32–42," *leqach* 1 (2001): 99–127.

8. Safe Spaces: Psalms of Lament and Modern Trauma Research

In many places in the psalms of lament, one finds metaphors that represent rescue and refuge. There is language describing a woven shield (Ps 5:12), a sheltering shield (7:11), the hand that holds (10:14), rescue (14:6), the waters of the rest (23:2), refuge and the shade of wings (27:1; 36:8), a safe place (59:17), the castle and the shadow of the mighty deity (91:1–2).

In more recent works that deal with the treatment of psychological trauma, the concept of "safe space" plays a significant role. The first step in coping with trauma is stabilization, communication, and security. The knowledge of an imaginary safe place in oneself that one can visit at any time, independent of external events, is crucial. This site forms an intrapsychic retreat that represents a refuge providing shelter during the processing of a traumatic experience.[33] The imaginative exercises of trauma therapy have at first the goal of setting good, controlled, regulated images of one's own making against unregulated mental images. Through this practice, one gains the experience of inner comfort and inner support, of absolute safety and security, and the experience of self-consolation. Imagining such a place is an essential step on the road to healing.[34] By means of an intervening inner image of safety, wounded people can withdraw inwardly to a safe space in times of stress.

The Old Testament scholar Frank Crüsemann was the first to notice that the image of a safe space bears a certain analogy to the psalms of lament. I thus wish to give Crüsemann the floor via a longer quote.

> Without straining the analogy, or even wanting to claim a complete identity, it still seems possible, in any case it is worthwhile to play it through and see a correlation here. God appears in these Psalms of lament as the safe space to which the supplicants flee. Here they seek safety and security. ... As Ps 31:21 states literally, God can "*hide*" threatened people "*in the hiding of your countenance*," and grants "*my refuge*" in the wilderness (Ps 55:8).
>
> By hiding even in the averted face of God, the supplicants can at any time withdraw to this imagined place of refuge. Even in times when God is hidden or absent, they induce His aid by at first imagining Him and assuming the presence of the Absent One by addressing and talking to Him. God as safe space—this image makes it possible to lament His turning away, to remember positive experiences, but also to articulate all reproaches against

---

33. Luise Reddemann, *Imagination als heilsame Kraft* (Stuttgart: Klett Cotta, 2007). See also http://www.luise-reddemann.info/.

34. See also the introduction to trauma research authored by Ruth Poser and the possibilities of using this for biblical interpretation. Ruth Poser, *Das Ezechielbuch als Traumaliteratur* (VTSup 154; Leiden: Brill, 2012), 57–119.

and fears of one's enemies, and indict them for their power, violence, and evil, to permit all feelings of guilt and failure; even an indictment against God is possible and permitted. ... God stands in the center as experience and hope of a safe place offering protection, whether near or far, present or future, a place that makes it possible to express every confidence, previously and remembered, still available and resilient, hoped-for and in the future.[35]

The Psalms do not begin like a therapy session with the image of a safe space. This often opens up only in the course of speaking. Safe spaces can be found throughout the Psalms; they grant a pause, a self-rescue, so that one may then go further and voice all of one's injuries and pain, without repressing or leaving anything out. The textual space of the psalm itself can become a safe space. As borrowed words, the words of the Psalms offer the possibility of "expressing feelings, while simultaneously leaving them inviolate."[36] It is borrowed words as well as one's very own words that are articulated in the language of the Psalms. In situations of utter powerlessness, it is important to know which words one may borrow—especially when one's own words fail and one's own throat is unable to articulate anything.

At the same time, the psalms of lament can connect the reader with other people, women and men, who have for millennia had similar experiences. Thus the textual space of the psalm turns into a safe and a protected space. This space can also become a wide realm, making freedom of movement and speech possible: "Thus, the lament itself becomes the source of their liberation"[37]—especially and precisely for women who have survived the experience of violence.

Translated from German by Carrie Dohe

---

35. Frank Crüsemann, "Der Gewalt nicht glauben: Hiobbuch und Klagepsalmen—zwei Modelle theologischer Verarbeitung traumatischer Gewalterfahrungen," in *Dem Tod nicht glauben: Sozialgeschichte der Bibel: Festschrift Luise Schottroff zum 70. Geburtstag* (ed. Frank Crüsemann et al.; Gütersloh: Gütersloher, 2004), 251–68, 265 (cursive in original). See also Renate Jost, "Trauma, Heilung und die Bibel," in *Dem Tod nicht glauben*, 269–92; esp. 280–81.
36. Crüsemann, "Der Gewalt nicht glauben," 9.
37. Konrad Raiser, "Klage als Befreiung," *Einwürfe* 5 (1988): 13–27.

Lamentations and Gender in Biblical Cultural Context

Nancy C. Lee

1. Introduction to Lamentations[1]

The book of Lamentations is one of the Megilloth (five scrolls) in the Hebrew Bible/Tanak read at annual Jewish festivals, in this case to commemorate the destruction of Jerusalem several times in history. It shares with the books of Ruth, Esther, and the Song of Songs (books also in the Megilloth) the inclusion of women's stories, voices, and perspectives. Lamentations is often regarded as composed by one or more eyewitnesses of the siege and destruction of Jerusalem by the Babylonians around 587 BCE and the exile of most of the Judean population. Christian Bibles place Lamentations just after the book of Jeremiah, following the Jewish tradition's attribution.[2] Four Hebrew manuscripts of Lamentations were discovered among the Dead Sea Scrolls.[3]

---

1. Biblical translations are the author's unless otherwise indicated.

2. Reflected by the superscription added to Lamentations in the Septuagint: "And it came to pass, after Israel was taken captive, and Jerusalem made desolate, Jeremias sat weeping and lamented this lamentation over Jerusalem" (Lam 1:1 LXX).

3. Besides a Qumran version of Lamentations (4QLam), there was also discovered a lament text from Qumran *close* to Lamentations. While many scholars suggest that the latter, 4Q179 (or 4Q Apocryphal Lamentations), was influenced by the biblical text, Tal Ilan suggests it was an "alternative version" of Lamentations before the MT was standardized: it contains more female references to more real women in the context, and more sympathetic renderings of the persona Jerusalem. "4Q179 is more female gendered than the masoretic text, and the masoretic text is more female gendered than 4QLam. This may point to the unstable character of the Lamentations texts during the Second Temple period regarding gender images"; see Ilan, "Gender and Lamentations: 4Q179 and the Canonization of the Book of Lamentations," *lectio difficilior* 2 (2008): http://www.lectio.unibe.ch/08_2/Tal_Ilan_Gender_of_Lamentations.html.

In comparison to many other biblical books, Lamentations has been rather neglected in the history of interpretation. This neglect may be due in part to the severance, in the Enlightenment period and afterward, of the traditional association with Jeremiah from the book, as well as the association of lament in the book with women, perhaps deemed less important by male interpreters, who dominated the field of biblical studies. Thus matters of gender have had an impact on how the book has been regarded in the canon.

A watershed study, however, was by Hedwig Jahnow (1923).[4] Though her work was overlooked for some time, she greatly enlarged the perspective on Lamentations, drawing on findings from anthropology and oral poetry, to show how dirges for the individual and the community across cultures share common features and help shed light on biblical texts and practice.[5] Prior to formal feminist criticism, Jahnow emphasized women in traditional cultures have played an important role worldwide in composing and performing laments in contexts of mourning. She suggested these customs shaped the book of Lamentations. While women were not given credit for composing any of Lamentations, recent studies have examined how the mourning context and echoes of the practice of women's laments might be embedded in the text.[6] Yet the possibility of a female poet composing any part of Lamentations has been largely neglected by scholars.[7] The greater trend has been to focus on the female voice of personified Jerusalem or Daughter Zion in the book,[8] implicitly regarded by many commentators as constructed by a male poet.

---

4. Hedwig Jahnow, *Das hebräische Leichenlied im Rahmen der Völkerdichtung* (BZAW 36; Giessen: Töpelmann, 1923).

5. Women sang dirges in ancient Israel (Jer 9:17–22; 2 Chr 35:25; Ezek 32:16), in the ancient Near East, and in many cultures worldwide, though men were not excluded from the practice (e.g., David's lament in 2 Sam 1:17–27).

6. See esp. Xuan Huong Thi Pham, *Mourning in the Ancient Near East and the Hebrew Bible* (Sheffield: Sheffield Academic, 1999). Archaeological and biblical evidence suggests women performed music and various genres in Israelite culture; see Carol Meyers, "Of Drums and Damsels," *BA* 54, no 1 (1991): 16–27; S. D. Goitein, "Women as Creators of Biblical Genres" (trans. Michael Carasik) *Prooftexts* 8 (1988): 1–33, 1–5.

7. Exceptions to this include Athalya Brenner and Fokkelien Van Dijk-Hemmes, *On Gendering Texts: Female and Male Voices in the Hebrew Bible* (Leiden: Brill, 1993), 83–90; Nancy C. Lee, *The Singers of Lamentations: Cities under Siege, From Ur to Jerusalem to Sarajevo* (BibIntS 60; Leiden: Brill, 2002), 12–37; and Mayer I. Gruber, "Women's Voices in the Book of Micah," *lectio difficilior* 1 (2007): http://www.lectio.unibe.ch/07_1/mayer_gruber_womens_voices.htm.

8. E.g., F. W. Dobbs-Allsopp, *Weep, O Daughter Zion: A Study of the City-Lament Genre in the Hebrew Bible* (BibOr 44; Rome: Pontifical Biblical Institute, 1993); Kathleen M. O'Connor, "Lamentations," in *The Women's Bible Commentary* (ed. Carol A. Newsom et al.; 3rd ed.; Louisville: Westminster John Knox, 2012), 278–82; Carleen R. Mandolfo, *Daughter*

Recent studies do not try to identify "the author" of Lamentations. Instead, some explain that the multiple voices in the book, including the voice of "Daughter Zion," are personae created by a single (usually assumed male) poet[9] who authored most of the work. Other scholars understand the multiple voices as those of real persons/singers in the context with different perspectives, including possibly a woman, whose creative expressions from their experiences were collected by an editor or scribe.

This author follows the latter, using an oral poetic approach. Whether chanted or sung, the lyrics are illuminated by comparing lament genres across cultures and understanding their forms and functions in different parts of the Bible. It is an approach that recognizes the sophisticated *oral poetic processes* of persons *in community* engaging their historical-political situations. Yet this approach affirms the work of feminist/womanist and other critics today who aim both to discern misogynous elements in the biblical texts and to recognize women's roles and voices in the Bible, in this case especially as lamenters and prophets. It takes seriously the possibility of women's actual contributions in composing biblical texts, no less than men, even in an androcentric culture.

Whether the book of Lamentations only includes a female persona constructed by a male poet, or also reflects a woman singer in her own right, the female voice certainly goes beyond women's traditional mourning expressions to lead a dialogical debate about God's punishing and violent role in the context. Does Lamentations significantly expand a female voice and perspective often missing in the biblical canon? Or does "the [male] poet" of Lamentations simply construct and control the speaking of a fictive female persona of the city, as some male prophets do? These are questions pertinent to the interpretation of Lamentations.[10]

In Lamentations the voices use two lament genres to express their grief with what has happened: the communal dirge (Lam 1, 2, and 4) and the lament prayer to God (in Lam 1, 2, 3, and 5).[11] The communal dirge, modified from funeral song for an individual's death (Heb. קינה), in the Bible is

---

Zion Talks Back to the Prophets (SemeiaSt 58; Atlanta: Society of Biblical Literature, 2007); Christl M. Maier, *Daughter Zion, Mother Zion: Gender, Space, and the Sacred in Ancient Israel* (Minneapolis: Fortress, 2008).

9. William Lanahan, "The Speaking Voice in the Book of Lamentations," *JBL* 93 (1974): 41–49, 41.

10. For a focus on Zion's voice see Maria Häusl, "Lamentations: Zion's Cry in Affliction," in *Feminist Biblical Interpretation: A Compendium of Critical Commentary on the Books of the Bible and Related Literature* (ed. Luise Schottroff and Marie-Theres Wacker; Grand Rapids: Eerdmans, 2012), 334–44.

11. There are a few examples of women identified as praying laments to God in the Hebrew Bible (e.g., Hannah in 1 Sam 1:15–16).

often uttered by prophets to warn a community that both disloyalty to God and social injustice shall lead to its social collapse, the "death" of the nation. Communal dirge was used by poets in Mesopotamia and in many cultures worldwide.[12] Lament prayers to the deity are often associated with this. Both of these plaintive genres regularly contain a "description of distress" and can be concerned about injustice. Yet the dirge signals the futilities of destruction and death, whereas the lament prayer, with its plea, raises hope—albeit dim in Lamentations—wherein God might intervene. Lament prayer also allows for confession to God, but not always, so may instead protest and defend innocence; this too is found in Lamentations.

Literary acrostics structure the chapters of Lamentations, using the twenty-two letters of the Hebrew alphabet. Commentators suggest the acrostic puts order on chaos, and conveys all possible suffering—or guilt—from "a to z" (א to ת). Nearly all the other acrostics in the Bible (in ten psalms) promote the idea of retributive justice, that people reap from God what they sow, and defend God as a righteous judge (צדיק). Such psalms espouse that the righteous are rewarded by God, the wicked are punished—a theological "order" hammered home by every letter (and line) of their acrostic form. Lamentations 1 follows this reasoning, using the alphabetic order. But Lam 2–4 present some dissident singers who rebel at the explanation of retributive justice in their complaining against God about the suffering and punishment of the *innocent*. Indeed, they *invert* letters of the alphabet, but to what end we shall see below.

Woven through the acrostic structure are techniques of poetic artistry. These include a קינה ("lament") rhythm, parallelism, chiasm, inclusio, repetition, and—as in the prophets—striking examples of double meaning and wordplay. Additionally, the first (likely male) voice personifies Jerusalem as a woman in a way typical of the prophets. However, is it also possible that a woman, from her experience, social role, and through her voice preserved in the text, spoke *on behalf of* the city? Some have suggested a woman skilled in dirge composing/singing in Israel is heard in Lamentations. This is certainly plausible, as women's laments across cultures have been a vehicle for dissident sociopolitical expression. And there have been historic instances in cultures where men in power have tried to curtail women's laments.[13] Yet most bib-

---

12. See Dobbs-Allsopp, *Weep, O Daughter Zion*. The rabbis titled the book of Lamentations קינות ("dirges") and used the term for communal lament psalms. Recognition of this genre in the canon is reflected in the later titles—θρῆνοι by the Septuagint and *Threni* by the Vulgate.

13. See discussion in Nancy C. Lee, *Lyrics of Lament: From Tragedy to Transformation* (Minneapolis: Fortress, 2010), 31–34; e.g., in classical Greece and possibly in early Chris-

lical commentators give the male prophets credit for adapting the women's dirge genre for their own oracles (e.g., Amos, Isaiah). In fact, in Lamentations the woman's voice is expressed primarily through the other lament form—the prayer. The instance of lament prayer as strong protest by women is not clearly evident elsewhere in the Hebrew Bible. Yet, with all social structures collapsing in this sixth-century crisis, a woman may have assumed such an exceptional speaking role.

2. Multiple Singers Express Their Sorrows: The Book of Lamentations

Let us now move to the text of Lamentations. Most commentators identify two key speakers in Lam 1–2; the first utilizes communal dirge speech primarily, like a male prophet; the second, like a woman concerned for the city's suffering, utilizes first-person lament prayer speech (1:9c, 11c–15b, 16–22; 2:20–22).

2.1. Lamentations 1: Singers Portray the Famous City's Downfall

As the book opens, the first lead voice expresses a communal dirge for the devastation of Jerusalem.[14]

> How lonely sits the city
> that once was full of people!
> How like a widow she has become,
> she that was great among the nations! (Lam 1:1 NRSV)

The first speaker portrays Jerusalem with similes and metaphors: like a widow weeping, a princess who has become a vassal, an abandoned promiscuous

---

tianity; thus Gail Holst-Warhaft, "Mourning in a Man's World: the *Epitaphios Logos* and the Banning of Laments in Fifth-Century Athens," in *Dangerous Voices: Women's Laments and Greek Literature* (London: Routledge, 1992), 4–6; and in early developing Islam, Suad Joseph and Afsaneh Najmabadi, eds., *Encyclopedia of Women and Islamic Cultures* (Leiden: Brill, 2003), 118–22; Leor Halevi, *Muhammad's Grave* (New York: Columbia University Press, 2007), 114–42.

14. As Jeremiah is the major prophet in this context, it is legitimate to ask whether Lamentations preserves *some* utterances of the figure of Jeremiah here, as one voice among many. The first voice in Lamentations is consistent with and suggestive of Jeremiah's voice, in that the individual artistry is strikingly parallel to the poetry of Jeremiah's voice in the book of Jeremiah, in terms of precise use of genre, phraseology, particular themes, and poetic techniques; Lee, *Singers of Lamentations*, 47–162.

woman, a grieving mother, a despised sinful woman,[15] a rape victim, a virgin trodden like grapes, and a woman ritually unclean due to her being violated or bloodied from injury. In her fall from power and honor, Jerusalem suffers and is abused, but the first speaker explains this by saying, "YHWH has made her suffer for the multitude of her transgressions" (v. 5) because "Jerusalem sinned grievously" (v. 8). With these characterizations, the first speaker is both judgmental and more sympathetic regarding Jerusalem's situation than some (male) prophetic rhetoric in this context (cf. Ezek 23). The speaker does not portray Jerusalem as an unfaithful wife to YHWH, though this is implicit given the larger context. Nor is God explicitly referred to as Jerusalem's husband, though in other biblical texts this is a common metaphor (Hos 1–3; Jer 3:1–3). Needless to say, feminist/womanist and other interpreters are troubled by the graphic description of abuse and punishment of women.

Besides personifying the city and country as female, the first speaker also sympathetically describes "real" women and girls suffering in the destruction as victims of war:[16] young girls grieve (1:4), children have gone away (1:5), elders and young girls mourn (2:10), infants cry to their mothers and die on their breasts (2:11, 19), young women of the city suffer (3:51), as do precious and thirsty children (4:2, 4), and most horrendously, mothers cannibalize children (4:10). Yet the speaker also describes the suffering of "all the people" in 1:11 and the fate of boys and men (e.g., priests in 1:4; princes in 1:6; rulers in 2:2; warriors in 2:3), and many times refers to the city's enemies.

The first speaker's dirge (with a rather detached tone) is interrupted in Lam 1:9c by the second voice, uttering an anguished lament (with typical elements of the address of the deity, a plea, and description of distress): "YHWH, look at my affliction, for the enemy has triumphed!"

Because of the juxtaposition of this plea to the description of personified Jerusalem in the nine verses prior, the book aims to have the reader understand that this lament is uttered by the female persona of Jerusalem. However, if we are to treat the voices in the book on an equal footing within their context, then it is also reasonable to regard the first voice as a prophet uttering a dirge for the personified city, and the second as a singer lamenting *on behalf of* the personified city. While the gender of neither voice is explicitly given, the larger context suggests the likelihood that the first voice is male as a typical

---

15. In Lam 1:8, Jerusalem has become a נִידָה (though NRSV has "mockery," the wordplay means also an outcast because of sin), but the similar-sounding נִדָּה, "impure one" (1:17), implies here rape and violation of the sanctuary (cf. 1:7, 10); contra those who read here a menstruant, also not a cause of guilt in the Bible, see Jacob Milgrom, *Leviticus 1–16* (AB 3; New York: Doubleday, 1991), 38, 744–46, 948–53.

16. O'Connor, "Lamentations," 190.

prophet, and the second voice is female, typical of a lamenter needing comfort in a mourning context. Her plea about the enemy is answered then by the first singer, and so a call-and-response pattern begins unfolding between them.

> Enemies have stretched out their hands over all her precious things;
> she has even seen the nations invade her sanctuary;
> those whom you forbade to enter your congregation. (1:10 NRSV)

It is apparent that the first voice's lyrics refer primarily to the city persona, yet most commentators hear a double meaning in these lines, of the enemy's rape of a woman in this war context. While the first voice goes on to describe the people's suffering from hunger, the second voice interjects again.

> Look, O Lord, and see how worthless I have become.
> Is it nothing to you, all you who pass by?
> Look and see if there is any sorrow like my sorrow,
> which was brought upon me,
> which the Lord inflicted on the day of his fierce anger. (1:11c–12 NRSV)

Thus far, both speakers are in agreement with prophetic theology, that Jerusalem's demise is God's punishment for the people's sin. However, in the following ten verses of lyric, the woman's voice expresses an *expanded accusation against God* for how he has treated her and the inhabitants of the city. The first speaker responds with an affirmation that YHWH has done this (v. 15c). Yet she goes on,

> For these things I weep; my eyes flow with tears;
> for a comforter is far from me, one to revive my courage;
> my children are desolate, for the enemy has prevailed. (1:16 NRSV)

Her grief is not just as a city persona but also as a real woman mourning in anguish as a mother for her dying children.[17] The lyrics weave together these female sufferings.[18]

In verse 17, the first voice says YHWH has "commanded" against the people, bringing on their foes to Jerusalem's detriment. Yet the female voice

---

17. On this theme, see Tod Linafelt, *Surviving Lamentations: Catastrophe, Lament and Protest in the Afterlife of a Biblical Book* (Chicago: University of Chicago Press, 2000), 50–58; on female metaphors for Zion and Jerusalem throughout the Bible, including as mother, and in Lamentations, see Maier, *Daughter Zion, Mother Zion*, 141–60, 198–217.

18. One is reminded of two layers of suffering in the book of Jeremiah, the imminent suffering of Jerusalem the prophet warns about, and his own suffering in the context.

says something about YHWH's "proclaiming" in Lam 1:18a: "*Innocent* ["righteous," צדיק] is YHWH, *but* I *rebel* against his speech!" The translation of her emphatic statement may not be a straightforward matter in this context when her possible tone is considered. The traditional translation is "YHWH is in the right, for I have rebelled against his word,"[19] and is thus a confession. Yet this misses the irony of how *this speaker* employs the phrase for *this* context.[20] The term usually carries a legal connotation and is used as a "declaration of acquittal" to proclaim someone's innocence. William Holladay convincingly argues that when Jeremiah uses the formula in his personal lament in Jer 12:1, he twists its meaning into "bitter sarcasm" toward YHWH.

> Thou art innocent [צדיק], YHWH,
> whenever I lodge a complaint with thee;
> yet I would pass judgment upon thee. (Jer 12:1)[21]

Most of the translations and commentators soften this abrasive line. Indeed, the Hebrew of the statement could be translated: "You are innocent, YHWH, *but* I will lodge a complaint with you; *indeed*! I would assert justice with you!"

The woman speaker's tone is likely congruent with Jeremiah's basic complaint. In the remainder of Lam 1 and 2—and the first speaker will soon join her complaint—the woman's voice is a "rebellion" that is *theological*—against *the nature of YHWH's excessive punishment*. She continues speaking by turning away from an unresponsive YHWH, and again beseeches those around her (cf. v. 12): "Hear, now! all [you] peoples, and see my pain. My young women and my young men have gone into captivity" (1:18b). After more speech in verse 19 about how her lovers (a metaphor for political allies) have failed her, Jerusalem turns to YHWH one last time in Lam 1 with yet another lament. She intensifies the poetic expression of her suffering and further emphasizes her "rebelling" by the use of the double root of the verb in Hebrew.

> Look! YHWH, how distressed I am! My insides churn.
> My heart is in tumult within me. Indeed! I certainly rebel. (1:20)

---

19. Most commentators follow the traditional reading, while a few also hear a protest in the statement: Theophile J. Meek, "The Book of Lamentations," in *The Interpreter's Bible* (New York: Abingdon-Cokesbury, 1956), 6:3–38, 14; S. Paul Re'emi, *God's People in Crisis: A Commentary on the Books of Amos and Lamentations* (ITC; Grand Rapids: Eerdmans, 1984), 89–90.

20. On Jeremiah's use of the formula, see William Holladay, "Style, Irony, and Authenticity in Jeremiah," *JBL* 81 (1962): 44–54, 49–50.

21. Ibid., 49–50.

Her increasing defiance after previous weeping bursts forth with the reason for her outcry: "because in the street the sword bereaves, in the house—death!" (1:20c).

Her not keeping silent before YHWH is likely also considered "rebellious" because in the larger context YHWH had ordered Jeremiah and the people to no longer lament to him (Jer 7:16; 11:14; 14:11; 15:1). Indeed, God called instead for the mourning women to raise dirges of death in Jer 9. Yet here the woman's voice (ingeniously speaking as Jerusalem) is ignoring that decree. The people's laments to God will not be stopped. Also, to speak out to YHWH about the horrors is implicitly to call God's actions into question, of punishing with violence. To lament is also to express their need for the absent "comforter" to intervene, YHWH, who is presently withholding comfort or rescue.

The woman's voice closes Lam 1—the longest of her speeches. While it does include her confession, at the end she sets God apart from the enemies, not with praise of God or remembrance of former rescue, but with an implicit, ironic, motivating reminder, that you, YHWH, *ought to be different* from the enemies, and she calls for their punishment.

> They hear how I groan:[22] "there is no one comforting me."
> All my enemies hear of my trouble;
> they rejoice that you have done it. (1:21ab)

2.2. Lamentations 2: The Woman's Lament Draws Out The Detached Male Singer's Emotions over War's Devastation

The first voice of Lam 1 also opens Lam 2. His rhetoric has shifted, however, to join more fully the aims of the woman's voice. He now adds to the accusation of God with another long litany of God's destroying actions against the city (2:1–17), caused by divine anger, causing the collapse of all the city structures of Jerusalem. In all this, the poet emphasizes how "God has become like an enemy" (v. 5). In verses 9 and 10 he subtly shifts the focus from the collapse of city structures to the collapse of human beings' bodies to the ground in mourning. Neither his voice, nor the woman's previously, have offered any positive expressions about YHWH in the context, which would have been typical in lament prayer.

By verse 11, the poet's demeanor shifts considerably when he himself collapses into weeping and lament for all the suffering he sees, especially the

---

22. Following MT.

fainting of infants in the city streets. In this pivotal verse, the phrase, "daughter of my people" (בת־עמי) appears for the first time in the book.²³

> My eyes are poured out with weeping;
> my stomach churns; my bile is poured out on the ground
> because of the destruction of the daughter of my people,
> because infants and babes faint in the streets of the city. (2:11 NRSV)

Most commentators simply read "daughter of my people" as another appellative for the personification of Jerusalem or Daughter Zion. They implicitly agree with modern renderings, such as in the NRSV above, that the previous word, "destruction," is in construct with "daughter of my people." However, this phrase can be translated just as accurately, without disturbing the Hebrew syntax, as "My eyes are poured out with weeping; … because of the destruction, *daughter of my people.*" That is, the language allows for the possibility that the male poet makes a comment about his weeping and mourning to a real woman in the context—whom he calls "daughter of my people."²⁴ Such a communal setting at least of a small group of survivors would be expected in the context, and such voices in dialogue are everywhere evident. This "daughter's" identity and role are not made clear, but commentators have noted that wherever this phrase appears in the Bible (in Isaiah, Jeremiah, and Lamentations), it always appears in proximity to weeping and mourning.²⁵ Once again, the question is raised, does the book only personify and make female Jerusalem speak? Or is there the possibility of a real woman participating in the situation, as the first speaker is? And is "daughter of my people" a reference to the woman who spoke in Lam 2, for herself and for the city of Jerusalem?

Meanwhile, the male voice continues, graphically describing the suffering of babies with their mothers (v. 12), and then addresses the female figure in verse 13. Again, are the references only to the personified city, or to a woman suffering as he is, or to a mother who needs comforting? Perhaps over time, all these are alluded to by the inclusive nature of the lyric. He says,

---

23. "Daughter of my people" appears only fifteen times in the Hebrew Bible, most often in Jeremiah, once in First Isaiah, and five times in Lamentations (2:11; 3:48; 4:3, 6, 10).

24. The occurrence of the phrase in the context of Isa 22:4 may have had a similar purpose (where Isaiah expresses his weeping for the destruction of the land), and in most other cases. Importantly, the plural of the phrase with "your people"—"daughters of your people"—is used by the prophet Ezekiel to critique *female prophets* in his context.

25. Joseph Henderson, "Who Weeps in Jer VIII 23 (IX 1)? Identifying the Dramatic Speakers in the Poetry of Jeremiah," *VT* 52 (2002): 196–206; Lee, *Singers of Lamentations*, 63–64; Lee, "Prophetic '*Bat-'Ammi*' Answers God and Jeremiah," *lectio difficilior* 2 (2009): http://www.lectio.unibe.ch/09_2/lee.html.

How can I strengthen you? To what can I compare you,
daughter of Jerusalem/Daughter Jerusalem?
To what can I liken you,[26] that I may comfort you,
virgin daughter of Zion/virgin Daughter Zion?
For as great as the sea is your crashing; Who can heal you?" (Lam 2:13)

The male voice tries to comfort her, further describing the city's suffering (vv. 14–17), yet in these verses, he *reverses* the normal letter order of the acrostic (v. 16), by uttering a line that begins with פ instead of ע.[27] The פ line describes her enemies; the ע line describes YHWH's carrying out his verbal threat against her to destroy her. The poet here echoes her earlier complaint about YHWH's speech in Lam 1:18. It is thus now with Lam 2:18 that he makes a dramatic and urgent call to the woman *to mourn* again; when she did so previously, she followed with vociferous lament prayer to YHWH, as will ensue also here.

O Wall of Daughter Zion!
Let tears run down like a torrent, day and night;
Do not let yourself grow numb; do not let your eyes cease. (Lam 2:18)

Note the peculiar reference to the person or persona as "wall" and the subsequent appeal to "cry out in the night, at the beginning of the watches" (v. 19).

The primary and growing complaint of these dissident lamenters is their witnessing the suffering of innocent children (an inversion of justice), who are victimized by the "retributive justice" noted earlier. Indeed, the *lead dissident* in this development in the book is *the woman lamenting* for her children. Now, in the acrostic in Lam 2, the usual order of two letters of the alphabet is reversed by the first poet (ע and פ, just preceding the צ letter). The צ letter in the acrostic psalms noted earlier often begins a familiar line that YHWH is "righteous" (צדיק), and this is precisely the statement (with that word) the woman's voice had uttered in that line of Lam 1:18, "righteous [צדיק] is YHWH," which was interpreted as ironic. Here in Lam 2:18, however, the first poet *reverses* these expected letters, thus calling attention to the use of the next צ line for something else entirely—not God's righteous qualities (צדיק)—rather he appeals to the woman to "cry out" (צעק) in lament (2:18), thus sympathetically joining her rhetorical effort.[28] Importantly, the

---

26. LXX has "who will *save* you or comfort you?"

27. Epigraphic evidence shows that the Hebrew alphabet was sometimes written with varying letter orders in earlier periods, but this explanation for the inversions in Lamentations is unlikely, since the standard alphabetical order had been established.

28. The reversal of the acrostic order in Lam 2 by the first poet is maintained by him

only other instance of an acrostic in the Hebrew Bible with these inverted letters is *in the lament* comprising Pss 9–10.

So the woman laments with great distress about the loss of the children she bore and nursed, and people killed and lying in the streets, and says directly to God, "on the day of your anger you have killed them, slaughtering without mercy"; she concludes her lament here with the final line in 2:22: "those whom I bore and reared my enemy has destroyed." It appears that the acrostic structure, and the rupture of that order, is part of the very rhetorical and theological purpose of these struggling lyricists, as they push back against a heavy-handed and simplistic explanation of divine-retributive corporate punishment that means the suffering and deaths of innocent children. Lamentations thus engages theodicy, the question of God's (in)justice, but the real impact of the rhetoric is embedded in the details, pathos, and artistry of the voices of real people. It should be apparent by now that the woman's voice in Lamentations goes well beyond women's traditional mourning. In all this, the female voice transcends accepted gender roles.

As numerous commentators have highlighted, women in the biblical culture typically sang victory songs for and in praise of Israelite warriors, favored by God, when they returned from battle. Women prophets composed a variation of the victory song, praising God for the rescue (as Miriam and Deborah).[29]

Yet in the book of Lamentations, the Judean warriors were defeated by the enemy. No doubt the hope was that the Judeans would be victorious, perhaps with the aid of an expected ally like Egypt against the Babylonians, in which case a woman or women would have risen to dance and sing a victory song in praise of Jerusalem's warriors and of God, who brought them victory.[30] Instead, what we have here in Lamentations is *entirely the opposite outcome*—not just a military defeat but also complete annihilation—and this for *God's chosen city of David, Zion*, where the temple of God's abode stood, which many thought could never be violated.

The woman singing on behalf of the city and the people in Lamentations—instead of singing praise to God for bringing them victory, rescue, salvation—must sing devastating, earthshaking news. She laments with disappointed anguish and complains against God for failing them, for acting instead *as their enemy*. Would anyone be allowed to sing this way in the official

---

again in Lam 3 still in dialogue with the woman, whose voice returns in chapter four with a rejoinder to complete the acrostic reversal (v. 17).

29. Goitein, "Women as Creators," 5–7; Brenner and Van Dijk-Hemmes, *On Gendering Texts*, 32–43.

30. Women announce victory in song in Ps 68:12; Goitein, "Women as Creators," 6.

temple liturgy of Israel?³¹ For these lyrics convey a theological crisis greater than any other in ancient Israel, when most (male) leaders had failed and all patriarchal social institutions in Jerusalem had collapsed. For all this she complains bitterly. Her tone is in the spirit of Moses' complaints (Num 11), and of Miriam's complaints (Num 12). Such laments are still an expression of faith. They are used regularly by prophets in the Bible. Therefore, it is reasonable to raise the question as to whether this distinctive female voice in Lamentations might be a female prophet. Is she a personification or a person? Either way, it is a singular development in the lyrical tradition of Israel and suggests why "her" songs, their songs, were preserved as Scripture.³²

2.3. Lamentations 3: A Male Warrior Responds! Lamenting His Mistreatment by God Who Is Like an Enemy, Yet Still Trusting in YHWH

This rhetorical, theological battle grows in Lam 3:1, when a new voice is heard, a man (גבר, suggestive of a warrior) who has seen and experienced defeat and much suffering. His personal description of distress continues and expands the vociferous complaints of the previous two speakers with a lengthy litany of what God has done against him (3:1–18). His soliloquy, however, is interrupted by his own turn to lament directly to God in prayer (3:19–20) and by a turn of his thoughts away from his complaints. He remembers God's acts of covenantal love; he says they have not ended, that divine mercies have not disappeared. The speaker casts his lot with God and therefore finds a quiet place of hope. This is the first instance of a voice in the book remembering God's positive attributes, typical of the Psalms.

The warrior's pause elicits a new voice in response beginning in verse 25. Sounding much like Job's friends, this voice defends God's ways and calls on the warrior to stop such severe complaints and instead to confess in silence.

> It is good that one should wait quietly for the salvation of the Lord.
> It is good for one to bear the yoke in youth,
> to sit alone in silence when the Lord has imposed it. (3:26–28 NRSV)

This second, new voice, apparently after listening to what has come before, objects to those who have been loudly complaining against God, and explains that the suffering is a punishment for sin, defends God, and says, "Let us lift

---

31. Perhaps the attribution of all of Lamentations to Jeremiah made it possible for her voice to be included in the canon.

32. See Lee, *Singers of Lamentations*, 67–73.

up our hearts as well as our hands to God in heaven" in confessional prayer (v. 41).

Unsurprisingly, this statement elicits a reaction from the first speakers! Probably it is the woman who angrily responds, directing a prayer to God in verses 42–44 after hearing the above, but with another lament to God.

> We have transgressed and rebelled—you have not forgiven!
> You have wrapped yourself with anger and pursued us;
> you have killed, you have not pitied.
> You have wrapped yourself with a cloud so that no prayer can pass through!
> (3:42–44)

2.4. Lamentations 4: First Voice Returns to Describe People's Suffering Caused by Corrupt Religious Leaders

In Lam 4, it appears that the first voice that opened the book returns, and continues with another communal dirge, further describing in graphic detail the devastation that has unfolded against the city's inhabitants. He especially describes the suffering and deaths of children, the downfall of the upper classes of the population, and the guilt and exile of priests and false prophets. The woman's individual voice is not expressed at all, but may be the source of the brief communal lament in verses 17–20. A direct address by the first voice to personified Zion in the last verse (4:22) simply states, "your" punishment is complete, and he (God) will not prolong your exile; thus this chapter closes.

2.5. Lamentations 5: A Final Voice with Female Perspectives Expresses the People's Lament to an Absent God

The book of Lamentations closes in chapter 5 with a communal lament to God that suggests a time after the frenzied catastrophe, when those remaining in the land attempt to carry on and survive war's deprivations. This lament (using not "I" language, but "we" language) appeals to God, expressing the voice of the people who still suffer.

As both primary poetic voices in Lam 1–2 spoke of men and women suffering in the community, so too do the voices of Lam 5 speak of the suffering of men and women, including giving attention to orphans and widows (vv. 2–3). The concern about securing water in verse 4 may suggest a woman's point of view, since women typically collected water for a household. Twice the collective voice mentions the difficulty of "getting bread" (vv. 6, 9), a responsibility usually held by women, and speaks of how their skin is "black as an oven from the scorching heat of famine" (v. 10). There is reference to how women and virgins are raped (v. 11); "young men are compelled to grind" with the millstone (v. 13), an ironic reversal, since this was normally an occupation of women and slaves.[33] In verses 12–14 the collective voice refers to princes, elders, young men, boys, and old men, and says, "young men have left their music" (v. 14b). Immediately following this, verse 15a renders a gender-matched parallelism, saying, "the joy of *our* hearts has ceased; *our* dancing has been turned to mourning," activities often ascribed to women.

Though this communal lament affirms God's enduring reign (v. 19), it also presents the voice of one who has witnessed the demise of Zion, and with it the end of the ideology of Zion's inviolability; this is not a lament of the Judean remnant in Babylonian exile who would receive words of consolation and future restoration of Zion from Second Isaiah. These are the ones left behind, who feel utterly abandoned. There may be a sardonic tone to their affirmation of God's sovereignty,[34] for the poet ironically contrasts YHWH's *everlasting* reign with YHWH's *perpetual* forgetting of the people.

> Why have you forgotten us completely?
> Why have you forsaken us these many days?
> Restore us to yourself, O Lord, that we may be restored;
> renew our days as of old—unless you have utterly rejected us,
> and are angry with us beyond measure. (5:20–22 NRSV)

These verses and the book as a whole leave the people in anguished doubt and with unanswered questions about whether God will continue in relationship with them. In spite of all the laments, and this final plea, God never speaks or answers their lament in the book of Lamentations.[35]

---

33. See Exod 11:5; Judg 9:53; 2 Sam 11:21; Isa 47:2.

34. Maier, *Daughter Zion*, 158, interprets that the community's affirmation of YHWH's enthronement forever suggests that they are still holding on to the preexilic ideology of Zion.

35. A number of scholars have explored the ways in which the poetry of prophetic voices in Second Isaiah renders God answering some of the precise laments of the female voice in the book of Lamentations; thus Norman Gottwald, "Social Class and Ideology in Isaiah 40–55: An Eagletonian Reading," *Semeia* 59 (1992): 43–57; Carol A. Newsom, "Response to Norman Gottwald, 'Social Class and Ideology in Isaiah 40–55: An Eagletonian Reading,'" *Semeia* 59 (1992): 73–78; Patricia Tull, *Remember the Former Things: The Recollection of Previous Texts in Second Isaiah* (SBLDS 161; Atlanta: Scholars Press, 1997); Maier, *Daughter Zion*, 161–210.

3. Distinctive Contributions and Themes from the Female Voice in Lamentations

In summary, contrary to the male-dominant attribution of all of Lamentations to Jeremiah, the text of Lamentations reveals a strong female voice, taking the important lead in expressing complaint about God's violent punishing, in which she is joined in partnership by the male voice in Lam 1–2. Her voice contributes the following elements, which are also key themes in the book: (1) she utters confession but also a severe and large amount of complaint language against God unprecedented in the Bible, matched only by the complaint poetry of Jeremiah and Job; (2) she does not herself construct Jerusalem (and judge her) as the metaphors of male prophets do, yet she sometimes, but not always, speaks as the city persona who admits sin and suffers; (3) she uses the accusation element of the lament prayer and dirge genres, often performed by women, to complain against God; (4) she speaks on behalf of the city to God, and to the people, perhaps functioning as a prophetic "sentinel"[36] (e.g., "wall" of Zion), both in empathetic identification with and in criticism of its leaders and people; (5) she speaks both as a mother who has lost children herself and as the persona of the city as a mother losing her children; (6) she influences the more detached first male voice to join her in mourning, and perhaps influences the male warrior to offer his own lament; thus she facilitates the grief process for the community; (7) she ignores the didactic voice of Lam 3, who seeks to silence laments, with her further lament and challenge to God; (8) she persists in challenging the theology and ideology of divine-retributive justice, which causes the suffering of innocent children, and thus is a forerunner to the debate in the book of Job; and finally (9) her laments are addressed by prophetic voices in Second Isaiah's oracles.

4. Perspectives on Lamentations and Women in the Bible

Interpretive work on the book of Lamentations suggests the following questions, which are of ongoing consideration: (1) Is it possible to retrieve a real

---

36. "Sentinel" from the Hebrew root צפה ("to watch" for the city or country). This is an often overlooked metaphor for prophets. The prophets as sentinels are depicted as those chosen and designated to watch and listen and announce an alarm, or news to the city or people that they hear from God (prophets are referred to as sentinels in Hos 9:8; Mic 7:4, 7; Jer 6:17; Hab 2:1; Ezek 3:17; 33:1–6; Isa 21:6; 52:8). Sometimes the prophet's words as sentinel are spoken *as the city's voice*, perhaps since the sentinel was stationed as a regular part of the city's structure, posted on the *wall* or watchtower of the city, as a watchman for a runner or chariot bringing important news.

woman composer's work and voice in the book of Lamentations, or is the woman's voice simply a constructed persona of a presumed male poet, or of male redaction? (2) Apart from later canonization processes, is it possible that men sympathetic to women in ancient Israel, who were in control of the redaction of Lamentations, included a woman's voice without recasting it in strictly male terms? (3) Or is the female voice in Lamentations "double-voiced"?[37] (4) How does the personifying of Jerusalem/Zion serve women's interests, and how does it hurt women's interests? How does it serve or hurt everyone's interests for a common good? (5) Looking beyond the personification of Jerusalem only in prophetic books, can we find "real" women's voices represented, as singers, or especially unnamed women prophets there? What about their lyric style might identify them as such?

---

37. Speaking according to dominant male culture, and at the same time as a marginal voice in the context; see Brenner and Van Dijk-Hemmes, *On Gendering Texts*, 27, following Elaine Showalter's model.

Shulammite:
The Woman "at Peace" in the Song of Songs

Gianni Barbiero

1. Introduction

The woman is surely the protagonist of the Song of Songs.[1] This is the simple fact that meets the eye even on a superficial reading of the poem. Not only does her voice characterize the prologue and the epilogue of the book, but she is also the speaker in most of the verses of the Song.[2] These two details convey the unusual nature of this work within the broad sweep of the Old Testament. If there is a book in which the "depatriarchalization" of the word of God, so desired by feminist exegesis, has a place,[3] it is precisely the Song of Songs.[4]

The father is never spoken of in the Song. While the usual term in the Hebrew Bible to indicate the family is "the house of the father," the Song speaks rather of "the house of my mother" (3:5; 8:2). Even the brothers are placed in a strongly negative light, as representatives of the patriarchal family from which the Song clearly distances itself (see 1:6; 8:8–9).[5]

---

1. Here I acknowledge three women who have inspired and corrected this contribution with female intelligence: Silvia Ahn (Seoul), Emanuela Zurli (Rome), and Irmtraud Fischer (Graz). Aknowledgment is also due to the English translator of the text, Michael Tait, and to the revisor, Gerard Sloyan.

2. According to my count, the woman utters 61.5 verses out of a total of 117, while those uttered by the man are 38.5. (The others are uttered by the "chorus" or by the author himself.)

3. See Phyllis Trible, "Depatriarchalizing in Biblical Interpretation," *JAAR* 41 (1973): 30–48; repr. in *The Jewish Woman: New Perspectives* (ed. Elizabeth Koltun; New York: Schocken, 1976), 217–40.

4. Not for nothing have a good two volumes of the *Feminist Companion* been devoted to feminist exegesis of the Song of Songs; see Athalya Brenner, ed., *A Feminist Companion to the Song of Songs* (FCB 1; Sheffield: Sheffield Academic, 1993); Athalya Brenner and Carol R. Fontaine, eds., *The Song of Songs* (FCB 2/6; Sheffield: Sheffield Academic, 2000).

5. The father is never spoken of in the poem. His absence is a significant *argumentum*

To speak of the woman of the Song is simply to speak of the Song itself: it is the voice of the woman.[6] The female figure that it presents is complex, at times apparently contradictory.[7] But the different aspects are unified in a profoundly coherent image.

2. In His Eyes I Have Found Peace

The woman of the Song is called "Shulammite" (see 7:1). The etymology and the meaning of the name are debated: at any rate, the link with שלום, "peace," seems certain. The term appears strange in the context, which speaks instead of war: the same verse makes allusion to the "dance of the two camps." The juxtaposition "war/peace" returns in 8:10, when the woman, in reply to the brothers who want to erect a wall and battlements to defend her chastity, retorts with irritation: "I am a wall and my breasts are like towers: but, in his eyes, I have become like one who has found peace."[8]

The maiden of the Song is a woman with self-consciousness, one who does not wish to be held in tutelage, who knows how to defend herself ("I am a wall"). At the same time, she declares that she has yielded in the face of love's assault, finding there her peace.[9] She has found that peace not by resisting but by laying down her arms. Her "defense" was in relation to that which was not love. Once she recognized that what was coming to face her was love, the woman ceased her struggle and declared her surrender. This is just what the

---

a silentio: it finds a parallel in the New Testament, where, among the members of the new family that Christ promises to his followers are brothers and sisters, mother and children, but not father (see Mark 10:30). On the condition of women in the patriarchal society of the OT, see Irmtraud Fischer, "Donne nell'Antico Testamento," in *Donne e Bibbia: Storia ed esegesi* (ed. Adriana Valerio; La Bibbia nella Storia 21; Bologna: Dehoniane, 2006), 161–64.

6. I do not wish to enter into the debate as to whether the author was a woman. This is secondary; see in this respect J. Cheryl Exum, *Song of Songs* (OTL; Louisville: Westminster John Knox, 2005), 65: "The sex of the author cannot be deduced from the poem."

7. So that Garbini, for example, detects three different types of woman in the poem: the married woman, the free woman (in the sense of "free love"), the prostitute; see Giovani Garbini, *Cantico dei cantici* (Biblica 2; Brescia: Paideia, 1992), 308–13. In my opinion, it is more a question of different aspects of the one figure.

8. [Translator's note: In the Italian original Gianni Barbiero translated the verses of the Song himself. The English translation reproduces his translation in English.]

9. The author plays on the two possible meanings of מוצאת: *qal* participle of מצא, "find," and *hiphil* participle of יצא, "make go out." The meaning in this latter case is understood in the light of Deut 20:10–11 as a surrender, a "seeking peace."

woman expresses in the parallel passage, 2:4: "His banner over me is love."[10] The woman yields not to force but to love.

The expression "in his [the beloved man's] eyes" is significant. It says that the woman finds peace not in herself but in her man: she is made for him. The woman realizes herself only in the loving relation with her partner.

The ensuing *waṣf*, 7:2–11, is built up ideally on the contrasting word pair "peace/war," which was introduced in 7:1.[11] To the semantic field of "peace" belong the "rounded," welcoming, parts of the female body (hips, navel, belly, breasts, vv. 2–4), while those that are straight (neck, nose, head, vv. 5–6) evoke the warlike, defensive aspect of her personality.[12]

In fact, the woman is not simply the object of the man's attempts; she too attacks with the might of a host drawn up for battle (6:4, 10). The lexeme דגל, "banner of war," which in 2:4 describes the man's attack, is employed in 6:4, 10, to describe that of the woman. The man feels threatened by her glances to the point of requesting her to turn them away from him (6:5), but he too, in the end, declares himself conquered, climbing up on to the war chariots of his assailant ("My desire has carried me on to the chariots of my noble people," 6:12).[13]

It is clear, then, that the strength that the woman possesses is not her own but that of love, which she personifies. It is the same invincible strength—since love is as strong as and stronger than death (8:6–7)—that her beloved represents for her. A strange war indeed, which is won by losing! A strange peace, which is attained by means of war! To attain peace, one must allow oneself to be overwhelmed, be turned upside down by the force of love.[14]

The strength of the woman of the Song is paradoxical precisely because it is unarmed and weak. Immediately before 6:4–12, we come across the nocturnal encounter with the watchmen: "They struck me, they wounded me, they took away my mantle, the watchmen of the walls" (5:7). The two "forces" are

---

10. The term דגל certainly does not indicate the sign of an inn. In the Song, it always has the sense of "banner of war" (see 5:10; 6:4; 6:10). Moreover, in 2:4, it is found not over the "banqueting chamber" but "over me" (עלי). The image is that of a city that has been conquered, over which the victor raises his banner.

11. The same can also be said of the preceding *waṣf*, 6:4–12, characterized by the programmatic phrase: "You are *fair* as Tirzah, my friend, lovely as Jerusalem, *terrible* as a host drawn up for battle" (6:4; cf. 6:10). See Gianni Barbiero, "Die 'Wagen meines edlen Volkes' (Hld 6,12): Eine strukturelle Analyse," *Bib* 78 (1997): 174–89.

12. For this reading of the *waṣf* in 7:2–6, see Mary Timothea Elliott, *The Literary Unity of the Canticle* (EHS; Frankfurt am Main/Bern: Lang, 1989), 165–66.

13. For an interpretation of this *crux interpretum*, I refer to Gianni Barbiero, *Song of Songs: A Close Reading* (trans. Michael Tait; VTSup 144; Leiden: Brill, 2011), 355–61.

14. The brothers also want their sister's peace, but without love.

thus laid side by side: on the one hand, the brute force of arms and violence and, on the other, the unarmed force of love, which seems to succumb to violence but which, in the end, is the victor.

3. How Fair You Are, My Friend!

The feminine ideal set down at the conclusion of the book of Proverbs is that of an efficient housewife (see Prov 31:10–31). As for beauty, the sage warns: "Charm is deceptive and beauty is fleeting; the woman who fears the Lord is to be praised" (Prov 31:30).[15]

By contrast, it is beauty above all that the Song praises in the woman. The two most recurrent lexemes are נאוה (1:5, 10; 2:14; 4:3; 6:4) and יפה (1:8, 15[2×]; 2:10, 13; 4:1[2×], 7, 10; 5:9; 6:1, 4, 10; 7:7), which refer almost exclusively to her.[16] The first time the vocabulary of beauty appears, it is she who speaks: "I am black but beautiful, O daughters of Jerusalem" (1:5). It is a beauty contest that is here being announced. The woman of the Song is being confronted with the artificial charm of the city girls and declares, by contrast, her fresh and authentic beauty: rough as the black tents of the desert nomads, but nonetheless worthy of the refined curtains that adorn the palace of Solomon. She is not being presumptuous.

On four occasions, in fact, her beauty is acknowledged by the chorus. Three times with the refrain: "You, O fairest among women" (1:8; 5:9; 6:1), which, on the one hand, confirms the estimation of herself that she gives in 1:6 and, on the other hand, suggests that beauty is a female prerogative: the man is characterized in other ways. The chorus that utters this phrase in 5:9 and 6:1 is that of the daughters of Jerusalem, the very same who in 1:6 had been presented as her rivals. In 1:8, it is probably the shepherds, that is, the companions of the beloved man, who are praising the "shepherdess." The fourth time, the chorus is that of the "daughters, queens, and concubines" who make up the harem of Solomon: "Who is this, who looks down like the dawn, fair

---

15. It has to be said, however, that Prov 5:19 carries a different tone: here the beauty of the bride is praised by the words "loving deer, attractive gazelle [חן]." On the role of the woman in the book of Proverbs, see Fischer, "Donne nell'Antico Testamento," 177–78; and the essay of Christl M. Maier in this volume.

16. It is only in 1:16 that, in conformity with that reciprocity that characterises the Song, the woman replies to the compliment of her man (1:15) in the same tone; thus the Song also recognizes male beauty. But the emphasis is undoubtedly placed on that of the woman. On beauty in the Old Testament, see Claudia Rakel, *Judit—über Schönheit, Macht und Widerstand im Krieg: Eine feministisch-intertextuelle Lektüre* (BZAW 334; Berlin: de Gruyter, 2003), 202–28.

as the moon, bright as the sun, terrible as a host drawn up for battle?" (6:10). The comparison with the cosmic phenomena raises the beloved woman above all other women, although they, like the queens, are on the highest rung of the social scale. She is being carried up to a superhuman, heavenly level. Perhaps in no other place in the Song is there such a clear perception of the quasi-divine character of the woman.[17] Moreover, it is significant that the likeness with God is seen from the point of view of beauty.

In every other instance the woman's beauty is sung of by the man. Each *waṣf* begins and ends with the praise of female attractiveness: "How fair you are, my friend, how fair!" (4:1; cf. 1:15). The repetition expresses the stammering of one who has been overwhelmed by an apparition that renders him incapable of saying anything else; he knows only how to repeat the same words.

"You are as fair as Tirzah, my friend, lovely as Jerusalem" (6:4). The term of comparison associates the woman with the history and geography of Israel according to a procedure typical of the Song. In his beloved, the man enjoys the promised land, the beauty and bounty that are God's gift to his people. In particular, in the Psalms Jerusalem is said to be the "perfection of beauty" (Ps 50:2; cf. 48:3).

Each time, having contemplated the body of the woman, the conclusion of her beloved is similar: "You are all fair, my friend, in you there is no blemish" (4:7); "How fair you are, how sweet, O love, in [your] pleasures" (7:7). Here, with the term "sweet" (נָעֵם), the enjoyable is added to the aesthetic dimension of love.

Elsewhere, there are particular aspects of feminine attractiveness that the beloved man praises: "Your cheeks are beautiful between ear pendants, your neck circled by pearls" (1:10); "Your voice is sweet and your face lovely" (2:14); "Your speech is beautiful" (4:3); "How fair are your feet in their sandals" (7:2). It is not only the external aspect of the woman that he admires but also her interior, revealed by her discourses, as evidenced also by the particular importance given to the eyes, arguably the most spiritual part of the person (see 1:15; 4:1; 6:5; 7:5).

The expression in 2:10, 13, is worth pointing out: "Rise up, my friend, my fair one, and go." To the affirmation of the beauty of his woman, the beloved man adds the detail that this beauty belongs to him, it is his ("*my* fair one!"), thus anticipating what the woman will affirm a little further on in the refrain of mutual belonging (see 2:16). This declaration precedes the request to leave the family nest and dare the adventure of love. The woman needs someone to

---

17. Hans-Peter Müller, "Begriffe menschlicher Theomorphie: Zu einigen *cruces interpretum* in Hld 6,10," *ZAH* 1 (1988): 112–21.

tell her that she is beautiful, desirable, and desired so as to be able to break the shell that holds her shut in "behind the wall" (2:9).

According to the Genesis account, God made the woman so as to be "a helper, as his partner" (עזר כנגדו, Gen 2:18, 20), his mirror.[18] In the woman, the man is reflected so that he knows who he really is. It could be said that the Song sees the matter from the woman's point of view, namely, that the man now is the mirror for her, the one who tells her about her true identity. The woman needs the man in order to perceive her own beauty.

4. Well of Living Water

The counterbalancing of "peasant woman/shepherdess" and "daughters of Jerusalem," which is introduced in 1:5–8, should be related to a leitmotif of the Song: the "nature/city" opposition.[19] Corresponding to a widespread tendency in the Hellenistic period (one thinks of bucolic poetry),[20] the ideal place for love, according to the Song, is unspoiled nature. Here are the forces of life, not in the city, whose walls of stone are dead.

Beyond the particular historical moment, in this return to nature the Song stresses some fundamental aspects of love and in particular of the female figure. When Adam calls his wife "Eve," he explains this name as "mother of all living" (Gen 3:20), that is, he establishes a fundamental link between the woman and life. The emphasis on nature is explained in this light.

In 2:7, there appears for the first time the refrain of the awakening, which will then be repeated in 3:5 and 8:4, with slight variations: "I charge you, daughters of Jerusalem, by the gazelles or by the wild deer: do not rouse, do

---

18. For a reading of Gen 2 that respects the reciprocity of the genders, see Irmtraud Fischer, "Egalitär entworfen—hierarchisch gelebt: Zur Problematik des Geschlechterverhältnisses und einer genderfairen Anthropologie im Alten Testament," in *Der Mensch im alten Israel: Neue Forschungen zur alttestamentlichen Anthropologie* (ed. Bernd Janowski and Kathrin Liess; HBS 59; Freiburg: Herder, 2005), 265–98, 269–70; Mercedes Navarro Puerto, "Divine Image and Likeness: Women and Men in Genesis 1–3 as an Open System in the Context of Genesis 1–11," in *Torah* (ed. Irmtraud Fischer et al.; The Bible and Women: An Encyclopaedia of Exegesis and Cultural History 1.1; Atlanta: Society of Biblical Literature, 2011), 193–249, 218–21.

19. On this contrast, see Hans-Josef Heinevetter, *"Komm nun, mein Liebster, Dein Garten ruft Dich!" Das Hohelied als programmatische Komposition* (BBB 69; Frankfurt: Athenäum, 1988), 179–90.

20. Together with a growing critical consent, I place the Song in the Hellenistic period, primarily on linguistic criteria, but also on grounds of cultural homogeneity; see, to this effect, Ludwig Schwienhorst-Schönberger, "Das Hohelied," in *Einleitung in das Alte Testament* (ed. Erich Zenger et al.; 8th ed.; Stuttgart: Kohlhammer, 2012), 474–83.

not waken love until it wishes." In 1:5, the "daughters of Jerusalem" were contrasted with the peasant woman burned by the sun; now they are counterposed to the wild animals, which are the personification of the forces of life. In these animals, it is Love itself called to witness to the oath, which in 8:6 will be called "flame of Yah." Love comes from there, from the uncontaminated kingdom of nature, not from society. It is not society's business, therefore, to dictate any laws to love. In the case in point, it is not its role to say when love must cease.[21]

The "nature/city" opposition explains the juxtaposition of the two songs placed at the beginning and the end of the body of the poem, 2:8–17 + 3:1–5; and 7:12–14 + 8:1–4,[22] respectively, with the effect of inclusion. In 2:8–17, it is the beloved man who calls on the woman to leave her home and go out into the countryside in blossom (2:10, 13); in 7:12–14, the parts are reversed and it is she who invites him to go out: "Come, my beloved, let us go out into the country" (7:12). The "country" is first and foremost the environment of love: "There I will give you my love" (7:13). The woman of the Song does not dwell in the city, but "in the gardens" (8:13), and the place of love is "under the apple tree" (8:5). The bed to which the woman invites her beloved is a bed in fresh grass, its ceiling made up of high trees of cedar and cypress (1:16–17) and its sides henna bushes and flowering vines (7:12–13).[23]

But nature is not merely the environment of love; it is also a metaphor for the bodies of the two lovers, which flower like the vines and the pomegranates: "*Our* vineyards are in flower" (2:15). In particular, the vegetative metaphor refers to the body of the woman: "We shall see whether the vine has budded, whether the buds have opened, whether the pomegranate trees are in flower" (7:13; cf. 6:11). The vine and the pomegranate are symbols of the female body, as are the garden and the vineyard in accordance with the primitive identification of the woman with the earth.

---

21. We understand "to rouse love" not as rousing a love that did not exist before (according to 2:6, the two lovers were united in an embrace), but as "rousing" the lovers from that sleep of love, of which 7:10 MT speaks. The expression is practically equivalent to "disturbing" love. See Brian P. Gault, "A 'Do Not Disturb' Sign? Reexamination of the Adjuration Refrain in Song of Songs," *JSOT* 36 (2011): 93–104.

22. It is my conviction that the Song is not an anthology of love songs but a poetic unity cleverly structured into a prologue (1:2–2:7), an epilogue (8:5–14), and two main sections: 2:7–5:1 and 5:2–8:4, in which the voices of the woman, the man, and the chorus alternate (see Barbiero, *Song of Songs*, 17–24).

23. I translate the term כפרים in 7:12 with "henna bushes." It can indicate "villages" only with difficulty. In the villages, the two lovers would not be any more alone than in the city from which they wish to escape.

This background explains the use of vegetable and animal metaphors in the description of the woman's body by contrast with that of the man, who is compared to a statue of ivory and gold (see 5:10–16): "Your eyes are doves behind your veil. Your hair, like a flock of goats gamboling down from the mountains of Gilead. Your teeth, like a flock of ewes coming out of their bath, ready for the shearing, all of them the mothers of twins; none has lost her young" (4:1–3). As Keel explains, it is not solely or primarily the external form of the metaphors that counts but, so to speak, the soul of the things.[24] In his woman, the man experiences the living forces of nature, namely of the animals and the plants. In particular, the woman personifies the rich land of Israel, the gift that God has made to his people. This is a gift the bounty of which it would be a sin to doubt (see Num 13:25–33).

It is in such a context that we should place the description of the "garden" in 4:12–16. The veiled allusion is to the woman's womb. The "shoots" (v. 13) refer to the pubic hair, and the words "stopped fountain, sealed spring" (v. 12) allude to the virginity of the "sister bride," as the parallel of Prov 5:15–18 confirms. The water metaphor returns in verse 15: "Spring of the gardens, well of living water, springing up from Lebanon." Water is an image of life, by contrast with the desert, the image of death: without water, life is impossible. Perhaps there is also an allusion to the maternal liquid in which the fetus swims. The link with life is underlined by the adjective "living" (חיים). It cannot but remind one of the "well of living water" of Jer 2:13 and 17:13. This is not a case of trivialization of a religious concept[25]—far from it. The woman is associated with God himself, the fountain of life, to whom, moreover, the phrase "springing up from Lebanon" alludes. Behind the metaphor of Lebanon, with its perennial snows, it is legitimate to catch a glimpse of the fountain of all life (cf. Jer 18:14), from which even human maternity draws its origin.

5. My Very Own Vineyard I Have Not Kept

The attitude of the brothers, who are preoccupied with protecting the virginity of their little sister at all costs (8:9), finds its correspondence in the prologue

---

24. Othmar Keel, *Deine Blicke sind Tauben: Zur Metaphorik des Hohen Liedes* (SBS 114/115; Stuttgart: Katholisches Bibelwerk, 1984), 27–30; Keel, *The Song of Songs: A Continental Commentary* (trans. Frederick J. Gaiser; Minneapolis: Fortress, 1994), 139–47.

25. Against those who speak of the "mockery" and "iconoclasm" in the use the Song makes of religious language to speak of erotic love, see André LaCocque, *Romance, She Wrote: A Hermeneutical Essay on Song of Songs* (Harrisburg, Pa.: Trinity Press International, 1998), passim, e.g., 128; Enrica Salvaneschi, *Cantico dei cantici Interpretatio ludica* (Genova: Il Melangolo, 1982), 54.

(1:6). They have probably noticed that she has taken a fancy to some young man and have taken it upon themselves to divert her from such fantasies: "My mother's sons were angry with me; they put me in charge of the vineyards." The keeping of the vineyards must have been an onerous task, designed to keep her from unsuitable companions.

The vineyard, however, is also a metaphor for the woman, whether because of the woman-earth equation or because the vines produce wine, a metaphor for love (see 1:2; 4:10; 7:10). Thus "to watch over the vineyards" comes to mean "to guard chastity." Such a meaning is clearly understood in 8:11–12, where "keepers of the vineyard" are mentioned.

In this sense we should understand 1:6: "My very own vineyard I have not kept!" The passage from the concrete to the figurative sense is expressed in the words: "*My* vineyard." The woman adds (literally): "that which is *mine*." The specification is superfluous, but it has the sense of a sorrowful protest: it is mine and not theirs. It is my business to make decisions about my body and no one else's.

Norbert Lohfink has seen the song of a prostitute in these words.[26] In my opinion, they agree rather with the character of the woman of the Song, which is profoundly moral and not moralistic. Among other things, these words correspond to the statement of 8:10: "In his eyes I have become like one who has found peace." That peace is found not by remaining shut up in the house, by suffocating the voice of love, but by welcoming it; it is the voice of God. The woman of the Song knows well the value of chastity (see 7:14). But this cannot be an external imposition, which obeys laws that are foreign to love: it must be a decision of the woman herself ("*my* vineyard, *my* very own," 1:6; 8:12). Here one grasps the modernity of the image of the woman put forward by the Song. One might say that the heroine of this book is a forerunner of the movement for women's liberation without being, on this account, outside the Old Testament's vision of the family. It is enough to think, for example, of the figure of Ruth, who slips under Boaz's cover by night and for this reason is accounted blessed (Ruth 3:1–15).

The poetic drama then associates the guardian of the vineyards with the figure of the shepherdess who at high noon goes in search of her beloved: "Tell me, O love of my soul, where do you pasture your flock, where do you rest it at noon, so that I may not look like a prostitute behind the flocks of your companions" (1:7). The term עטיה, literally "veiled," recalls Tamar, the daughter-in-law of Judah, who had put on the prostitutes' veil to seduce him

---

26. Norbert Lohfink, "Review of Roland E. Murphy, The Wisdom Literature (FOTL 13)," *TP* 58 (1983): 239–41, here 240.

and have a son with him (see Gen 38:15–16). The Genesis author does not condemn as immoral the behavior of Tamar but rather that of Judah the patriarch, his respectability notwithstanding. Returning to the text of the Song, it has the woman ashamed; she does not wish to go around asking people the whereabouts of her man lest she seem up to no good.

The reply of the chorus is surprising: "If you do not know, O most beautiful among women, go out in the tracks of the flock, and pasture your little goats beside the tents of the shepherds" (1:8). The tents of the shepherds were precisely where she did not wish to go, in order to avoid people's chatter. The chorus urges the young woman not to worry about this but to confront it by following the voice of love. The little goats, like the gazelles and the wild deer, are the personification of love, which the woman is called to follow, without worrying that people will mistake her for a prostitute (1:7). In fact, in 3:1–5 and 5:6–8, the shepherdess will go out at night through the town's streets and squares in search of her beloved, running into the watchmen, who will take her for a prostitute and treat her as such. But she will find her beloved.

The advice of the chorus, "Go out" (צְאִי־לָךְ), brings this passage close to the "Go!" (לְכִי־לָךְ) of 2:10, 13. It is a reminder of the exodus dimension of love that echoes the vision of Gen 2:24: "Therefore a man leaves his father and his mother and cleaves to his wife, and they two become one flesh." To leave the nuclear family in order to form a new family is a traumatic change that can be compared to the leaving of the mother's womb; it is the adventure of birth to life, and it is rendered possible by love. The verbs "go out" and "go" are the same that characterize the adventures of Abraham and Moses. In particular, the reference to the "Go forth" (לֶךְ־לְךָ) of Gen 12:1 is unmistakable. To the voice of God, which calls one to leave one's own land to go toward an unknown country, is added the voice of love which, as Song 8:6 explains, is none other than the voice of God.

In Gen 2:24, the subject of the verb is the man (as it will be in Gen 12:1). In the Song, it is the woman who is to abandon her home, as if the author wished to rewrite the story of the garden of Eden from a feminine point of view.[27]

6. My Beloved Is Mine and I Am His

Three times there resounds the refrain of mutual belonging. The first is in 2:16, at the end of the first song of the woman (2:8–17): "My beloved is mine and I am his: he grazes among the lotus flowers."[28] Here, it follows the request

---

27. See Karl Barth, *Die kirchliche Dogmatik* (Vol. 3.2; Zürich: EVZ, 1948), 355.
28. We thus translate the Hebrew שׁוֹשַׁנָּה, by analogy with the Egyptian *sšn*; see also

to catch the "foxes" that could spoil "our vineyards in blossom" (v. 15). What is forbidden to the foxes is granted to the beloved: the young deer grazes among the lotus flowers that grow on the body of the woman, while the foxes would ruin her "vineyard." The reason for the difference is expressed by the refrain of mutual belonging: "I am his." And therefore my vineyard is also his; he is not committing theft, unlike the foxes. The belonging of the woman to the man is, then, balanced by his belonging to her: "My beloved is mine."

At the basis of this affirmation stands the narrative of Gen 2. When God brings the woman to Adam,[29] Adam exclaims exultantly: "Now at last: this is bone of my bone and flesh of my flesh. Therefore she shall be called woman [אשה], because she was taken from man [איש]" (Gen 2:23). "Bone of my bone and flesh of my flesh" expresses the concept that is expressed in the Song by the formula: "My beloved is mine, and I am his." By contrast with the account of the garden of Eden in Genesis, the phrase is now uttered by the woman, as is usual in the Song.

Mary Elliott speaks of a "mirroring dynamic," in which the affirmations made of one of the lovers are then referred to the other.[30] Thus it is explained that the lotus flowers found in her breast and in her womb (2:16; 4:5; 7:3) are also on his lips (5:13). The myrrh that runs from her hands (5:5) likewise flows from his lips (5:13). If he is enchanted, speechless before her beauty, (1:15; 4:1), she experiences the same wonder before him (1:16). The lovers have sibling bodies. Not for nothing will he call the woman "my sister, my bride" (4:9, 10, 12; 5:1, 2). In exchange, she proposes the desire that her beloved will be "like a brother to me, suckled at the breast of my mother" (8:1). In effect, the formula of Gen 2:23 is a formula of complete consanguinity.

Perhaps the mirroring dynamic is nowhere more evident than in the description of the eyes. His eyes are compared to doves (5:12), as are hers (1:15; 4:1), but the description of 5:12 is more extensive: "His eyes like doves … , placed on a full bath." To this image corresponds that of her eyes in 7:5: "Your eyes pools of Heshbon at the gate of Bath-Rabbim." A comparison between the two images yields his eyes (doves) as reflected in hers (pools); the likeness is the "mirror" of Gen 2.

Keel, *Deine Blicke sind Tauben*, 63–78; S. F. Grober, "The Hospitable Lotus: A Cluster of Metaphors: An Inquiry into the Problem of Textual Unity in the Song of Songs," *Semitics* 9 (1984): 86–112.

29. For a nonmasculinist reading of the creation of woman from "man," see Walter Vogels, "'It Is Not Good That the 'Mensch' Should Be Alone; I Will Make Him/Her a Helper Fit for Him/Her' (Gen 2,18)," *EgT* 9 (1978): 9–35.

30. Elliott, *Literary Unity of the Canticle*, 246–51.

To make it clear that the two lovers are on the same plane and there is no superiority of one over the other—since true love does not tolerate inequalities!—the second time the refrain of mutual belonging is sounded the order is inverted: "I am my beloved's, and my beloved is mine" (6:3). Here, too, the formula fits into the context coherently. The woman had lost her beloved and had sought him in distress through the streets of the city, involving the daughters of Jerusalem in her search (5:6–8). In response to their inquiry she describes at length his face and figure, which prove to be of the same precious materials as her own (5:10–16). This makes her certain that her beloved can only have retired into his garden, that is, to her (6:2).

The mutual belonging of the lovers is again expressed at the end of the first part of the Song, at the conclusion of 4:8–5:1. The beloved ends his song with praise of the "garden": "Garden enclosed, my sister, my bride!" (4:12)—praise of her continence but also an implicit request for an opening of what is closed. The woman understands and comes to meet the request of her spouse, bidding first the winds to blow, spreading the perfumes of the garden: "Make my garden breathe: let its balms spread" (4:16a). Then comes the consent: "Let my beloved come into his garden and taste its delicious fruits" (4:16b). What was "*my* garden" now becomes "*his* garden," the garden of her beloved. It belongs no more to the bride but to her beloved; she has given it to him. He understands and exclaims with joy: "I have come into *my* garden, my sister, my bride" (5:1).

We have spoken of the woman's bodily continence. It is signified explicitly in the expression "garden enclosed ... sealed spring" (4:12). But the closing is not an end in itself; it is aligned to the gift. The garden is closed so as to be opened to the beloved. And the opening occurs from the inside. The latch on the door is firmly in the woman's hands. It is she who has to open it each time! Love cannot be other than a free gift freely bestowed.

The theme of the latch recurs in the following song, in which, in the face of her hesitations, the beloved man tries to open the door with his hands, seeking to release the latch; but he does not succeed (5:2–4). The gate to her room cannot be opened from the outside. It is the beloved woman who must rise and open it (5:5–6). Now the meeting can take place. But it is too late! The man is tired of waiting and has fled. In the idyll of the Song, suffering and misunderstanding creep in as in every concrete story of love.[31]

---

31. For this reading of the episode, see Keel, *The Song of Songs*, 192–94. The author thinks of the experience, frequent among married couples, of the lack of coincidence in the inclination to make love ("Phasenverschiebung der Gefühle"). See also Peter Chave, "Toward a Not Too Rosy Picture of the Song of Songs," *Feminist Theology* 18 (1998): 41–53.

The third time in which the refrain of mutual belonging resounds is 7:11: "I am my beloved's, and his desire is for me [עָלַי תְּשׁוּקָתוֹ]." With these words, the woman refers to what the man had expressed in 7:9–10: "I said to myself: I will climb [אֶעֱלֶה] up the palm." The preposition עַל takes up again the verb אעלה exactly. By saying "I am my beloved's," she expresses her assent to his desire, in the same way as, in 5:1, she had made of "my" garden "his" garden.

The term used to express "desire" is not accidental, but refers to Gen 3:16.[32] After the fall, God expresses its consequences for the woman thus: "I will greatly multiply your pain in childbearing: in pain shall you bring forth children. Your desire [תְּשׁוּקָתֵךְ] shall be for your husband, but he shall be your master." Here, sexual desire is seen as the origin of the submission of woman with regard to man, but this does not correspond to the original plan of God; it is made by the Genesis author to be the fruit of sin, which has damaged the relation between the sexes.[33]

The text of the Song deliberately brings the male-female relation back to the way it was before the fall, when desire was something positive that did not lead to the subjugation of woman. Keel rightly speaks of "lifting the curse"[34] and Trible of "love redeemed."[35]

7. Who Is This Who Rises from the Desert?

Following the descriptions of nature in 2:8–17 and 7:12–14 are depictions of love in the town (3:1–5 and 8:1–4, respectively). The contrast is deliberate: both times the town is presented as potentially hostile to love. The refrain of awakening that concludes the two passages (3:5 and 8:4) has the sense of a bitter protest against the inappropriate interference of town society in the love of the two young people.

In 3:1–5, the town is characterized by the "watchmen" (v. 3). The woman turns to them to obtain information in her nocturnal search: "Have you seen the love of my soul?" As expected, her question receives no reply. What do the watchmen know about love? In the other nocturnal search, in 5:6–7, they end up by striking and stripping the girl, taking her for a prostitute. Indeed, a girl who walks the streets at night seeking information about her loved one from passersby does not fall within the parameters of the normal behavior of social

---

32. The term תְּשׁוּקָה appears again in Biblical Hebrew only in Gen 4:7, in a negative sense as in 3:16.
33. See Fischer, "Donne nell'Antico Testamento," 271.
34. Keel, *The Song of Songs*, 251–52.
35. Phyllis Trible, "Love's Lyric Redeemed," in Brenner, *A Feminist Companion to the Song of Songs*, 100–120.

respectability. In Prov 7:6–27, the foreign woman from whom the sage seeks to keep his distance is painted along these lines as well.

The woman of the Song is not exemplary in her observance of the town rules. Love has about it something of the anarchic, which upsets not only the life of the individual but also the life of society. In his description of the woman's body, besides the beautiful, Apollonian character, the man sketches its vital, Dionysian aspect present, for example, in his description of her hair: "Your hair like a flock of goats gamboling down from the mountains of Gilead." Luxuriant hair is a sign of strength, as recalled by Samson (see Judg 16:17, 22) and the Song of Deborah (Judg 5:2). In Ps 68:22, the enemy of God has a "shaggy" head, as a sign of his rebellion; "shaggy" too is the goat of Gen 37:21, as well as the demon of Lev 17:7 and Isa 13:21.[36] In Greek mythology, one thinks of the god Pan and the satyrs who accompanied him. The comparison of the goats, which are black and descend in disorderly fashion leaping down the slope of the mountain, underlines this aspect, in contrast with the orderly procession of the white ewes coming out of the cleansing bath.

In the vision of the Song, love comes from the fields (2:7; 3:5), from the mountains (2:8; 4:8), from the desert (3:1; 8:5)—in a word, from untamed nature. But it does not remain there. Contrary to the movement of the going out of love is that of "coming in." Here, too, the woman is the protagonist. She is the one who in 3:4 introduces her man into the family: "I held him tight and would not let him go until I had brought him into the house of my mother, into the chamber of her who conceived me." The image returns in 8:2, presented as a dream, a desire: "I would lead you, I would bring you into the house of my mother."

The "house of the mother" is not only the building but also the family. If, in 3:4 and 8:2, it is her mother who is mentioned, in two other places it is his mother who is spoken of. In 8:5, in the immediate context of 8:2, the place of love is described thus: "Under the apple tree I awakened you, there your mother travailed, there she travailed and gave you to the light." The bride is superimposed on the mother, takes the role in the man's life, which was that of his mother, generating her spouse for new life.[37] The expression "under the apple tree" is not to be taken literally. The allusion is rather to the normal room of a house in the town, where the man was conceived and brought to the light. Love transforms walls of stone into a tree full of life.

---

36. See Keel, *Song of Songs*, 141.

37. Daniel Lys, *Le plus beau chant de la création: Commentaire du Cantique des cantiques* (LD 51; Paris: Cerf, 1968), 284: "Finally, I aroused you to a new birth, the one of love." See also Elliott, *Literary Unity of the Canticle*, 193.

The second mention of his mother is in 3:11: "Go out, O daughters of Zion, and behold King Solomon and the crown with which his mother has crowned him on the day of his wedding, the day of the joy of his heart." The mother has to be present at the nuptial feast. It is she who crowns her son, as if passing the witness of the female role to the bride. Besides the mother the "daughters of Zion" are also present, viewed now in a highly positive light as the society that welcomes and legitimizes sexual love. In the same song, there is mention of the armed escort that accompanies the litter of the bride (3:7–8). Society that elsewhere comes under the scourge of disapproval is here recognized as playing an essential role.

In 3:6, the refrain "Who is this who rises from the desert?" appears for the first time (see again 6:10 and 8:5). The answer to the question is given in verse 10, when, in the description of Solomon's litter, it is said that its interior is "adorned with the love of the daughters of Jerusalem." Thus we have a metonymy to indicate the bride, who, in her turn, symbolizes the love of the daughters of Jerusalem.[38]

The desert, the place of origin of the "litter," has in fact its own dangers (3:8), from which the sixty valiant men-at-arms have to defend the litter. Thus in 4:8 the man urges his woman to come away from the "desert": "With me from Lebanon, my bride, with me from Lebanon come. Look from the summit of Amana, from the peak of Senir and Hermon, from the lairs of the lions, from the mountains of the panthers!" Like the desert, the mountains are the habitat of wild animals, of the savage forces of life that also have a destructive character and must be educated to come into contact with the "town" or the "city." The journey of love, therefore, goes from the desert to the garden. Its itinerary is sketched in 4:8–5:1; the garden, described in the concluding passage (4:12–5:1), is at the same time a metaphor for the woman and a place of love.[39]

The appellation "bride" characterizes the whole of the poem in 4:8–5:1, where it resounds a good six times (4:8, 9, 10, 11, 12; 5:1). One cannot say that the Song is proposing a love without a home or laws.[40] On the other hand, it is curious that the use of the term "bride" is restricted to the passage in question.

---

38. In this respect, see Elliott, *Literary Unity of the Canticle*, 88; Gianni Barbiero, "Die Liebe der Töchter Jerusalems: Hld 3,10b MT im Kontext vom 3,6–11," *BZ* 39 (1995): 96–104.

39. On the significance of the garden in the Song, see Heinevetter, "Komm nun, mein Liebster," 179–90; Francis Landy, *Paradoxes of Paradise: Identity and Difference in the Song of Songs* (BLS 7; Sheffield: Almond, 1983), 189–210.

40. Contra, among others, André LaCocque, *Romance, She Wrote*, 8: "The entire Song strums the chord of 'free love,' neither recognized nor institutionalized."

The usual title with which the man addresses his woman is רַעְיָתִי, a term that indicates a relation of friendship, one that has not been ratified by an institutional contract. That can be explained, perhaps, by the progressive maturing of love, but it is possible, also, that the author does not see that opposition between the two terms that has become established in Western society. The "bride" does not cease to be "friend." The bond that unites the spouses is not primarily an institutional one: it is, in fact, love.

The journey toward the city is presented again in the epilogue (8:5–14), which begins with the desert (8:5) and ends with the garden (8:13: "You who dwell in the gardens"). As if welcoming the invitation of 4:8 ("*With me* from Lebanon"), the woman is no longer alone in this journey: she is "leaning on her beloved" (8:5). In dialogue with her is the chorus of the daughters of Jerusalem, evoked in the previous verse in a decidedly negative light. Apparently, they have accepted the woman's rebuke, and, from an attitude hostile to love, they have been converted to one that is respectful and welcoming, like that described in the parallel passage, 3:6–11. Thus the woman proceeds toward the city, bearing there the critical demands of love.

Criticism is introduced in 8:7: "If a man were to give all the wealth of his house in exchange for love, scorn is all he would obtain." The woman establishes the primacy of love over commerce, a primacy important to affirm in the world of the Song (and not only there!), in which marriages of convenience were the custom. This is spoken of again in 8:11–12, where there is criticism of the harem of Solomon, to whom every keeper of the "vineyard" must bring "a thousand shekels of silver." Solomon, here, is the representative of the kind of society the woman of the Song, in agreement with the statement in 8:7b, holds in contempt because it thinks it possible to buy love with money.

Song 6:8 also speaks of Solomon's harem: "Sixty are the queens, eighty the concubines, and maidens without number." Against the multiplicity of women in the harem, the beloved man counterposes the uniqueness of his woman: "Unique is my dove, my perfect one, the only one of her mother, the darling of the one who conceived her" (6:9). This is a clear protest against polygamy, a practice that must have been widespread in the society of the time and one the author holds to be incompatible with the dignity of women.

Speaking of Deut 6:4–5, Lohfink stresses the profound analogy between monolatry and monogamy.[41] Just as the God of Israel is one (Deut 6:4), so the woman of the Song is one (6:9). Just as the God of Israel is jealous (Exod 34:14; Deut 4:24; 5:9), so is the beloved woman because love is jealous (cf. 8:6): it

---

41. See Norbert Lohfink and Jan Bergman, "אֶחָד *'echādh*," *TDOT* 1:193–201, here 196–97.

tolerates no rivals. While the "many" remain on the earth, the "one" is aligned with the heavenly phenomena; its place is heaven, the place of God (6:10).

8. Set Me as a Seal upon Your Heart

The "seal" is spoken of twice in the Song. The first occasion is in 4:12. In the expression "sealed spring," we have seen an image of the chastity of the bride. The term appears for the second time in 8:6: "Set me as a seal upon your heart, as a seal upon your arm." In 4:12, the seal witnessed to the fact that the "gate" had not been opened. Now that the union has been consummated, it confirms the indissolubility of that union. Nothing can put asunder the two lovers united in their embrace.[42]

The statements that follow have to be understood as an explanation of the indissolubility of the union: they are, in fact, connected by means of the causal particle כי: "*because* love is strong as death, jealousy relentless as the grave." Mention of jealousy allows us to understand that the union is threatened by promiscuity, something that goes against the very nature of love.[43] From a psychological point of view, women are strictly monogamous in love.[44] This is confirmed strongly here at the climax of the poem, not in the name of any institution but of love itself. Love has laws that are no less demanding than human laws.

The other statement in the phrase is also to be understood in this light. Love is "strong as death," because it is just as demanding and relentless; it seeks everything, it demands the surrender of life on behalf of one's beloved. But love is also stronger than death, as is affirmed in verse 7: "The great waters—that is, those of death[45]—cannot quench love." Death is another "rival" that threatens to snatch the woman from her man, but it will not succeed in doing so. What follows explains why: "Its darts are darts of fire, a flame of Yah." Since love is a flame of YHWH, death is powerless against it. The man of the Old

---

42. This is alluded to by the expressions "on your heart," "on your arm," both of which take up the description of the embrace in 8:3.

43. Cf., in the same sense, Mal 2:14–16.

44. See Günter Krinetzki, *Kommentar zum Hohenlied: Bildsprache und theologische Botschaft* (BET 16; Frankfurt am Main: Lang, 1981), 185. It is interesting to note that the Old Testament legislation speaks only of a man's jealousy (see Num 5:11–31). A woman was to have only one man, while a man could have as many women as he wished. In reality, however, female jealousy is also well known in the Old Testament (see Gen 16:1–5).

45. See Herbert G. May, "Some Cosmic Connotations of *Mayim Rabbim* 'Many Waters,'" *JBL* 74 (1955): 9–21.

Testament knows that nothing and no one can separate him from his God (cf. Isa 43:2–3; Ps 16:9–11).

This affirmation seems to be contradicted by the conclusion of the poem, 8:14:[46] "Flee, my beloved, be like a gazelle or a young stag, on the mountains of balms." The beginning and end of the epilogue are linked by means of an inclusion. In both, the theme is the relation of the woman with her man while the two central compositions, 8:8–10 and 8:11–12, concern the woman's relation with society. In fact, the man seems to refer to society in verse 13: "My companions are attentive to your voice." After the woman has spoken to the "companions," she addresses the last word to her beloved ("Let *me* hear it").

The word is that recorded above: "Flee!" It is an important word, for it concludes not only the epilogue of the Song but also the whole poem. To think that, as is often the case,[47] we have here a displaced text that has been added subsequently to the poem is a convenient escape technique. Moreover, the explanation according to which "flee" would be another way of saying "come" does not agree with the meaning of the word ברח, which indicates taking one's distance from a definite place or person. Furthermore, verses 5–6 of the same chapter have represented the two lovers in a close embrace; the request to approach, therefore, would not make sense.

In my opinion, it is precisely the structural relationship of verses 13–14 with verses 5–6, the beginning and end of the epilogue, which explains the verb "flee" in verse 14. It stands, that is, in antithesis to the request of verse 6: "Set me as a seal upon your heart." If verse 6 shows the need for the union, an indissoluble union of the two lovers, verse 14 points to the antithetical need for having one's own space. Verse 6 speaks of a "jealousy" that has something positive about it but also has negative implications because it can lead to possessiveness. The union of the two lovers must not become a fusion that annihilates the individuality of each partner. It is only insofar as one is really oneself that one can make a free gift of oneself; otherwise, love is subjugation, the annihilation of the other. Love has need not only of union but also of distance, and it is this that the woman seeks with the verb "flee." In verse 4, the woman requested the daughters of Jerusalem not to rouse Love "before

---

46. In my opinion, 8:5–14 constitutes a firmly structured literary unit, which makes up the poem's epilogue. See Gianni Barbiero, "'Leg mich wie ein Siegel—Fliehe, mein Geliebter': Die Spannung in der Liebesbeziehung nach dem Epilog des Hohenliedes," in *Studien zu alttestamentlichen Texten* (SBAB 34; Stuttgart: Katholisches Bibelwerk, 2002), 185–98; Barbiero, "L'amore, 'fiamma di Jah': Una lettura contestuale di Ct 8,5–7.13–14," in *Corpo e religione* (ed. Gaspare Mura and Roberto Cipriani; Rome: Città Nuova, 2009), 443–57.

47. For all these, the verdict of Landy (*Paradoxes of Paradise*, 133) holds good: "Following the credo (= 8:6), the Song has nothing more to say."

it wishes." Now, in verse 14, is the moment in which Love itself decides to "awaken," to loosen the embrace.

This distancing, however, is not aimed at a rupture in the relation but at its deepening. The direction of flight is the "mountains of balms," which we know to be a metaphor of the female body.

Union, then, but, at the same time, otherness. Ultimately, it is this that allows dialogue. The alternation—the collision, even—between the voices reflects the dialectic of the human being. Dialogue is a characteristic of the Song, which confers a profoundly "personal"[48] character on the poem.

In theological terms, one could speak of the "immanence" and "transcendence" of the relationship of love. Love unites the man to the woman so that they become "one flesh" (Gen 2:24). But even when the two regain their original unity, when their two bodies beat in unison, the lovers are still conscious of being two.[49] Each remains his or herself, with his or her own mystery.

Human love is shown to be the most adequate metaphor for God, a God who is not solitary but, according to Christian faith, a trinity of persons in union for all eternity without ever being "confused." Moreover, in the Old Testament, the prophets had glimpsed the theological dimension of human love: the love story of Hosea became the symbol of the relationship between God and his people. It is no surprise that first Israel—and later the church—were able to read in the Song the story of their own relationship with God.

Translated from Italian by Michael Tait

---

48. On the dialogic character of the Song, see Jean-Pierre Sonnet, "Le Cantique, entre érotique et mystique: sanctuaire de la parole échangée," NRTh 119 (1997): 481–502.

49. Armand Abécassis, "Espaces de lecture du Cantique des Cantiques en contexte juif," in Les nouvelles voies de l'exégèse, en lisant le Cantique des Cantiques: XIX congrès de l'ACFEB, Toulouse 2001 (ed. J. D. Jacques Nieuviarts and Pierre Debergé; LD 190; Paris: Cerf, 2002), 185–96, 190: "The other, who builds up and partcipates in this union, remains other, he is never reached at the point where he finds himself, he remains, so to speak, foreign to all knowledge of himself, to all power over him, to all manipulation. He remains, we can say, transcendent, that is, outside and above, since he provokes the responsibility with regard to himself."

Part 4
Ambivalent Role Models: Women in Narrative Texts

Ruth and Naomi Reclaim Their Lives and Memories

Miren Junkal Guevara Llaguno

1. Introduction

Augustine of Hippo, considering the value of time, says in *Confessions*: "The present considering the past is the memory" (11.20.26).[1] Memory, then, evokes what has been lived, loved, suffered, and enjoyed and brings these things to enrich, illuminate, and direct the present.

The book of Ruth is, for many reasons, a book about memory. Most likely written during the postexilic period, this short story of only four chapters evokes a distant time in Israelite history—the conflictive and convulsive time of the judges; it relates a story both about women shaken by strokes of fate that they must survive and about King David's family.

The force with which the protagonists, Ruth and Naomi, both foreigners and widows, vindicate the reality of women, foreigners, and the substance of the Torah converts the book into a tool that honors their lives and memories and avoids "losing everything like a bubble in the wind."[2]

2. Memory of the Feminine World in the Bible

If choosing the title of a book, like that of a business or a movie, helps its author organize its content, center its purpose, and communicate quickly with its reader, a good title also helps the recipients to direct their expectations, to reject the offer, and even to worry or be curious. So what, then, does the title of this book tell us?

---

1. Saint Augustine, *Confessions* (trans. Henry Chadwick; New York: Oxford University Press, 1991), 235.

2. Antonio Machado, "Desgarrada la nube," in *Soledades* (ed. Antonio Machado; Buenos Aires: Tecnibook Ediciones, 2011), 46.

In the first place, the book is called "Ruth," the name of a woman. Together with Esther and Judith, it is one of the three books in the Septuagint named after a woman. From the oldest canonical lists,[3] the book is known by this name—"Ruth"—a name that appears for the first time in Ruth 1:4, and is repeated nine times in the book before disappearing from the Bible. The name is never again used to refer to a woman. The title is not, however, trying to identify its author, and in fact Jewish tradition attributes the book to Samuel. The title also does not identify the main character, Naomi, even though it is she who appears most, and is related to all of the people in the story.[4] The title does, however, suggest the possibility that a female author wrote the book[5] and offers possible female role models to women. This idea, then, allows for possible deep transformations in both the feminine world and in the societies in which women live.

In this sense, the title could be considered *pro-vocative*, that is, evocative of the feminine world in the Bible that often seems trapped in books authored by men and whose setting is reduced to the domestic environment. And if the Bible—like any other piece of literature from the ancient Near East—expresses the identity of a character, his or her place in the story, and his or her relationship with the community through the choice of a name, then choosing a character as the title of a book would expressly highlight this person's story, world, voice, pronouncements, and denouncements. And "the house of Israel is built on people; maintained by names full of stories, or better, stories full of meaningful names."[6] In this sense, we affirm that the title of the book is a move to avoid the warning of Louise Otto-Peters, a pioneer of the fight for women's rights in the mid-nineteenth century: "The history of all times, and of today especially, teaches that … women will be forgotten if they forget to think about themselves."[7]

---

3. According to Vílchez, the oldest witness is the Babylonian Talmud, which in *Baba Batra* 14b names the book and places it at the head of the Writings. See José Vílchez Líndez, *Rut y Ester* (Nueva Biblia Española. Narrations 2; Estella: Verbo Divino, 1998), 25.

4. About the pertinence of naming this book for Naomi, see Zefira Gitay, "Ruth and the Women of Bethlehem," in *Ruth and Esther* (ed. Athalya Brenner; FCB 2/3; Sheffield: Sheffield Academic, 1999), 178–90, 186.

5. Irmtraud Fischer, *Women Who Wrestled with God: Biblical Stories of Israel's Beginnings* (trans. Linda M. Maloney; Collegeville, Minn.: Liturgical Press, 2005), 129.

6. Mercedes Navarro Puerto, *Los libros de Josué, Jueces y Rut* (Guía Espiritual del Antiguo Testamento; Barcelona/Madrid: Ciudad Nueva, 1995), 137. For a striking example, see the genealogies in 1 Chr 1–9 analyzed by Sara Japhet in this volume.

7. Louise Otto-Peters, "Die Frauen Zeitung," in *Heroinas* (Madrid: Mueso-Thyssen-Bornemisza/Fundación Caja Madrid, 2011), 59. For the English citation, see http://www.womeninworldhistory.com/wisdom.html.

2.1. The Meaning of the Protagonist's Name

In biblical literature, marked by a definite male slant, the attention to detail with feminine names can give us a lot of information about the character herself.[8] For some time it was thought that the name Ruth came from the root רע, "close friend" (in the book, "friend, companion"). Since Hans Bruppacher published his work, however, authors have accepted that the origin of the name must be related to רוה, "to give water to, to satisfy." Ruth, then, would have to mean "the one who alleviates, or comforts."[9] Perhaps the book evokes, in the first place, the people who care for others, watch over them, and knit webs of solidarity to help them. The choice of the two protagonists' names is thus truly paradigmatic. We must keep in mind the fact that the one who alleviates or comforts (Ruth) sees her name fully realized when her mother-in-law Naomi (she who pleases, helps) fully reclaims her life at the end of the story. In 1:20 she asks the women of Bethlehem to call her Mara ("bitter") like the waters the Israelites could not drink in the desert (Exod 15:23). And thus, as she herself will remind us in the life of Naomi, Dolores Aleixandre says: "Now in my old age I have managed to understand that I received my name at birth from an unfulfilled promise. Now it has become reality and I see how the Lord has driven our lives toward understanding the meanings of our names."[10]

The relationship between these two women is established at the beginning of the story through the male characters. Naomi is Elimelech's wife and the mother of Mahlon and Chilion; Ruth is one son's wife, but we do not know which one until the end of the story (Ruth 4:9). It is only the disappearance of the men that allows for a direct relationship between the two women: the text says that Ruth is Naomi's daughter-in-law (Ruth 1:6),[11] and her daughter (Ruth 1:11), and also that Naomi is Ruth's mother-in-law (Ruth 1:14). It is in this relationship that the two women will be seen by everyone, through to the last scene in the story. Of course, it is the quality of their relationship that is going to allow them both to fulfill their names, as Dolores Aleixandre says.

The meaning of this relationship is established at Ruth's decision to "cling," דבק, to her mother-in-law (Ruth 1:14). Her independence in deciding about

---

8. Karla G. Bohmbach, "Names and Naming in the Biblical World," in *Women in Scripture: A Dictionary of Named and Unnamed Women in the Hebrew Bible* (ed. Carol L. Meyers; Grand Rapids: Eerdmans, 2000), 33–39, here 33.

9. Ernst A. Knauf, "Ruth la moabite," *VT* 44 (1994): 547–48, 547.

10. Dolores Aleixandre, "Buscadoras de un nombre: memoria de Naomi," *Reseña Bíblica* 71 (2011): 4–10, here 7.

11. At the beginning, the story mentions two daughters-in-law, Ruth and Orpah. For my purposes, however, I am only going to consider Ruth.

her own family, law, and religion is going to create a guideline for women's mobility from the traditional feminine space (what happens "behind closed doors; the family-domestic world," untimely and uncreative …) to the public sphere dominated by men. The verb דבק, which we translate as "to cling to," or "to follow to the point of giving everything for another," is not an infrequently used term in Hebrew. It tends to be used to describe devotion to God (Deut 4:4) as well as a firm loyalty and depth, even erotic, that distinguishes relationships between people. It is used, thus, to refer to marriage (Gen 2:24; 34:3; Josh 23:12; 1 Kgs 11:2), loyalty to the king (2 Sam 20:2), and friendship (Prov 18:24). This verb then defines a personal link that requires a sacrifice of one's own self in order to unite with another. It appears another three times in the book (Ruth 2:8, 21, 23), always to refer to the relationship that Ruth must establish with Boaz's employees. That is, the use of the verb reveals a transition in Ruth's affection. She begins her story clinging to her mother-in-law and ends clinging to Boaz, who will restore the life and memory of both women.

The radical nature of Ruth's obligation to Naomi is explained immediately after Orpah, her sister-in-law, has decided to follow her mother-in-law's advice. This radicalism is made palpable in her entreaty "do not press me to leave you and to turn back from following you" (1:16) because the verb עזב, "to leave," is the same used in Gen 2:24 to refer to how the man leaves his mother after finding his wife, thus reinforcing the depth of the commitment that Ruth wants to make to Naomi.

The content of this promise is explained in the words that mark the new relationship: "where you go I will go; where you lodge I will lodge; your people shall be my people and your God my God" (Ruth 1:16). These words are heard immediately after Ruth has rejected Naomi's suggestion that she return "to her mother's house" (Ruth 1:8). This detail tells us that Ruth has decided autonomously about the law, because Naomi suggests that her daughters-in-law do what she herself plans: to return to her place of birth, as established by law (Gen 38:11). Judah suggests this to his daughter-in-law Tamar, and Lev 22:13 advises the same in the case of the priest's daughter. Not only this, but in the context of the verse (1:9), Ruth also decides to reject a new marriage.

On the other hand, the expression "return to your mother's house" is actually so strange that some versions written after the Masoretic text[12] change it. The phrase only appears three times in the Old Testament (Gen 24:28; Song 3:4; 8:2) and in all cases refers to stories about women who make their own

---

12. Carol L. Meyers, "Returning Home: Ruth 1:8 and the Gendering of the Book of Ruth," in *A Feminist Companion to Ruth* (ed. Athalya Brenner; FCB 3; Sheffield: Sheffield Academic, 1993), 85–114, here 92.

decisions about their future and who also influence other people—stories that take place in the family environment and that show the intelligence and perspicacity of their protagonists.[13]

The reference to "your mother's house" has also been studied as an indicator of a female author who vindicates the "mother's house" (noting the participation of women therein) as opposed to the "father's house" as a patriarchal unit, the nucleus of a family's economic activity, and a reference to property. All of this shows the family structure not in the light of power hierarchy, but rather in the light of gender and thus as a unit both productive and reproductive. Additionally, it vindicates the memory of the family that the woman abandoned as a consequence of being married.[14]

Last, Ruth demonstrates the solidity of her promise by turning her back on her own gods and "clinging" to Naomi's God. Given that she had met the Israelites in Moab, the knowledge that Ruth could have of the God of Israel would not have been received in the public sphere (through a community). Ruth has found Israel's God, to whom she decides "to cling," in the domestic sphere and, principally, through contact with her mother-in-law. Their cohabitation in Moab allows her to understand what is meant by a life supported by faith in the God of Israel and its provident action, even in adversity.[15] If the news that reaches Moab ("YHWH has visited his people and given them food" [Ruth 1:6]) is so believable that it causes her to risk going to Bethlehem with her mother-in-law, it is because Naomi's God reveals himself to be worthy. Ruth's decision, then, shows her to be a woman with the capacity for choice. And her choice is motivated by the affection she has for her mother-in-law and not for reasons of gender, ethnicity, or religion.[16]

In what way does Ruth enrich our view of reality? In the first place, Ruth chooses a commitment to her mother-in-law over her own ethnic and family group, over a new marriage arranged by her family[17] and even over her own gods. This indicates that Ruth, upon understanding the conflict that has arisen because of the death of the men, has decided to resolve it not in terms of justice and law but rather in terms of personal attachment and separation. Ruth

---

13. Jenni R. Ebeling, *Women's Lives in Biblical Times* (New York: T&T Clark, 2010), 28.
14. Ibid., 86.
15. Roberta T. Apfel and Lise Grondahl, "Feminine Plurals," in *Reading Ruth: Contemporary Women Reclaim a Sacred Story* (ed. Judith A. Kates and Gail Twersky Reimer; New York: Ballantine, 1996), 55–64, here 59.
16. Navarro Puerto, *Los libros de Josué, Jueces y Rut*, 138.
17. Ebeling, *Women's Lives in Biblical Times*, 82: "Even though mothers could be involved in marriage negotiations, the language used in the arrangements is male: a woman is given, taken, sent for, captured or even purchased in the case of a slave wife."

has chosen to free her mother-in-law from the isolation and pain that their situation could cause instead of following what is prescribed by the law. Ruth has assumed responsibility for her, and this action will cause the personal links between the two women to strengthen to the point that they will recover the lives that they carry within their names.

In this way, Ruth has given us keys to use in examining our own interpersonal relationships. As Roberta T. Apfel and Lise Grondahl note, the verb דבק, which does not have pejorative meaning in the Bible, can be understood today as referring to something unhealthy, capable of eliminating autonomy and the power of decision; from their psychiatric point of view, however, the authors observe that the richness of some relationships thus established can contribute to our condition as people.[18]

Additionally, by offering a new dimension of reality—the idea that taking care of another invites the management of interpersonal relationships through a perspective illuminated by the principle of responsibility[19]—Ruth reminds us that we form part of a web of relationships in which some of us depend on others. This dependence demands both a care for the fabric of social links that allow for this responsibility and an attention to the abandonment and social exclusion that can sometimes result. We should be cautious, however, when dealing with the relationship between mother- and daughter-in-law and avoid generalizing its value and presenting it as a model for all women.[20]

2.2. The Women of Bethlehem as Protagonists

After examining the capacity of Ruth's name to enrich women's imagination, let us spend time with a group of women from Bethlehem, an anonymous chorus whose participation is the key for understanding Ruth and Naomi's return to Bethlehem.[21] The women of Bethlehem (Ruth 1:19; 4:14) play a crucial role in the story because they provide the setting for the process that will return life and memory to Naomi and, through "clinging" to her, also to Ruth.

---

18. Apfel and Grondahl, "Feminine Plurals," 59–60.

19. Ellen F. Davis, "'All that You Say, I Will Do': A Sermon on the Book of Ruth," in *Scrolls of Love: Ruth and the Song of Songs* (ed. Peter S. Hawkins and Lesleigh C. Stahlberg; New York: Fordham University Press, 2006), 3–8, here 4.

20. Feminist exegesis in the context of Asia provides interesting warnings about this; see Ana May Say Pa, "Reading Ruth 3:1–5 from an Asian Woman's Perspective," in *Engaging the Bible in a Gendered World: An Introduction to Feminist Biblical Interpretation in Honor of Katharine Doob Sakenfeld* (ed. Linda Day and Carolyn Pressler; Louisville: Westminster John Knox, 2006), 47–59, here 49.

21. Rachel Minc, "Le role du choeur feminine dans le livre de Ruth," *BVC* 77 (1967): 71–76.

In Ruth 1:19, they are not explicitly cited, but the verb ותאמרנה, "the women said," is in the feminine plural, which allows us to identify the women of Bethlehem as the subject of the sentence; in Ruth 4:17 they are השכנות, "women of the neighborhood."[22] Our protagonists have created ties of solidarity and friendship with these women, especially when, as a consequence of marriage, they have joined a social group that was different from theirs.[23] Their reception of Ruth and Naomi, who are returning from Moab, shows emotion and agitation, but also happiness (cf., e.g., the happiness of the women who receive David in 1 Sam 18:7). The women serve as a mouthpiece for the surprise provoked in Bethlehem when Naomi returns ten years after emigrating to Moab: widow, without children, with no sign of having prospered economically and also in the company of a Moabite.

The question "Can this be Naomi?" suggests that the years passed and suffering caused by the tragedy in Moab have left traces on Naomi's face. She arrives, also, without the men who brought her into the public sphere. Naomi's answer explains that her new identity is found in the changing of her name. She who left alive, fecund, and accompanied (Ruth 1:21) returns "bitter" (Ruth 1:20). It is these women's words, however, at the end of the story that rehabilitate Naomi's life and memory. They do this by "clinging" to Ruth, who is no longer the Moabite, but rather "your daughter-in-law who loves you so much," and who seems to have been forgotten during the arrival (Ruth 1:19-21). The chorus of women thus serves the memory of both. The daughter-in-law, who arrives "clinging" to Naomi and unacknowledged, returns life to her. If we understand life to mean the sustenance provided by alimentation (Lam 1:11, 19), then the Hebrew expression להשיב נפש could be translated as "it will restore your life" or "it will return your vitality" (Ruth 4:15).[24]

It is worth noting that we can find one of the theological messages of our book in the voice of the women's chorus. The book of Ruth teaches that two things are outside of the control of biblical men: the fecundity of a woman and of the earth, both signs of God's action. The women who receive Naomi "empty" proclaim that she once again experiences life and fecundity thanks to the fact that Ruth has clung to her and has become "more to you than seven sons" (Ruth 4:15).[25] The action of returning a person to life, an action of which God is usually the subject, is attributed to Ruth, an instrument of

---

22. The term only appears here and in Exod 3:22.
23. Carol L. Meyers, "Women of the Neighbourhood," in Brenner, *Ruth and Esther*, 110–17, 119.
24. The expression להשיב נפש, "to restore vitality/life," also appears in Job 33:30.
25. Keep in mind that "seven" traditionally represents perfection and also the ideal number of children (1 Sam 2:5; Job 1:2; 42:13; Jer 15:9) and that men were, in general,

divine providence. Note that God does not appear even once directly communicating with protagonists in revelations or religious acts.[26] However, the fecundity of the earth, the other symbol of God's action, which mobilizes the return of Ruth and Naomi (announced in Ruth 1:6), is also undertaken thanks to women when Ruth collects food in Boaz's fields and brings abundant amounts to her mother-in-law (Ruth 2:1; 3:16).

3. The Memory of the Foreigners

The story of Ruth, a story of poor women who support one another when their lives and memories are at stake, comes together with biblical literature as a paradigmatic example of what we know today as the "processes of empowerment." According to these processes, individuals or collectives who have been excluded from the system and denied the capacity of choice speak and make decisions and acquire in these circumstances the capacities that they had been denied.

The book begins with the emigration of the family of Elimelech, a Jew from Bethlehem, to Moab; the marriage of his sons with two women from the country (Ruth 1:1–4); and the death of all the men. This story is linked very quickly with another that is similar: the emigration of the women of the family to their homeland. The narrator places both stories in parallel and tells them from the Israelite's perspective to create, from within, a rereading that can perhaps reaffirm values that were being questioned when the story was written.[27] Thus the reader does not have the impression that the emigration to Moab was difficult for Elimelech and his people; the text does not suggest that there is any conflict. However, the continual reference to the daughter-in-law's Moabite origin and the silence of the women when she enters the town with her mother-in-law cause the reader to be suspicious about the women's return.

Indeed, from the beginning to the end, the author makes note of the fact that Ruth belongs to Moab. In fact, the term "Moabite" accompanies the proper noun six times: three times from the narrator (Ruth 1:22; 2:2, 21), once from Boaz's servants (Ruth 2:6) and twice from Boaz himself (Ruth 4:5, 10).

---

preferred over women. Timothy D. Finlay, *The Birth Report Genre in the Hebrew Bible* (FAT 12; Tübingen: Mohr Siebeck, 2005).

26. Katharine D. Sakenfeld, *Ruth* (IBC; Louisville: Westminster John Knox, 1999), 16: "Readers are invited to look for the human component in the blessings they receive, and, like Ruth specially, to live in such a way that their own actions become the channel for God's blessings upon those around them."

27. The postexilic time of Ezra and Nehemiah's reforms.

The narrator emphasizes this so that the reader never loses sight of the protagonist's origin. Not only this, but Ruth also interprets her ethnic condition as the reason for her exclusion when, in her dialogue with Boaz, the relative from Bethlehem who accommodates her on his land, she presents herself as a "foreigner" (Ruth 2:10). In this case, she uses the term נכריה, which not only refers to the "foreigner" (גר) to whom Israelite legislation gives certain rights (Exod 12:48; Lev 19:33; 23:35, 47; Num 9:14; 15:14; Deut 10:18; 24:17; 27:19), but also to the "alien" who does not have any links and who, for this reason, is part of a lower social order. In fact, Robert Martin-Achard[28] and Paul Humbert[29] emphasize the meaning that נכרי has in the family sphere. It designates the person who is not recognized as a member, the woman who is not integrated into the clan and is definitively socially disqualified.

The choice of Moab as a homeland for Ruth, the titular woman, is fairly paradoxical[30] if one considers the fact that relations between Moab and Israel entail a long history of agreements and disagreements in which women play an important role. Moab, a town with which Israel is linked by kinship (Deut 2:8–9), is disdained for its incestuous origins (Gen 19:30–38), for not accommodating Israel upon its return from Egypt, even for seeking to place a curse on them at the oracles of the prophet Balaam (Num 22–24), and because the daughters of Moab have corrupted the men of Israel (Num 25). This conflictive history has sealed the Moabites' exclusion from the Israelite assembly (Deut 23:3–6). Such exclusion is the most serious and irremediable of any group mentioned in the Torah.[31]

As in all stories of exclusion, the prejudices that are consolidated throughout time make a peaceful relationship between the parties impossible. The author most likely chose the paradigm of exclusion, the Moabites, and in particular the female Moabites, in order to make the reader think about a new type of relationship that could be instituted with the excluded people, who are in our story represented by the Moabites. In other words, the author thinks not only about the assimilation or conversion of non-Israelites but also about

---

28. Robert Martin-Achard, "נֵכָר stranger," *TLOT* 2:739–41.

29. Cited by Jack M. Sasson, *Ruth: A New Translation with a Philological Commentary and a Formalist-Folklorist Interpretation* (JHNES; Baltimore: Johns Hopkins University Press, 1979), 51.

30. André LaCocque, "Subverting the Biblical World: Sociology and Politics in the Book of Ruth," in Hawkins and Stahlberg, *Scrolls of Love*, 20–30, 24.

31. In the same chapter it is pointed out: "You shall not abhor an Edomite, for he is your brother; you shall not abhor an Egyptian, because you were a sojourner in his land. The children of the third generation that are born to them may enter the assembly of the Lord" (Deut 23:7–8).

the need to energize in Israel a kind of relationship with foreigners based on values and not prejudices. Nothing in the text suggests a negative view of the Moabites: we actually see the opposite.[32] In fact, for some people, Ruth presents an inclusive and even universalist image of the people of Israel.[33] Now, in order to discover these values, we have to go to the text itself and see two elements that provide a key to construct a discourse about "the others," a discourse that, free of prejudices, is capable of seeing others as completely necessary in constructing one's own identity.

The first element is dialogue. In the book of Ruth, fifty-six of its eighty-six verses form part of a dialogue. In fact, dialogue is the instrument with which the plot is structured, giving it a cinematographic agility.[34] Additionally, all of the characters have been created to communicate with each other; the narrator limits himself to presenting them and giving them the chance to speak and thus additionally suggests the value of the cooperative over the hierarchical.[35] If we keep in mind the agreement from a psychological, scientific, and philosophical perspective that the construction of identity is the fruit of a dialogical process,[36] an analysis of the dialogues in which Ruth's social and personal identities[37] are explained reveals the message the book wants to impart about the Moabites. I will examine three dialogues that signal key moments in the story: the reception by the women of Bethlehem (1:19–20), the dialogue between Ruth and Boaz in the field (2:5–12), and the dialogue at the doors of the city at the end of the story (4:9–11).

In the first dialogue, the women of Bethlehem completely ignore the Moabite. This exclusion has perhaps been started by Naomi, who quiets her after her daughter-in-law decides to "cling to her" (1:14, 17). When Ruth speaks, Naomi's silence continues: "When Naomi saw that she was determined to go with her, *she said no more to her*" (1:18).

In the second dialogue, Boaz becomes the first person in Bethlehem to notice Ruth's presence; upon visiting his field, he sees her. The question "Whose maiden is this?" (2:5) starts a dialogue with his servant. This dialogue

---

32. Ruth A. Putnam, "Friendship," in Kates and Reimer, *Reading Ruth*, 44–54, here 46.
33. Donn F. Morgan, *Between Text and Community: The "Writings" in Canonical Interpretation* (Minneapolis: Fortress, 2007), 51.
34. Navarro Puerto, *Los libros de Josué, Jueces y Rut*, 167.
35. Meyers, "Returning Home," 92–93.
36. Andrés Escarbajal Frutos and Andrés Escarbajal de Haro, *La interculturalidad: Desafío para la educación* (Madrid: Dykinson, 2007), 39.
37. Lupicinio Íñiguez, "Identidad: de lo personal a lo social: Un recorrido conceptual," in *La constitución social de la subjetividad* (ed. Eduardo Crespo; Madrid: Catarata, 2001), 209–25.

places Ruth at the forefront of the narration to present her not only with her social identity, her Moabite origin, but also with her personal identity, that of having decided to "cling" to her mother-in-law. It is this identity that is going to become significant for Boaz, who will publicly praise Ruth's חסד, her goodness, her big heart (3:10). Said in another way, the virtue that accompanies her actions[38] renders her worthy of God's blessing and an exemplary woman. In the book of Ruth, חסד also appears in 1:8 and 2:20 as a divine attribute that is revealed in how people act. Thus Naomi asks for God's חסד for her daughters-in-law, the same that they have given to her; and she blesses God because the figure of Boaz as גאל ("rescuer") expresses the חסד of YHWH over them. Finally, Boaz sees חסד in all of Ruth's personal history. Additionally, this virtue becomes the key that unites the destinies of Ruth and Boaz, the "powerful man" (2:11) and the "strong woman" (3:11), since divine חסד is expressed through the actions of both.

The last dialogue, between the people and the elders at the door of Bethlehem, links Ruth with the great matriarchs of Israel, thus tying her closely to the history of the Israelite people. Different from the Israelite heroines Deborah or Miriam, Ruth becomes a heroic figure for having carried the limits of goodness further than one would hope for or imagine, thus making goodness (חסד) a rule for relationships with foreigners.[39] The excluded minority represented by Ruth teaches Israel that חסד is the key to empowering foreigners—a symbol of those who are excluded—in the midst of the people. Additionally, her autonomy and decision-making power, based in that same attitude, offer women keys to empowerment.[40] Also, Ruth represents anyone who dares to break down barriers, to fight to go further than what is thought possible.

This paradigm of fighting against exclusion comes back to us when we consider the reality of those women who, having to confront economic, political, or gender conditions that excluded them from their people, were capable of reinventing their future.[41] Thinking about migrant women who go to the first world to look for work in order to be able to survive, many

---

38. As Joüon notes, Ruth's first act of חסד is not having abandoned her mother-in-law; the second, having wanted to give descendants to her father-in-law, preferring to marry the "rescuer" Boaz over any other young man. Perhaps the reference to the poor young ones is an allusion to the servants behind whom she gleaned in the fields. Paul Joüon, *Ruth: Commentaire philologique et exégétique* (SubBi 9; Roma: Institut Biblique Pontifical, 1986), 74.

39. Susanne Klingenstein, "Circles of Kinship: Samuel's Family Romance," in Kates and Reimer, *Reading Ruth*, 199–210, 202.

40. Judith A. Kates, "Women at the Center: Ruth and Shavuot," in Kates and Reimer, *Reading Ruth*, 187–98, 198.

41. Sarojini Nadar, "A South African Indian Womanist Reading of the Character of

people interpret[42] the story of Ruth to reclaim the unimaginable: that they are accepted—and integrated—especially when dealing with women who are severely poor or belong to excluded groups.

> Ruth, a foreign and excluded woman, was capable of making an offer that responded to the core problem. Love helps Ruth to rescue identity, communal spirit, happiness of life, faith, hope and future for Naomi's people (Ruth 4:11–16). She, the excluded one, gives her life to the reconstruction of a foreign people whom she takes as her own. In the alliance that she made with Naomi, she embraces this people's destiny which then comes to be her own. She does this because of friendship and also through the deep solidarity that unites the poor.[43]

The title of the book can empower the Moabites, rehabilitate their memory, and also show the existence of a world outside of Israel where the Jews are present and YHWH accompanies them. In this sense, Ruth highlights theological traditions present in the Bible that, far from presenting an exclusive theology, call attention to the need to recuperate the inclusion of all human beings in one space.[44]

4. The Substantial Memory of the Torah

The book of Ruth, whose position in the canon changes depending on whether we speak of the Hebrew text or the Septuagint, contains a memory of Torah traditions that convert the familiar past of Israel in a permanent and interpolating present. It is probably for this reason that it became part of the small collection of the Megilloth, five books that are read in synagogue liturgy during the most important holidays of the Jewish calendar. The reading of Ruth is given during the Festival of Weeks (Shavuot), a holiday of biblical origin (Exod 34:22; Lev 23:15–21; Num 28:26–31) that is celebrated, in the first place, at the beginning of the wheat harvest, the same season in which the

---

Ruth," in *Other Ways of Reading: African Women and the Bible* (ed. Musa W. Dube; Atlanta: Society of Biblical Literature, 2001), 159–75.

42. Bonnie Honig, "Ruth, the Model Émigrée: Mourning and the Symbolic Politics of Immigration," in Brenner, *Ruth and Esther*, 50–74; Brenner, "Ruth as Foreign Worker and the Politics of Exogamy," in Brenner, *Ruth and Esther*, 158–62; Kwok Pui-lan, *Post-Colonial Imagination and Feminist Theology* (Louisville: Westminster John Knox, 2005).

43. Mercedes Lopes, "Alianza por la vida: Una relectura de Rut a partir de las culturas," *RIBLA* 26 (1997): 96–101.

44. Tamara Cohn Eskenazi interprets the book of Ruth in the same way as an answer to the exclusion of foreign women in Ezra-Nehemiah; see her contribution in this volume.

nucleus of Ruth's story takes place (Ruth 1:22; 2:23); but since rabbinical times it also commemorates the gift of the Torah to the sons of Israel (b. Pesaḥ. 68b).

4.1. Celebrating the Gift of the Torah from New Perspectives

At the beginning of her study of Ruth and Shavuot, Judith A. Kates questions the meaning of reading the book during this holiday.[45] The question is not rhetorical, nor can it be answered today with traditional explanations.[46] Tackling this question and looking for new perspectives that add meaning to a reading of the book as an updated memory of the Torah can be extremely suggestive. Note that everything said, pointed out, or whispered here will legitimize the Torah.

Our task, following traditional parameters, must be in the first place to attend to references to legal precepts in the Torah that, whether explicitly or implicitly, appear in the text.[47] There are already a number of studies dealing with this question, to which I will direct the reader. In recent years, new studies have developed in another interesting area: the analysis of explicit or implicit allusions to the narrations of the Torah and its principal characters, the patriarchs and matriarchs that have built the house of Israel. It is precisely into these allusions that I propose to delve in order to discover how they challenge our own story. First, I will examine explicit references, those that are perfectly recognizable in the text or the tradition that is being reread; I will continue then with implicit references, that is, the suggestion—subtle and veiled at times—of themes, figures, or traditions of the Torah.

4.2. The Explicit Rereading of Narrative Torah Texts

The book of Ruth contains two explicit references to narrations of the Torah in which women are protagonists. They are Ruth 4:11, "May YHWH make the woman, who is coming into your house, like Rachel and Leah, who together built up the house of Israel"; and 4:12, "through the children that YHWH will give you by this young woman, may your house be like the house of Perez, whom Tamar bore to Judah." Both texts are put in the mouths of the people[48]

---

45. Kates, "Women at the Center," 188.
46. Adele Berlin, "Ruth and the Continuity of Israel," in Kates and Reimer, *Reading Ruth*, 255–60, 255.
47. The legal plot of the story explicitly combines two married legal institutions of the Torah: the levirate law (Deut 25) and the rescue law (Lev 25:23–38). The social legislation to benefit widows, orphans, and foreigners is implicitly noted (Lev 19:9–10; Deut 24:19).
48. Sakenfeld, *Ruth*, 76, speculates about a possible female presence in the group.

and the elders assembled at the doors to the city; both are directed at Boaz as prayers of blessing on his upcoming marriage.

This blessing includes two petitions. Through reference to Jacob's wives (who "built his house"), the first petition asks that in Ruth the fecundity she carries in her name be visible, a fertility that was hidden during ten years of marriage to Mahlon in Moab (they did not have children) and that could now be consummated. Additionally, this petition gives Ruth a foundational value[49] that will manifest itself when she becomes an ancestor of David, the new dynasty that will unite Israel.[50] It is worth noting that this scene harks back directly to the levirate legislation (Deut 25), but with a notable change: it is not the male/brother-in-law who builds his brother's house, but a woman—Ruth, evoking Leah and Rachel—who fulfills this duty. There is a move from the legal realm to the family sphere, a step that will be sealed when the neighbors proclaim, "A son has been born to Naomi" (Ruth 4:17). In this way, we see the difference between the male world, which takes pleasure in Boaz's luck in bearing many sons through Ruth, and the female world, which publicly proclaims how Naomi's name has finally been fulfilled.[51]

The second petition completes the first because it compares Ruth to Tamar, two foreign women who take the reins of their lives with autonomy and decisiveness. The story's goal is to emphasize Ruth's capacity to put herself in another's place and to show how this is the key to a fertile life, capable of bringing vitality to the lineage she joined.[52] The reference to the stories of the matriarchs appeals, additionally, to the need to overcome certain biblical stereotypes we continue to use today. Indeed, an inattentive reading of women's texts leads us to believe—at times—stories of biblical heroines who frequently fight over a man. It is true that the story of the two sisters, Leah and Rachel, presents this trait and underlines how the dependence on a man generates competition and violence among women. However, it is no less true that its mention in Ruth's blessing allows our memory to question the values that guide our interpersonal relationships.

On the other hand, the use of the body as a weapon against men to claim rights—a resource that is still used today in relations among the sexes—if indeed present in Ruth's story (3:3-4), is destroyed precisely by the words of Boaz, who approves of the woman not because she offers her body but because of her goodness and charity (Ruth 3:10). Thus one has to read the story as

---

49. Note the implicit reference to 2 Sam 7:27.
50. Luis Alonso Schökel, *Rut, Tobías, Judit Ester* (Los Libros Sagrados 8; Madrid: Cristiandad, 1973), 22.
51. Aleixandre, "Buscadoras de un nombre," 7.
52. Kates, "Women at the Center," 196.

"a story of family loyalty along the lines of the old customs and laws"[53] that denounce the recourse to force or power because these corrupt the dynamic of life inherent in all families. The story of Ruth, who is "outside the law," invites us to be givers of a life that is—beyond mere reproduction—capable of building a history of a family and people without exclusions and with values learned and imitated from Israel's God.

4.3. The Memory of Implicit References[54]

The first implicit reference is found in Ruth 1:1, when we receive news of a family's emigration as a consequence of hunger in their homeland. We have many biblical testimonies of the Israelite's custom to emigrate to Egypt in times of need. In the patriarchal stories, Abraham (Gen 12:10), Isaac (Gen 26:1), and Jacob (Gen 41:43–57; 42:5; 43:1) emigrate because "there was hunger in the land." Abraham and Isaac are forced to lie about their marriages, and Jacob's children suffer because they are foreigners. In Ruth's story, hunger mobilizes the emigration of the Ephrathites to Moab, but those who emigrate are poor and seem to start with nothing; they mix with the inhabitants of the country, become poorer still, and then die. The last of these stories can be told because the women, taking into their own hands a present with few guarantees of life, leave to find a future that YHWH seems to guarantee. Different from the trips of the patriarchs, always centered on men, in which women follow (the men decide on and determine duration and itinerary), the book of Ruth presents a trip taken by two women alone. Additionally, they enter a world over which they have no control, and they resolve difficulties not through lies but rather through the firm closeness between them. Fortunately, the author enables us to enter their world and hear their dialogues, a feature that is not offered to us in the stories of the patriarchs' migration.

The second reference is found in Ruth 2:11, where Ruth "clings" to her mother-in-law like a husband to his wife (Gen 2:24). Within the frame of rereading the Torah, this relationship again confronts us with patterns that play out in our interpersonal relations and tend to underline equilibrium, the existence of common worlds. We have seen already how the narration questions the stereotype of relationships between daughters-in-law and their

---

53. Alonso Schökel, *Rut, Tobías, Judit Ester*, 19.
54. This theme has been deeply studied by Irmtraud Fischer, "The Book of Ruth: A 'Feminist' Commentary to the Torah?" in Brenner, *Ruth and Esther*, 24–49. Others, following her study and as Judith A. Kates notes, have wanted to move beyond traditional exegesis; e.g., Berlin, "Ruth and the Continuity of Israel," 255–60; and Kates herself, "Women at the Center," 187–98.

mothers-in-law, a piece of imagery usually filled with conflictive stories.[55] However, the story also invites us to integrate compromises that, in some way, challenge the barriers of age, race, nationality, or religion.[56] Rebecca Alpert, for example, explains how reading this book has helped lesbians illuminate their situation within the Jewish context.[57] In fact, due to the strong connotations of the word "cling," "Ruth will assume (together with the role of daughter-in-law) another role in the narration, that of 'husband,' because she will be the sustenance of her mother-in-law (Ruth 2:2–3), who, in her way will assume the role of 'father,' making sure that her daughter-in-law finds a good husband (Ruth 3:1–5)."[58]

The third implicit reference is also found in Ruth 2:11: "you left your father and mother and your native land." The text echoes the stories of Abraham and Rebecca. In Gen 12:1, Abraham receives the order to leave his land and his father's house and to go to a land unknown to him, which will be shown to him; Rebecca, then, also leaves her land and her father's house (Gen 24:4–9, 58) to go to a land and family that are unknown. Now, as opposed to Abraham and Rebecca, who immigrated accompanied either by their families or in order to start a new family, Ruth leaves her family behind with no expectation of having another.[59]

Echoing 2 Sam 7:27, the fourth reference (Ruth 4:11) suggests a breaking with the stereotypes, related to the construction of Israel's identity. Let us not forget that Israel is a people firmly supported in the mutual compromise of love and fidelity that they have agreed on with God. Also, "Ruth is incorporated into this world, and an expression of this is, in the first place, her own persona, and secondly, the son of her womb."[60] This theme also challenges us to consider the means by which we affirm our religious identities. Such

---

55. They can found their relationships on cooperation and not competition; see Julie Ley C. Chu, "Returning Home: The Inspiration of Rule Differentiation in the Book of Ruth for Taiwanese Women," *Semeia* 78 (1997): 47–53, here 51–52.

56. Apfel and Grondahl, "Feminine Plurals," 57: "The Ruth-Naomi relationship is more than just a model of two people relating across culture, age, and status. It is a model of a mutual, non-judgmental, accepting, caring, devoted relationship between people who might be expected to quarrel, compete, and find conflict. This type of relationship is found nowhere else in the Bible, and indeed is rare in the world's literature."

57. Rebecca T. Alpert, "Finding out Past: A Lesbian Interpretation of the Book of Ruth," in Kates and Reimer, *Reading Ruth*, 91–96, here 93.

58. Elisa Estévez, "Un alegato a favor del mestizaje: el libro de Ruth," *Reseña Bíblica* 40 (2003): 23–31, here 29.

59. Kates, "Women at the Center," 191.

60. Elisa Estévez, "Función socio-histórico y teológica del libro de Rut," *Miscelánea Comillas* 59 (2001): 685–707, here 700.

religious self-assertion can oscillate between the negation of the other and the uncritical assimilation of the dominant religion and identity.

Last, in the second genealogy of chapter 4, the expression ואלה תולדות ("these are the descendants," Ruth 4:18) reminds us of the *toledot* formulas present in Genesis (2:4; 5:1; 6:9; 10:1; 11:10, 27; 25:12, 19; 36:1; 37:2). These *toledots* structure the book and contribute, together with the family stories, to presenting the world as a great family and underlining the importance of sociopolitical questions. Now, of course, all *toledot* are male centered, and the author of the book of Ruth incorporates them into the story to include a perspective that considers women's roles in Israel in biblical tradition. Perhaps all of these reasons are sufficient to respond to the question that Judith A. Kates posed at the beginning of this section: "Its women characters challenge the Jewish world to live up to Torah ideals and, in so doing, make manifest to us what sort of society—what sort of people—the Torah is supposed to create."[61]

5. Conclusion

At the beginning of this essay, I noted the capacity of memory to envision the force and vitality of the past and to neutralize the ease of forgetting. The trip that we have taken through the book of Ruth legitimizes it, without a doubt, as a book of memory. This memory visualizes for its readers at all times the need to open paths toward the empowerment and inclusion of all those human beings who are still today separated from decision-making centers and excluded from a worthy social life, here represented by two poor, widowed, foreign women. This memory emphasizes the force of solidarity, of clinging to others to travel with them, down a privileged road, where structures can be built that are capable of generating life, culture, and development. This memory savors and deepens inheritance and shared tradition, converting both to a key not only to forming one's own identity but also to opening oneself to others. May this reading, contemplation, and memory of the book of Ruth not only wear out its pages but also show them to be alive and capable of generating hope.

Translated from Spanish by Anna Deckert

---

61. Kates and Reimer, *Reading Ruth*, xix.

Interpreting Esther: Categories, Contexts, and Creative Ambiguities

Susan Niditch

1. Introduction to Esther: Content and Methodological Challenges

The book of Esther might be regarded as a kind of Cinderella tale. The Persian monarch Ahasuerus (Xerxes) has eliminated his queen Vashti for refusing to appear at his behest in front of him and his drunken entourage. A beautiful orphan girl raised by Mordecai, her cousin, a member of the Jewish community living in exile, Esther is selected among all the maidens of the kingdom to become the new queen of Persia. This traditional theme concerning the rise of Esther is joined by others including the rivalry between the courtiers Haman and Mordecai, the plot against the king's life foiled by Mordecai, and the threat of extermination leveled against Esther's people, the Jews, a disaster she herself is able to prevent by intervening with the king. The rescue is enshrined in the festival of Purim, established at the end of the narrative.

The style of the book of Esther is densely repetitive, hyperbolic, and at times comic. The king plans not just to kill the Jews but also to destroy, to kill, and to cause them to perish (7:4; 8:11). The people who are threatened do not merely fast, but fast, weep, wail, and wear sackcloth and ashes (4:3). The bigger-than-life characters are also hyperbolic: The beauty and wisdom of Esther are incomparable, the villainy of Haman extraordinary, the foolishness of Ahasuerus undeniable, the goodness of Mordecai exemplary. Qualities of goodness and evil, wisdom and foolishness are drawn starkly. It is important to note that all the good and wise characters are Jewish, the evil and foolish ones are not. Esther is a Persian-period work that portrays Jews in the marginal position of the conquered. They are under threat and subject to false accusation even though they are the king's most loyal subjects. They are able to survive by the exercise of their own wits. The deity is barely mentioned, if at all (4:14). The book of Esther reinforces a positive view of Jewish identity, resilience, and self-reliance in the context of foreign domination.[1]

The book of Esther with its female hero and its themes of tyranny, oppression, marginalization, and liberation is an especially rich source of feminist reflection and reception. Purim plays, reenactments of the tale of the Esther, were the common stock of Purim celebrations at synagogue and Hebrew school celebrations in my youth. Every little girl wanted to play the part of Esther, who was viewed as a beautiful, courageous savior queen. In my early twenties, Esther became to many Jewish women an epitome of the archetypal, passive woman whose road to success was derived from the controlling men around her. Her physical, bodily capital seemed central to her career, as did her skills as an ideal hostess and preparer of food—not, in short, a good role model for feminists. Of course, both of these culturally laden assumptions about Esther simplify the biblical character and the spectrum of interpretations that can be or have been offered.

The study of Esther is complicated by a variety of challenging ambiguities and questions that have been addressed in various ways by scholars of women's studies over the last several decades. How are power and status defined in gendered terms? Do portrayals of women in literature exist iconically apart from composers and contexts? Are certain aspects of female portrayal universal, even biological, in origin, or are all portrayals ultimately cultural constructions? Do we seek to understand portrayals of women such as Esther within their own sociohistorical contexts, however we reconstruct or define these settings, or as sources for appropriation, interpretation, and investment with meanings that are relevant to subsequent writers?

My study of Esther begins by offering some heuristic categories in feminist interpretation that help to frame an understanding of the biblical character and her variegated reception history. Having provided these descriptive categories for engagement with Esther, I review a number of interpretations and perceptions of Esther that both reflect and have shaped worldviews in a range of cultural settings. Certain recurring threads emerge in the interpretation of Esther that transcend the particular settings of those who receive and

---

1. For a reading from this perspective, see Klara Butting, "Esther: About Resistance against Anti-Semitism and Sexism," in *Feminist Biblical Interpretation: A Compendium of Critical Commentary on the Books of the Bible and Related Literature* (ed. Luise Schottroff and Marie-Theres Wacker; Grand Rapids: Eerdmans, 2012), 207–20. Feminist interpretations in German-speaking scholarship include Marie-Theres Wacker, *Ester: Jüdin—Königin—Retterin* (Stuttgart: Katholisches Bibelwerk, 2006); and Aurica Nutt and Stephanie Feder, eds., *Esters unbekannte Seiten: Theologische Perspektiven auf ein vergessenes biblisches Buch: Festschrift für Marie-Theres Wacker* (Mainz: Grünewald, 2012).

respond to the fifth-century-BCE work. These interpretations, in turn, relate in complex and revealing ways to our understanding of the ancient narrative in its own social context, complicating and enriching the process of exegesis. The essay concludes with my own suggestions about the biblical figure of Esther, an analysis influenced by colleagues in the field of folklore studies; with a view of Esther as exemplifying women's backdoor power; with a reflection on the theme of woman as a civilizing force; and with thoughts on the holiday of Purim as it relates to themes of liberation, colonialism, and feminism.

2. Categories

The first category is traditionalist acceptance. This method of reading, often rooted in normative assumptions, approaches biblical portrayals of women positively and unapologetically as models for contemporary women. Traits of courage and forbearance are found in traditional roles of wife and mother. The women are sometimes selected by the deity for special roles, but there is no shame in taking a back seat to husbands and fathers in the exercise of power. Those who espouse traditionalist acceptance claim to take the Bible on its own terms, but often ignore nuances and tensions implicit in the biblical tales or the larger tradition, for example, Esther's marriage to an uncircumcised foreigner, a foolish, narcissistic, self-indulgent man. This marriage, pushed by Esther's guardian, her cousin Mordecai, does not seem to trouble the biblical author of the Hebrew Esther, but poses a problem in the larger Jewish tradition, as responses in the Greek Esther and rabbinic commentaries indicate.

In contrast to acceptance, a deceptively simple response to biblical portrayals of women, is the second category, rejectionism. An eloquent and exemplary voice in this category is that of Carol P. Christ. Christ notes that she herself was trained as a scholar of the Hebrew Scriptures and that as a young adult she sought meaningful life models in the Bible. As her thinking developed, however, she came to believe that the Hebrew Bible is not useful "as a basis for [her] feminist vision." Rejecting the models provided by Scripture, Christ discovered the goddess, writing "Not until I said Goddess did I realize that I had never felt fully included in the fullness of my being as a woman in masculine or neuterized imagery for divinity."[2] One might argue that the book of Esther has no reference to God and that its heroine provides a flesh-and-blood model for female empowerment and noble action. Christ herself notes that some of her feminist colleagues do "work within biblical

---

2. Carol P. Christ, *The Laughter of Aphrodite: Reflections on a Journey to the Goddess* (San Francisco: Harper & Row, 1988), 67.

traditions to reform or transform them so that they will reflect a feminist vision of the equality of women."[3] This brings us to the third category of approaches to women in the Bible, selective appropriation and adaptation.

Between those who uncritically accept the tradition and those who espouse reasoned rejection are those who find certain aspects of biblical material empowering to women but other themes and motifs oppressive and offensive. Aspects accepted or rationalized or adjusted will differ from period to period and author to author, but all in this category want to find their worldviews in Scripture even while acknowledging that apologies and adaptations must be made. Examples of selective biblical appropriation are offered in the many thoughtful works by Phyllis Trible.

Trible, for example, rescues Eve from a long history of Western interpretations of Gen 2–3 that blame woman for death and the loss of paradise. She points to Eve's positive qualities as a seeker of wisdom, a bringer of culture who displays a capacity for leadership rather than passivity and a secondary status.[4] In the same article, Trible suggests that the woman in the Song of Songs offers a positive model of independence and sensuality. In this way, Trible as a feminist Christian appropriates the biblical text.

The final category is "structured empathy," a phrase created by the scholar of comparative religion Ninian Smart.[5] The phrase "structured empathy" implies the scholar's desire to understand and identify with the way others believe—others who lived before us or who live in contemporary cultures different from our own. Such scholars seek to comprehend the way other human beings, set in social groups, make sense of the world. They approach this search with openness toward the subjects of study, but with no need to appropriate their worldviews. The investment in this sort of study of sacred texts is thus different from the investment of appropriators. Those who approach a work such as Esther with structured empathy, however, make no claim of absolute objectivity. Our selves and our contexts always intrude and influence our interpretation.

2.1. Acceptance

The nineteenth-century corpus of works by women who interpret Esther is rich in traditional acceptance. In her 1842 work, *Heroines of Sacred History*,

---

3. Ibid., 58.

4. Phyllis Trible, "Depatriarchalizing in Biblical Interpretation," in *The Jewish Woman: New Perspectives* (ed. Elizabeth Koltun; New York: Schocken, 1976), 217–40.

5. Ninian Smart, *Worldviews: Crosscultural Explorations of Human Beliefs* (New York: Scribner's, 1983).

Eliza Steele presents Esther as a fine example of "woman's self-sacrifice and filial obedience."[6] Steele describes Esther as "a beautiful example of the duty we owe our guardians and aged relatives."[7] A similar interpretation of Esther's initiative and selflessness is found in a mid-twentieth-century assessment by Edith Deen, a best-selling Christian writer whose popular works have reached millions of readers. Deen writes that Esther had "the sound judgment, fine self-control, and the ability to think of others first."[8]

These characterizations of Esther reflect some of the same spirit of traditional acceptance found in the interpretation of evangelical Christian writer Lisa Ryan. A former Miss California, actress, and TV producer, Ryan is especially interested in Esther as a model for contemporary young women. Her book *For Such a Time as This*, written in the genre of inspirational literature for young women, treats Esther as a model of the feminine with qualities of tenderness, compassion, self-sacrifice, and mothering, "a reflection of the heart of God" that all women should embrace.[9] For her, Esther's beauty is rooted in her character rather than in superficial makeup and finery. The king loves her because "she is a breath of fresh air."[10] Such is the beauty she urges readers to find in themselves. Esther's obedience is moreover exemplary. Young women need to follow the advice of wise mentors such as Mordecai. As a former beauty pageant competitor, Ryan identifies with Esther and, like the biblical writer, sees no problem in the competition for the king's affection. In fact, she describes Esther's waiting to hear about the king's response as follows: "The Queen of Persia is—envelope please ..."[11] Ryan's is a full-throated appropriation as identification.

The thread of acceptance thus includes women commentators from the nineteenth century, the mid-twentieth century, and contemporary evangelical culture. Piety, beauty, selflessness, self-control, and quiet courage lead to acts of heroism. Other interpreters, however, suggest that such a portrayal contributes to a stereotype that reinforces passivity, powerlessness, and superficial physical qualities.

---

6. Cited by Joyce Zonana, "Esther, Vashti, and the Duty of Disobedience in Nineteenth Century Hermeneutics," in *Through a Glass Darkly: Essays in the Religious Imagination* (ed. John C. Hawley; New York: Fordham University Press, 1996), 228–49, here 230.

7. Ibid., 239.

8. Edith Deen, *All the Women of the Bible* (London: Independent, 1959), 124.

9. Lisa Ryan, *For Such a Time as This: Your Identity, Purpose, and Passion* (Sisters, Ore.: Multnomah, 2001), 17.

10. Ibid., 82.

11. Ibid., 103.

2.2. Rejectionism

The rejectionist position points to the negative effects such views of Esther have on young women and gender relations. Mary Gendler writes,

> What about Esther do I find objectionable? In most ways she sounds like an ideal woman—beautiful, pious, obedient, courageous. And it is just this which I find objectionable. Esther is certainly the prototype—and perhaps even a stereotype—of the ideal Jewish woman—an ideal which I find restrictive and repressive. ... Ahasuerus can be seen not only as an Ultimate Authority who holds vast power over everyone, but more generally as male, patriarchal authority in relation to females.[12]

Esther Fuchs,[13] Alice Laffey,[14] and Bea Wyler[15] share Gendler's position and see Esther as contributing to a portrait of woman as passive sex object, able to succeed only by pleasing men and by conforming to a male-centered view of women. The rejectionist/substitution position thus finds a place in the larger field of women and religion, as feminist studies rooted in the women's movement of the 1970s and 1980s inform women's capacity to appropriate or identify with a character such as Esther. Gendler does suggest, however, that Vashti provides a better model than Esther for young women in her defiance of the patriarchal, authoritarian king and his entourage. In this way, Gendler is able to find some redeeming features in the biblical story and Jewish tradition, all of which provides a segue to the category of selective appropriation.

---

12. Mary Gendler, "The Restoration of Vashti," in *The Jewish Woman* (ed. Elizabeth Koltun; New York: Schocken, 1976), 242, 245.

13. Esther Fuchs, "Status and Role of Female Heroines in the Biblical Narrative," *The Mankind Quarterly* 23 (1983): 149–60.

14. Alice L. Laffey, *An Introduction to the Old Testament: A Feminist Approach* (Philadelphia: Fortress, 1988), 216–17. Writing from a "womanist" position, South African scholar Sarojini Nadar suggests that Esth 2 is a "text of terror" and that this passage "colludes in the approval of the rape of women." See Nadar, "'Texts of Terror' Disguised as the 'Word of God': The Case of Esther 2:1–18 and the Conspiracy of Rape in the Bible," *Journal of Constructive Theology* 10 (2004): 59–79, 70.

15. Bea Wyler, "Esther: The Incomplete Emancipation of a Queen," in *A Feminist Companion to Esther, Judith, and Susanna* (ed. Athalya Brenner; FCB 7; Sheffield: Sheffield Academic, 1995), 111–35, 134–35.

2.3. SELECTIVE APPROPRIATION AND ADAPTATION

Vashti's role in the rise of Esther is of particular interest to a range of biblical appropriators. Lucinda B. Chandler, a contributor to Elizabeth Cady Stanton's 1890s project *The Woman's Bible*, embraces the portrayal of Vashti "as a sublime representative of all self-centered women. Rising to the heights of self-consciousness and of self-respect, she takes her soul into her own keeping, and though her position both as wife and queen are jeopardized, she is true to the Divine aspirations of her nature."[16] As Joyce Zonana notes, "liberal feminist readers in the nineteenth century might find in Esther an empowering story of women's emergence from oppression: a story of divine providence that could amply justify—and represent—the contemporary struggle for women's social advancement and emancipation."[17] Esther was also a source of appropriation and inspiration to a range of nineteenth-century American abolitionists including Maria Stewart, Sojourner Truth, and Angelina Grimké. These women identified with the biblical heroine as one who risked speaking out, challenging the legal authority in a situation of oppression. As Susan Zaeske writes of Grimké, "[She] fuses herself with Esther to create a supplicating yet radical model of female activism."[18]

A revealing modern example of selective appropriation and adaptation is Diane Wolkstein's retelling of Esther for young readers aged eight to twelve years.[19] Wolkstein makes Ahasuerus into a jolly paternal figure rather than a dirty old man. Modern girls can identify with Esther's story without being made uncomfortable, as Wolkstein focuses on Esther's courage, her intelligence, her capacity to adapt to changing circumstances, and her ultimate success in saving her people. Esther is desexualized and the whole tale rendered less violent. In my own view, Wolkstein might have challenged even young readers to deal with troubling aspects of the biblical portrayal. Perhaps her version reflects a contemporary postfeminist world.

Acknowledging that Esther's sexually charged subversiveness was toned down for young appropriators when she herself was a child, writer and editor Celina Spiegel notes that as an adult she has come to realize that Esther's power and her people's salvation lie in her sexuality: "It is not merely Esther's

---

16. Elizabeth Cady Stanton and the Revising Committee, *The Woman's Bible* (Seattle: Seattle Coalition on Women and Religion, 1974), 87.

17. Zonana, "Esther," 230.

18. Susan Zaeske, "Unveiling Esther as a Pragmatic Radical Rhetoric," *Philosophy and Rhetoric* 33 (2000): 193–220, 214.

19. Diane Wolkstein, "Esther's Story," in Brenner, *A Feminist Companion to Esther, Judith and Susanna*, 198–206.

beauty, however, but her sexuality to which the Jews owe their salvation—and this distinction is what is so startling and powerful about the story, even to modern readers. Esther's sexuality is presented as the embodiment of Jewish virtues."[20] Spiegel's view of Esther is thus evocative both of Trible's appropriation of the female speaker in the Song of Songs and of the writings of modern feminists such as Camille Paglia who emphasize the positive power of women's expressed sexuality.[21]

2.4. Structured Empathy

Modern scholars who engage in structured empathy worry less about relevance and appropriation than about understanding Esther in the context of early Judaism. They employ a diverse range of methodological approaches and concepts to frame their work. A number of scholars view the characterization of Esther in terms of issues relevant to the survival of a persecuted minority population. Sidnie White (Crawford) points to Esther as an excellent example of the way the weak in a culture manage to achieve "basic survival." She writes, "They must adjust to their lack of immediate political and economic power to learn to work within the system to gain what power they can."[22] Esther's strength and wisdom lie in her capacity to adjust to the changing and insecure fortunes of the marginal, to use anything that enhances her advantage including beauty, sex appeal, and men's susceptibility to women's emotion.[23] In a similar vein, I describe Esther's "collaboration with tyranny" as a necessary expedient for the powerless, the author's view of what it is to be wise for Jews in the setting of exile and for women in the workaday world of gender relations as he understands them.[24]

---

20. Celina Spiegel, "The World Remade: The Book of Esther," in *Out of the Garden: Women Writers on the Bible* (ed. Christina Büchmann and Celina Spiegel; New York: Fawcett Columbine, 1994), 191–203, 202.

21. For an excellent review article that concludes by embracing this theme of women's empowerment, see Gail Twersky Reimer, "Eschewing Esther/Embracing Esther: The Changing Representation of Biblical Heroines," in *Talking Back: Images of Jewish Women in American Popular Culture* (ed. Joyce Antler; Hanover, N.H.: Brandeis University Press, 1998), 207–19.

22. Sidnie Ann White, "Esther: A Feminine Model for Jewish Diaspora," in *Gender and Difference in Ancient Israel* (ed. Peggy L. Day; Minneapolis: Fortress, 1989), 161–77, 166–67. See also Susan Niditch, *Underdogs and Tricksters: A Prelude to Biblical Folklore* (San Francisco: Harper & Row, 1987), 141–45.

23. White, "Esther," 167–68, 171.

24. The phrase is that of David Daube, *Collaboration with Tyranny in Rabbinic Law* (The Riddell Memorial Lectures 1965; London: Oxford University Press, 1965).

Another useful observation is that the tale of Esther is a bildungsroman of sorts in which the heroine develops and matures.²⁵ Her passive beauty, her acceptance of guidance under Mordecai and then under the chief eunuch, her capacity to be molded by men—her helpers in the traditional narrative pattern of the underdog—characterize the young Esther described as בתולה, an adolescent, a young woman who has reached puberty but who is not yet fulfilling adult roles.²⁶

At Esth 4:15-16 comes the transformation of Esther's character, her passage into adulthood and psychological maturity as she takes responsibility for the lives of her people and actively takes control of the situation. She orders Mordecai to instruct all the Jews of Susa to hold a fast on her behalf. She then holds the banquets,²⁷ cleverly wooing Haman into unsuspecting and hubristic complacency while reminding her husband of her charms, finally climatically revealing her ethnic identity and convincing the king of Haman's villainy. The Jews' fortunes are reversed because of Esther's intervention. In chapter 8, Esther has the power to place Mordecai over the house of Haman (8:2), power to see that Haman's edict is reversed and that the Jews may defend themselves (8:8), and in 9:29-32 she is declared to lend her authority through letters to the celebration of Purim.

Sidnie White thus suggests that Esther's seeming passivity before the transformation in chapter 4 is essential to understanding one theme of the work dealing with maturation, the acceptance of responsibility and moral autonomy, matters essential to the successful development of men and women. However, we need to ask further what this mature and active Esther, successful within the parameters of the narrative, indicates about its creator's attitudes to women, about woman as a component of his cultural and symbolic map. How were Esther's audience of men and women expected to react to Esther? What messages does the tale reinforce?

---

25. Niditch, *Underdogs*, 135, 138; White, "Esther," 169-72; Linda Day, *Esther* (AOTC; Nashville: Abingdon, 2005), 6; Zaeske, "Unveiling Esther," 203; Leila L. Bronner, "Reclaiming Esther: From Sex Object to Sage," *JBQ* 26 (1998): 4-10, 5-6. As the title of the article suggests, Bronner is concerned to appropriate Esther and takes issue with rejectionist positions. As with a number of the selective appropriators and traditional acceptors discussed above, Bronner glances over troubling aspects of the narrative that could be interpreted to suggest that Mordecai furthers his career at court and protects the fortunes of his people by offering up his ward to serve the king's pleasure.

26. Peggy L. Day, "From the Child Is Born the Woman: The Story of Jephthah's Daughter," in Day, *Gender and Difference*, 58-74, 59-60.

27. On the banquet motif, see Sandra Beth Berg, *The Book of Esther: Motifs, Themes, and Structure* (Missoula, Mont.: Scholars Press, 1979), 31-35; Claudia V. Camp, *Wisdom and the Feminine in the Book of Proverbs* (Sheffield: Almond, 1985), 133-36.

Exploring key turning points outlined above, Lillian R. Klein interprets Esther from the perspective of "shame and honor" as they relate to gender in the traditional culture of Esther's world. She writes, "The text allows that, in threatening situations, social paradigms may be creatively interpreted as long as the prescribed gender role is publicly observed. Powerless women—and Jews—can invoke power as long as they maintain required appearances."[28]

3. My Reading of Esther

My own approach to Esther under the rubric of structured empathy is strongly influenced by the field of folklore studies, and begins with comparative studies offered by colleagues who study the role and portrayal of heroines in traditional literatures. Emphases are on women who succeed by indirect means, the theme of women as a civilizing force, and questions concerning gender and voice.

3.1. Feminism, Folklore, and "Dancing with Chains"

Margaret Beissinger works in the narrative traditions of Romanian and Roma or gypsy cultures, with special interests in women's studies, oral literatures, and epic. Beissinger explores portrayals of various "Penelope" figures in Balkan tradition, women left behind the lines during the absence of their husbands or fiancées who are off fighting a long war.[29] The ideal is for the woman to remain faithful, and those who take their lives into their own hands and choose a new suitor are punished, reinforcing, at least overtly, the male control over females and the androcentric, patriarchal bent of the dominant culture. She points out, however, that some of the faithful women find other ways to subvert the system. Influenced by the work of Lillian Doherty,[30] Beissinger notes that

> feminist criticism of literature frequently takes two forms: critical and utopian. Critical or "closed" feminist readings show how women in literature reflect gender constraints ... the ways in which male power is imposed on

---

28. Lillian R. Klein, "Honor and Shame in Esther," in Brenner, *A Feminist Companion to Esther, Judith and Susanna*, 149–75, 175.

29. Margaret Beissinger, "Gender and Power in the Balkan Return Song," *Slavic and East European Journal* 45, no. 3 (2001): 403–30.

30. Lillian Doherty, *Siren Songs: Gender, Audiences, and Narrators in the Odyssey* (Ann Arbor: University of Michigan Press, 1995).

female society. ... By contrast, utopian or "open" feminist readings seek nuances within literature that allow for new affirmations of identity.[31]

In Doherty's words the latter approach attempts to "identify openings that undercut ostensible patterns of meaning."[32]

In the field of biblical studies, the work of Esther Fuchs, whose views on Esther are placed above in the category of rejectionism, might also be described as critical and closed in orientation. In Fuchs's view, for example, although the annunciation scenes in Genesis do centrally feature women and suggest that the women are privy to divine communication, these scenes function not to enhance women's status but to propagandize for the very roles in society that demean and subjugate women.[33] J. Cheryl Exum, author of several classic works on biblical women, allows for more openness. As she notes,

> Power is the ability to gain compliance with one's wishes and to achieve one's ends. Authority is culturally legitimated power, a power recognized by society and distributed according to a hierarchical chain of command and control. The matriarchs do not have authority; they are subordinate to their husbands. But they are not powerless. ... Sarah and Rebecca illustrate how women can have power in areas not normally accorded them by working through those in authority.[34]

The same might be said of Esther. Her relationship with Ahasuerus, her capacity to make herself desirable, her playing on the food-providing, nurturing roles of woman allow her a backdoor means of achieving her ends.

The second folklorist whose fascinating work is relevant to the characterization of Esther is Margaret Mills, a scholar who has explored Afghan traditional literature, working in Afghanistan before the wars, with a variety of local storytellers, male and female. She, like Beissinger, is interested in the way in which women caught in patriarchal cultures manage "to dance with chains on."[35] She is also interested in the links between content, genre, and gender, providing important suggestions as we speculate about the possibility of women's voices in biblical narrative. In Afghan culture, "men

---

31. Beissinger, "Gender and Power," 404.

32. Doherty, *Siren Songs*, 40.

33. Esther Fuchs, "The Literary Characterization of Mothers and Sexual Politics in the Hebrew Bible," in *Feminist Perspectives on Biblical Scholarship* (ed. Adela Yarbro Collins; Chico, Calif.: Scholars Press, 1985), 117–36.

34. J. Cheryl Exum, *Fragmented Women: Feminist (Sub)versions of Biblical Narratives* (Valley Forge, Pa.: Trinity Press International, 1993), 136–37.

35. So Mills in a lecture at Amherst College, fall 2009.

tend to tell stories about men, whereas women tell stories about men and women."[36] She finds it particularly interesting that women tend "not to masculinize" female heroines as she would expect them to if they "envied men's social options."[37] "Women," she notes, however, "readily identify dramatic potential in the women's world,"[38] with its themes of courtship, marriage, and kinship. In the case of Esther with its foreign, royal, urbane, and courtly setting, the woman's world involves the harem, courtship becomes a matter of winning favor with the king, and kinship relations are transformed into a matter of furthering her high-placed cousin's political aims and her people's well-being. Nevertheless, realms of male and female are clearly demarcated, as are all relationships and social spaces in the hierarchical society pictured by the author. The queen risks death by appearing at the inner court without the king's request (Esth 4:11).

Beissinger and Mills thus explore the ways in which women find means of survival, self-promotion, creativity, and self-expression within certain circumscribed and potentially limiting gender boundaries. In this way, within the context of the social world in which the work was composed and received, Esther might be viewed as partaking of a female voice that asserts woman's significance and power, albeit within the contours of a man's world. Contributing to this backdoor self-assertion is the theme of woman as a civilizing force.

3.2. Woman as a Civilizing Force

Building on themes emphasized by my colleagues, I suggest that the characterization of Esther is informed by the archetype of woman as a civilizing force.[39] Esther is one of a host of wise biblical heroines described in scenes with powerful male characters. The women change the heroes' minds so that the course of events is altered and the women's situation or the status of those

---

36. Margaret A. Mills, "Sex Role Reversals, Sex Changes, and Transvestite Disguise in the Oral Tradition of a Conservative Muslim Community in Afghanistan," in *Women's Folklore, Women's Culture* (ed. Rosan A. Jordan and Susan J. Kalčik; Philadelphia: University of Pennsylvania Press, 1985), 187–213, 188.

37. Ibid., 188–89.

38. Margaret A. Mills, "Gender and Verbal Performance Style in Afghanistan," in *Gender, Genre, and Power in South Asian Expressive Traditions* (ed. Arjun Appadurai et al.; Philadelphia: University of Pennsylvania Press, 1991), 56–77, 72.

39. Material that follows reprises in part my discussion in "Short Stories: The Book of Esther and the Theme of Woman as a Civilizing Force," in *Old Testament Interpretation Past, Present, and Future: Essays in Honor of Gene M. Tucker* (ed. James Luther Mays et al.; Nashville: Abingdon, 1995), 195–209.

whose cause they advocate is improved. Frequently, danger to them or to those they represent is averted. Even more important for the theme of civilizing, they tame the men whom they address, powerful men who are not using their power wisely but who appear foolish, violent, willing to destroy innocent victims or unable to show mercy.

Esther is in this category, as is Abigail (1 Sam 25), who convinces David in the bandit period of his career not to take vengeance on her husband's household (1 Sam 25:1–13). Also in the category of civilizing force are the woman of Tekoa hired by David's general Joab to perform an act of mediation between David and his estranged son Absalom (2 Sam 14) and the wise woman of Abel Beth-maacah, who intervenes between her townsmen and Joab concerning an enemy of David's state who has taken refuge in her city (2 Sam 20:4–22). Claudia V. Camp has explicitly or implicitly taken stock of many of the ways of these wise women.[40]

The women present themselves in stereotypical biblical feminine roles that are regarded as positive in the ancient Israelite tradition. They are appealingly ripe with nonthreatening sexuality or are mother-like. Esther and Abigail are beauties and offer the men food and drink, playing the woman's role as provider in the private realm.[41] The woman of Tekoa presents herself as a concerned and suffering mother while the wise woman of Abel Beth-maacah begs Joab not to destroy this ancient town, which is "a mother in Israel." Moreover, the women convince with words carefully and cleverly chosen to enhance the self-esteem of those they address, while they place themselves in the background even as they speak. A good example in Esther is found at 8:5: "If it please the king … and if I have found favor in his sight, and if the matter seems right before the king. …" Esther Fuchs nicely describes Queen Esther's language as "placatory" and "ingratiating."[42] Abigail's interaction with David at 1 Sam 25:24, 28, the woman of Tekoa's approach to David at 2 Sam 14:12, 17, and the wise woman's interaction with Joab at 2 Sam 20:18–19 are similarly diplomatic and ingratiating.[43]

---

40. Camp, *Wisdom*, 42, 85–87, 133–36, 90–96, 120–24, 133–36, 143–45.

41. Ibid., 80–81.

42. Fuchs, "Female Heroines," 156.

43. Susan Zaeske's philosophy-of-rhetoric approach leads to similar emphases concerning the characterization of Esther, and Zaeske sees this ingratiating tone and supplicatory stance as sources of empowerment ("Unveiling Esther," 202–3); see also my *Folklore and the Hebrew Bible* (Minneapolis: Fortress, 1993), 69–70. On the wise women in 2 Samuel and the use of sayings as a diplomatic means of criticism, a way in which the weaker can approach the stronger, see Claudia V. Camp, "The Wise Women of 2 Samuel: A Role Model for Women in Early Israel?" *CBQ* 43 (1981): 21, 23.

The women succeed by making themselves seem small, dependent, and unimportant while flattering the men to make them feel as if all power resides with them. The women's rhetoric also suggests that the men are fair, good men of self-discipline who know how to control their power and use it properly, which is, in fact, precisely not the case for Ahasuerus, David, and Joab. The Persian king has abused his power in accepting plans to destroy good and loyal citizens; David later grabs Bathsheba's sexuality contrary to accepted mores and kills her husband, Uriah the Hittite, to cover up the woman's pregnancy; Joab kills his brother's slayer, but, whereas Abner kills unavoidably in war, Joab takes vengeance in an ambush, perhaps not only to avenge his brother but also to remove a rival general who now vies for David's patronage. Each of these men exemplifies a particular sort of macho arrogance and displays an undisciplined and unbridled aggressiveness, undertaking action not circumscribed by proper thought or consideration of consequences, and evidencing, in short, a lack of wisdom.

All four representations of interactions between powerful men and the women who influence them are rooted in notions of mother as teacher even, a Freudian would say, as the mother-teacher sometimes mixes with the mother-as-lover. Claudia Camp has explored these boundaries in representations of Woman Wisdom,[44] who is the archetypal civilizing force of Israelite classical literature, at God's side in creation, drawing the young man to her with words of love, nurturing, and encouragement, helping him to avoid the impetuous adolescent side of himself prone to violence, illicit sex, and other harmful aggressive activities.

3.3. Social Critique, Cultural Model: Whose Voice?

On the one hand, all of these images of the way men and women interact are reactionary, for true power arrangements are not altered and the women achieve their objectives by working within that system—by helping to build up the confidence of those in power so that they can be helpful to the woman's objectives, at least this time.

On the other hand, these scenes, stories, and characterizations have a subversive underside. As women hear or create such typological scenes, they learn that they can be wise, wiser than the men, and that they can take some measure of control. Even more subversively, these women's words and deeds may serve as powerful social critique, perhaps a self-critique and a critique of their

---

44. Camp, *Wisdom*. For personified wisdom see also the essay by Gerlinde Baumann in this volume.

culture by men, when they are the composers of one or another of the tales. One thinks of the *Iliad*, in which the words of women might be interpreted as questioning the agonistic, male-dominated ethos of their warrior husbands.[45]

These various complaints of women are complex markers of cultural attitudes toward the accepted or proverbial ways of men and women, for while the critiques in the women's voice stand, the ways of the world and the ways of men—be they violent, foolhardy, or reckless—are not expected to change. And yet, apart from the culture at large, in individual situations and on individual men, the influence and therefore the responsibility of the women can be deemed to be considerable. These works, at least in their final form, were no doubt written and preserved by men, members of scribal elites.

Esther, Abigail, and the wise women of 2 Samuel are ultimately ways in which men can express their conscience and their best side, but through these women the superego prods in a nonthreatening and nonintrusive way. Ancient Israelite women, while not encouraged to feminist liberation by these models, were no doubt reinforced in their belief in the truth of Nancy Astor's saying, "I married beneath me. All women do." Paradoxically, the inner self-esteem lent to women by this belief tends to reinforce the outer status quo.[46] Additional ways to look at portrayals of Esther's story are offered by a number of contemporary scholars of folklore, feminism, and ritual.

4. Purim as Portrayed and Received

A discussion of the holiday of Purim, which is said to be established at the end of the book of Esther as a celebratory response to the survival of the Jews of Persia, provides another opportunity to explore ancient contexts and modern interpretations from women's studies perspectives. The description of the founding of the holiday emphasizes the mood of the day, ritual activities, and reasons for the feast. These are to be days of feasting and gladness on which portions of food are to be sent as gifts from Jew to Jew and presents offered to the poor. Because the Jews have been saved from their enemies, "grief has been turned to joy and mourning to a holiday" (9:22). Purim is thus a holiday of reversals, reciprocity, and generosity. A folk etymology is provided for the holiday rooted in the word פור, for lot; lots were cast to select the day of the Jews' destruction (3:7).

---

45. See, e.g., the exchange between Andromache and Hektor in *Iliad* 6:406–465.

46. For an interesting and thoughtful discussion of women's voice and the implicit ambivalences in the portrayal of wise women, see Athalya Brenner and Fokkelien Van Dijk-Hemmes, *On Gendering Texts: Female and Male Voices in the Hebrew Bible* (Leiden: Brill, 1993), 129. Brenner's comments dovetail nicely with the discussion above, although she and I reach somewhat different conclusions.

Esther herself is involved in the establishment of Purim, providing, with Mordecai, written authority for the celebration (9:29–32). In the ancient Esther tradition, the establishment of the holiday thus features a powerful foundational role for the queen. Purim is integrally related to her activities and status. What, however, is the holiday's relationship to the questions about gender and power with which this essay begins?

In U.S. history, abolition, women's suffrage, African American civil rights, and gay rights are often seen as part of a chain of comparable phenomena, each building on the other. A similar equation might be drawn between themes in the book of Esther concerning the saving of the Jews, an event commemorated by Purim, and the aspirations of women in Judaism, symbolized by Esther's relationship to the events surrounding the holiday and the establishment of Purim itself. This set of connections, however, is complicated, and each member of the set poses problems of interpretation.

On the one hand, the Jews are saved, and Esther does play a central role in their salvation. On the other hand, the insecurity of a marginal people living in exile cannot be erased. Nothing guarantees that a similar crisis, a threat to the Jews' very existence, might not arise again. Does Purim have to do with genuine liberation? Similarly, Esther's success involves the deployment of precisely those characteristics that are rooted in her subservient womanly position and status. Is the celebration of Purim actually a reminder to women that they must use their power carefully, only behind the scenes? This would seem to be a pale sort of liberation indeed. It can be argued, moreover, that the Jews' escape makes them accomplices in a colonialist tyrant's exercise of power. Does Esther's role as his queen similarly undermine women's aspirations? In this way, like the narrative and the characterization of Esther as heroine, the holiday associated with the narrative and with Esther herself has a somewhat tortured or equivocal relationship to questions concerning women's identity and sense of self-worth.

It is significant that the holiday itself as biblically described has to do with chance (the drawing of lots), the reversal of fortunes (the saving of the Jews, Mordecai, and Esther, and the death of Israel's enemies, Haman included), the overt, ritualized manifestation of joyfulness, and the emphasis on community with the exercise of care for the less fortunate and the exchange of commensal gifts. Purim is perhaps less about liberation than about a temporary break from an all-too-unliberated reality. As such, Purim takes its place among a host of traditional celebrations that emphasize "the reversal of the normal course of events and the social order."[47]

---

47. Shifra Epstein, "The 'Drinking Banquet' (Trink-Siyde): A Hasidic Event for Purim," *Poetics Today* 15 (1994): 133–52, 135.

4.1. Purim Celebrations: Gender and Appropriations

The biblical message about celebrating Purim with gladness and joy has been put into action in a variety of customs and ritual forms including plays (Purim-shpil), processions, drinking banquets, and ritual actions during the reading of the Esther scroll at synagogue such as noisemaking to drown out the name of Haman. Drawing on the work of folklorist Barbara Babcock, Shifra Epstein compares Purim to a host of other "festivals, carnivals, and spectacles" and notes that "given the conservatism of traditional Judaism, such activities as masquerades, pranks, drinking bouts, parodies and theatricals" purposely invert or contradict expected behaviors and norms.[48] She suggests that "all of these festive features serve to reinforce the idea of a holiday on which unusual behavior is not only tolerated, but actively encouraged."[49] Many of these aspects of carnival throughout most of the twentieth century have been male-dominated events.

The ninetieth- and twentieth-century Purim plays explored by folklorist Barbara Kirshenblatt-Gimblett regularly feature countercultural and antiestablishment plots dealing with smugglers and brigands. The plays send the message "that justice resides outside the official system, that the law is often ineffectual, and that nonviolent breaches of the law ... may be necessary for survival in an unjust and capricious world—themes of the original Purim story."[50] The actors in these Yiddish theatrical performances, undertaken in the private homes of well-to-do hosts, were generally "boys and unmarried men."[51] The small troupe of actors thus constituted a kind of young men's club, and although the plays challenge aspects of the status quo, norms regarding the status of women are not included in this form of social criticism.

Contemporary drinking banquets celebrated by Bobover Hasidim provide another challenge to norms in the context of a men's club. Epstein notes, however, that the "*trink-siyde*, which celebrates the actions of a heroic woman, Esther, is a male festivity that almost completely excludes women."[52] Women are confined to a women's section, although "no one notices or cares if the women ... peer over the *mehize* (partition). This kind of behavior by women

---

48. Epstein, "The 'Drinking Banquet,'" 134; see also Barbara Babcock, ed., *The Reversible World: Symbolic Inversion in Art and Society* (Ithaca, N.Y.: Cornell University Press, 1978), 31.
49. Epstein, "The 'Drinking Banquet,'" 134.
50. Barbara Kirshenblatt-Gimblett, "Contraband: Performance, Text and Analysis of a Purim-shpil," *The Drama Review* 24 (1980): 5–16, 9.
51. Ibid., 6.
52. Epstein, "The 'Drinking Banquet,'" 140.

would not be tolerated on other occasions during the year."[53] Women's intrusion is thus allowed as a mild and temporary reversal of norms in this very Orthodox, conservative group of Hasidim. Contemporary non-Hasidic celebrations of Purim, however, offer new possibilities for a challenge to norms, a form of inspiration and advocacy concerning the place of women in Judaism. The links between liberation from tyrants, Esther's prominence in the ancient narrative, the challenge to sexual stereotypes, and Jewish feminist aspirations are made overt.

4.2. New Women's Rituals for Purim

Examples abound of new rituals for Purim inspired by women's religious aspirations in Judaism and the larger concern with contemporary gender issues. Just as some have appropriated and adapted the narrative tradition of Esther through a process of exegesis, so the holiday of Purim itself has been transformed and rendered newly meaningful to women.

One trend involves the creation of flags featuring or evoking Esther, Vashti, or both women. The flags are raised and waved at the mention of the women's names during the public reading of the Esther scroll, a counterpoint to the noisemaking that traditionally accompanies the reading of the name Haman, a sound that is supposed to drown out mention of the villain. The flags are works of artistic imagination whose very creation can be a sacred, self-defining, ritual act. The use of the flags in the context of ritual reading contrasts with what one writer describes as the "negative sound" of the noisemaker, which tends "to put Haman, hatred, and sometimes the valorization of violent acts of retribution at the center of communal celebrations of Purim."[54] Rather, the flags point to "the experiences of women," Jewish and non-Jewish.

Another essay, by Erika Katske, asks how the festival of Purim can provide an opportunity "to bring attention to deeply ingrained societal perceptions of women and to take action towards new and healthier understandings and representations of women's beauty."[55] She describes the way in which creating art

---

53. Ibid.

54. Tamara Cohen, "Taking Back Purim," originally published in *A Different Purim Sound: Waving Flags and Ringing Bells, An Exhibition of Esther and Vashti Purim Flags by Jewish Artists* (Ma'yan exhibition catalog), 2 (now available at http://www.ritualwell.org/ritual/taking-back-purim). On violent retribution and Purim, see Elliott Horowitz, *Reckless Rites: Purim and the Legacy of Jewish Violence* (Princeton: Princeton University Press, 2006).

55. Erika Katske, "Transforming Purim," *Ma'yan Journey*, winter 2001, http://www.ritualwell.org/ritual/transforming-purim.

(Purim masks, group collages) and taking action (e.g., by organizing events, group performances, and displays that explore feminist themes) can infuse the holiday with new meaning for contemporary Jewish women.

5. Pulling Threads Together

The study of themes pertaining to women in Esther and the discussion of women's interpretations of Esther have been framed by four categories: acceptance, rejectionism, appropriation, and structured empathy. These categories have been shown to be far more porous and overlapping than one might expect. Currents in particular periods—social, cultural, and scholarly—do indeed influence views of Esther, for example, the women's movement of the 1970s and 1980s or contemporary postfeminism. Worldviews, however, are not confined to certain times. Views of Vashti, found among the suffragettes of the early twentieth century, are similar to those expressed by modern Jewish feminists. If women share attitudes concerning authority, power, and gender, they tend to reach many of the same conclusions about the portrayal of women in Esther. A similar connection is found between a range of nineteenth-century Protestant women's treatments of Esther and the interpretations of contemporary evangelical women.

Certain culturally constructed archetypes have enormous staying power and seem to transcend particular periods: the self-sacrificing woman; the woman who achieves her goals through beauty and charm; the woman as a civilizing force. Such archetypes, as they relate to Esther, are deeply rooted in complex gender relations that allow women backdoor power within the contours of an overtly male-centered construction of culture.

The field of folklore studies provides an important methodological dimension in the analysis of Esther's narrative patterns and characterizations and raises questions about women's voices. This comparative work is a means of exploring ways in which the biblical Esther reflects the concerns and orientations of its composers and audiences. The study of the holiday of Purim as a festival of inversions that challenges social norms relates beautifully to a variety of questions concerning Esther traditions and gender.

Susanna, Example of Virtue and Daniel's Female Counterpart

Isabel Gómez-Acebo

1. The Book of Daniel

The book of Daniel underwent a process of stringing together its stories due to the memory of Babylonian captivity, an experience that remained vivid in Israel.[1] These events were transmitted without proper names, which facilitated their attribution to specific characters in other parts of the story. The original text was written in Hebrew and, when it was translated to Greek, posterior additions were made, as with the story of Susanna and the Elders, which gives the text a female protagonist and a more novelistic character.

We have two versions of Susanna's story—the one known as Theodotion, long and well written, preferred by the church, and the OG-Daniel (Old Greek Daniel), which appeared in the Septuagint and is much shorter and possibly older.[2] Both are surely Greek translations of Aramaic or Hebrew stories, written long ago, and linked to an oral tradition that continued evolving through the years.[3]

---

1. In Qumran, eight fragments of the book of Daniel have been found (1Q71; 1Q72; 4Q112; 4Q113; 4Q114; 4Q115; 4Q116; 6Q7) and seven more of texts from the Daniel tradition.
2. The Theodotion version was the one most utilized in the Greek church between the years 150–200 CE, a process that was also started in the Latin church. Because of this, the LXX version practically disappeared until the year 250 CE except in three manuscripts. See the interesting study by Christina Leisering, *Susanna und der Sündenfall der Ältesten: Eine vergleichende Studie zu den Geschlechterkonstruktionen der Septuaginta- und Theodotionfassung von Dan 13 und ihren intertextuellen Bezügen* (Exegese in unserer Zeit 19; Münster/Vienna: LIT, 2008).
3. For the origin of the texts, their comparison and canonization, see Carey A. Moore, *Daniel, Esther and Jeremiah: The Additions* (AB 44; Garden City, N.Y.: Doubleday, 1977), 79–92.

I believe the idea that both narrations were included in the book of Daniel is valid (even though they could have been written at the end of the Persian Empire),[4] between the first and second centuries before Christ, by Jews, who added to or adapted previous manuscripts and Babylonian traditions in the custom of their people. It is possible that the original story was composed in Babylon, but its Jewish form points us toward educated writers, possibly living in Jerusalem. The same can be said of the final Hebrew version, which was written during the Maccabean revolt, inside a wisdom circle that valued divination.[5]

1.1. THE SOCIOPOLITICAL SITUATION

The introduction of Hellenistic thought into the Jewish world began with the arrival of the armies of Alexander the Great and grew due to the changes Palestine suffered during the second and first centuries BCE. After the Battle of Panium (200 BCE), Antiochus III (the Great) resumed the government in the area and proved to be very generous with those Jews who looked kindly on his Hellenistic reign. This approval of foreign customs caused many to consider their own customs to be antiquated and an impediment to the progress brought with the new morals. The political instability that was rampant during the wars caused the disintegration of a community that until that point had been closed, and allowed, upon breaking open, for the appearance of different ways of thinking that would affect the theological sphere. All of these changes motivated an internal conflict between cosmopolitan Jews and those who wanted to stay loyal to their traditional ways. The latter considered some Hellenistic proposals anathema to their beliefs and opted to develop a stronger national identity.[6]

---

4. Giovanni Garbini, "Hebrew Literature in the Persian Period," in *Temple and Community in the Persian World* (ed. Tamara Cohn Eskenazi and Kent Richards; vol. 2 of *Second Temple Studies*; ed. Lester L. Grabbe; JSOTSup 175; Sheffield: Sheffield Academic, 1994), 180–89, speaks of the large amount of Hebrew literature produced during this period.

5. See Gerhard von Rad, *The Theology of Israel's Prophetic Traditions* (vol. 2 of *Old Testament Theology*; trans. D. M. G. Stalker; Louisville: John Knox, 2001), 301–15: "Daniel and Apocalyptic."

6. For more information on this, see James K. Aitken, "Judaic National Identity," in *Judah between East and West: The Transition from Persian to Greek Rule (ca. 400–200 BCE)* (ed. Lester L. Grabbe and Oded Lipschits; Library of Second Temple Studies 75; New York: T&T Clark, 2011), 36–40; Richard Horsley and Patrick Tiller, "Ben Sira and the Sociology of the Second Temple," in *Studies in Politics, Class and Material Culture* (ed. Philip R. Davies and John Halligan; vol. 3 of *Second Temple Studies*; ed. Lester L. Grabbe; JSOTSup 340; Sheffield: Sheffield Academic, 2002), 74–107.

The opening of new commerce routes led to the birth of a class of people who did not belong either to the central government or to the priesthood. In the countryside, overwhelmingly abandoned by governors, the rural nouveau riche were in command together with the elders, who enjoyed great power in their communities.[7] A new class of intellectual independent scribes emerged, like Ben Sira, who used their knowledge to defend the Jewish identity that was under attack. It is within this group that we find our authors.[8]

1.2. The Cultural Situation

The exchange between different Hellenistic kingdoms and Greek as the lingua franca favored a situation in which the intellectual classes had access to manuscripts that circulated through trade routes. Within this framework, to adopt Foucault's language, the book of Daniel should be understood within "a system of references to other books, other texts, other sentences: like a knot inside a large net."[9]

Who influenced our authors? We can affirm that they were familiar with Jewish tradition, Greek literature, and some customs and texts from the Oriental courts, which can be seen by the placement of their story in Babylon. A

---

7. James Pasto, "The Origin, Expansion and Impact of the Hasmoneans in Light of Comparative Ethnographic Studies," in Davies and Halligan, *Studies in Politics, Class and Material Culture*, 189. The Zenon papyri show that these rural communities had sufficient capacity to resist possible official interference in subjects related to their localities.

8. I refer to those who wrote the story of Susanna and to those alluded to at the beginning. The importance of this period for the emergence of Judaism and Christianity has produced many studies, among them Jon L. Berquist, ed., *Approaching Yehud: New Approaches to the Study of the Persian Period* (SemeiaSt 50; Atlanta: Society of Biblical Literature, 2007); Berquist, *Judaism in Persia's Shadow: A Social and Historical Approach* (Minneapolis: Fortress, 1995); Philip R. Davies, ed., *Persian Period* (vol. 1 of *Second Temple Studies*; ed. Lester L. Grabbe; JSOTSup 117; Sheffield: Sheffield Academic, 1991); Eskenazi and Richards, *Temple and Community in the Persian World*; Davies and Halligan, *Studies in Politics, Class and Material Culture*; Grabbe and Lipschits, *Judah between East and West*. About women, see Tal Ilan, *Jewish Women in Greco-Roman Palestine* (Peabody, Mass.: Hendrickson, 1996); Ilan, *Integrating Women into Second Temple History* (Peabody, Mass.: Hendrickson, 2001).

9. Michel Foucault, *The Archeology of Knowledge* (trans. A. M. Sheridan Smith; London: Tavistock, 1974), 23. For intertextuality, see Richard Bautch, "Intertextuality in the Persian Period," in Berquist, *Approaching Yehud*, 25–35; or some classic works such as Terry Eagleton, *Literary Theory: An Introduction* (Oxford: Basil Blackwell, 1983); and Julia Kristeva, *Desire in Language: A Semiotic Approach to Literature and Art* (New York: Columbia University Press, 1980).

good knowledge of the Bible allowed them to support their threatened Jewish identity, which was linked to their historical narratives and legendary figures.

The starting point to possibly relate Susanna to Daniel can be seen in the similarity of their lives with that of the patriarch Joseph (Gen 37–50), a variation on the story of the deposed and restored governor, a classic in Babylonian literature, *Ludlul bel nemeqi*.[10] Joseph is sold by his brothers because of envy, and in the house of his new master the Egyptian wife offers him sexual relations, which the young man declines. As in Susanna's story, the spiteful lover accuses him before the servants of the house of seeking to seduce her, and as a result the Jew is arrested and jailed in the king's prison.

In jail, he has the chance to interpret the dreams of two palace officers, and one of them, reinstated in office, remembers him when no wizard in the court is capable of understanding the pharaoh's dream. Joseph's explanation convinces the monarch, who sends him to manage the land that has been prophesied to have seven years of abundance followed by seven years of hardship. This story is similar to that of Daniel in the Babylonian court, and in this way unites the dissimilar lives of Susanna and Daniel. Susanna's story is told with plots frequent in popular literature: the spiteful lover who swears vengeance against the desired woman and only the child or the crazy person is capable of uncovering the truth, because he says what he thinks without being affected by societal norms.[11]

The text of Isa 52:13–53:12, about the suffering servant, a figure who through pain gives light and salvation to his companions, also plays an important role. The martyrdom of the mother and her seven children (2 Macc 7:1–42) is a show of interest in this figure in this moment. The story became famous because of the centrality that Hellenism gave to the individual, which allowed people's lives to be put forth as examples even when these people were neither kings nor priests nor notable within the community. Any human being could, with his or her acts, light the path for other people, including women.[12]

We can see a certain analogy between Susanna's, David's, and Bathsheba's (2 Sam 11:1–17) stories. The king, upon seeing Uriah's wife naked while bathing, sends for her and has sexual relations with her that end with an unwanted

---

10. Donald J. Wiseman, "A New Text of the Babylonian Poem of the Righteous Sufferer," *Anatolian Studies* 30 (1980): 101–7, cited by Karel van der Toorn, "Scholars at the Oriental Court," in *The Book of Daniel: Composition and Reception* (ed. John J. Collins and Peter W. Flint; VTSup 83.1; Leiden: Brill, 2002), 43.

11. The most famous of these stories is *The Emperor's New Clothes*.

12. Sylvie Honigman, "King and Temple in 2 Maccabees: The Case for Continuity," in Grabbe and Lipschits, *Judah between East and West*, 25, emphasizes the importance that individuals were gaining with the arrival of Hellenism.

pregnancy. In order to avoid gossip, he sends her fooled husband to the front lines of battle so that he will die. This is a story that plays with eroticism, power, and death, which is explicated by the characters of the elders in Susanna's story.[13]

Greek novels also influenced the story. The literacy rate had risen, and these readings were very popular, especially in the female world. Their creation was similar to the creation of the book of Daniel; they were based on an amalgamation of popular stories and legends whose principal figures offered examples of how to behave in life. The protagonists were characterized by their youth, beauty, and faithfulness in love, to which they adhered strongly enough to endanger their own lives.[14] They often prayed to gods who, when all seemed lost, returned to them the freedom of which they dreamed. The women's behavior was especially exemplary. Jewish stories did differ from Greek stories, however, in that their heroines were presented alone.[15]

The first of the novels we have is *Chaereas and Callirhoe*, written by Chariton of Aphrodisias in the first century CE. Although his story takes place in Syracuse in the fourth century BCE, many passages recall what happened in Susanna's story. Callirhoe, a woman of great beauty, is unjustly accused of adultery (1.2.6), and before her punishment she is unclothed (1.13.14) before many people, who admire her beauty. Her rejected lovers plot that she be punished by death.

Many exegetes consider the possibility that the female protagonists of Jewish books, such as Esther, Judith, and even Susanna, are formed on patterns similar to those found in Greek novels, knowing of the success that this literature had by adding an erotic dimension to its stories. This inclusion was facilitated by the fact that the prophets had already used this practice when they denounced Israel as an unfaithful wife.[16]

---

13. For a study of these stories in which Bathsheba appears guilty for sleeping with David, see Ester Fuchs, *Sexual Politics in the Biblical Narrative: Reading the Hebrew Bible as a Woman* (JSOTSup 310; Sheffield: Sheffield Academic, 2000), 118–39.

14. For the characteristics of Greek novels, see Mari Cruz Herrero Ingelmo, *La novela griega antigua* (Madrid: Akal Clásica, 1987), 7–27 (introduction). The book reproduces the novel I cite.

15. Lawrence M. Wills, ed., *Ancient Jewish Novels: An Anthology* (Oxford: Oxford University Press, 2002), 5.

16. Renita J. Weems, *Battered Love: Marriage, Sex, and Violence in the Hebrew Prophets* (2nd ed.; Minneapolis: Fortress, 1996), refers in detail to these images in the prophets.

2. The Texts Warn about the Dangers of Power

2.1. Human Power

Daniel, a young, faithful, and sophisticated Jew, arrives at the top of the Babylonian government thanks to his wisdom and culture, two qualities that, besides divination, increased people's influence in primitive cultures. Susanna, in contrast, moves within the rural world, and her relationship to power is seen through her spouse, the rich man in the village, who offers his house for meetings with his neighbors and for the settlement of court cases.

The power that surrounds Susanna, in addition to her husband's riches, is one wielded by a pair of elders, governors of the small community in which she lives. Infatuated with the young woman, they decide to trap her when she is alone and force her to have sexual relations with them. Angry when she declines, they start a libelous process to condemn her to death.

The young woman possesses qualities highly valued by the author, who uses them as an example because they form part of the identity of the chosen people: she is of their race, has received a careful religious education, and is beautiful and virtuous, a paragon of qualities that are worth more than all the power and kingdoms in the world.[17]

In all cultures, power is assumed to include the right to sex, whether through raping the women of the vanquished or accosting the wives of subordinates, while in the home men have imposed their right and forced even daughters or sisters against their will. In the Bible there are many tales of sexual abuses against women that are not condemned by the authors. In order to give wives to Benjamin's clan, other tribes do not hesitate to take the young virgins of Shiloh (Judg 21:19–23). Amnon, infatuated with his sister, does not hesitate to rape her and deny her a later marriage (2 Sam 13:15); the great patriarch Abraham offers his wife Sarah to the pharaoh in exchange for a flock of animals (Gen 12:14–17), a story that is repeated with Abimelech in Gen 20:2. The worst example is offered by the prophets, making God the subject of violent acts against his unfaithful wife who dared defy social order. In all of these cases, the powerful, whether husband, father, governor, or brother, had the right and the power to reprimand his subordinate.[18]

---

17. Geoffrey D. Miller, *Marriage in the Book of Tobit* (Deuterocanonical and Cognate Literature Studies 10; Berlin: de Gruyter, 2011), 34–91, highlights the qualities that a male Jew faithful to YHWH should look for in a wife, and that are in accord with the description of Susanna in the text.

18. Weems, *Battered Love*, 68–80, offers one of the best surveys of this violence against unfaithful Israel.

Although it is not elaborated, in Susanna's story one can also see a theme of envy. The elders hold the governorship of the village, but they have to hold their trials in a house lent to them by the wealthy Joakim, which makes them dependent on him. The Bible advises with one of the Ten Commandments: "You shall not covet your neighbor's house; you shall not covet your neighbor's wife" (Exod 20:17). A way to recoup one's anger is to cuckold the enemy, sleeping with his wife, who, if she is pretty, will yield double satisfaction.

Our two protagonists suffer from the havoc of this unjust power. The envy of Daniel's companions causes them to denounce Daniel for not having prostrated himself before the golden image the king has had erected; for this denial he is punished with seclusion in a den of hungry lions. In the Babylonian world, lions were used as a metaphor for designating "hostility and competition among the wise men of the court," a theme that is used in the book of Daniel to change his enemies into real beasts.[19]

In the case of Susanna, the predators are the elders who govern the small, exiled Jewish community. They participate in a prestigious institution, known for its knowledge of the law and its administration of justice. But they accost the young woman and thus transgress their duties as pastors of the village. They are two men who go after the same woman, while in the Bible we sometimes see two women fighting over one man. But here there is a third man involved, Susanna's husband, who is the legitimate owner of the desired body. This prohibited fruit, possessed by the rich man of the village, adds a sickness to their desire.

The two versions of Susanna's story clearly show that power must be opposed when it is not exercised with fairness, but that opposition on a political level would be suicide because of Israel's weakness. The fight must take place on a religious level, where fragility is supplemented by God's power. Such a scenario is exemplified by Susanna's attitude.

2.2. Divine Power

The divine person moves behind the scenes like a mute spectator who waits to see the end of the story before interfering. Divine sovereignty over temporal powers, which forget they are only commissioned, is obvious. We hear through Daniel the interpretation of the dream that worried Nebuchadnezzar, according to which the kingdom would slip through his fingers "until

---

19. Van der Toorn, "Scholars at the Oriental Court," 43. Power always manages to create laws in its own interest; see Michel Foucault, *Discipline and Punish: The Birth of the Prison* (trans. A. Sheridan; London: Lane, 1977), 48–49.

you know that the Most High has sovereignty over the kingdom of mortals" (Dan 4:22; NRSV 4:25). It does not seem that these words make an impression on the king. It is only when the prophecy comes true that we hear: "reason returned to me and I blessed the Most High" (Dan 4:31; NRSV 4:34), a flash of wisdom that allows God, as he did with Job, to return to him the glory he had lost.

Susanna's elders also have time to recognize their error through the poor use they make of their power. They do not, however, say one word of repentance, and are thus condemned to death.

Both texts are based on the idea that God punishes the bad and rewards the good, those who stay faithful to the torah and resist corrupt rulers, whether Gentiles or Jews. Their heroes are willing to sacrifice their lives before giving up their convictions.

Susanna's prayer is a determining factor in the story. Naked before the community during the trial, the largest embarrassment to which a woman could be subjected, she rises without pause and, standing upright, sends a prayer to a God who seems in that moment absent.[20] It is an affecting scene designed to stay in the readers' memory: the innocence of a young woman facing the malicious libel of a group of elders; the fragility of the weak in front of constituted power; the mass of an apathetic people who do not react against a possible injustice until shaken by a young, wise prophet.

The accused has faith in YHWH because she knows his character and starts her plea with a phrase that relates him to time, "Oh eternal God!" (Dan 13:42 = Sus 1:42 NRSV), which is the equivalent of saying: "You know what happened, I am innocent."[21] It is a cry of pain before injustice, which neither asks for anything nor reproaches God for not having intervened: she simply presents him with the facts in the hope that he will act in her favor. On the edge of the precipice, she demonstrates that she is capable of maintaining her faith when all appears lost; a faith that is given to her by God himself, who has awakened a patient faith redressed in active hope.[22] God listens to her, takes pity on her, and sends her the young Daniel as a savior.

---

20. To understand the magnitude of the offense, we find in the haggadah examples of modest women who cover their heads even at home, see Ilan, *Jewish Women in Greco-Roman Palestine*, in particular the section titled "Head Covering," 129–32. In the Mishnah, in trials for adultery, hair is let loose and clothes are torn, except in the case of women who are very beautiful (Sotah 1:5).

21. The titles applied to God tended to be placed at the beginning of prayers; see Patrick D. Miller, *They Cried to the Lord: The Form and Theology of Biblical Prayer* (Minneapolis: Fortress, 1994), 58.

22. Samuel E. Balentine, *Prayer in the Hebrew Bible: The Drama of Divine-Human*

The prayer of the protagonist is a recurring theme in situations of weakness suffered by many biblical women. Judith in her prayer reminds God of his deeds for Israel and presents him as "God of the afflicted, helper of the oppressed, an upholder of the weak, a protector of the forlorn, a savior of them that are without hope" (Jdt 9:11). The case of Queen Esther is similar. She sees herself alone and needs to intercede for her people by speaking with her husband, the king. Her prayer echoes glorious past deeds in order to deliver to Yhwh "the cry of the desperate" (Esth 4:17 LXX addition).

The Bible talks about these women when Israel is in danger. In these moments, all social convictions fall, and what is important is saving the nation, using all possible talent. Agustina de Aragón, Joan of Arc, Cleopatra, Queen Zenobia of Palmyra—all were women who came from anonymity to take care of their people during difficult times. All of them are seen as threats once the danger is over, because they show that a female government is possible. The solution, necessary to return to the status quo, is to make them disappear. The people's historical memory, however, is not erased, and the women's deeds are repeatedly narrated.

Did Susanna come to the defense of a people in danger? Our authors believed she did. The Jews were going through rough times, they were persecuted for staying faithful, or they were threatened by a wave of thought that was considered to be more in accord with the times. For a pious man, the threat of enemies on a battlefield was preferable to the slow infiltration of Hellenism into faithful hearts, something that broke their faith.

As the situation is extreme, God appears and frees Daniel and Susanna. He no longer acts for himself as he did before. He uses messengers or intermediaries, to whom he gives the freedom to move within parameters of his choosing. In the case of Susanna, the intermediary is Daniel, a young man who is linked to two classic figures in the Jewish world: the prophet and the wise man, used by God to guide the people. Susanna's mediation is produced because of her refusal, which leads to a public trial in which her value, piety, and virtue stand out. These three qualities generate a light that can guide, like a lighthouse on a path, a weak and badly governed people.

Dialogue (OBT; Minneapolis: Fortress, 1993), 187; Rainer Albertz, "Personal Piety," in *Religious Diversity in Ancient Israel and Judah* (ed. Francesca Stavrakopoulou and John Barton; New York: T&T Clark, 2010), 135–49.

3. The Symbolic World

Numerous cultures use the image of women to symbolize cities and communities. In the Bible, Israel appears in the female role of YHWH's wife and mother of the people. She is not a woman faithful to her husband: she prostitutes herself with foreign lovers, and God punishes her. This negative image of Israel is made more and more extravagant, both in attitude and punishment, which culminate in the texts of the prophet Ezekiel (chapters 16 and 23); today we would consider such behavior violence against women.[23] Susanna's image as an honest and faithful wife, capable of defending herself against a sexual attack despite risks to her own life, offers a counterpoint to this development in Israel.

In metaphorical discourse, the woman's beautiful and desirable body becomes a symbol for talking about problems in the social body: women and cities should guard their walls and access points because the arrival of intruders will pollute and harm them. With this parallelism, illicit sexual relations are compared to social relations that compromise the people and should be avoided at all cost. For this reason, those who oppose the power of the intruders are placed as guardians of all points of access.[24]

In Susanna's story there are doors that open and close. Those that stay open allow the entrance of the elders into the garden, threatening Israel with impurity symbolized in the body of a woman. This woman is attacked and maligned for not wanting to open her own door.[25] The immoral attitude of those who should defend the law not only hurts them but also affects the entire social body, whereas those who are faithful to YHWH and his covenant strengthen the religious community.

In adding Susanna's story to the book, our authors directed attention to the fragile and vulnerable collectives in communities that serve to represent the people. Susanna, together with Judith and Jael (Judg 4:17–22; 5:24–27), are paradigmatic cases of women who, despite their little strength, can overcome their opponents. They manage to defeat the powerful not alone, but pray

---

23. See Athalya Brenner, "The Hebrew God and His Female Complements," in *Reading Bibles, Writing Bodies: Identity and the Book* (ed. Timothy K. Beal and David M. Gunn; London: Routledge, 1997), 64.

24. John W. Wright, "A Tale of Three Cities: Urban Gates, Squares and Power in Iron Age II, Neo-Babylonian and Achaemenid Judah," in Davies and Halligan, *Studies in Politics, Class and Material Culture*, 19–50, explores in detail what doors and walls represent in Israelite cities.

25. Mary Douglas has best analyzed societies' self-defense: "we" against those from outside, "the others," and the way in which bodily control constitutes an expression of social control; see Mary Douglas, *Natural Symbols: Explorations in Cosmology* (London: Barrie & Rockliff, 1970), 71, 103.

to God, who helps them with his power. The image of the pleading Susanna allows us to see the "rest" of Israel, this small group that knew how to stay faithful to its creed, even in difficult circumstances.

In the Old Testament, women serve as mediators between God and certain men, as in the case of Moses, who lives thanks to a group of women (Exod 1–3), and Abigail, who stops David's vengeance against her husband (1 Sam 25:1-42). In our story, Susanna's mediation has served to highlight the maliciousness of the elders who hurt the community.

4. What Does Susanna Add to the Story of Daniel?

Can a short story of a page and a half add something of interest to a book as long as Daniel? What does Susanna contribute to the story of the male hero?

From the situation in Palestine, we can infer that the ancient authors, illustrious and faithful men, were worried about the people oppressed by unscrupulous governors, both foreign and Israelite. Their subjects did not dare to stand up to them and were even tempted to imitate their actions, which seemed beneficial and were not punished. The ethics of Israel, a strongly marked part of its identity, is questioned, seriously harming its image and future.

In order to stop this aberration, joined to the old legendary figure of Daniel, the story of Susanna and the Elders adds a tale that takes place in different circumstances. Daniel walks among the foreign governors, while Susanna deals with the powerful people from her own village. The common people cannot see themselves reflected in Daniel's story because he offers a model of behavior for Jews who govern, for the wise and the scribes in their own circle.

Susanna's story introduces other parameters; she is not among the governing class and lives among the people, in everyday life both in the Diaspora and in Israel; she highlights a problematic use of the torah, a basic pillar of Judaism, when two witnesses agree to manipulate it. Susanna's case, however, provides an example of what is happening in many communities, in order to alert recipients to similar dangers and offer an alternative.[26]

To show the weakness of the people, the text uses a woman, the wife of a rich man who does not defend her. No one helps her, and she has neither the knowledge nor the cultural information that Daniel has received at court. Yet she has learned faith and the history of salvation from her family through stories of the deeds of a merciful God in favor of Israel. The young woman not

---

26. For a reading of the book of Susanna in painting, see Dan W. Clanton, *The Good, the Bold and the Beautiful: The Story of Susanna and Its Renaissance Interpretations* (LHBOTS 430; New York: T&T Clark, 2006).

only refrains from prostituting herself with alien lovers, as Israel did, but also risks her life for not complying. It is her faith, ignorant in mundane knowledge but rich in knowledge of the divine, that the story presents to people who find themselves in a similar situation, in order that they might have a model. The social weakness in which Israel is engulfed does not preclude fighting, as this woman has shown. The strength of her faith allows her to challenge the governors of her community and to deny their desires.

Susana is a paragon of publicly expressed convictions. Naked before the assembly, she is not afraid, she does not cover her body, but she screams her prayer aloud so that everyone can see and hear her, though God is the recipient of her words. More than fidelity, the defense of faith demands a raising of one's voice when it is crushed, even though it may seem futile because no one listens.

Hers is the cry of the innocent, of the poor and weak who have no human support, a theme that recurs in Judaism and in the Greek novels of the period.[27] The story, however, presents us with an inversion of values: the weak turn to a God who is in favor of their disgrace, and will win a battle that, in any other moment, would have been lost.

Apart from the principal characters, the actors that appear in these stories can be divided into three categories: the bad, the good, and the numerous. Susanna's story is written for this last group, so that they avoid evil and fight against it. It shows them the way to hold their heads high and their faith firm. Its authors have lost hope of converting the powerful (an idea latent in Daniel), and Susanna serves as their role model. The individualistic ideas of Greece, though, also influenced these Jewish authors, who advocate that any human being, even a woman, can serve as a light for the people.

Susanna is the last in a saga of women who take a step forward. Some, like Deborah, lead frightened groups of people (Judg 4–5); others, like Judith or Jael, kill the adversary general; Queen Esther convinces her husband to annul a decree of the Jews' extermination; while the mother of the Maccabees encourages her children not to falter at the moment of martyrdom (2 Macc 7), an image that is very close to that of our protagonist. Susanna would never know if her example serves and is imitated, but her story in the Bible adds feminine life to Jewish faith.

The story has nothing that can be compared to modern feminism. However, the figure of Susanna, like that of other heroines in these Jewish books,

---

27. In Hellenistic novels of this period, such as *Chariton and Callirrhoe* or *Leucippe and Clitophon*, weakness tends to be found in women; see Achilles Tatius, *Leucippe and Clitophon* (trans. S. Gaselee; LCL 45; London: Heinemann, 1961).

has opened doors for other female protagonists, unthinkable until these moments. These women have confronted powerful men, and won, showing that female leadership is possible and the process of a people's liberation is only complete when both sexes fight to achieve it.[28]

The story has a happy ending. The people are glad to see that a young man has shown himself to be more useful and honest than the partial governors of the village community. The husband and family of the young woman see that her honor has not been stained, and the young Daniel begins to make himself a legend of wisdom.

We still need to ask about the young wife, whose feelings are not mentioned. In my view, one may rightly surmise that this episode would have had emotional repercussions. She receives no praise for refusing the elders, although she has almost been condemned to death. Her relationship with her husband, who does not defend her, would have deteriorated—although the law did not allow for spousal declarations. Susanna's contacts with the members of her community may not be the same either. She has appeared naked or unclothed in their presence, and every time she is with someone, she will feel that they are imagining her thus.

The authors of our story have ruined Susanna's (fictive?) life—have they not? They have possibly done so without realizing they have because, like the God of the prophets, they only see one side of the equation. Once they have used her image for their intentions, they make her disappear because she is no longer needed. The same thing happens with other biblical women, like Esther, Judith, Deborah, and Jael. Their images and gestures are used when the circumstances require it, and once they are no longer needed, they leave the scene without a sound, leaving behind only the example of a life to be imitated.

The message to the hurt and subjugated community is clear. Neither ignorance nor weakness is an excuse to give in to this type of power, which is diminished because God comes to the defense of the innocent who cry for help. Political leadership, however strong it may be, will give in to divine power, which is always greater. Susanna, as a faithful and virtuous woman, who stands and implores YHWH in her most difficult moment, is the best example that readers can imitate when they seek to preserve their religious identity—and Israel can imitate her as well, because every little bit helps.

Translated from Spanish by Anna Deckert and Christl M. Maier

---

28. André LaCocque, *The Feminine Unconventional: Four Subversive Figures in Israel's Tradition* (Minneapolis: Fortress, 1990), 20.

Bibliography

Abécassis, Armand. "Espaces de lecture du Cantique des Cantiques en contexte juif." Pages 185–96 in *Les nouvelles voies de l'exégèse, en lisant le Cantique des Cantiques: XIX congrès de l'ACFEB, Toulouse 2001*. Edited by Jacques Nieuviarts and Pierre Debergé. LD 190. Paris: Cerf, 2002.

Abraham, Kathleen. "West Semitic and Judean Brides in Cuneiform Sources from the Sixth Century B.C.E.: New Evidence from a Marriage Contract from al-Yahudu." *AfO* 51 (2005–6): 198–219.

Ahituv, Shmuel. *Echoes from the Past: Hebrew and Cognate Inscriptions from the Biblical Period*. Jerusalem: Carta Press, 2008.

Aitken, James K. "Judaic National Identity." Pages 36–48 in *Judah between East and West: The Transition from Persian to Greek Rule (ca. 400–200 BCE)*. Edited by Lester L. Grabbe and Oded Lipschits. Library of Second Temple Studies 75. New York: T&T Clark, 2011.

Albertz, Rainer. "Personal Piety." Pages 135–48 in *Religious Diversity in Ancient Israel and Judah*. Edited by Francesca Stavrakopoulou and John Barton. New York: T&T Clark, 2010.

Aleixandre, Dolores. "Buscadoras de un nombre: Memoria de Noemí." *Reseña Bíblica* 71 (2011): 4–10.

Alkier, Stefan. "Intertextualität—Annäherungen an ein texttheoretisches Paradigma." Pages 1–26 in *Heiligkeit und Herrschaft: Intertextuelle Studien zu Heiligkeitsvorstellungen und zu Psalm 110*. Edited by Dieter Sänger. BThS 55. Neukirchen-Vluyn: Neukirchener, 2003.

Alonso Schökel, Luis. *Proverbios y Eclesiástico*. Los Libros Sagrados 8.1. Madrid: Cristiandad, 1968.

———. *Rut, Tobías, Judit, Ester*. Los Libros Sagrados 8. Madrid: Cristiandad, 1973.

Alonso Schökel, Luis, and Cecilia Carniti. *I Salmi*. Vols. 1–2. Roma: Borla, 1992–93.

Alpert, Rebecca T. "Finding Our Past: A Lesbian Interpretation of the Book of Ruth." Pages 91–96 in *Reading Ruth: Contemporary Women Reclaim a Sacred Story*. Edited by Judith A. Kates and Gail Twersky Reimer. New York: Ballantine, 1996.

Anaya Luengo, Pedro Raúl. *El hombre, destinatario de los dones de Dios en el Qohélet*. Bibliotheca Salmanticensis. Estudios 296. Salamanca: Publicaciones Universidad Pontificia, 2007.

Apfel, Roberta T., and Lise Grondahl. "Feminine Plurals." Pages 55–64 in *Reading Ruth: Contemporary Women Reclaim a Sacred Story*. Edited by Judith A. Kates and Gail Twersky Reimer. New York: Ballantine, 1996.

Assmann, Jan. *Ma'at: Gerechtigkeit und Unsterblichkeit im Alten Ägypten*. Munich: Beck, 1990.
Augustine, Saint. *Confessions*. Translated by Henry Chadwick. Oxford World's Classics. New York: Oxford University Press, 1991.
Auwers, Jean-Marie. *La composition littéraire du Psautier: Un état de la question*. Paris: Gabalda, 2000.
Avnery, Orit. "The Threefold Cord: Interrelations between the Books of Samuel, Ruth and Esther." Ph.D. diss., Bar Ilan University, 2011 (Hebrew).
Baarda, Tjitze. "The Sentences of the Syriac Menander (Third Century A.D.): A New Translation and Introduction by T. Baarda." Pages 583–606 in *Expansions of the "Old Testament" and Legends, Wisdom and Philosophical Literature, Prayers, Psalms and Odes, Fragments of Lost Judeo-Hellenistic Works*. Vol. 2 of *The Old Testament Pseudepigrapha*. Edited by James H. Charlesworth. Garden City, N.Y.: Doubleday, 1985.
Babcock, Barbara, ed. *The Reversible Worlds: Symbolic Inversion in Art and Society*. Ithaca, N.Y.: Cornell University Press, 1978.
Bail, Ulrike. *Gegen das Schweigen klagen: Eine intertextuelle Studie zu den Klagepsalmen Ps 6 und Ps 55 und der Erzählung von der Vergewaltigung Tamars*. Gütersloh: Gütersloher, 1998.
———. "Hautritzen als Körperinszenierung der Trauer und des Verlustes im Alten Testament." Pages 54–80 in *"Dies ist mein Leib": Leibliches, Leibeigenes und Leibhaftiges bei Gott und den Menschen*. Edited by Jürgen Ebach et al. Jabboq 9. Gütersloh: Gütersloher, 2006.
———. "The Psalms: Who Is Speaking May Be All That Matters." Pages 180–91 in *Feminist Biblical Interpretation: A Compendium of Critical Commentary on the Books of the Bible and Related Literature*. Edited by Luise Schottroff and Marie-Theres Wacker. Grand Rapids: Eerdmans, 2012.
———. "Susanna verlässt Hollywood: Eine feministische Auslegung von Dan 13." Pages 91–98 in *Gott an den Rändern: Sozialgeschichtliche Perspektiven auf die Bibel*. Edited by Ulrike Bail and Renate Jost. Gütersloh: Gütersloher, 1996.
———. "Wehe, kein Ort, nirgends ... Überlegungen zum Sprachraum der Klagelieder Jeremias." Pages 81–90 in *Time—Utopia—Eschatology*. Edited by Charlotte Methuen. Jahrbuch der ESWTR 7. Leuven: Peeters, 1999.
Bail, Ulrike, et al., eds. *Bibel in gerechter Sprache*. 4th ed. Gütersloh: Gütersloher Verlagshaus, 2011.
Balentine, Samuel E. *Prayer in the Hebrew Bible: The Drama of Divine-Human Dialogue*. Minneapolis: Fortress, 1993.
Balla, Ibolya. *Ben Sira on Family, Gender, and Sexuality*. Deuterocanonical and Cognate Literature Studies 8. Berlin: de Gruyter, 2011.
Barbiero, Gianni. "L'amore, 'fiamma di Jah': Una lettura contestuale di Ct 8,5–7.13–14." Pages 443–57 in *Corpo e religione*. Edited by Gaspare Mura and Roberto Cipriani. Rome: Città Nuova, 2009.
———. "'Di Sion si dirà: ognuno è stato generato in essa': Studio esemplare del Sal 87." Pages 209–64 in *Biblical Exegesis in Progress: Old and New Testament Essays*.

Edited by Jean-Noël Aletti and Jean-Louis Ska. AnBib 176. Rome: Pontifical Biblical Institute, 2009.

———. "'Leg mich wie ein Siegel auf dein Herz—Fliehe, mein Geliebter': Die Spannung in der Liebesbeziehung nach dem Epilog des Hohenliedes." Pages 185–98 in *Studien zu alttestamentlichen Texten*. SBAB 34. Stuttgart: Katholisches Bibelwerk, 2002.

———. "Die Liebe der Töchter Jerusalems: Hld 3,10b MT im Kontext vom 3,6–11." *BZ* 39 (1995): 96–104.

———. *Song of Songs: A Close Reading*. Translated by Michael Tait. VTSup 144. Leiden: Brill, 2011.

———. "Die 'Wagen meines edlen Volkes' (Hld 6,12): Eine strukturelle Analyse." *Bib* 78 (1997): 174–89.

Barstad, Hans M. "After 'the Myth of the Empty Land': Major Challenges in the Study of Neo-Babylonian Judah." Pages 3–20 in *Judah and the Judeans in the Neo-Babylonian Period*. Edited by Oded Lipschits and Joseph Blenkinsopp. Winona Lake, Ind.: Eisenbrauns, 2003.

Barth, Karl. *Die kirchliche Dogmatik*. Vol. 3.2. Zürich: EVZ, 1948.

Bauks, Michaela, and Gerlinde Baumann. "Im Anfang war ... ? Gen 1,1ff und Prov 8,22–31 im Vergleich." *BN* 71 (1994): 24–52.

Baumann, Gerlinde. "A Figure with many Facets: The Literary and Theological Functions of Personified Wisdom in Proverbs 1–9." Pages 44–78 in *Wisdom and Psalms*. Edited by Athalya Brenner and Carole R. Fontaine. FCB 2/2. Sheffield: Sheffield Academic, 1998.

———. *Love and Violence: Marriage as Metaphor for the Relationship between YHWH and Israel in the Prophetic Books*. Translated by Linda M. Maloney. Collegeville, Minn.: Liturgical Press, 2003 (German original 2000).

———. *Die Weisheitsgestalt in Proverbien 1–9: Traditionsgeschichtliche und theologische Studien*. FAT 16. Tübingen: Mohr Siebeck, 1996.

———. "'Zukunft feministischer Spiritualität' oder 'Werbefigur des Patriarchats'? Die Bedeutung der Weisheitsgestalt in Prov 1–9 für die feministisch-theologische Diskussion." Pages 135–52 in *Von der Wurzel getragen: Christlich-feministische Exegese in Auseinandersetzung mit Antijudaismus*. Edited by Luise Schottroff and Marie-Theres Wacker. BibIntS 17. Leiden: Brill, 1996.

Bautch, Richard. "Intertextuality in the Persian Period." Pages 25–35 in *Approaching Yehud: New Approaches to the Study of the Persian Period*. Edited by Jon L. Berquist. SemeiaSt 50. Atlanta: Society of Biblical Literature, 2007.

Bazyliński, Stanislaw. "Psalm 87: Motivation for Pilgrimage." Pages 71–90 in *Nova et Vetera: Miscellanea in onore di padre Tiziano Lorenzin*. Edited by Luciano Fanin. Studi religiosi. Padova: Edizioni Messaggero, 2011.

Beissinger, Margaret. "Gender and Power in the Balkan Return Song." *Slavic and East European Journal* 45, no. 3 (2001): 403–30.

Ben-Barak, Zafrira. "The Status and Right of the gĕbîrâ." *JBL* 110 (1991): 23–34.

Berg, Sandra Beth. *The Book of Esther: Motifs, Themes, and Structure*. Missoula, Mont.: Scholars Press, 1979.

Berlin, Adele. "Ruth and the Continuity of Israel." Pages 255–60 in *Reading Ruth: Contemporary Women Reclaim a Sacred Story*. Edited by Judith A. Kates and Gail Twersky Reimer. New York: Ballantine, 1996.

Berlyn, P. J. "The Great Ladies." *JBQ* 24 (1996): 26–35.

Berquist, Jon L. *Judaism in Persia's Shadow: A Social and Historical Approach*. Minneapolis: Fortress, 1995.

Berquist, Jon L., ed. *Approaching Yehud: New Approaches to the Study of the Persian Period*. SemeiaSt 50. Atlanta: Society of Biblical Literature, 2007.

Bester, Dörte. *Körperbilder in den Psalmen: Studien zu Psalm 22 und verwandten Texten*. FAT 2/24. Tübingen: Mohr Siebeck, 2007.

Bird, Phyllis A. "'Frauenarbeit' und die Sphäre des Religiösen im alten Israel: Überlegungen zur Kontinuität und Diskontinuität in häuslichen und kultischen Rollen anhand von Trauerriten." Pages 23–35 in *Geschlechterdifferenz, Ritual und Religion*. Edited by Elmar Klinger et al. Würzburg: Echter, 2003.

Bohmbach, Karla G. "Names and Naming in the Biblical World." Pages 33–39 in *Women in Scripture: A Dictionary of Named and Unnamed Women in the Hebrew Bible*. Edited by Carol L. Meyers. Grand Rapids: Eerdmans, 2000.

Booij, Thijs. "Some Observations on Psalm LXXXVII." *VT* 37 (1987): 16–25.

Botterweck, G. Johannes, and Helmer Ringgren, eds. *Theological Dictionary of the Old Testament*. Translated by D. E. Green. 15 vols. Grand Rapids: Eerdmans, 1974–2006.

Bowen, Nancy R. "A Fairy Tale Wedding? A Feminist Intertextual Reading of Psalm 45." Pages 53–71 in *A God So Near: Essays on Old Testament Theology in Honor of Patrick D. Miller*. Edited by Brent A. Strawn and Nancy R. Bowen. Winona Lake, Ind.: Eisenbrauns, 2003.

———. "The Quest for the Historical Gĕbîrâ." *CBQ* 63 (2001): 597–618.

Braude, William G., trans. *The Midrash on Psalms*. Vol. 1. 3rd ed. Yale Judaica Series 13. New Haven: Yale University Press, 1976.

Braulik, Georg. "Das Deuteronomium und die Bücher Ijob, Sprichwörter, Rut." Pages 61–138 in *Die Tora als Kanon für Juden und Christen*. Edited by Erich Zenger. HBS 10. Freiburg: Herder, 1996.

Brenner, Athalya, ed. *A Feminist Companion to the Song of Songs*. FCB 1. Sheffield: Sheffield Academic, 1993.

———. "Figurations of Women in Wisdom Literature." Pages 50–66 in *A Feminist Companion to Wisdom Literature*. Edited by Athalya Brenner. FCB 9. Sheffield: Sheffield Academic, 1995.

———. "The Hebrew God and His Female Complements." Pages 56–72 in *Reading Bibles, Writing Bodies: Identity and the Book*. Edited by Timothy K. Beal and David M. Gunn. London: Routledge, 1997.

———. "Ruth as Foreign Worker and the Politics of Exogamy." Pages 158–62 in *Ruth and Esther*. Edited by Athalya Brenner. FCB 2/3. Sheffield: Sheffield Academic, 1999.

Brenner, Athalya, and Carole R. Fontaine, eds. *The Song of Songs*. FCB 2/6. Sheffield: Sheffield Academic, 2000.

Brenner, Athalya, and Fokkelien van Dijk-Hemmes. *On Gendering Texts: Female and Male Voices in the Hebrew Bible*. BibIntS 1. Leiden: Brill, 1993.

Brockmöller, Katrin. *"Eine Frau der Stärke—wer findet sie?" Exegetische Analysen und intertextuelle Lektüren zu Spr 31,10-31*. BBB 147. Berlin: Philo, 2004.

Bronner, Leila L. "Reclaiming Esther: From Sex Object to Sage." *JBQ* 26 (1998): 4-10.

Brunner, Hellmut. *Altägyptische Weisheit: Lehren für das Leben*. Darmstadt: Wissenschaftliche Buchgesellschaft, 1988.

Bush, Frederick. *Ruth/Esther*. WBC 9. Waco, Tex.: Word, 1996.

Butting, Klara. *Die Buchstaben werden sich noch wundern: Innerbiblische Kritik als Wegweisung feministischer Hermeneutik*. Berlin: Alektor, 1994.

———. "Esther: About Resistance against Anti-Semitism and Sexism." Pages 207-220 in *Feminist Biblical Interpretation: A Compendium of Critical Commentary on the Books of the Bible and Related Literature*. Edited by Luise Schottroff and Marie-Theres Wacker. Grand Rapids: Eerdmans, 2012.

———. "'Die Töchter Judas frohlocken' (Ps 48,12): Frauen beten Psalmen." *BK* 1 (2001): 35-39.

Cady, Susan, Maria Ronan, and Hal Taussig, eds. *Sophia: The Future of Feminist Spirituality*. New York: Harper & Row, 1986.

Calduch-Benages, Nuria. "The Absence of Named Women from Ben Sira's Praise of the Ancestors." Pages 301-17 in *Rewriting Biblical History: Essays on Chronicles and Ben Sira in Honour of Pancratius C. Beentjes*. Edited by Jeremy Corley and Harm van Grol. Deuterocanonical and Cognate Literature Studies 7. Berlin: de Gruyter, 2011.

———. "Aromas, fragancias y perfumes en el Sirácida." Pages 15-30 in *Treasures of Wisdom: Studies on Ben Sira and the Book of Wisdom: Festschrift M. Gilbert*. Edited by Nuria Calduch-Benages and Jacques Vermeylen. BETL 143. Leuven: Peeters, 1999.

———. "Ben Sira y las mujeres." *Reseña Bíblica* 41 (2004): 37-44.

———. "'Cut Her Away from Your Flesh': Divorce in Ben Sira." Pages 81-95 in *Studies in the Book of Ben Sira: Papers of the Third International Conference on the Deuterocanonical Books, Shime'on Centre, Pápa, Hungary, 18-20 May, 2006*. Edited by Géza G. Xeravits and József Zsengellér. JSJSup 127. Leiden: Brill, 2008.

———. *En el crisol de la prueba: Estudio exegético de Sir 2,1-18*. Asociación Bíblica Española 32. Estella: Verbo Divino, 1997.

———. "Jesus and Wisdom." Pages 109-40 in *The Perfume of the Gospel: Jesus' Encounters with Women*. Theologia 8. Rome: Gregorian and Biblical Press, 2012.

———, ed. *El Libro de Ben Sira (Sirácida o Eclesiástico)*. Reseña Bíblica 41. Estella: Verbo Divino, 2004.

———. "La mujer en la versión siríaca (Peshitta) de Ben Sira: ¿Sesgos de género?" Pages 686-93 in *Congreso Internacional "Biblia, memoria histórica y encrucijada de culturas."* Edited by Jesús Campos Santiago and Víctor Pastor Julián. Zamora: Asociación Bíblica Española, 2004.

Camp, Claudia V. "Understanding a Patriarchy: Women in Second Century Jerusalem Through the Eyes of Ben Sira." Pages 1-40 in *"Women Like This": New Perspec-*

tives on Jewish Women in the Graeco-Roman World. Edited by Amy-Jill Levine. Atlanta: Scholars Press, 1991.

———. *Wisdom and the Feminine in the Book of Proverbs.* Bible and Literature 11. Sheffield: Almond, 1985.

———. *Wise, Strange and Holy: The Strange Woman and the Making of the Bible.* JSOTSup 320. Sheffield: Sheffield Academic, 2000.

———. "The Wise Women of 2 Samuel: A Role Model for Women in Early Israel?" *CBQ* 43 (1981): 14–29.

Carruthers, Jo. *Esther through the Centuries.* Blackwell Bible Commentary. Oxford: Blackwell, 2008.

Cavicchia, Alessandro. *Le sorti e le vesti: La "Scrittura" alle radici del messianismo giovanneo tra re-interpretazione e adempimento: Sal 22 (21) a Qumran e in Giovanni.* Tesi Gregoriana. Serie Teologia 81. Rome: Editrice Pontificia Università Gregoriana, 2010.

Ceresko, Anthony R. "The Function of Antanaclasis ($mṣ'$ 'to find'//$mṣ'$ 'to reach, overtake, grasp') in Hebrew Poetry, Especially in the Book of Qoheleth." *CBQ* 44 (1982): 551–69.

Chave, Peter. "Toward a Not Too Rosy Picture of the Song of Songs." *Feminist Theology* 18 (1998): 41–53.

Childs, Brevard. *Myth and Reality in the Old Testament.* SBT 27. London: SCM, 1960.

Christ, Carol P. *The Laughter of Aphrodite: Reflections on a Journey to the Goddess.* San Francisco: Harper & Row, 1988.

Christianson, Eric S. *Ecclesiastes through the Centuries.* Blackwell Bible Commentary. Oxford: Blackwell, 2007.

Chu, Julie Ley C. "Returning Home: The Inspiration of Role Differentiation in the Book of Ruth for Taiwanese Women." *Semeia* 78 (1997): 47–53.

Clanton, Dan W. *The Good, the Bold and the Beautiful: The Story of Susanna and Its Renaissance Interpretations.* LHBOTS 430. New York: T&T Clark, 2006.

Clines, David J. A. *Job 1–20.* WBC 17. Dallas, Tex.: Word, 1989.

———. *Ezra, Nehemiah, Esther.* NCB. Grand Rapids: Eerdmans, 1984.

Coggins, Richard J. *Sirach.* Guides to the Apocrypha and Pseudepigrapha 6. Sheffield: Sheffield Academic, 1998.

Cohen, Shaye J. D. "Solomon and the Daughter of Pharaoh: Intermarriage, Conversion, and the Impurity of Women." *JANES* 16–17 (1984–85): 23–37.

Cohen, Tamara. "Taking Back Purim." In *A Different Purim Sound: Waving Flags and Ringing Bells: An Exhibition of Esther and Vashti Purim Flags by Jewish Artists* (Ma'yan's exhibition catalog). n.d. Online: http://www.ritualwell.org/ritual/taking-back-purim.

Collins, John J. *Jewish Wisdom in the Hellenistic Age.* OTL. Louisville: Westminster John Knox, 1997.

Conzelmann, Hans. "Die Mutter der Weisheit." Pages 225–34 in *Zeit und Geschichte: Dankesgabe an Rudolf Bultmann zum 80. Geburtstag.* Edited by Erich Dinkler. Tübingen: Mohr Siebeck, 1964.

Cornelius, Izak. *The Iconography of the Canaanite Gods Reshef and Ba'al: Late Bronze and Iron Age I Periods (c 1500–1000 BCE)*. OBO 140. Fribourg: University Press; Göttingen: Vandenhoeck & Ruprecht, 1994.

Cowley, Arthur E., ed. *Aramaic Papyri of the Fifth Century B.C.* Oxford: Clarendon, 1923.

Crüsemann, Frank. "Der Gewalt nicht glauben: Hiobbuch und Klagepsalmen—zwei Modelle theologischer Verarbeitung traumatischer Gewalterfahrungen." Pages 251–68 in *Dem Tod nicht glauben: Sozialgeschichte der Bibel: Festschrift für Luise Schottroff zum 70. Geburtstag*. Edited by Frank Crüsemann, Marlene Crüsemann, Claudia Janssen, Rainer Kessler, and Beate Wehn. Gütersloh: Gütersloher, 2004.

Curtis, Edward L. *The Book of Chronicles*. ICC. Edinburgh: T&T Clark, 1952.

D'Alario, Vittoria. *Il libro del Qohelet: Struttura letteraria e retorica*. RivBSup 27. Bologna: Dehoniane, 1993.

———. "Liberté de Dieu ou destin? Un autre dilemme dans l'interprétation du Qohélet." Pages 457–63 in *Qohelet in the Context of Wisdom*. Edited by Antoon Schoors. BETL 136. Leuven: Peeters, 1998.

Dahood, Mitchell. "Qohelet and Recent Discoveries." *Bib* 39 (1958): 302–18.

Daube, David. *Collaboration with Tyrannny in Rabbinic Law*. The Riddell Memorial Lectures 37. London: Oxford University Press, 1965.

Davidson, Andrew B. "Sirach's Judgment of Women." *ExpTim* 6 (1984–85): 402–4.

Davies, Philip R., ed. *Persian Period*. Vol. 1 of *Second Temple Studies*. Edited by Lester L. Grabbe. JSOTSup 117. Sheffield: Sheffield Academic, 1991.

Davies, Philip R., and John Halligan, eds. *Studies in Politics, Class and Material Culture*. Vol. 3 of *Second Temple Studies*. Edited by Lester L. Grabbe. JSOTSup 340. Sheffield: Sheffield Academic, 2002.

Davis, Ellen F. "'All That You Say, I Will Do': A Sermon on the Book of Ruth." Pages 3–8 in *Scrolls of Love: Ruth and the Song of Songs*. Edited by Peter S. Hawkins and Lesleigh C. Stahlberg. New York: Fordham University Press, 2006.

Day, Linda. *Esther*. AOTC. Nashville: Abingdon, 2005.

Day, Peggy L. "From the Child is Born the Woman: The Story of Jephthah's Daughter." Pages 58–74 in *Gender and Difference in Ancient Israel*. Edited by Peggy L. Day. Minneapolis: Fortress, 1989.

Deen, Edith. *All the Women of the Bible*. London: Independent, 1959.

Deissler, Alfons. *Die Psalmen*. Die Welt der Bibel. Düsseldorf: Patmos, 1964.

Die Bibel in Elberfelder Übersetzung. 4th ed. Sonderausgabe der revidierten Fassung 1992. Paderborn: Voltmedia, 2005.

Demosthenes, Pseudo-. "Against Neaera." In *Women's Life in Greece and Rome: A Source Book in Translation*. Edited by Mary R. Lefkowitz and Maureen B. Fant. Baltimore: Johns Hopkins University Press, 1992.

Dieckmann, Detlef, and Dorothea Erbele-Küster, eds. *Du hast mich aus meiner Mutter Leib gezogen: Beiträge zur Geburt im Alten Testament*. Neukirchen-Vluyn: Neukirchener, 2006.

Dobbs-Allsopp, Frederick W. *Weep, O Daughter Zion: A Study of the City-Lament Genre in the Hebrew Bible*. BibOr 44. Rome: Pontifical Biblical Institute, 1993.

Doherty, Lilian. *Siren Songs: Gender, Audiences, and Narrators in the Odyssey.* Ann Arbor: University of Michigan Press, 1995.

Donbaz, Veysel, and Matthew W. Stolper. *Istanbul Murašû Texts.* Leiden: Nederlands Historisch-Archaeologisch Instituut te Istanbul, 1997.

Dor, Yonina. "The Composition of the Episode of the Foreign Women in Ezra IX–X." *VT* 53 (2003): 26–47.

———. *Have the "Foreign Women" Really been Expelled? Separation and Exclusion in the Restoration Period.* Jerusalem: Hebrew University Magnes Press, 2006 (Hebrew).

Douglas, Mary. *Natural Symbols: Explorations in Cosmology.* London: Barrie & Rockliff, 1970.

Duesberg, Hilaire, and Irénée Fransen. *Ecclesiastico.* La Sacra Bibbia volgata latina e traduzione italiana dai testi originali illustrate con note critiche e commentate a cura di Mons. Salvatore Garofalo. Antico Testamento sotto la direzione di P. Giovanni Rinaldi C.R.S. Torino/Rome: Marietti, 1966.

Duhm, Bernard. *Die Psalmen erklärt.* KHC 14. Freiburg im Breisgau: Mohr Siebeck, 1899.

Eagleton, Terry. *Literary Theory: An Introduction.* Oxford: Basil Blackwell, 1983.

Ebach, Jürgen. "Fremde in Moab—Fremde aus Moab: Das Buch Ruth als politische Literatur." Pages 277–304 in *Bibel und Literatur.* Edited by Jürgen Ebach and Richard Faber. Munich: Fink, 1995.

———. *Hiobs Post: Gesammelte Aufsätze zum Hiobbuch, zu Themen biblischer Theologie und zur Methodik der Exegese.* Neukirchen-Vluyn: Neukirchener, 1995.

Ebeling, Jenni R. *Women's Lives in Biblical Times.* New York: T&T Clark, 2010.

Ecker, Gisela. "Trauer zeigen: Inszenierung und Sorge um den Anderen." Pages 9–25 in *Trauer tragen—Trauer zeigen: Inszenierungen der Geschlechter.* Edited by Gisela Ecker. Munich: Fink, 1999.

Edelman, Diana. *The Origins of the Second Temple: Persian Imperial Policy and the Rebuilding of Jerusalem.* London: Equinox, 2005.

Egger-Wenzel, Renate. "'Denn harte Knechtschaft und Schande ist es, wenn eine Frau ihren Mann ernährt' (Sir 25,22)." Pages 23–49 in *Der Einzelne und seine Gemeinschaft.* Edited by Renate Egger-Wenzel and Ingrid Krammer. BZAW 270. Berlin: de Gruyter, 1998.

Elliott, Mary T. *The Literary Unity of the Canticle.* EHS 23. Theologie 371. Frankfurt am Main: Lang, 1989.

Ellis, Teresa A. "Is Eve the 'Woman' in Sirach 25:24?" *CBQ* 73 (2011): 723–42.

Emerton, John A. "The Problem of Psalm LXXXVII." *VT* 50 (2000): 183–99.

Engel, Helmut. "Weisheit Salomos." *Das wissenschaftliche Bibellexikon im Internet* (2005). Online: http://www.wibilex.de.

Epstein, Shifra. "The 'Drinking Banquet' (Trink-Siyde): A Hasidic Event for Purim." *Poetics Today* 15 (1994): 133–52.

Erbele-Küster, Dorothea. *Beten als Akt des Lesens: Eine Rezeptionsästhetik der Psalmen.* WMANT 87. Neukirchen-Vluyn: Neukirchener, 2001.

Escarbajal Frutos, Andrés, and Andrés Escarbajal de Haro. *La interculturalidad: Desafío para la educación.* Madrid: Dykinson, 2007.

Eskenazi, Tamara Cohn. "Ezra-Nehemiah." Pages 116–23 in *The Women's Bible Commentary*. Edited by Carol A. Newsom and Sharon H. Ringe. Louisville: Westminster John Knox, 1992.

———. "Ezra-Nehemiah." Pages 192–200 in *The Women's Bible Commentary*. Edited by Carol A. Newsom, Sharon H. Ringe, and Jacqueline E. Lapsley. 3rd ed. Louisville: Westminster John Knox, 2012.

Eskenazi, Tamara Cohn, and Tikva Frymer-Kensky. *The JPS Bible Commentary: Ruth*. Philadelphia: Jewish Publication Society, 2011.

Eskenazi, Tamara Cohn, and Eleanore P. Judd. "Marriage to a Stranger in Ezra 9–10." Pages 266–85 in *Temple and Community in the Persian Period*. Edited by Tamara Cohn Eskenazi and Kent H. Richards. Vol. 2 of *Second Temple Studies*. Edited by Lester L. Grabbe. JSOTSup 175. Sheffield: JSOT Press, 1994.

Estes, Daniel J. "What Makes the Strange Woman of Proverbs 1–9 Strange?" Pages 151–69 in *Ethical and Unethical in the Old Testament: God and Humans in Dialogue*. Edited by Katherine Dell. LHBOTS 528. New York: T&T Clark, 2010.

Estévez, Elisa. "Un alegato a favor del mestizaje: el libro de Rut." *Reseña Bíblica* 40 (2003): 23–31.

———. "Función socio-histórica y teológica del libro de Rut." *Miscelánea Comillas* 59 (2001): 685–707.

Exum, J. Cheryl. *Fragmented Women: Feminist (Sub)versions of Biblical Narratives*. Valley Forge, Pa.: Trinity Press International, 1993.

———. "Is This Naomi?" Pages 129–74 in *Plotted, Shot and Painted: Cultural Representations of Biblical Women*. JSOTSup 215. Edited by J. Cheryl Exum. Sheffield: Sheffield Academic, 1996.

———. *Song of Songs*. OTL. Louisville: Westminster John Knox, 2005.

Faust, Avraham. "Settlement Dynamics and Demographic Fluctuations in Judah from the Late Iron Age to the Hellenistic Period and the Archaeology of Persian Period Yehud." Pages 23–51 in *A Time of Change: Judah and Its Neighbours in the Persian and Early Hellenistic Periods*. Edited by Yigal Levin. New York: T&T Clark, 2007.

Fewell, Danna Nolan, ed. *Reading between Texts: Intertextuality and the Hebrew Bible*. Louisville: Westminster John Knox, 1992.

Fewell, Danna Nolan, and David M. Gunn. "Boaz, Pillar of Society: Measures of Worth in the Book of Ruth." *JSOT* 45 (1989): 45–59.

———. *Compromising Redemption: Relating Characters in the Book of Ruth*. Louisville: Westminster John Knox, 1990.

———. "Is Coxon a Scold? On Responding to the Book of Ruth." *JSOT* 45 (1989): 39–43.

———. "'A Son Is Born to Naomi!': Literary Allusions and Interpretation in the Book of Ruth." *JSOT* 40 (1988): 99–108.

Finlay, Timothy D. *The Birth Report Genre in the Hebrew Bible*. FAT 2/12. Tübingen: Mohr Siebeck, 2005.

Fisch, Harold. "Ruth and the Structure of Covenant History." *VT* 32 (1982): 425–37.

Fischer, Irmtraud. "The Book of Ruth: A 'Feminist' Commentary to the Torah?" Pages 24–49 in *Ruth and Esther*. Edited by Athalya Brenner. FCB 2/3. Sheffield: Sheffield Academic, 1999.

———. "Donne nell'Antico Testamento." Pages 161–96 in *Donne e Bibbia: Storia ed esegesi*. Edited by Adriana Valerio. La Bibbia nella Storia 21. Bologna: Dehoniane, 2006.

———. "Egalitär entworfen—hierarchisch gelebt: Zur Problematik des Geschlechterverhältnisses und einer genderfairen Anthropologie im Alten Testament." Pages 265–98 in *Der Mensch im alten Israel: Neue Forschungen zur alttestamentlichen Anthropologie*. Edited by Bernd Janowski and Kathrin Liess. HBS 59. Freiburg: Herder, 2005.

———. "Frauen in der Literatur (Altes Testament)." *Das wissenschaftliche Bibellexikon im Internet* (2008). Online: http://www.wibilex.de.

———. *Gotteslehrerinnen: Weise Frauen und Frau Weisheit im Alten Testament*. Stuttgart: Kohlhammer, 2006.

———. *Gottesstreiterinnen: Biblische Erzählungen über die Anfänge Israels*. 3rd ed. Stuttgart: Kohlhammer, 2006.

———. "Israel's Senses for the Sensual God." *TD* 53 (2006): 137–42.

———. "Ist der Tod nicht für alle gleich? Sterben und Tod aus der Genderperspektive." Pages 87–108 in *Tod und Jenseits im alten Israel und seiner Umwelt: Theologische, religionsgeschichtliche, archäologische und ikonographische Aspekte*. Edited by Angelika Berlejung and Bernd Janowski. FAT 64. Tübingen: Mohr Siebeck, 2009.

———. *Rut*. HTKAT. Freiburg: Herder, 2001.

———. "Rut/Rutbuch." *Das wissenschaftliche Bibellexikon im Internet* (2006). Online: http://www.wibilex.de.

———. *Women Who Wrestled with God: Biblical Stories of Israel's Beginnings*. Translated by Linda M. Maloney. Collegeville, Minn.: Liturgical Press, 2005.

Fischer, Irmtraud, and Mercedes Navarro Puerto with Andrea Taschl-Erber, eds. *Torah*. The Bible and Women: An Encyclopaedia of Exegesis and Cultural History 1.1. Atlanta: Society of Biblical Literature, 2011.

Fontaine, Carole R. "Ecclesiastes." Pages 161–63 in *Women's Bible Commentary*. Edited by Carol A. Newsom and Sharon H. Ringe. 2nd ed. Louisville: Westminster John Knox, 1998.

———. "Proverbs." Pages 153–60 in *Women's Bible Commentary*. Edited by Carol A. Newsom and Sharon H. Ringe. 2nd ed. Louisville: Westminster John Knox, 1998.

Foote, Catherin J. *Survivor Prayers: Talking with God about Childhood Sexual Abuse*. Louisville: Westminster John Knox, 1994.

Foucault, Michel. *The Archeology of Knowledge*. Translated by A. M. Sheridan Smith. London: Tavistock, 1974.

———. *Discipline and Punish: The Birth of the Prison*. Translated by Allan Sheridan. London: Lane, 1977.

Fox, Michael V. *Proverbs 1–9*. AB 18A. New York: Doubleday, 2000.

Frettlöh, Magdalene L. "Der auferweckte Gekreuzigte und die Überlebenden sexueller Gewalt: Kreuzestheologie genderspezifisch wahr genommen." Pages 77–104 in *Das Kreuz Jesu: Gewalt—Opfer—Sühne*. Edited by Rudolf Weth. Neukirchen-Vluyn: Neukirchener, 2001.

———. *Theologie des Segens: Biblische und dogmatische Wahrnehmungen*. 2nd ed. Gütersloh: Kaiser/Gütersloher, 1998.

Fuchs, Esther. "The Literary Characterization of Mothers and Sexual Politics in the Hebrew Bible." Pages 117–36 in *Feminist Perspectives on Biblical Scholarship*. Edited by Adela Yarbro Collins. Chico, Calif.: Scholars Press, 1985.

———. *Sexual Politics in the Biblical Narrative: Reading the Hebrew Bible as a Woman*. JSOTSup 310. Sheffield: Sheffield Academic, 2000.

———. "Status and Role of Female Heroines in the Biblical Narrative." *The Mankind Quarterly* 23 (1983): 149–60.

Fünfsinn, Bärbel, and Carola Kienel, eds. *Psalmen leben: Frauen aus allen Kontinenten lesen biblische Psalmen neu*. Hamburg: EB, 2002.

Garbini, Giovanni. *Cantico dei cantici*. Biblica 2. Brescia: Paideia, 1992.

———. "Hebrew Literature in the Persian Period." Pages 180–89 in *Temple and Community in the Persian World*. Edited by Tamara Cohn Eskenazi and Kent H. Richards. Vol. 2 of *Second Temple Studies*. Edited by Lester L. Grabbe. JSOTSup 175. Sheffield: Sheffield Academic, 1994.

Gault, Brian P. "A 'Do Not Disturb' Sign? Reexamination of the Adjuration Refrain in Song of Songs." *JSOT* 36 (2011): 93–104.

Gendler, Mary. "The Restoration of Vashti." Pages 241–47 in *The Jewish Woman: New Perspectives*. Edited by Elizabeth Koltun. New York: Schocken, 1976.

Gilbert, Maurice. "Ben Sira et la femme." *RTL* 7 (1976): 426–42.

———. "Siracide." *DBSup* 12 (1996): 1389–437.

Gillingham, Susan E. *Psalms through the Centuries*. Blackwell Bible Commentary. Oxford: Blackwell, 2007.

Gillmayr-Bucher, Susanne. "Body Images in the Psalms." *JSOT* 28, no. 3 (2004): 301–26.

———. "Emotion und Kommunikation." Pages 278–89 in *Biblische Anthropologie: Neue Einsichten aus dem Alten Testament*. Edited by Christian Frevel. QD 237. Freiburg: Herder, 2010.

———. "Rauchende Nase, bebendes Herz: Gefühle zur Sprache bringen." *BK* 67 (2012): 21–25.

Gitay, Zefira. "Ruth and the Women of Bethlehem." Pages 178–90 in *Ruth and Esther*. Edited by Athalya Brenner. FCB 2/3. Sheffield: Sheffield Academic, 1999.

Goitein, S. D. "Women as Creators of Biblical Genres." Translated by Michael Carasik. *Prooftexts* 8 (1988): 1–33.

Goldingay, John. *Psalms*. Vol. 2. Baker Commentary on the Old Testament Wisdom and Psalms. Grand Rapids: Baker Academic, 2006.

Goodfriend, Elaine. "Yitro." Page 407 in *The Torah: A Women's Commentary*. Edited by Tamara Cohn Eskenazi and Andrea L. Weiss. New York: UTJ, 2008.

Gorges-Braunwarth, Susanne. *"Frauenbilder—Weisheitsbilder—Gottesbilder" in Spr 1–9: Die personifizierte Weisheit im Gottesbild der nachexilischen Zeit*. Exegese in unserer Zeit 9. Münster: LIT, 2002.

Gottwald, Norman. "Social Class and Ideology in Isaiah 40–55: An Eagletonian Reading." *Semeia* 59 (1992): 43–57.

Goulder, Michael D. "Ruth: A Homily on Deuteronomy 22–25?" Pages 307–19 in *Of Prophets' Visions and the Wisdom of Sages: FS R. N. Whybray*. Edited by Heather A. McKay and David J. A. Clines. JSOTSup 162. Sheffield: Sheffield Academic, 1993.

Grabbe, Lester L., and Oded Lipschits. *Judah between East and West: The Transition from Persian to Greek Rule (ca. 400–200 BCE)*. Library of Second Temple Studies 75. New York: T&T Clark, 2011.

Grober, S. F. "The Hospitable Lotus: A Cluster of Metaphors: An Inquiry into the Problem of Textual Unity in the Song of Songs." *Semitics* 9 (1984): 86–112.

Grohmann, Marianne. *Fruchtbarkeit und Geburt in den Psalmen*. FAT 53. Tübingen: Mohr Siebeck, 2007.

Gruber, Mayer I. "Women's Voices in the Book of Micah." *lectio difficilior* 1 (2007). Online: http://www.lectio.unibe.ch/07_1/mayer_gruber_womens_voices.htm.

Gueuret, Agnès. "Observations sur Qohélet." *Sémiotique et Bible* 127 (2007): 25–39.

Gunkel, Hermann. *Die Psalmen übersetzt und erklärt*. 4th ed. HKAT 2/2. Göttingen: Vandenhoeck & Ruprecht, 1926.

Halevi, Leor. *Muhammad's Grave*. New York: Columbia University Press, 2007.

Harris, Scott L. *Proverbs 1–9: A Study of Inner-Biblical Interpretation*. SBLDS 150. Atlanta: Scholars Press, 1995.

Häusl, Maria. "Lamentations: Zion's Cry in Affliction." Pages 334–44 in *Feminist Biblical Interpretation: A Compendium of Critical Commentary on the Books of the Bible and Related Literature*. Edited by Luise Schottroff and Marie-Theres Wacker. Grand Rapids: Eerdmans, 2012.

Hausmann, Jutta. "Beobachtungen zu Spr 31,10–31." Pages 261–66 in *Alttestamentlicher Glaube und biblische Theologie: Festschrift für H. D. Preuß zum 65. Geburtstag*. Edited by Jutta Hausmann and Hans J. Zobel. Stuttgart: Kohlhammer, 1992.

Healey, John F. "Mot." Pages 598–603 in *Dictionary of Deities and Demons in the Bible*. Edited by Karel van der Toorn, Bob Becking, and Pieter W. van der Horst. 2nd ed. Leiden: Brill; Grand Rapids: Eerdmans, 1999.

Heinevetter, Hans-Josef. *"Komm nun, mein Liebster, Dein Garten ruft Dich!" Das Hohelied als programmatische Komposition*. BBB 69. Frankfurt am Main: Athenäum, 1988.

Henderson, Joseph. "Who Weeps in Jer VIII 23 (IX 1)? Identifying the Dramatic Speakers in the Poetry of Jeremiah." *VT* 52 (2002): 196–206.

Herrero Ingelmo, Mari Cruz. *La novela griega antigua*. Madrid: Akal Clásica, 1987.

Herrmann, Christian. *Ägyptische Amulette aus Palästina/Israel: 1. Mit einem Ausblick auf die Rezeption durch das Alte Testament*. OBO 138. Fribourg: Universitätsverlag; Göttingen: Vandenhoeck & Ruprecht, 1994.

Herzer, Jens. "Freund und Feind: Beobachtungen zum alttestamentlich-frühjüdischen Hintergrund und zum impliziten Handlungsmodell der Gethsemane-Perikope Mk 14,32–42." *leqach* 1 (2001): 99–127.

Holladay, William. "Style, Irony, and Authenticity in Jeremiah." *JBL* 81 (1962): 44–54.

Holst-Warhaft, Gail. *Dangerous Voices: Women's Laments and Greek Literature*. London: Routledge, 1992.

Honig, Bonnie. "Ruth, the Model Emigrée: Mourning and the Symbolic Politics of Immigration." Pages 50–74 in *Ruth and Esther*. Edited by Athalya Brenner. FCB 2/3. Sheffield: Sheffield Academic, 1999.

Honigman, Sylvie. "King and Temple in 2 Maccabees: The Case for Continuity." Pages 91–130 in *Judah between East and West: The Transition from Persian to Greek Rule (ca. 400–200 BCE)*. Edited by Lester L. Grabbe and Oded Lipschits. Library of Second Temple Studies 75. New York: T&T Clark, 2011.

Horowitz, Elliott. *Reckless Rites: Purim and the Legacy of Jewish Violence.* Princeton: Princeton University Press, 2006.

Horsley, Richard, and Patrick Tiller. "Ben Sira and the Sociology of the Second Temple." Pages 74–107 in *Studies in Politics, Class and Material Culture.* Edited by Philip R. Davies and John Halligan. Vol. 3 of *Second Temple Studies.* Edited by Lester L. Grabbe. JSOTSup 340. Sheffield: Sheffield Academic, 2002.

Horst, Pieter W. van der. "Images of Women in the Testament of Job." Pages 93–116 in *Studies on the Testament of Job.* Edited by Michael A. Knibb and Pieter W. van der Horst. SNTSMS 66. Cambridge: Cambridge University Press, 1989.

Horton, Ernest. "Koheleth's Concept of Opposites as Compared to Samples of Greek Philosophy and Near and Far Eastern Wisdom Classics." *Numen* 19 (1972): 1–21.

Ilan, Tal. "Gender and Lamentations: 4Q179 and the Canonization of the Book of Lamentations." *lectio difficilior* 2 (2008). Online: http://www.lectio.unibe.ch/08_2/Tal_Ilan_Gender_of_Lamentations.html.

———. *Integrating Women into Second Temple History.* Peabody, Mass.: Hendrickson, 2001.

———. *Jewish Women in Greco-Roman Palestine.* Peabody, Mass.: Hendrickson, 1996.

Íñiguez, Lupicinio. "Identidad: de lo personal a lo social: Un recorrido conceptual." Pages 209–25 in *La constitución social de la subjetividad.* Edited by Eduardo Crespo. Madrid: Catarata, 2001.

Jahnow, Hedwig. *Das hebräische Leichenlied im Rahmen der Völkerdichtung.* BZAW 36. Giessen: Töpelmann, 1923.

Jenni, Ernst, and Claus Westermann, eds. *Theological Lexicon of the Old Testament.* Translated by Mark E. Biddle. 3 vols. Peabody, Mass.: Hendrickson, 1997.

Japhet, Sara. *1 and 2 Chronicles: A Commentary.* OTL. London: SCM, 1993.

———. "The Expulsion of the Foreign Women: The Legal Basis, Precedents, and Consequences for the Definition of Jewish Identity." Pages 141–61 in *"Sieben Augen auf einem Stein" (Sach 3,9): Studien zur Literatur des Zweiten Tempels: Festschrift für Ina Willi-Plein.* Edited by Friedhelm Hartenstein and Michael Pietsch. Neukirchen-Vluyn: Neukirchener, 2007.

———. *From the Rivers of Babylon to the Highlands of Judah: Collected Studies on the Restoration Period.* Winona Lake, Ind.: Eisenbrauns, 2006.

———. *The Ideology of the Book of Chronicles and Its Place in Biblical Thought.* 3rd ed. Frankfurt am Main: Lang, 1989. Repr., Winona Lake, Ind.: Eisenbrauns, 2009.

———. "The Israelite Legal and Social Reality as Reflected in Chronicles: A Case Study." Pages 233–44 in *Sha'arei Talmon: Studies in the Bible, Qumran, and the Ancient Near East Presented to Shemaryahu Talmon.* Edited by Michael Fishbane et al. Winona Lake, Ind.: Eisenbrauns, 1992. Repr. as pages 79–91 in Sara Japhet. *From the Rivers of Babylon to the Highlands of Judah: Collected Studies on the Restoration Period.* Winona Lake, Ind.: Eisenbrauns, 2006.

———. "The Prohibition of the Habitation of Women: The *Temple Scroll*'s Attitude toward Sexual Impurity and Its Biblical Precedents." In *Comparative Studies in Honor of Yohanan Muffs. JANES* 22 (1993): 69–87. Repr. as pages 268–88 in Sara

Japhet, *From the Rivers of Babylon to the Highlands of Judah: Collected Studies on the Restoration Period*. Winona Lake, Ind.: Eisenbrauns, 2006.

———. "Was David a Judahite or an Ephraimite? Light from the Genealogies." Pages 297–306 in *Let Us Go Up to Zion: Essays in Honour of H. G. M. Williamson on the Occasion of His Sixty-Fifth Birthday*. Edited by Mark Boda and Iain Provan. VTSup 153. Leiden: Brill, 2012.

Johnson, Marshall D. *The Purpose of the Biblical Genealogies*. 2nd ed. Cambridge: Cambridge University Press, 1989.

Joseph, Suad, and Afsaneh Najmabadi, eds. *Encyclopedia of Women and Islamic Cultures*. Vol. 1. Leiden: Brill, 2003.

Jost, Renate. *Freundin in der Fremde: Rut und Noomi*. Stuttgart: Quell, 1992.

———. "Trauma, Heilung und die Bibel." Pages 269–92 in *Dem Tod nicht glauben: Sozialgeschichte der Bibel: Festschrift für Luise Schottroff zum 70. Geburtstag*. Edited by Frank Crüsemann et al. Gütersloh: Gütersloher, 2004.

Joüon, Paul. *Ruth: Commentaire philologique et exégétique*. Rome: Institut Biblique Pontifical, 1986.

Joüon, Paul, and Takamitsu Muraoka. *A Grammar of Biblical Hebrew*. 2nd ed. SubBi 27. Rome: Gregorian and Biblical Press, 2009.

Karrer, Martin, et al., eds. *Septuaginta Deutsch: Erläuterungen und Kommentare*. 2 vols. Stuttgart: Deutsche Bibelgesellschaft, 2011.

Karrer-Grube, Christiane. "Ezra and Nehemiah: The Return of the Others." Pages 192–206 in *Feminist Biblical Interpretation: A Compendium of Critical Commentary on the Books of the Bible and Related Literature*. Editedy by Luise Schottroff and Marie-Theres Wacker. Grand Rapids: Eerdmans, 2012.

Kates, Judith A. "Women at the Center: Ruth and Shavuot." Pages 187–98 in *Reading Ruth: Contemporary Women Reclaim a Sacred Story*. Edited by Judith A. Kates and Gail Twersky Reimer. New York: Ballantine, 1996.

Katske, Erika. "Transforming Purim." *Ma'yan Journey* (Winter 2001). Online: http://www.ritualwell.org/ritual/transforming-purim.

Kayatz, Christa. *Studien zu Prov. 1–9: Eine form- und motivgeschichtliche Untersuchung unter Einbeziehung ägyptischen Vergleichsmaterials*. WMANT 22. Neukirchen-Vluyn: Neukirchener, 1966.

Keel, Othmar. *Corpus der Stempelsiegel-Amulette aus Palästina/Israel: Von den Anfängen bis zur Perserzeit*. Katalogband II: Von Bahan bis Tel Eton. Mit Beiträgen von Daphna Ben-Tor, Baruch Brandl und Robert Wenning. OBO Series Archaeologica 29. Fribourg: Academic Press; Göttingen: Vandenhoeck & Ruprecht, 2010.

———. *Deine Blicke sind Tauben: Zur Metaphorik des Hohen Liedes*. SBS 114/115. Stuttgart: Katholisches Bibelwerk, 1984.

———. *Die Geschichte Jerusalems und die Entstehung des Monotheismus*. Orte und Landschaften der Bibel 4/1. Göttingen: Vandenhoeck & Ruprecht, 2007.

———. *Gott weiblich: Eine verborgene Seite des biblischen Gottes*. Liebefeld: Bibel + Orient Museum, 2008.

———. *Jahwes Entgegnung an Ijob: Eine Deutung von Ijob 38–41 vor dem Hintergrund der zeitgenössischen Bildkunst*. FRLANT 121. Göttingen: Vandenhoeck & Ruprecht, 1978.

———. *The Song of Songs: A Continental Commentary*. Translated by Frederick J. Gaiser. Minneapolis: Fortress, 1994.
———. *The Symbolism of the Biblical World: Ancient Near Eastern Iconography and the Book of Psalms*. Translated by Timothy J. Hallett. Winona Lake, Ind.: Eisenbrauns, 1997.
———. *Die Weisheit spielt vor Gott: Ein ikonographischer Beitrag zur Deutung des mesaḥäqät in Sprüche 8,30f*. Fribourg: Universitätsverlag; Göttingen: Vandenhoeck & Ruprecht, 1974.
———. *Die Welt der altorientalischen Bildsymbolik und das Alte Testament: Am Beispiel der Psalmen*. 5th ed. Göttingen: Vandenhoeck & Ruprecht, 1996.
Keel, Othmar, and Christoph Uehlinger. *Gods, Goddesses, and Images of God in Ancient Israel*. Translated by Allan W. Mahnke. Minneapolis: Fortress, 1996.
———. *Göttinnen, Götter und Gottessymbole: Neue Erkenntnisse zur Religionsgeschichte Kanaans und Israels aufgrund bislang unerschlossener ikonographischer Quellen*. 5th ed. QD 134. Freiburg: Herder, 2001.
Keel, Othmar, and Silvia Schroer. *Eva—Mutter alles Lebendigen: Frauen- und Göttinnenidole aus dem Alten Orient*. 3rd ed. Fribourg: Academic Press, 2011.
———. *Schöpfung: Biblische Theologien im Kontext altorientalischer Religionen*. 2nd ed. Fribourg: Universitätsverlag; Göttingen: Vandenhoeck & Ruprecht, 2008.
Kelso, Julie. *O Mother, Where Art Thou? An Irigarayan Reading of the Book of Chronicles*. London: Equinox, 2007.
Kessler, Rainer. "Männertränen." Pages 30–34 in *Gotteserdung: Beiträge zur Hermeneutik und Exegese der Hebräischen Bibel*. Stuttgart: Kohlhammer, 2006.
———. "'Zänkisches Weib' und 'Tüchtige Hausfrau': Blicke auf Frauen in jüdischen Schriften aus persischer und hellenistischer Zeit." Pages 1–10 in *Zwischen Vernunft und Gefühl: Weibliche Religiosität von der Antike bis heute*. Edited by Christa Bertelsmeier-Kierst. Kulturgeschichtliche Beiträge zum Mittelalter und der frühen Neuzeit 3. Frankfurt am Main: Lang, 2010.
Kimchi, David. *Commento ai Salmi*. Vol. 2. Edited by Luigi Cattani. Tradizione d'Israele 6. Roma: Città Nuova, 1995.
Kirshenblatt-Gimblett, Barbara. "Contraband: Performance, Text and Analysis of a Purim-shpil." *The Drama Review* 24 (1980): 5–16.
Kittel, Rudolf. *Die Psalmen*. 4th ed. KAT 13. Leipzig: Deichert, 1922.
Klein, Lillian R. "Honor and Shame in Esther." Pages 149–75 in *A Feminist Companion to Esther, Judith and Susanna*. Edited by Athalya Brenner. FCB 7. Sheffield: Sheffield Academic, 1995.
Kletter, Raz, et al. *Yavneh I: The Excavation of the "Temple Hill" Repository Pit and the Cult Stands*. OBO Series Archaeologica 30. Fribourg: Academic Press, 2010.
Klingenstein, Susanne. "Circles of Kinship: Samuel's Family Romance." Pages 199–210 in *Reading Ruth: Contemporary Women Reclaim a Sacred Story*. Edited by Judith A. Kates and Gail Twersky Reimer. New York: Ballantine, 1996.
Kloppenborg, John S. "Isis and Sophia in the Book of Wisdom." *HTR* 75 (1982): 57–84.
Knauf, Ernst A. "Ruth la moabite." *VT* 44 (1994): 547–48.
Knoppers, Gary N. "Intermarriage, Social Complexity, and Ethnic Diversity in the Genealogy of Judah." *JBL* 120 (2001): 15–30.

Koosed, Jennifer L. *(Per)mutations of Qohelet: Reading the Body in the Book*. LHBOTS 429. New York: T&T Clark, 2006.

Korenhof, Mieke. "Spr. 8,22-31: Die 'Weisheit' scherzt vor Gott." Pages 118–26 in *Feministisch gelesen*. Vol. 1. Edited by Eva Renate Schmidt et al. Stuttgart: Kreuz, 1988.

Kraeling, Emil G., ed. *The Brooklyn Museum Aramaic Papyri: New Documents of the Fifth Century B.C. from the Jewish Colony at Elephantine*. New Haven: Yale University Press, 1953.

Kraus, Wolfgang, et al., eds. *Septuaginta Deutsch: Das griechische Alte Testament in deutscher Übersetzung*. Stuttgart: Deutsche Bibelgesellschaft, 2009.

Krinetzki, Günter. *Kommentar zum Hohenlied: Bildsprache und theologische Botschaft*. BBET 16. Frankfurt am Main/Bern: Lang, 1981.

Kristeva, Julia. *Desire in Language: A Semiotic Approach to Literature and Art*. New York: Columbia University Press, 1980.

Krüger, Thomas. "'Frau Weisheit' in Koh 7,26?" *Bib* 73 (1992): 394–402.

Kwok, Pui-lan. *Post-colonial Imagination and Feminist Theology*. Louisville: Westminster John Knox, 2005.

Labahn, Antje, and Ehud Ben Zvi. "Observations on Women in the Genealogies of 1 Chronicles 1–9." *Bib* 84 (2003): 457–78.

LaCocque, André. *The Feminine Unconventional: Four Subversive Figures in Israel's Tradition*. Minneapolis: Fortress, 1990.

———. *Romance, She Wrote: A Hermeneutical Essay on Song of Songs*. Harrisburg, Pa.: Trinity Press International, 1998.

———. "Subverting the Biblical World: Sociology and Politics in the Book of Ruth." Pages 20–30 in *Scrolls of Love: Ruth and the Song of Songs*. Edited by Peter S. Hawkins and Lesleigh C. Stahlberg. New York: Fordham University Press, 2006.

Laffey, Alice L. "I and II Chronicles." Pages 110–15 in *The Women's Bible Commentary*. Edited by Carol A. Newsom and Sharon H. Ringe. Louisville: Westminster John Knox, 1992.

———. *An Introduction to the Old Testament: A Feminist Approach*. Philadelphia: Fortress, 1988.

Lanahan, William. "The Speaking Voice in the Book of Lamentations." *JBL* 93 (1974): 41–49.

Lancellotti, Angelo. *I Salmi: Versione—introduzione—note*. Nuovissima versione della Bibbia dai testi originali 18/C. Rome: Paoline, 1984.

Landy, Francis. *Paradoxes of Paradise: Identity and Difference in the Song of Songs*. Sheffield: Almond, 1983.

Lang, Bernhard. *Frau Weisheit: Deutung einer biblischen Gestalt*. Düsseldorf: Patmos, 1975.

———. *Wisdom in the Book of Proverbs: A Hebrew Goddess Redefined*. New York: Pilgrim, 1986.

———. "Women's Work, Household and Property in Two Mediterranean Societies." *VT* 54 (2004): 188–207.

Lange, Armin. *Weisheit und Torheit bei Kohelet und in seiner Umwelt: Eine Untersuchung ihrer theologischen Implikationen*. EHS 23. Theologie 433. Frankfurt am Main: Lang, 1991.

Larkin, Katrina J. A. *Ruth and Esther.* OTG. Sheffield: Sheffield Academic, 1996.
Lavoie, Jean-Jacques. *La pensée du Qohélet: Étude exégétique et intertextuelle.* Héritage et projet 49. Québec: Fides, 1992.
Lee, Nancy C. *Lyrics of Lament: From Tragedy to Transformation.* Minneapolis: Fortress, 2010.
———. "Prophetic 'Bat-'Ammî' Answers God and Jeremiah." *lectio difficilior* 2 (2009). Online: http://www.lectio.unibe.ch/09_2/lee.html.
———. *The Singers of Lamentations: Cities Under Siege, From Ur to Jerusalem to Sarajevo.* BibIntS 60. Leiden: Brill, 2002.
Leehan, James. *Defiant Hope: Spirituality for Survivors of Family Abuse.* Louisville: Westminster John Knox, 1993.
Lefkowitz, Mary R., and Maureen B. Fant. *Women's Life in Greece and Rome: A Source Book in Translation.* Baltimore: Johns Hopkins University Press, 1992.
Leisering, Christina. *Susanna und der Sündenfall der Ältesten: Eine vergleichende Studie zu den Geschlechterkonstruktionen der Septuaginta- und Theodotionfassung von Dan 13 und ihren intertextuellen Bezügen.* Exegese in unserer Zeit 19. Münster/Wien: LIT, 2008.
LeMon, Joel M. *Yahweh's Winged Form in the Psalms: Exploring Congruent Iconography and Texts.* OBO 242. Fribourg: Academic Press; Göttingen: Vandenhoeck & Ruprecht, 2010.
Levin, Yigal. "Understanding Biblical Genealogies." *CurBS* 9 (2001): 11–46.
Levison, Jack. "Is Eve to Blame? A Contextual Analysis of Sirach 25:24." *CBQ* 47 (1985): 617–23.
Lichtheim, Miriam. *Late Egyptian Wisdom Literature in the International Context: A Study of Demotic Instructions.* OBO 52. Fribourg: Universitätsverlag; Göttingen: Vandenhoeck & Ruprecht, 1983.
Liesen, Jan. "Strategical Self-references in Ben Sira." Pages 63–74 in *Treasures of Wisdom: Studies in Ben Sira and the Book of Wisdom: Festschrift M. Gilbert.* Edited by Nuria Calduch-Benages and Jacques Vermeylen. BETL 143. Leuven: Peeters, 1999.
Linafelt, Tod. *Surviving Lamentations: Catastrophe, Lament and Protest in the Afterlife of a Biblical Book.* Chicago: University of Chicago Press, 2000.
———. "The Undecidability of *brk* in the Prologue of Job and Beyond." *BibInt* 4 (1996): 165–72.
Lippmann, Walter. *Public Opinion.* New York: Macmillan, 1922. Repr., 1949.
Lohfink, Norbert. "Besprechung von: R. E. Murphy, The Wisdom Literature (FOTL 13)." *TP* 58 (1983): 239–41.
———. "War Kohelet ein Frauenfeind? Ein Versuch, die Logik und den Gegenstand von Koh. 7,23–8,1a herauszufinden." Pages 259–87 in *La Sagesse de l'Ancien Testament.* Edited by Maurice Gilbert. BETL 51. Gembloux-Leuven: Leuven University Press, 1979.
Lopes, Mercedes. "Alianza por la vida: Una relectura de Rut a partir de las culturas." *RIBLA* 26 (1997): 96–101.
Lurker, Manfred. *Wörterbuch biblischer Bilder und Symbole.* 2nd ed. Munich: Kösel, 1978.

Luzzatto, Amos. *Chi era Qohelet?* Brescia: Morcelliana, 2011.
Lys, Daniel. *Le plus beau chant de la création: Commentaire du Cantique des cantiques.* LD 51. Paris: Cerf, 1968.
MacDowell, Douglas M. *The Law in Classical Athens.* Ithaca, N.Y.: Cornell University Press, 1978.
Machado, Antonio. *Soledades.* Buenos Aires: Tecnibook Ediciones, 2011.
Mack, Burton L. *Logos und Sophia: Untersuchungen zur Weisheitstheologie im hellenistischen Judentum.* SUNT 10. Göttingen: Vandenhoeck & Ruprecht, 1973.
Magonet, Jonathan. *Schöne, Heldinnen, Narren: Von der Erzählkunst der Hebräischen Bibel.* Gütersloh: Gütersloher, 1996.
Maier, Christl M. "'Begehre nicht ihre Schönheit in deinem Herzen' (Prov 6,25): Eine Aktualisierung des Ehebruchsverbots aus persischer Zeit." *BibInt* 5 (1997): 46–63.
———. "Body Imagery in Psalm 139 and its Significance for a Biblical Anthropology." *lectio difficilior* 2 (2001). Online: http://www.lectio.unibe.ch/01_2/m.htm.
———. *Daughter Zion, Mother Zion: Gender, Space, and the Sacred in Ancient Israel.* Minneapolis: Fortress, 2008.
———. "Der Diskurs um interkulturelle Ehen in Jehud als antikes Beispiel von Intersektionalität." Pages 129–53 in *Doing Gender—Doing Religion: Fallstudien zur Intersektionalität im frühen Judentum, Christentum und Islam.* Edited by Ute Eisen et al. WUNT 302. Tübingen: Mohr Siebeck, 2013.
———. *Die "fremde Frau" in Proverbien 1–9: Eine exegetische und sozialgeschichtliche Studie.* OBO 144. Fribourg: Universitätsverlag; Göttingen: Vandenhoeck & Ruprecht, 1995.
———. "Proverbs: How Feminine Wisdom Comes into Being." Pages 255–72 in *Feminist Biblical Interpretation: A Compendium of Critical Commentary on the Books of the Bible and Related Literature.* Edited by Luise Schottroff and Marie-Theres Wacker. Grand Rapids: Eerdmans, 2012.
———. "Psalm 87 as a Reappraisal of the Zion Tradition and Its Reception in Galatians 4:26." *CBQ* 69 (2007): 473–86.
———. "Weisheit (Personifikation) (AT)." *Das wissenschaftliche Bibellexikon im Internet* (2007). Online: http://www.wibilex.de.
———. "'Zion wird man Mutter nennen': Die Zionstradition in Psalm 87 und ihre Rezeption in der Septuaginta." *ZAW* 118 (2006): 582–96.
Maier, Christl M., and Karin Lehmeier. "Witwe." Pages 667–68 in *Sozialgeschichtliches Wörterbuch zur Bibel.* Edited by Frank Crüsemann et al. Gütersloh: Gütersloher, 2009.
Maier, Christl M., and Silvia Schroer. "Job: Questioning the Book of the Righteous Sufferer." Pages 221–39 in *Feminist Biblical Interpretation: A Compendium of Critical Commentary on the Books of the Bible and Related Literature.* Edited by Luise Schottroff and Marie-Theres Wacker. Grand Rapids: Eerdmans, 2012.
Malamat, Abraham. "Origins and the Formation Period." Pages 63–66 in vol. 1 of *A History of the Jewish People.* Edited by Hayim H. Ben-Sasson. Cambridge: Harvard University Press, 1976.
———. "Tribal Societies: Biblical Genealogies and African Lineage Systems." *Archives Européennes de Sociologie* 14 (1973): 126–36.

Mandolfo, Carleen R. *Daughter Zion Talks Back to the Prophets: A Dialogic Theology of the Book of Lamentations*. SemeiaSt 58. Atlanta: Society of Biblical Literature, 2007.
Manicardi, Luciano. "Sion, la 'città di Dio' (Sal 87)." *Parola Spirito e Vita* 50 (2004): 83–102.
Mannati, Marina. *Psaumes 73 à 106*. Vol. 3 of *Les Psaumes*. Cahiers de la Pierre-qui-Vive. Paris: Desclée de Brouwer, 1967.
Marböck, Johannes. "Das Buch Jesus Sirach." Pages 408–16 in *Einleitung in das Alte Testament*. Edited by Erich Zenger et al. 7th ed. Stuttgart: Kohlhammer, 2008.
———. *Sirach 1–23*. HTKAT. Freiburg: Herder, 2010.
———. *Weisheit im Wandel: Untersuchungen zur Weisheitstheologie bei Ben Sira*. 2nd ed. BZAW 272. Berlin: de Gruyter, 1999.
Marsman, Hennie J. *Women in Ugarit and Israel: Their Social and Religious Position in the Context of the Ancient Near East*. OtSt 49. Leiden: Brill, 2003.
May, Herbert G. "Some Cosmic Connotations of *Mayim Rabbîm* 'Many Waters.'" *JBL* 74 (1955): 9–21.
Mazzinghi, Luca. "The Verbs מצא 'to Find' and בקש 'to Search' in the Language of Qohelet: An Exegetical Study." Pages 91–120 in *The Language of Qohelet in Its Context: Essays in Honour of Prof. A. Schoors on the Occasion of His Seventieth Birthday*. Edited by Angelika Berlejung and Pierre van Hecke. OLA 164. Leuven: Peeters, 2007.
McKinlay, Judith E. *Gendering Wisdom the Host: Biblical Invitations to Eat and Drink*. JSOTSup 216. Gender, Culture, Theory 216. Sheffield: Sheffield Academic, 1996.
Meek, Theophile J. "The Book of Lamentations." Pages 3–38 in vol. 6 of *The Interpreter's Bible*. New York: Abingdon-Cokesbury, 1956.
Meyers, Carol. "Archaelogy—A Window to the Lives of Israelite Women." Pages 61–108 in *Torah*. Edited by Irmtraud Fischer and Mercedes Navarro Puerto with Andrea Taschl-Erber. The Bible and Women: An Encyclopaedia of Exegesis and Cultural History 1.1. Atlanta: Society of Biblical Literature, 2011.
———. *Discovering Eve: Ancient Israelite Women in Context*. New York: Oxford University Press, 1988.
———. "Grinding to a Halt: Gender and the Changing Technology of Flour Production in Roman Galilee." Pages 65–74 in *Engendering Social Dynamics: The Archaeology of Maintenance Activities*. Edited by Sandra Montón-Subías and Margarita Sánchez-Romero. BAR International Series 186. Oxford: Archeopress, 2008.
———. "Of Drums and Damsels." *BA* 54 (1991): 16–27.
———. "Returning Home: Ruth 1.8 and the Gendering of the Book of Ruth." Pages 85–114 in *A Feminist Companion to Ruth*. Edited by Athalya Brenner. FCB 3. Sheffield: Sheffield Academic, 1993.
———. "'To Her Mother's House': Considering a Counterpart to the Israelite *Bet ab*." Pages 39–51 in *The Bible and the Politics of Exegesis: Essays in Honor of Norman K. Gottwald on His Sixty-Fifth Birthday*. Edited by David Jobling et al. Cleveland: Pilgrim, 1991.
———. "'Women in the Neighborhood' (Ruth 4.17): Informal Female Networks in Ancient Israel." Pages 110–27 in *Ruth and Esther*. Edited by Athalya Brenner. FCB 2/3. Sheffield: Sheffield Academic, 1999.

Meyers, Eric M. "The Shelomit Seal and the Judean Restoration: Some Additional Considerations." *ErIsr* 18 (1985): 33*–38*.
Michel, Diethelm. *Untersuchungen zur Eigenart des Buches Qohelet*. BZAW 183. Berlin: de Gruyter, 1989.
Midrash Rabbah Translated into English with Notes, Glossary and Indices under the Editorship of Rabbi Dr. M. Freedman and Maurice Simon. Vol. 1. 3rd ed. London: Soncino, 1961.
Miles, Johnny. *Constructing the Other in Ancient Israel and the USA*. The Bible in the Modern World 32. Sheffield: Sheffield Phoenix, 2011.
Milgrom, Jacob. *Leviticus 1–16*. AB 3. New York: Doubleday, 1991.
Miller, Geoffrey D. *Marriage in the Book of Tobit*. Deuterocanonical and Cognate Literature Studies 10. Berlin: de Gruyter, 2011.
Miller, Patrick D. *They Cried to the Lord: The Form and Theology of Biblical Prayer*. Minneapolis: Fortress, 1994.
Mills, Margaret A. "Gender and Verbal Performance Style in Afghanistan." Pages 56–77 in *Gender, Genre, and Power in South Asian Expressive Traditions*. Edited by Arjun Appadurai et al. Philadelphia: University of Pennsylvania Press, 1991.
———. "Sex Role Reversals, Sex Changes, and Transvestite Disguise in the Oral Tradition of a Conservative Muslim Community in Afghanistan." Pages 187–213 in *Women's Folklore, Women's Culture*. Edited by Rosan A. Jordan and Susan J. Kalčik. Philadelphia: University of Pennsylvania Press, 1985.
Minc, Rachel. "Le rôle du chœur féminin dans le livre de Ruth." *BVC* 77 (1967): 71–76.
Minissale, Antonino. *Siracide (Ecclesiastico)*. Nuovissima versione della Bibbia dai testi originali 23. Rome: Paoline, 1980.
Moore, Carey A. *Daniel, Esther and Jeremiah: The Additions*. AB 44. Garden City: Doubleday, 1977.
Moosbach, Carola. *Gottesflamme Du Schöne: Lob- und Klagegebete*. Gütersloh: Gütersloher, 1997.
Mopsik, Charles. *La Sagesse de ben Sira: Traduction de l'hébreu, introduction et annotation par Charles Mopsik*. Collection "Les Dix Paroles." Paris: Verdier, 2003.
Morgan, Donn F. *Between Text and Community: The "Writings" in Canonical Interpretation*. Minneapolis: Fortress, 2007.
Morla Asensio, Víctor. *Eclesiástico: Texto y Comentario*. El Mensaje del Antiguo Testamento 20. Estella: Verbo Divino, 1992.
Müller, Hans-Peter. "Begriffe menschlicher Theomorphie: Zu einigen *cruces interpretum* in Hld 6,10." *ZAH* 1 (1988): 112–21.
Müllner, Ilse. *Das hörende Herz: Weisheit in der hebräischen Bibel*. Stuttgart: Kohlhammer, 2006.
———. "Klagend laut werden: Frauenstimmen im Alten Testament." Pages 69–85 in *Schweigen wäre gotteslästerlich: Die heilende Kraft der Klage*. Edited by Georg Steins. Würzburg: Echter, 2000.
Nadar, Sarojini. "A South African Indian Womanist Reading of the Character of Ruth." Pages 159–75 in *Other Ways of Reading: African Women and the Bible*. Edited by Musa W. Dube. Atlanta: Society of Biblical Literature, 2001.

———. "'Texts of Terror' Disguised as the 'Word of God': The Case of Esther 2:1–18 and the Conspiracy of Rape in the Bible." *Journal of Constructive Theology* 10 (2004): 59–79.

Nauck, August. *Tragicorum Graecorum Fragmenta: Supplementum adiecit Bruno Snell.* Hildesheim: Georg Olms Verlagsbuchhandlung, 1964.

Navarro Puerto, Mercedes. "Divine Image and Likeness: Women and Men in Genesis 1–3 as an Open System in the Context of Genesis 1–11." Pages 193–249 in *Torah.* Edited by Irmtraud Fischer and Mercedes Navarro Puerto with Andrea Taschl-Erber. The Bible and Women: An Encyclopaedia of Exegesis and Cultural History 1.1. Atlanta: Society of Biblical Literature, 2011.

———. *Los libros de Josué, Jueces y Rut.* Guía Espiritual del Antiguo Testamento. Barcelona/Madrid: Ciudad Nueva, 1995.

Neher, Martin. *Wesen und Wirken der Weisheit in der Sapientia Salomonis.* BZAW 333. Berlin: de Gruyter, 2004.

Nelson, Harold H. *The Wall Reliefs.* Vol. 1.1 of *The Great Hypostyle Hall at Karnak.* OIP 106. Chicago: Oriental Institute of the University of Chicago, 1981.

Newsom, Carol A. "Response to Norman Gottwald, 'Social Class and Ideology in Isaiah 40–55: An Eagletonian Reading.'" *Semeia* 59 (1992): 73–78.

———. "Woman and the Discourse of Patriarchal Wisdom: A Study of Proverbs 1–9." Pages 142–60 in *Gender and Difference in Ancient Israel.* Edited by Peggy L. Day. Minneapolis: Fortress, 1989.

Niditch, Susan. *Folklore and the Hebrew Bible.* Minneapolis: Fortress, 1993.

———. "Short Stories: The Book of Esther and the Theme of Woman as a Civilizing Force." Pages 195–209 in *Old Testament Interpretation Past, Present, and Future: Essays in Honor of Gene M. Tucker.* Edited by James Luther Mays, David L. Petersen, and Kent Harold Richards. Nashville: Abingdon, 1995.

———. *Underdogs and Tricksters: A Prelude to Biblical Folklore.* San Francisco: Harper & Row, 1987.

Nielsen, Kirsten. *Ruth: A Commentary.* OTL. Louisville: Westminster John Knox, 1997.

Nissinen, Martti. "Song of Songs and Sacred Marriage." Pages 173–218 in *Sacred Marriages: The Divine-Human Sexual Metaphor from Sumer to Early Christianity.* Edited by Martti Nissinen and Risto Uro. Winona Lake, Ind.: Eisenbrauns, 2008.

Nutt, Aurica, and Stephanie Feder, eds. *Esters unbekannte Seiten: Theologische Perspektiven auf ein vergessenes biblisches Buch: Festschrift für Marie-Theres Wacker.* Mainz: Grünewald, 2012.

O'Connor, Kathleen M. "Lamentations." Pages 187–91 in *The Women's Bible Commentary.* Edited by Carol Newsom and Sharon H. Ringe. 2nd ed. Louisville: Westminster John Knox, 1998.

———. "Lamentations." Pages 278–82 in *The Women's Bible Commentary.* Edited by Carol A. Newsom, Sharon H. Ringe, and Jacqueline E. Lapsley. 3rd ed. Louisville: Westminster John Knox, 2012.

Oded, Bustenay. "Where Is 'The Myth of the Empty Land' to Be Found?—Myth versus History." Pages 55–74 in *Judah and the Judeans in the Neo-Babylonian Period.*

Edited by Oded Lipschits and Joseph Blenkinsopp. Winona Lake, Ind.: Eisenbrauns, 2003.

Pahk, Johan Y.-S. *Il canto della gioia in Dio: L'itinerario sapienziale espresso dall'unità letteraria in Qohelet 8,16–9,10 e il parallelo di Gilgameš Me. Iii.* Dipartimento di Studi Asiatici. Series Minor 52. Naples: Istituto Universitario Orientale, 1996.

———. "The Significance of אשר in Qoh. 7,26: More Bitter Than Death Is the Woman, if She Is a Snare." Pages 373–83 in *Qohelet in the Context of Wisdom*. Edited by Antoon Schoors. BETL 136. Leuven: Peeters, 1998.

———. "A Syntactical and Contextual Consideration of 'iš in Qoh. IX 9." *VT* 51 (2001): 370–80.

Pasto, James. "The Origin, Expansion and Impact of the Hasmoneans in Light of Comparative Ethnographic Studies." Pages 166–201 in *Studies in Politics, Class and Material Culture*. Edited by Philip R. Davies and John Halligan. Vol. 3 of *Second Temple Studies*. Edited by Lester L. Grabbe. JSOTSup 340. Sheffield: Sheffield Academic, 2002.

Petersen, Silke. *Brot, Licht und Weinstock: Intertextuelle Analysen johanneischer Ich-bin-Worte*. NovTSup 127. Leiden: Brill, 2008.

Pham, Xuan Huong Thi. *Mourning in the Ancient Near East and the Hebrew Bible*. Sheffield: Sheffield Academic, 1999.

Philip, Tarja S. *Menstruation and Childbirth in the Bible: Fertility and Impurity*. New York: Lang, 2006.

Pietersma, Albert, and Benjamin G. Wright, eds. *A New English Translation of the Septuagint and the Other Greek Translations Traditionally Included under That Title*. Oxford: Oxford University Press, 2007.

Pomeroy, Sarah B. *Xenophon, Oeconomicus: A Social and Historical Commentary with a New English Translation*. Oxford: Clarendon, 1994.

Poser, Ruth. *Das Ezechielbuch als Traumaliteratur*. VTSup 154. Leiden: Brill, 2012.

Potts, Timothy F., et al. "Preliminary Report on the Eighth and Ninth Seasons of Excavations by the University of Sydney at Pella (Tabaqat Fahl), 1986 and 1987." *ADAJ* 32 (1988): 115–49.

Putnam, Ruth A. "Friendship." Pages 44–54 in *Reading Ruth: Contemporary Women Reclaim a Sacred Story*. Edited by Judith A. Kates and Gail Twersky Reimer. New York: Ballantine, 1996.

Rad, Gerhard von. *The Theology of Israel's Prophetic Traditions*. Vol. 2 of *Old Testament Theology*. Translated by D. M. G. Stalker. Louisville: Westminster John Knox, 2001.

———. *Weisheit in Israel*. 3rd ed. Neukirchen-Vluyn: Neukirchener, 1985.

———. *Wisdom in Israel*. Nashville: Abingdon, 1972.

Raiser, Konrad. "Klage als Befreiung." *Einwürfe* 5 (1988): 13–27.

Rakel, Claudia. *Judit—über Schönheit, Macht und Widerstand im Krieg: Eine feministisch-intertextuelle Lektüre*. BZAW 334. Berlin: de Gruyter, 2003.

Rapp, Ursula. "Der gottesfürchtigen Frau ein guter Mann? Zur Lektüre der Aussagen über gute und schlechte Ehefrauen im Sirachbuch." Pages 325–38 in *Auf den Spuren der schriftgelehrten Weisen: FS J. Marböck*. Edited by Irmtraud Fischer et al. BZAW 331. Berlin: de Gruyter, 2003.

———. "Weisheitsbeziehung und Geschlechterverhältnis: Untersuchungen zu Texten über Frauen und Ehe im Buch Jesus Sirach." Habilitationsschrift. Universität Bamberg, 2010.
Ravasi, Gianfranco. *Il Cantico dei Cantici*. Bologna: Dehoniane, 1992.
———. *Il Libro dei Salmi: Commento e attualizzazione*. Vol. 2. Lettura pastorale della Bibbia 14. Bologna: EDB, 1983.
———. "A Sion tutti sono nati! L'universalismo del salmo 87." *Parola Spirito e Vita* 16 (1979): 53–63.
———. "L'universalismo dei Salmi 8—47—87." *RivB* 43 (1995): 77–84.
Reddemann, Luise. *Imagination als heilsame Kraft*. Stuttgart: Klett Cotta, 2007.
Reʻemi, S. Paul. *God's People in Crisis: A Commentary on the Books of Amos and Lamentations*. ITC. Grand Rapids: Eerdmans, 1984.
Reimer, Gail Twersky. "Eschewing Esther/Embracing Esther: The Changing Representation of Biblical Heroines." Pages 207–19 in *Talking Back: Images of Jewish Women in American Popular Culture*. Edited by Joyce Antler. Hanover, N.H.: Brandeis University Press, 1998.
Rienstra, Marchienne Vroon. *Swallow's Nest: A Feminine Reading of the Psalms*. Grand Rapids: Eerdmans, 1992.
Riesener, Ingrid. "Frauenfeindschaft im Alten Testament? Zum Verständnis von Qoh 7,25-29." Pages 193–207 in *"Jedes Ding hat seine Zeit...": Studien zur israelitischen und altorientalischen Weisheit: Diethelm Michel zum 65. Geburtstag*. Edited by Anja A. Diesel et al. BZAW 241. Berlin: de Gruyter, 1996.
Roth, Martha T. "The Dowries of the Women of the Itti-Marduk-Balatu Family." *JAOS* 111, no. 1 (1991): 19–37.
Rudman, Dominic. "Woman as Divine Agent in Ecclesiastes." *JBL* 116 (1997): 411–27.
Ryan, Lisa. *For Such a Time as This: Your Identity, Purpose, and Passion*. Sisters, Ore.: Multnomah, 2001.
Sakenfeld, Katharine D. *Ruth*. IBC. Louisville: Westminster John Knox, 1999.
Salvaneschi, Enrica. *Cantico dei cantici: Interpretatio ludica*. Genova: Il Melangolo, 1982.
Sasson, Jack M. *Ruth: A New Translation with a Philological Commentary and a Formalist-Folklorist Interpretation*. JHNES. Baltimore: Johns Hopkins University Press, 1979.
Say Pa, Ana May. "Reading Ruth 3:1-5 from an Asian Woman's Perspective." Pages 47–59 in *Engaging the Bible in a Gendered World: An Introduction to Feminist Biblical Interpretation in Honor of Katharine Doob Sakenfeld*. Edited by Linda Day and Carolyn Pressler. Louisville: Westminster John Knox, 2006.
Scaiola, Donatella. *Rut: Nova versione, introduzione e commento*. I libri biblici Primo Testamento 23. Milan: Paoline, 2009.
———. "I Salmi imprecatori: il linguaggio violento dei Salmi: Preghiera e violenza." *RStB* 1–2 (2008): 61–79.
Schäfer, Peter. *Mirror of His Beauty: Feminine Images of God from the Bible to the Early Kabbalah*. Princeton: Princeton University Press, 2002.

Schellenberg, Annette. *Erkenntnis als Problem: Qohelet und die alttestamentliche Diskussion um das menschliche Erkennen.* OBO 188. Fribourg: Universitätsverlag; Göttingen: Vandenhoeck & Ruprecht, 2002.

Schimanowski, Gottfried. *Weisheit und Messias: Die jüdischen Voraussetzungen der urchristlichen Präexistenzchristologie.* WUNT 17. Tübingen: Mohr Siebeck, 1985.

Schipper, Bernd U. "Die Lehre des Amenemope und Prov 22,17–24,22—eine Neubestimmung des literarischen Verhältnisses." *ZAW* 117 (2005): 53–72 (part 1) and 232–48 (part 2).

Schoors, Antoon. "L'ambiguità della gioia in Qohelet." Pages 278–80 in *Il libro del Qohelet: Tradizione, redazione, teologia.* Edited by Giuseppe Bellia and Angelo Passaro. Cammini nello Spirito. Biblica 44. Milan: Paoline, 2001.

———. "Words Typical of Qohelet." Pages 17–39 in *Qohelet in the Context of Wisdom.* Edited by Antoon Schoors. BETL 136. Leuven: Peeters, 1998.

Schroer, Silvia. "Ancient Near Eastern Pictures as Keys to Biblical Texts." Pages 31–60 in *Torah.* Edited by Irmtraud Fischer and Mercedes Navarro Puerto with Andrea Taschl-Erber. The Bible and Women: An Encyclopaedia of Exegesis and Cultural History 1.1. Atlanta: Society of Biblical Literature, 2011.

———. "Frauenkörper als architektonische Elemente: Zum Hintergrund von Ps 114,12." Pages 425–50 in *Bilder als Quellen/Images as Sources: Studies on Ancient Near Eastern Artefacts and the Bible Inspired by the Work of Othmar Keel.* OBO special edition. Edited by Susanne Bickel et al. Fribourg: Academic Press and Göttingen: Vandenhoeck & Ruprecht, 2007.

———. *Die Ikonographie Palästinas/Israels und der Alte Orient: Eine Religionsgeschichte in Bildern (IPIAO).* Vol. 2, Mittelbronzezeit (2008). Vol. 3, Spätbronzezeit (2011). Fribourg: Academic Press.

———. "'Im Schatten deiner Flügel': Religionsgeschichtliche und feministische Blicke auf die Metaphorik der Flügel Gottes in den Psalmen, in Ex 19,4; Dtn 32,11 und in Mal 3,20." Pages 296–316 in *"Ihr Völker alle, klatscht in die Hände!" FS für Erhard S. Gerstenberger zum 65. Geburtstag.* Edited by Rainer Kessler et al. Exegese in unserer Zeit 3. Münster: LIT, 1997.

———. "Liebe und Tod im Ersten (Alten) Testament." Pages 35–52 in *Liebe und Tod: Gegensätze—Abhängigkeiten—Wechselwirkungen.* Edited by Peter Rusterholz and Sara M. Zwahlen. Bern: Haupt, 2006.

———. *Die Tiere in der Bibel: Eine kulturgeschichtliche Reise.* Freiburg: Herder, 2010.

———. "Wisdom: An Example of Jewish Intercultural Theology." Pages 555–65 in *Feminist Biblical Interpretation: A Compendium of Critical Commentary on the Books of the Bible and Related Literature.* Edited by Luise Schottroff and Marie-Theres Wacker. Grand Rapids: Eerdmans, 2012.

———. *Wisdom Has Built Her House: Studies on the Figure of Sophia in the Bible.* Collegeville, Minn.: Liturgical Press, 2000 (German original 1996).

———. "Die Zweiggöttin in Palästina/Israel: Von der Mittelbronze IIB-Zeit bis zu Jesus Sirach." Pages 201–25 in *Jerusalem: Texte—Bilder—Steine.* Edited by Max Küchler and Christoph Uehlinger. NTOA 6. Göttingen: Vandenhoeck & Ruprecht, 1987.

Schroer, Silvia, ed. *Images and Sources, Images and Gender: Contributions to the Hermeneutics of Reading Ancient Art.* Göttingen: Vandenhoeck & Ruprecht, 2006.

Schroer, Silvia, and Othmar Keel. *Vom ausgehenden Mesolithikum bis zur Frühbronzezeit.* Vol. 1 of *Die Ikonographie Palästinas/Israels und der Alte Orient: Eine Religionsgeschichte in Bildern (IPIAO).* Fribourg: Academic Press, 2005.

Schroer, Silvia, and Thomas Staubli. *Body Symbolism in the Bible.* Translated by Linda M. Maloney. Collegeville, Minn.: Liturgical Press, 2001 (German original 1998).

Schwienhorst-Schönberger, Ludger. "Das Hohelied." Pages 474–83 in *Einleitung in das Alte Testament.* Edited by Erich Zenger et al. 8th ed. Stuttgart: Kohlhammer, 2011.

———. *Nicht im Menschen gründet das Glück (Koh 2,24): Kohelet im Spannungsfeld jüdischer Weisheit und hellenistischer Philosophie.* HBS 2. Freiburg: Herder, 1994.

Seidl, Theodor. "Tänzerinnen, Weberinnen, Klagefrauen: Spuren von Frauenrollen in den Kulten des Alten Israel." Pages 105-29 in *Geschlechterdifferenz, Ritual und Religion.* Edited by Elmar Klinger et al. Würzburg: Echter, 2003.

Simian-Yofre, Horacio. "Conoscere la sapienza: Qohelet e Gen 2–3." Pages 314–36 in *Il libro del Qohelet: Tradizione, redazione, teologia.* Edited by Giuseppe Bellia and Angelo Passaro. Cammini nello Spirito. Biblica 44. Milano: Paoline, 2001.

Sinnott, Alice M. *The Personification of Wisdom.* SOTSMS. Aldershot: Ashgate, 2005.

Skehan, Patrick W., and Alexander A. Di Lella. *The Wisdom of Ben Sira: A New Translation with Notes by Patrick W. Skehan, Introduction and Commentary by Alexander A. Di Lella.* AB 39. New York: Doubleday, 1987.

Smart, Ninian. *Worldviews: Crosscultural Explorations of Human Beliefs.* New York: Charles Scribner's Sons, 1983.

Smend, Rudolph. *Die Weisheit Jesus Sirach.* Berlin: Reimer, 1906.

Solé i Auguets, Maria Claustre. *Déu, una paraula sempre oberta: El concepte de Déu en el Qohèlet.* Collectània Sant Pacià 65. Barcelona: Facultat de Teologia de Catalunya, 1999.

Sonnet, Jean-Pierre. "Le Cantique, entre érotique et mystique: sanctuaire de la parole échangée." *NRTh* 119 (1997): 481–502.

Spiegel, Celina. "The World Remade: The Book of Esther." Pages 191–203 in *Out of the Garden: Women Writers on the Bible.* Edited by Christina Büchmann and Celina Spiegel. New York: Fawcett Columbine, 1994.

Stanton, Elizabeth Cady, and the Revising Committee. *The Woman's Bible.* Seattle: Seattle Coalition on Women and Religion. 1895-98. Repr., 1974.

Staubli, Thomas. *Begleiter durch das Erste Testament.* Düsseldorf: Patmos, 1999.

———. "Land der sprießenden Zweige." *BK* 60 (2005): 16–22.

Steck, Odil Hannes. "Zion als Gelände und Gestalt: Überlegungen zur Wahrnehmung Jerusalems als Stadt und Frau im Alten Testament." *ZTK* 86 (1989): 261–81.

Stolper, Matthew W. *Entrepreneurs and the Empire: The Murašû Archive, the Murašû Firm, and Persian Rule in Babylonia.* Leiden: Nederlands Historisch-Archaeologisch Instituut te Istanbul, 1985.

Strotmann, Angelika. "Sirach (Ecclesiasticus): On the Difficult Relation between Divine Wisdom and Real Women in an Androcentric Document." Pages 539–54 in *Feminist Biblical Interpretation: A Compendium of Critical Commentary on the Books of the Bible and Related Literature.* Edited by Luise Schottroff and Marie-Theres Wacker. Grand Rapids: Eerdmans, 2012.

Sutter Rehmann, Luzia. "Testament of Job: Job, Dinah and Their Daughters." Pages 586–95 in *Feminist Biblical Interpretation: A Compendium of Critical Commentary on the Books of the Bible and Related Literature*. Edited by Luise Schottroff and Marie-Theres Wacker. Grand Rapids: Eerdmans, 2012.

Talshir, Zipora. *1 Esdras: A Text Critical Commentary*. Atlanta: Society of Biblical Literature, 2001.

Tan, Nancy Nam Hoon. *The "Foreignness" of the Foreign Woman in Proverbs 1–9: A Study of the Origin and the Development of a Biblical Motif*. BZAW 381. Berlin: de Gruyter, 2008.

Tanner, Beth LaNeel. *The Books of Psalms through the Lens of Intertextuality*. Studies in Biblical Literature 26. New York: Lang, 2001.

Tatius, Achilles. *Leucippe and Clitophon*. Translated by S. Gaselee. LCL 45. London: Heinemann, 1961.

Terrien, Samuel. "The Omphalos Myth and the Hebrew Religion." *VT* 20 (1970): 314–38.

Toorn, Karel van der. "Scholars at the Oriental Court." Pages 37–55 in *The Book of Daniel: Composition and Reception*. Edited by John J. Collins and Peter W. Flint. VTSup 83.1. Leiden: Brill, 2002.

Trenchard, Warren C. *Ben Sira's View of Women: A Literary Analysis*. BJS 38. Chico, Calif.: Scholars Press, 1982.

Trible, Phyllis. "Depatriarchalizing in Biblical Interpretation." *JAAR* 41 (1973): 30–48. Repr., pages 217–40 in *The Jewish Woman: New Perspectives*. Edited by Elizabeth Koltun. New York: Schocken, 1976.

———. *God and the Rhetoric of Sexuality*. London: SCM, 1992.

———. "Love's Lyric Redeemed." Pages 100–120 in *A Feminist Companion to the Song of Songs*. Edited by Athalya Brenner. FCB 1. Sheffield: Sheffield Academic, 1993.

Tull, Patricia. *Remember the Former Things: The Recollection of Previous Texts in Second Isaiah*. SBLDS 161. Atlanta: Scholars Press, 1997.

Vignolo, Roberto. "Il legame più complesso: Luci e ombre delle relazioni parentali nella Bibbia." Pages 147–215 in *Genitori e figli nella famiglia affettiva*. Edited Giuseppe Angelini. Disputatio. Milan: Glossa, 2002.

Vignolo, Roberto, and Laura Giangreco. "Paternità e maternità." Pages 980–85 in *Temi teologici della Bibbia*. Edited by Romano Penna et al. Dizionari San Paolo. Cinisello Balsamo: Edizioni San Paolo, 2010.

Vilchez Lindez, José. *Eclesiastés o Qohélet*. Nueva Biblia Española. Sapienciales 3. Estella: Verbo Divino, 1994.

———. *Rut y Ester*. Nueva Biblia Española. Narrations 2. Estella: Verbo Divino, 1998.

Vogels, Walter. "'It Is Not Good That the 'Mensch' Should Be Alone: I Will Make Him/Her a Helper Fit for Him/Her' (Gen 2,18)." *EgT* 9 (1978): 9–35.

Wachsmith, Curt, and Otto Hense, eds. *Ioannis Stobaei Anthologium*. Vol. 4 of *Anthologii libri quarti partem priorem ab Ottone Hense editam continens*. Berlin: Weidman, 1909.

Wacker, Marie-Theres. "Baruch: Mail form Distant Shores." Pages 531–38 in *Feminist Biblical Interpretation: A Compendium of Critical Commentary on the Books of the*

Bible and Related Literature. Edited by Luise Schottroff and Marie-Theres Wacker. Grand Rapids: Eerdmans, 2012.

———. "Books of Chronicles: In the Vestibule of Women." Pages 178–91 in *Feminist Biblical Interpretation: A Compendium of Critical Commentary on the Books of the Bible and Related Literature*. Edited by Luise Schottroff and Marie-Theres Wacker. Grand Rapids: Eerdmans, 2012.

———. *Ester: Jüdin—Königin—Retterin*. Stuttgart: Katholisches Bibelwerk, 2006.

———. "Tora für Frauen, verwirrende Beziehungen und eine geflügelte Gottheit: Genderforschung zum Alten Testament am Beispiel des Rut-Buches." *Concilium* 48, no. 4 (2012): 413–20.

Wacker, Marie-Theres, Klara Butting, and Gerard Minnaard, eds. *Ester: Mit Beiträgen aus Judentum, Christentum, Islam, Literatur, Kunst*. Wittingen: Erev-Rav, 2005.

Webster, Jane S. "Sophia: Engendering Wisdom in Proverbs, Ben Sira and the Wisdom of Solomon." *JSOT* 78 (1998): 63–79.

Weems, Renita. *Battered Love: Marriage, Sex, and Violence in the Hebrew Prophets*. 2nd ed. Minneapolis: Fortress, 1996.

Wertheimer, Solomon A., ed. *Batei Midrashot*. Vol. 2. 2nd ed. Jerusalem: Mosad ha-Rav Kuk, 1968.

West, Martin L., ed. *Archilochus, Hipponax, Theognidea*. Vol. 1 of *Iambi et elegi graeci ante Alexandrum cantati*. 2nd ed. Oxford: Oxford University Press, 1989.

———. *Hesiod, Works and Days: Edited with Prolegomena and Commentary by M. L. West*. Oxford: Clarendon, 1978.

Westbrook, Raymond. *Property and the Family in Biblical Law*. JSOTSup 113. Sheffield: Sheffield Academic, 1991.

White, Sidnie Ann. "Esther: A Feminine Model for Jewish Diaspora." Pages 161–77 in *Gender and Difference in Ancient Israel*. Edited by Peggy L. Day. Minneapolis: Fortress, 1989.

Whybray, Roger N. *The Book of Proverbs: A Survey of Modern Studies*. Leiden: Brill, 1995.

Willetts, Ronald F. *The Law Code of Gortyn, Edited with Introduction, Translation and a Commentary*. Berlin: de Gruyter, 1967.

Willi, Thomas. *1 Chr 1–10*. Vol 1 of *Chronik*. BKAT 24. Neukirchen-Vluyn: Neukirchener, 2009.

Willi-Plein, Ina. "'Eschet Chajil': Weisheit und Lebensart Israels in der Perserzeit." Pages 411–25 in *Exegese vor Ort: Festschrift für Peter Welten zum 65. Geburtstag*. Edited by Christl Maier et al. Leipzig: Evangelische Verlagsanstalt, 2001.

———. "Problems of Intermarriage in Postexilic Times." Pages 177*–89* in *Shai le-Sara Japhet: Studies in the Bible, its Exegesis and its Language*. Edited by Moshe Bar-Asher et al. Jerusalem: Mosad Bialik, 2007.

Wills, Lawrence M., ed. *Ancient Jewish Novels: An Anthology*. Oxford: Oxford University Press, 2002.

Winter, Urs. *Frau und Göttin: Exegetische und ikonographische Studien zum weiblichen Gottesbild im Alten Israel und in dessen Umwelt*. 2nd ed. OBO 53. Fribourg: Universitätsverlag; Göttingen: Vandenhoeck & Ruprecht, 1987.

———. "Der 'Lebensbaum' in der altorientalischen Bildsymbolik." Pages 57–88 in ... *Bäume braucht man doch: Das Symbol des Baumes zwischen Hoffnung und Zerstörung*. Edited by Harald Schweizer. Sigmaringen: Thorbecke, 1986.

———. "Der stilisierte Baum: Zu einem auffälligen Aspekt altorientalischer Baumsymbolik und seiner Rezeption im Alten Testament." *BK* 41 (1986): 171–77.

Wiseman, Donald J. "A New Text of the Babylonian Poem of the Righteous Sufferer." *Anatolian Studies* 30 (1980): 101–7.

Wolde, Ellen van. "The Development of Job: Mrs Job as Catalyst." Pages 201–21 in *A Feminist Companion to Wisdom Literature*. Edited by Athalya Brenner. FCB 9. Sheffield: Sheffield Academic, 1995.

Wolff, Hans Walter. *Anthropology of the Old Testament*. Translated by Margaret Kohl. London: SCM, 1974.

Wolkstein, Diane. "Esther's Story." Pages 198–206 in *A Feminist Companion to Esther, Judith and Susanna*. Edited by Athalya Brenner. FCB 7. Sheffield: Sheffield Academic, 1995.

Wright, John W. "A Tale of Three Cities: Urban Gates, Squares and Power in Iron Age II, Neo-Babylonian and Achaemenid Judah." Pages 19–50 in *Studies in Politics, Class and Material Culture*. Edited by Philip R. Davies and John Halligan. Vol. 3 of *Second Temple Studies*. Edited by Lester L. Grabbe. Sheffield: Sheffield Academic, 2002.

Wyler, Bea. "Esther: The Incomplete Emancipation of a Queen." Pages 111–35 in *A Feminist Companion to Esther, Judith and Susanna*. Edited by Athalya Brenner. FCB 7. Sheffield: Sheffield Academic, 1995.

Yoder, Christine R. *Wisdom as a Woman of Substance: A Socioeconomic Reading of Proverbs 1–9 and 31:10–31*. BZAW 304. Berlin: de Gruyter, 2001.

Zaeske, Susan. "Unveiling Esther as a Pragmatic Radical Rhetoric." *Philosophy and Rhetoric* 33 (2000): 193–220.

Zakovitch, Yair. *Das Buch Rut: Ein jüdischer Kommentar*. SBS 177. Stuttgart: Katholisches Bibelwerk, 1999.

Zapff, Burkard M. *Jesus Sirach 25–51*. NEchtB 39. Würzburg: Echter, 2010.

Zenger, Erich. *Das Buch Ruth*. ZBKAT 8. Zürich: Theologischer, 1986.

———. "'Wie das Kind bei mir …': Das weibliche Gottesbild von Ps 131." Pages 177–95 in *"Gott bin ich, kein Mann": Beiträge zur Hermeneutik der biblischen Gottesrede: FS für Helen Schüngel-Straumann zum 65. Geburtstag*. Edited by Ilona Riedel-Spangenberger and Erich Zenger. Paderborn: Ferdinand Schöningh, 2006.

———. "Zion, als Mutter der Völker in Psalm 87." Pages 117–50 in Norbert Lohfink and Erich Zenger. *Der Gott Israels und die Völker: Untersuchungen zum Jesajabuch und zu den Psalmen*. SBS 154. Stuttgart: Katholisches Bibelwerk, 1994.

Zonana, Joyce. "Esther, Vashti, and the Duty of Disobedience in Nineteenth Century Hermeneutics." Pages 228–49 in *Through a Glass Darkly: Essays in the Religious Imagination*. Edited by John C. Hawley. New York: Fordham University Press, 1996.

Zorell, Franciscus. *Lexicon Hebraicum Veteris Testamenti*. Rome: Pontifical Biblical Institute, 1984.

Contributors

Ulrike Bail is Extraordinary Professor of Old Testament at Ruhr-Universität Bochum, Germany. She is working as a freelance writer and teacher of German in Luxemburg. Her main research areas are the Psalms, traditions of lament, and prophets. In her interpretation, she uses literary methods as well as postmodern concepts of text and space in a feminist perspective. She is co-editor of *Bibel in gerechter Sprache* (Gütersloher, 2006; 4th ed., 2011), the new German translation of the Bible in inclusive language. She was awarded prizes for her book *Die verzogene Sehnsucht hinkt an ihren Ort: Literarische Überlebensstrategien nach der Zerstörung Jerusalems im Alten Testament* (Gütersloher, 2004) and for her poems. Recently she published the poem collection *Wundklee streut aus: 47 Gedichte über theodora* (Conte, 2011) and essays on Psalms, Habbakuk, and Zephaniah in *Feminist Biblical Interpretation: A Compendium of Critical Commentary on the Book of the Bible and Related Literature* (ed. L. Schottroff and M.-T. Wacker; trans. Lisa E. Dahill et al., Eerdmans, 2012). For more information, see www.ulrike-bail.de.

Gianni Barbiero, a member of the Roman-Catholic order of the Salesians of Don Bosco, is Professor of Old Testament Exegesis at the Pontifical Biblical Institute in Rome, Italy. He earned his PhD in 1988 and his habilitation in 1998 from St. Georgen (Frankfurt) supervised by Norbert Lohfink. He taught at Messina, Italy (1982–1992), and at the college of his religious order in Benediktbeuern, Germany (1992–2003). His current research focuses on Psalms, Song of Songs, and Jeremiah, as his recent publications demonstrate: *Il regno di JHWH e del suo Messia: Salmi scelti dal primo libro del Salterio* (Città Nuova, 2008); *Cantico dei Cantici* (Paoline, 2004); *Song of Songs: A Close Reading* (Brill, 2011); *"Tu mi hai sedotto, Signore": Le confessioni di Geremia alla luce della sua vocazione profetica* (Gregorian and Biblical Press, 2013).

Gerlinde Baumann is Extraordinary Professor of Old Testament at the University of Marburg, Germany, and research fellow at the University of Pretoria, South Africa. She works as a freelance translator, writer, editor, and lecturer. Her main research areas are wisdom literature, images of the divine, and hermeneutics of the Hebrew Bible. She has published numerous books and articles for academic and lay readers, among them *Die Weisheitsgestalt in Proverbien 1–9: Traditionsgeschichtliche und theologische Studien* (Mohr Siebeck, 1996); *Love and Violence: The Imagery of Marriage for YHWH and Israel in the Prophetic Books* (Liturgical Press, 2003; the German original received a prize in 2000); *Gottesbilder der Gewalt im Alten Testament verstehen* (Wissenschaftliche Buchgesellschaft, 2006; trans. to Brazilian Portuguese in 2011); and "Hermeneutical Perspectives on Violence against Women and on Divine Violence in German-Speaking Old Testament Exegesis," in *Global Hermeneutics? Reflections and Consequences* (ed. K. Holter and L.C. Jonker; IVBS online publication; see http://ivbs.sbl-site.org/uploads/JONKER~1.PDF).

Nuria Calduch-Benages, born in Barcelona, Spain, is Professor of Old Testament at the Pontifical Gregorian University in Rome, Italy. She edits book reviews for the journal *Biblica* (Pontifical Biblical Institute) and serves as consultant at the Cardinal-Bea-Center for Jewish Studies (Rome). She is Vice-President of the International Society for the Study of Deuterocanonical and Cognate Literature and editorial board member of *Estudios Bíblicos* and *Vetus Testamentum*. Her research focuses on wisdom literature, especially the book of Ben Sira. Among her recent publications are *En el crisol de la prueba: Estudio exegético de Sir 2,1–18* (Verbo Divino, 1997); with J. Liesen and J. Ferrer, *The Wisdom of the Scribe* (Verbo Divino, 2003); with J. Liesen, *History and Identity: How Israel's Later Authors Viewed Its Earlier History* (de Gruyter, 2006); *The Perfume of the Gospel: Jesus' Encounters with Women* (Gregorian and Biblical Press, 2012); and *Wisdom for Life* (de Gruyter, 2014).

Tamara Cohn Eskenazi is Professor of Bible at the Hebrew Union College–Jewish Institute of Religion in Los Angeles, California. She is editor-in-chief of *The Torah: A Women's Commentary* (Union of Reform Judaism Press, 2008), the winner (with Andrea L. Weiss) of the 2008 Jewish Book of the Year Award. She has served in several committees of the Society of Biblical Literature and on several editorial boards of leading journals. Her research focuses on the reconstruction of Jewish life in the Persian period, on the role of women in the biblical world, and on the significance of the Hebrew Bible for contemporary communities. She co-authored *The JPS Bible Commentary: Ruth* (with Tikva Frymer-Kensky; Jewish Publication Society, 2011), which won the National Jewish Book Award for Women Studies in 2012. She also received a National Endowment for the Humanities Fellowship for her project on "Out from the Shadows: Biblical Women in the Persian Period (Sixth to Fourth Centuries BCE)." A volume in her honor, titled *Making a Difference: Essays on Bible and*

Judaism in Honor of Tamara Cohn Eskenazi (ed. D. J. A. Clines et al.; Sheffield Phoenix) appeared in 2012.

Vittoria D'Alario is Professor of Old Testament at the Pontifical Faculty of Theology in South Italy (San Luigi Section) in Naples, Italy. Her main subject of research is the book of Qoheleth. She has authored numerous books and articles, including "L'assurdità del male nella teodicea del Qohelet," in *Initium Sapientiae: Scritti in onore di Franco Festorazzi nel suo 70° compleanno* (ed. R. Fabris; Dehoniane, 2000); "Struttura e teologia del libro del Qohelet," in *Il libro del Qohelet: Traduzione, redazione, teologia* (ed. G. Bellia and A. Pasaro; Paoline, 2001); "Qohelet e l'apocalittica: Il significato del termine 'olam in Qo 3,11," in *Tempo ed eternità: In dialogo con Ugo Vanni S.I.* (ed. A. Casalegno; Cinisello Balsamo, 2002); "Qoèlet," in *Temi teologici della Bibbia* (ed. R. Penna et al.; Cinisello Balsamo, 2010); and "Il silenzio di Dio nell'esperienza di Giobbe e di Qoelet," in *Ricercare la sapienza di tutti gli antichi (Sir 39, 1): Miscellanea in onore di Gian Luigi Prato* (ed. M. Milani and M. Zappella; Dehoniane, 2013).

Isabel Gómez-Acebo is Professor (emerita) at the Pontifical University of Comillas in Madrid, Spain. She is a founding member of the Association of Spanish Theologians (ATE) and of the School of Feminist Theology in Andalusia (EFETA; see http://www.efeta.org/EN/). Her research focuses on spirituality and female characters of the Bible. She has edited twenty-four volumes of the series En clave de mujer (Desclée de Brouwer). Her recent publications include "Personajes femeninos en el libro de Ester," *Reseña Bíblica* 56 (2007); *Lucas: Guía de lectura al evangelio de Lucas* (EVD, 2008); and "Aportaciones a la familia del Libro de la Vida," in *El libro de la Vida de santa Teresa de Jesús* (Burgos, 2011).

Miren J. Guevara Llaguno is Professor of Old Testament (Pentateuch and Historical Books) at the Faculty of Theology of the University of Granada, Spain, and also teaches in the postgraduate masters program in the Department of Semitic Studies. She is coordinator of university extension and Vice Director of the Department of Holy Scripture. Her research interests are the reception of the Hebrew Bible in the New Testament and the relationship between the Bible and culture, with a focus on the Bible in soap operas. She has authored *Esplendor en la diáspora: La tradición de José (Gn 37-50) y sus relecturas en la literatura bíblica y parabíblica* (Verbo Divino, 2006); *Proyecto Nazaret 1: En la Iglesia; 2: Comunidad de bienes* (with J. J. Gómez-Escalonilla, J. M. Rodríguez, and A. Villar; Edelvives and Verbo Divino, 2010); and *Los apócrifos posmodernos* (Edelvives, 2012).

Sara Japhet is Yehezkel Kaufmann Professor (emerita) of Bible at the Hebrew University of Jerusalem and until 2012 was editor of *Shnaton: An Annual for Biblical and Ancient Near Eastern Studies*. She held positions as chairperson and member of academic committees in Israel and abroad as well as prestigious visiting professorships in the United States and Europe. She served, among others, as the Chairperson of the Department of Bible at the Hebrew University of Jerusalem (1984–1986), the Chairperson of the Institute of Jewish Studies (1986–1989), the Director of the National and University Library (1997–2001), and the President of the World Union of Jewish Studies (2006–2009). In 2004 she was awarded the prestigious Israel Prize for Biblical Studies. Her research interests are the history, society, religion, and literature of Israel in the biblical period, biblical law and legal traditions, and the history of the interpretation of the Bible. She has widely published on Chronicles and the restoration period, for example, *The Ideology of the Book of Chronicles and Its Place in Biblical Thought* (3rd ed.; Eisenbrauns, 2009); *I and II Chronicles: A Commentary* (SCM, 1993; Herder, 2002–2003); *From the Rivers of Babylon to the Highlands of Judah: Collected Studies on the Restoration Period* (Eisenbrauns, 2006). She also authored books and articles on biblical exegesis, such as *Collected Studies in Biblical Exegesis* (Mosad Bialik, 2008) and *A Commentary on Ezra-Nehemiah* (Magnes, forthcoming).

Nancy C. Lee is Professor of Religious Studies at Elmhurst College near Chicago and Extraordinary Visiting Professor at the University of Stellenbosch in South Africa. In 1996–1997 she was a Fulbright Fellow to Croatia and Bosnia and co-founded the section on Lamentations in the Society of Biblical Literature. Her research focuses on lament traditions in the Hebrew Bible and across ancient and contemporary cultures, as reflected in her "Lamentations and Polemic: The Rejection/Reception History of Women's Lament ... and Syria," *Interpretation* 67 (2013). Another research topic is oral poetic artistry in the Hebrew Bible in relation to a Hebraic woman's lyrical tradition also utilized by women prophets. Her books include *The Singers of Lamentations: Cities under Siege, from Ur to Jerusalem to Sarajevo* (Brill, 2002); *Lyrics of Lament: From Tragedy to Transformation* (Fortress, 2010); and *Hannah and Hanneviʾah: Hearing a Woman's Lyrical Tradition and Women Biblical Prophets* (Wipf & Stock, forthcoming).

Christl M. Maier is Professor of Old Testament at the University of Marburg, Germany. In 2003–2006 she taught at Yale Divinity School, New Haven, Connecticut. She is editor-in-chief of Supplements to Vetus Testamentum and a member of the editorial boards of *lectio difficilior*, the *Journal of Biblical Literature*, and the *Journal for the Study of the Old Testament*. Her research focuses on prophecy and wisdom literature in the Hebrew Bible, with special interests in feminist hermeneutics and theories of space. Her recent publications include *Daughter Zion, Mother Zion: Gender, Space, and the Sacred in Ancient Israel* (Fortress, 2008); *Constructions of Space V: Place, Space, and Identity in the Ancient Mediterranean World* (co-edited with G. Prinsloo; Bloomsbury T&T Clark, 2013); and *Prophecy and Power: Jeremiah in Feminist and Postcolonial Perspective* (co-edited with C. J. Sharp; Bloomsbury T&T Clark, 2013).

Susan Niditch is Samuel Green Professor of Religion at Amherst College, Amherst, Massachusetts. She has widely published on biblical and Jewish women, war and ethics in the Hebrew Bible, and biblical and Jewish folklore. Her publications include *War in the Hebrew Bible: A Study in the Ethics of Violence* (Oxford University Press, 1993); *Judges: A Commentary* (Westminster John Knox, 2008); and *"My Brother Esau Is a Hairy Man": Hair and Identity in Ancient Israel* (Oxford University Press, 2008). A new book, forthcoming in the fall of 2015 (Yale University Press), is tentatively entitled "The Responsive Self: Personal Religion in Biblical Literature of the Neo-Babylonian and Persian Periods."

Donatella Scaiola is Professor at the Department of Missiology of the Pontifical Urbaniana University in Rome, Italy. She also teaches Biblical Hebrew at the Department of Theology and Old Testament Exegesis at the School of Theology of Northern Italy in Milan. She is a member of the Biblical Association of Italy (ABI) and serves as a representative of ABI at the Section of the Biblical Apostolate (SAB) as well as at the coordinating council of Italian Theologians. She is editor-in-chief of the journal *Parole di Vita* and a member of the editorial board of *Euntes Docete*. Her research focuses on the Psalms and the Twelve Prophets. Among her recent publications are *Servire il Signore: Linee di una teologia biblica della missione nell'Antico Testamento* (Urbaniana University Press, 2008); "I Salmi imprecatori; il linguaggio violento dei Salmi: Preghiera e violenza," *RStB* 1–2 (2008); and *Ruth* (Paoline, 2009); *I Dodici Profeti: Perché «Minori?»; Esegesi e teologia* (EDB, 2011); *Abdia, Giona, Michea* (Edizioni San Paolo, 2012); *Naum, Abacuc, Sofonia* (Edizioni San Paolo, 2013) and *La donna perfetta: Interpretazioni di un poema biblico* (EDB, 2014).

Silvia Schroer, a Roman Catholic theologian, is Professor of Old Testament and the Biblical World at the University of Bern, Switzerland. She is co-founder and (with Tal Ilan) co-editor of *lectio difficilior*, the first electronic journal for feminist exegesis in Europe (www.lectio.unibe.ch). Since 2011 she has been a member of the National Research Council of the Swiss National

Science Foundation (SNF). Being an expert in feminist interpretation and ancient Near Eastern iconography, she has published fundamental studies in these research areas, for example, a compendium of the history of religion in Palestine/Israel on the basis of iconographic findings titled *Die Ikonographie Palästinas/Israels und der Alte Orient: Eine Religionsgeschichte in Bildern*, vol. 1: *Vom ausgehenden Mesolithikum bis zur Frühbronzezeit* (with O. Keel; 3 vols.; Academic Press, 2005–2011). Many of her books have been translated into other languages, such as, *Wisdom Has Built Her House: Studies on the Figure of Sophia in the Bible* (trans. L. M. Maloney and W. McDonough; Liturgical Press, 2000). She also writes popular books for a wider audience interested in the Bible, among them *Eva—Mutter alles Lebendigen: Frauen- und Göttinnenidole aus dem Alten Orient* (with O. Keel; 3rd ed.; Academic Press, 2010) and *Menschenbilder der Bibel* (with T. Staubli; Patmos, 2014).

Index of Ancient Sources

Hebrew Bible/Old Testament

Genesis
- 1:1–2:4a — 62
- 1:2–3 — 166, 67
- 1:28 — 144
- 2 — 131
- 2–3 — 258
- 2:4 — 253
- 2:10–14 — 177
- 2:18 — 122, 220
- 2:20 — 220
- 2:21–22 — 154
- 2:23 — 225
- 2:24 — 224, 233, 240, 251
- 3:6 — 115
- 3:16 — 227
- 3:20 — 220
- 4:1 — 167
- 10 — 44
- 10:1 — 253
- 12:1 — 224, 252
- 12:10 — 251
- 12:14–17 — 280
- 19:30–38 — 159, 245
- 20:2 — 280
- 24:4–9 — 252
- 24:28 — 240
- 24:58 — 252
- 25:1–4 — 44
- 25:4 — 46
- 25:12–16 — 44
- 26:1 — 251
- 36 — 44
- 36:1 — 253
- 37–50 — 278
- 37:21 — 228
- 38 — 47, 159
- 38:11 — 25, 240
- 38:15–16 — 224
- 39:7–12 — 84
- 41:43–57 — 251
- 42:5 — 251
- 43:1 — 251

Exodus
- 1–3 — 285
- 1:15–22 — 159
- 12:48 — 245
- 13:21 — 69
- 15:23 — 239
- 19:4 — 140
- 19:15 — 21
- 20:17 — 281
- 21:2–6 — 48
- 34:14 — 230
- 34:22 — 248

Leviticus
- 7:11–21 — 29
- 17:7 — 238
- 19:9–10 — 249
- 19:33 — 245
- 22:13 — 25, 240
- 22:21 — 29
- 23:15–21 — 248
- 24:16 — 88
- 25:23–28 — 249

Numbers		16:17	228
9:14	245	21:19–23	280
12	209		
22–24	245	1 Samuel	
25	245	19:8–17	159
26:33	43, 46	25	159, 267
27:1–11	43	25:1–13	267
27:8	49	25:1–42	285
28:26–31	248	25:24	267
30	29	25:28	267
36:8	49		
		2 Samuel	
Deuteronomy		2:14–22	159
2:8–9	245	6:16	156
4:4	240	6:20–23	38
4:24	230	7:27	250
5:9	230	8:16	38
6:4–5	230–31	11:1–17	278–79
6:5	69	12	42, 187
7:1–6	22	13	36, 42, 190–93
10:18	245	13:15	280
12:9–10	69	13:19	191
20:19	154	13:20	190, 192,
23:3–6	245	14	36, 267
23:4–7	22, 24	14:12	267
24:17	90, 245	14:17	267
24:19	249	15:2	175
24:19–22	90	20	36
25	249	20:4–22	267
25:5–10	48	20:18–19	267
25:7	174	21:8–14	159
32:11	140	23:18	38
32:18	134		
		1 Kings	
Joshua		3:1	49
17:6	46	3:16–27	36
19:50	47	7:14	38
24:30	47	8:1–10	50
		9:24	39, 49
Judges		10:1–10	38
4–5	286	10:13	38
4:17–22	284	11	51
5:2	228	11:1–10	36
5:24–27	284	11:2	240
5:28–30	156	11:3	36

INDEX OF ANCIENT SOURCES

15:33	37	Ezekiel	
16:6	46	3:17	212
17:8–24	36	16	284
		16:25	116–17
2 Kings		23	202, 284
2:8	167	23:33	192
4:1	25	47:1–12	177
4:1–37	36		
9:30–34	156	Hosea	
11:1–16	38	1–3	202
11:2	40	9:8	212
12:22	40–41		
22:14–20	38	Micah	
25	42, 52	5:1	46
		7:4	212
Isaiah			
13:21	228	Psalms	
22:4	206	1	154
43:2–3	232	5:12	194
52:13–53:12	278	6	187
54:1	192	7:11	194
54:1–10	175	10:14	194
56:3–8	24	14:6	194
57:7	85	16:8–9	186
62:4	192	16:9–11	232
66:7–14	175	17:7–9	138
		17:15	135
Jeremiah		22:2–3	168
1:5	167–68	22:5–6	168
2:13	222	22:7–9	169
3:1–3	202	22:10	183
3:3–5	85	22:10–11	133–44, 168–70
4:17	192	23:2	194
6:17	212	24:2	178
7:16	205	27:1	194
9	205	27:10	171
9:17–21	191	28:2	183
11:14	205	31:14	192
12:1	204	31:17	137
14:11	205	31:21	194
15:1	205	36:7	161
17:8	154	40:7–11	161
17:13	222	41:13	137
51:43	190, 192	46:5	177
		50:2	219

INDEX OF ANCIENT SOURCES

Psalms (cont.)
51:1	187
55	190–93
55:4–6	192
55:7–9	193
55:14	191
57:2	138
59:8	185
59:17	194
61:4–5	138
63:2	185
63:8–9	138
68:22	228
69:13	174
70:3	171
71:5–9	171
71:13	171
71:17–18	171
71:24	171
72:1–2	161
85:14	161
87	172–78
87:1–3	174–75
87:4–6	175–76
87:7	177
90:2	134
91:1–2	194
91:1–5	138
102	180
102:1–8	184–85
102:9	185
104	142
104:29	137
109:4	180
111:10	64
118:19–20	175
127:5	174
130:2	138
131:1–2	170
131:2	134
139:13–16	166–68
139:15	134
144:12	154

Job
1:21	134
2:3	87
2:5	87
2:9	87–89
2:9 LXX	88–89
2:9–10	165
10:8–11	167
22:9	90
24:3	90
24:21	90
28	64, 73, 160–61
28:28	64
29:12–13	90
29:12–16	91
31:9–10	91
31:16–17	90
31:21	175
39–41	141–43
39	132
42:13	87
42:14–15	89
42:15	80

Proverbs
1–9	59–63, 66, 69, 74, 81, 83–86
1:2–3	160
1:7	64
1:8	29, 86, 91
1:20–21	59
1:20–33	59, 66
1:22–33	59, 61
2:6	84
2:17	84
3:16–17	59
3:16–18	61
3:18	61, 144
4:6	59, 61
4:8–9	59
5:3–5	99
5:3–14	29
5:9–10	82
5:9–14	84
5:15–18	222
5:15–19	84, 222

INDEX OF ANCIENT SOURCES

5:19	29, 218	12:26	79
6:20	29, 86, 91	14:1	80
6:20–35	29, 84	15:25	89
6:24	84	17:23	79
6:26	84	19:14	80, 120
7:1–27	29	21:9	81, 116
7:4	59, 61	21:19	116
7:6	154–56	22:14	83
7:6–27	228	22:17–23:11	132
7:14	84	22:22	174
7:14–15	29	23:10	89
7:14–20	84	23:27–28	83–84
7:16	82	25:1	78
7:16–17	29	25:8	116
7:22	97	25:17	116
7:25–27	99	25:20	116
7:26–27	85	25:24	116
8	59	26:1–4	118–19
8:1–3	59	26:7	116
8:1–21	160	27:15	81
8:4–11	59	31	30
8:4–36	61	31:1	86
8:11	81	31:1–9	28, 83
8:12–21	59	31:2	29
8:13	64, 66	31:10	28, 81
8:14–16	87	31:10–31	12, 28–29, 66, 81–83, 91, 218
8:15–16	61, 70, 160		
8:19	61, 66	31:11–12	118, 122–23
8:22	61	31:14	21
8:22–31	60, 64, 132, 162–63	31:15	28, 30
8:24–25	61	31:17	21
8:30	61	31:21	28
8:31	62	31:22	29
8:32–36	60	31:23	82, 123, 174
9:1–6	66, 81	31:24	28
9:1–9	59	31:26	87
9:10	64	31:28	29
9:11	59	31:30	218
9:13	84		
9:13–18	60	Ruth	
10:1	86	1:1	251
10:6	79	1:1–4	244
11:22	80	1:4	238
12:4	80	1:6	239, 241, 244
12:5	79	1:7	223

INDEX OF ANCIENT SOURCES

Ruth (cont.)		2:1–2	150
1:8	25–26, 240	2:4	217
1:11	239	2:6	221
1:14	239–40	2:7	152, 218, 220–21
1:16	240	2:8–17	221, 224–25
1:18	246	2:9	220
1:19	25, 243	2:10	219–20, 221, 224
1:20	239, 243	2:13	219–20, 221, 224
1:21	243	2:14	152, 218
1:22	244, 249	2:15	221, 225
2:2–3	252	2:16	150, 224–25
2:6	244	3:1–2	107
2:10	245	3:1–5	221, 224, 227
2:11	251–52	3:4	228, 240
2:16	25	3:5	215, 220, 228
2:17	244	3:6	229
2:20	247	3:8	229
2:21	244	3:11	229
2:22	25	4:1	153, 219, 225
2:23	249	4:1–3	222
3:1–15	223	4:4	144
3:3–4	250	4:7	219
3:10	245, 250	4:8	153, 229–230
3:11	245	4:8–5:1	226–29
3:16	244	4:12	222, 226
4	21	4:12–16	222
4:1–11	175	4:15	222
4:3	25	4:16	226
4:11	249–50, 252	5:1	226, 227
4:11–16	248	5:2–4	226
4:12	252	5:5–6	226
4:12–13	26	5:6–7	227
4:15	243	5:7	217
4:17	25, 243, 250	5:9	218
4:18	26, 253	5:12	225
4:18–22	26	5:13	150, 225
		6:1	218
Song of Songs		6:3	226
1:5	218, 221	6:4	217, 219
1:6	215, 218, 222–23	6:8	230
1:7	223	6:9	230
1:8	218, 224	6:10	219, 231
1:10	219	6:12	217
1:15	152, 219	7:1	216
1:16–17	221	7:2	219

INDEX OF ANCIENT SOURCES

7:2–11	217	8:1	96
7:3	144, 150	8:16–17	100
7:5	144, 225	9:1	104
7:7	218	9:1–12	103
7:7–10	144–45	9:2–3	104
7:9–10	227	9:7	105
7:11	227	9:9	94, 103–6
7:12–13	221	9:11–12	104
7:12–14	221, 227	9:12	98
8:1–4	227	12:9–10	101
8:2	215, 228, 240	12:13	107
8:4	220, 227		
8:5	221, 228, 230	Lamentations	
8:5–14	230–32	1	199–201
8:6	156–58, 221, 224, 230–31	1–2	201, 210, 212
8:6–7	217	1:1	201
8:7	230	1:1 LXX	197
8:8–9	215	1:5	202
8:8–10	144	1:8	202
8:9	222	1:9	202
8:10	216, 223	1:10	203
8:11–12	223, 230	1:11	202, 243
8:12	223	1:11–12	203
8:14	232	1:16	203
		1:18	204, 207
Qoheleth		1:19	243
1:3	93	1:20	204–5
2:8	14	1:21	205
3:8	99	2	199, 205–9
3:10	102	2–4	200
3:19–21	131	2:11	202
5:6	107	2:12	206
6:10–12	93	2:13	207
6:12	100–101	2:18	207
7:14	107	2:22	208
7:16	103	3	199, 209–10
7:23–24	96	3:1	209
7:23–27	94–99	3:26–28	209
7:25–26	97–99	3:41	209–10
7:26	92, 98, 99–101	3:42–44	210
7:26–28	94–95, 99–101	4	199, 210
7:27	101–2	4:22	210
7:27–29	101–3	5	199, 210–11
7:28	107, 202–3	5:2–3	210
7:29	95, 103	5:10	210

Lamentations (cont.)
5:11 210–11
5:12–14 211
5:20–22 211

Esther
2:1–8 27
3:7 269
4:3 255
4:10–17 27
4:11 266
4:14 256
4:15–16 263
4:17 283
7:4 255
8:2 263
8:5 267
8:8 263
8:11 255
9:22 269
9:29 27
9:29–32 27, 263, 270

Daniel
4:22 282
4:31 282
13:42 282

Ezra
2:65 14, 30
9–10 22–23, 50, 85
9:1–2 22
10:3 50
10:19 23
10:44 23

Nehemiah
5:1–13 14
5:17 14
6:14 22
7 13
7:67 14, 30
8:2–3 21
10:1–29 22
10:29–30 22

13:23–24 23
13:23–31 85
13:26 23, 51, 85

1 Chronicles
1–9 35, 42–47
1:1 34
1:32 46
2:3–4 47
2:16 38, 47
2:17 47
2:19 45
2:21 45
2:23 45
2:34–35 48–49
2:46 43, 45
2:48 43
2:50–54 45
2:50 43
3 47–48
3:17–24 47
3:19 43
3:19–20 47
4:2–4 45
4:4 43, 46
4:18 45
7:14 45
7:15 43
7:16 43
7:24 43, 46
7:30 42, 47
10 36
11 36
11:6 38
11:20 38
15:29 38
18:12 38
18:15 38
23 49
23:21–22 49
23:22 49
25:5 40
26:33 46

INDEX OF ANCIENT SOURCES 331

2 Chronicles		6:26	69
2:13	38	6:28	69
5:2–14	50	7:18–28	112
8:11	39, 49–50	7:19	112, 119
9:1–9	38	7:20–21	112
9:12	38	7:24–25	91, 111
11:18–22	39–40	7:26	112, 116, 117
13:21	40	8:3	73
15:13	41	9:1	112, 119
21:14	41	9:1–9	111
21:16–17	41	10:18	109
22:3	38	14:20–15:10	64, 65, 139
22:10–23:15	38	15:2	71
22:11–12	40	15:2–3	66
24:3	40	15:6	65
24:26	41	22:3–5	111
28:8	41	23:22–26	111
28:10	41	24	64, 67, 112, 177
28:15	41	24:1–22	65
29:9	41	24:3–7	67
31:16–18	40	24:4	69
31:19	40	24:8	69
34:22–28	38	24:9	69
35:25	41	24:10	67, 69, 121
36:17	41–42	24:13–22	68
36:22–23	34	24:18	66
		24:19–21	66, 68, 148
Deuterocanonical Writings		24:21	118
		24:23	64, 67
Judith		25:1	113
9:11	283	25:6	113
		25:13	113
2 Maccabees		25:13–26	112, 114–15, 123
7	286	25:15	116
7:1–42	278	25:15–26	91,
		25:16	114, 116
Ben Sira		25:17	113, 116
1:1–27	64	25:19	113
1:10–20	64, 66	25:20	115, 116, 117
1:20	144	25:21	114, 117, 120
1:26	64	25:22	115, 117
4:11–19	64	25:24	92, 115
4:14	68–69	25:25	114, 117
4:19	64–65	25:26	114, 118
6:18–37	64	26:1–4	91, 112, 118–19

INDEX OF ANCIENT SOURCES

Ben Sira (cont.)		6:22	70
26:1	118	7:7–22	70
26:3	118, 120, 122	7:12	73
26:5–12	112, 114–15, 119	7:15	70–71
26:7	113, 114, 116	7:21	70
26:7–12	91	7:22–8:1	70, 73
26:8	115, 117	7:25	73
26:9–12	117	7:28	71, 73
26:10	114, 115	8:1	73
26:12	116–17	8:2–20	70, 73
26:13–18	91, 112, 118–19, 117	8:13	71
26:14	119, 120	8:17	71
26:15	120	9:2	162
26:17–18	120–21	9:4	70, 151
26:22–27	91	9:9	70
33:20	117	10:15–21	73–74
33:27	112		
36:21–27	119, 122	New Testament	
36:24	123		
36:24–25	122	Mark	
36:25–27	123	10:30	216
40:1	134		
40:23	113	Pseudepigraphal Works	
42:5	112		
42:6	112, 113, 118	1 Esdras	
42:9–14	111	9:36	51
44–50	64, 109–10		
47:19	112, 117	Testament of Job	
50:12	154	23:2–10	89
51:13–26	64, 65	46	89
51:19–20	66		
51:23	65	Ancient Near Eastern Texts/ Documents	
Baruch			
3–4	73	Amenemope	
		7:11–14	89
Susanna	275–87		
		Ankhsheshonqy	
Wisdom		24–25	111
1:1	160	24:21	118
1:1–15	70		
1:6	71	Elephantine Papyri, Cowley	
3:12–14	71	C 7	20
6:12	72	C 10	20
6:12–21	71	C 22	20

INDEX OF ANCIENT SOURCES

Elephantine Papyri, Kraeling		Midrash Psalms	
K 2	19, 20	59	114
K 4	19		
K 5	19	ANCIENT AUTHORS	
K 7	20		
K 10	20	Chariton of Aphrodisias, *Chaereas and*	
K 12	20	*Callirhoe*	
		1.2.6	279
Gilgamesh Epic		1.13.14	279
3.12–13	106		
		Pseudo-Demosthenes, *Against Neaera*	
Gortyn–Codex		122	16
VI.1–2	17		
VII.1–10	17	Euripides, *Uncertain Fragments*	
VII.15	17	1059	113–14
VIII.20–22	17		
		Hesiod, *Works and Days*	
Ludlul bel nemeqi	278	695	113
		702	118
Moussaiff tablet	19		
		Greek Menander	
Murashu tablets	18	83	120
Pap. Insinger		Syriac Menander, *Sentences*	
8:10	114	118–22	120
9	111		
		Stobaeus	
QUMRAN		22–23	111
4Q179	197	Theognis	
		1225	118
4Q184	92		
		Xenophon, *Oeconomicus*	
4QLam	197	3.14–15	11–12
RABBINICAL WRITINGS		PATRISTIC WRITINGS	
b. Pesaḥ.		Augustine, *Confessions*	
68b	249	11.20.26	237
m. Sotah			
1:5	282		
Gen. Rab.			
17:2	122		

www.ingramcontent.com/pod-product-compliance
Lightning Source LLC
Chambersburg PA
CBHW021117300426
44113CB00006B/181